Language Planning and Policy in Europe, Vol.2

LANGUAGE PLANNING AND POLICY
Series Editors: Dr Richard B. Baldauf Jr., *University of Queensland, Brisbane, Australia*
and Professor Robert B. Kaplan, *University of Southern California, USA.*

Other Books in the Series
Language Planning and Policy in Africa, Vol. 1: Botswana, Malawi, Mozambique and South
Africa
    Richard B. Baldauf Jr. and Robert B. Kaplan (eds)
Language Planning and Policy in Europe, Vol. 1: Hungary, Finland and Sweden
    Robert B. Kaplan and Richard B. Baldauf Jr. (eds)

Other Books of Interest
Community and Communication: The Role of Language in Nation State Building and
European Integration
    Sue Wright
Can Threatened Languages be Saved?
    Joshua Fishman (ed.)
Language and Society in a Changing Italy
    Arturo Tosi
Language Planning: From Practice to Theory
    Robert B. Kaplan and Richard B. Baldauf Jr. (eds)
The Other Languages of Europe
    Guus Extra and Durk Gorter (eds)
Multilingualism in Spain
    M. Teresa Turell (ed.)
Beyond Boundaries: Language and Identity in Contemporary Europe
    Paul Gubbins and Mike Holt (eds)
Ideology and Image: Britain and Language
    Dennis Ager
Where East Looks West: Success in English in Goa and on the Konkan Coast
    Dennis Kurzon
English in Africa: After the Cold War
    Alamin M. Mazrui
Politeness in Europe
    Leo Hickey and Miranda Stewart (eds)
Language in Jewish Society: Towards a New Understanding
    John Myhill
Urban Multilingualism in Europe
    Guus Extra and Kutlay Yagmur (eds)
Cultural and Linguistic Policy Abroad: The Italian Experience
    Mariella Totaro-Genevois
Language Decline and Death in Africa: Causes, Consequences and Challenges
    Herman M. Batibo
In and Out of English: For Better for Worse
    Gunilla Anderman and Margaret Rogers (eds)

For more details of these or any other of our publications, please contact:
Multilingual Matters, Frankfurt Lodge, Clevedon Hall,
Victoria Road, Clevedon, BS21 7HH, England
http://www.multilingual-matters.com

LANGUAGE PLANNING AND POLICY

Language Planning and Policy in Europe, Vol. 2

The Czech Republic, The European Union and Northern Ireland

Edited by

Richard B. Baldauf Jr. and Robert B. Kaplan

MULTILINGUAL MATTERS LTD
Clevedon • Buffalo • Toronto

Library of Congress Cataloging in Publication Data
Language Planning and Policy in Europe/Edited by Robert B. Kaplan and Richard B.
Baldauf, Jr.
Language Planning and Policy
Includes bibliographical references.
1. Language planning–Europe. 2. Language policy–Europe. I. Kaplan, Robert B.
II. Baldauf, Richard B. III. Series.
P40.5.L352E854 2005
306.44'94–dc22   2005009432

British Library Cataloguing in Publication Data
A catalogue entry for this book is available from the British Library.

ISBN 1-85359-813-5 / EAN 978-1-85359-813-5 (hbk)

Multilingual Matters Ltd
UK: Frankfurt Lodge, Clevedon Hall, Victoria Road, Clevedon BS21 7HH.
USA: UTP, 2250 Military Road, Tonawanda, NY 14150, USA.
Canada: UTP, 5201 Dufferin Street, North York, Ontario M3H 5T8, Canada.

Material in this book has also appeared in the journal *Current Issues in Language Planning*
Vol. 2, No. 4; Vol. 3, No. 4 and Vol. 4, Nos 3&4.

Typeset by Archetype-IT Ltd (http://www.archetype-it.com).
Printed and bound in Great Britain by Short Run Press Ltd.

Contents

Series Overview 1

Language Policy and Planning in The Czech Republic,
The European Union and Northern Ireland: Some Common Issues
Richard B. Baldauf Jr. and Robert B. Kaplan 6

Language Management in the Czech Republic
J.V. Neustupný and Jiří Nekvapil 16

The European Union, its Institutions and its Languages:
Some Language Political Observations
T.J.M. van Els 202

An Update
T.J.M van Els 252

Language Planning in Northern Ireland
Diarmait Mac Giolla Chríost 257

An Update
Diarmait Mac Giolla Chríost 309

Biographical Notes on Contributors 313

Series Overview

Since 1998 and 1999 when the first six polity studies on Language Policy and Planning – addressing the language situation in a particular polity – were published in the *Journal of Multilingual and Multicultural Development*, 17 studies (since 1990 through the middle of 2004) have been published in *Current Issues in Language Planning*. These studies have all addressed, to a greater or lesser extent, 22 common questions or issues (Appendix A), thus giving them some degree of consistency. However, we are keenly aware that these studies have been published in the order in which they were completed. While such an arrangement is reasonable for journal publication, the result does not serve the needs of area specialists nor are the various monographs easily accessible to the wider public. As the number of available polity studies has grown, we have planned to update (where necessary) and republish these studies in coherent areal volumes.

The first such volume published concerned Africa (i.e., Botswana, Malawi, Mozambique and South Africa) (Baldauf & Kaplan, 2004), both because a significant number of studies had become available and because Africa constituted an area that is significantly under-represented in the language planning literature and yet is marked by extremely interesting language policy and planning issues. The second volume dealt with Europe (i.e., Hungary, Finland and Sweden) (Kaplan & Baldauf, 2005). This third volume also focuses on Europe, and includes The Czech Republic, the European Union and Northern Ireland, again examining polities that have not been the subject of a great deal of published language planning and policy activity. These will shortly be followed by other areal volumes, focusing perhaps on Latin America, The Middle East, or Asia.

We hope that these areal volumes will better serve the needs of specialists. It is our intent to continue to publish other areal volumes subsequently as sufficient studies are completed. We will do so in the hope that such volumes will be of interest to areal scholars and others interested in language policies and language planning in geographically coherent regions. The areas in which we are planning to produce future volumes, and some of the polities that may be included are:

Europe (3), including the Baltic States, Ireland, Italy and Malta;
Asia, including Bangladesh, Chinese Characters, Malaysia, Nepal, Singapore and Taiwan;
Latin America, including Ecuador, Mexico and Paraguay;
Pacific Basin, including Fiji, the Philippines and Vanuatu;
Africa (2), including Algeria, Côte d'Ivoire, Nigeria, Tunisia and Zimbabwe.

In the mean time, we will continue to bring out *Current Issues in Language Planning*, adding to the list of polities available for inclusion in areal volumes. At this point, we cannot predict the intervals over which such volumes will appear, since those intervals will be defined by the ability of contributors to complete work on already contracted polity studies.

Assumptions Relating to Polity Studies

There are a number of assumptions that we have made about the nature of language policy and planning that have influenced the nature of the studies presented. First, we do not believe that a broader and more coherent paradigm addressing the complex questions of language policy / planning development is yet available. On the other hand, we do believe that the collection of a large body of more or less comparable data and the careful analysis of that data will give rise to a better paradigm. Therefore, in soliciting the polity studies, we have asked each of the contributors to address some two-dozen questions (to the extent that such questions were pertinent to each particular polity); the questions were offered as suggestions of topics that might be covered. (See Appendix A.) Some contributors have followed the questions rather closely; others have been more independent in approaching the task. It should be obvious that, in framing those questions, we were moving from a perhaps inchoate notion of an underlying theory. The reality that our notion was inchoate becomes clear in each of the polity studies.

Second, we have sought to find authors who had an intimate involvement with the language planning and policy decisions made in the polity about which they were writing; i.e., we were looking for insider knowledge and perspectives about the polities. However, as insiders are part of the process, they may find it difficult to take the part of the 'other' – to be critical of that process. But it is not necessary, or even appropriate, that they should be – this can be left to others. As Pennycook (1998: 126) argues:

> One of the lessons we need to draw from this account of colonial language policy [i.e. Hong Kong] is that, in order to make sense of language policies we need to understand both their location historically and their location contextually. What I mean by this is that we can not assume that the promotion of local languages instead of a dominant language, or the promotion of a dominant language at the expense of a local language, are in themselves good or bad. Too often we view these things through the lenses of liberalism, pluralism or anti-imperialism, without understanding the actual location of such policies.

While some authors do take a critical stance, or one based on a theoretical approach to the data, many of the studies are primarily descriptive, bringing together and revealing, we hope, the nature of the language development experience in the particular polity. We believe this is a valuable contribution to the theory / paradigm development of the field. As interesting and challenging as it may be to provide a priori descriptions of the nature of the field (e.g., language management, language rights, linguistic imperialism) based on partial data – nor have we been completely immune from this ourselves (e.g. Kaplan and Baldauf, 2003, Chapter 12) – we believe the development of a sufficient data base is an important prerequisite for paradigm development.

An Invitation to Contribute

We welcome additional polity contributions. Our views on a number of the issues can be found in Kaplan and Baldauf (1997); sample polity monographs have appeared in the extant issues of *Current Issues in Language Planning*. Interested authors are invited to contact the editors, present a proposal for a monograph, and provide a sample list of references. It is also useful to provide a brief biographical note, indicating any personal involvement in language planning activities in the polity proposed for study as well as any relevant research/publication in LPP. All contributions should, of course, be original, unpublished works. We expect to work with contributors during the preparation of monographs. All monographs will, of course, be reviewed for quality, completeness, accuracy, and style. Experience suggests that co-authored contributions may be very successful, but we want to stress that we are seeking a unified monograph on the polity, not an edited compilation of various authors' efforts. Questions may be addressed to either of us.

Robert B. Kaplan   Richard B. Baldauf, Jr.
rkaplan@olypen.com   rbaldauf@bigpond.com

References

Kaplan, R.B. and Baldauf, R.B., Jr (2003) *Language and Language-in-Education Planning in the Pacific Basin.* Dordrecht: Kluwer.

Kaplan, R.B. and Baldauf, R.B., Jr (eds) (2004) *Language Planning and Policy in Africa. I: Botswana, Malawi, Mozambique and South Africa.* Clevedon: Multilingual Matters.

Kaplan, R.B. and Baldauf, R.B., Jr (1997). *Language Planning From Practice to Theory.*Clevedon, Avon: Multilingual Matters.

Kaplan, R.B. and Baldauf, R.B., Jr (eds) (2005). *Language Planning and Policy in Europe I: Hungary, Finland and Sweden.* Clevedon: Multilingual Matters.

Pennycook, A. (1998) *English and the Discourses of Colonialism.* London and New York: Routledge.

Appendix A

Part I: The Language Profile of . . .

1. Name and briefly describe the national/official language(s) (*de jure* or *de facto*).
2. Name and describe the major minority language(s).
3. *Name and describe the lessor minority language(s) (include 'dialects', pidgins, creoles and other important aspects of language variation)*; the definition of minority language / dialect / pidgin will need to be discussed in terms of the sociolinguistic context.
4. *Name and describe the major religious language(s)*; In some polities religious languages and/or missionary policies have had a major impact on the language situation and provide *de facto* language planning. In some contexts religion has been a vehicle for introducing exogenous languages while in other cases it has served to promote indigenous languages.
5. Name and describe the major language(s) of literacy, assuming that it is / they are not one of those described above.
6. Provide a table indicating the number of speakers of each of the above languages, what percentage of the population they constitute and whether those speakers are largely urban or rural.

7. Where appropriate, provide a map(s) showing the distribution of speakers, key cities and other features referenced in the text.

Part II: Language Spread

8. Specify which languages are taught through the educational system, to whom they are taught, when they are taught and for how long they are taught.
9. Discuss the objectives of language education and the methods of assessment to determine that the objectives are met.
10. To the extent possible, trace the historical development of the policies/ practices identified in items 8 and 9 (may be integrated with 8/9).
11. Name and discuss the major media language(s) and the distribution of media by socio-economic class, ethnic group, urban/rural distinction (including the historical context where possible). For minority language, note the extent that any literature is (has been) available in the language.
12. How has immigration effected language distribution and what measures are in place to cater for learning the national language(s) and/or to support the use of immigrant languages.

Part III: Language Policy and Planning

13. Describe any language planning legislation, policy or implementation that is currently in place.
14. Describe any literacy planning legislation, policy or implementation that is currently in place.
15. To the extent possible, trace the historical development of the policies/ practices identified in items 13 and 14 (may be integrated with these items).
16. Describe and discuss any language planning agencies/organisations operating in the polity (both formal and informal).
17. Describe and discuss any regional/international influences affecting language planning and policy in the polity (include any external language promotion efforts).
18. To the extent possible, trace the historical development of the policies/ practices identified in items 16 and 17 (may be integrated with these items).

Part IV: Language Maintenance and Prospects

19. Describe and discuss intergenerational transmission of the major language(s); (is this changing over time?).
20. Describe and discuss the probabilities of language death among any of the languages/language varieties in the polity, any language revival efforts as well as any emerging pidgins or creoles.
21. Add anything you wish to clarify about the language situation and its probable direction of change over the next generation or two.
22. Add pertinent references/bibliography and any necessary appendices (e.g., a general plan of the educational system to clarify the answers to questions 8, 9 and 14).

Language Policy and Planning in The Czech Republic, the European Union and Northern Ireland: Some Common Issues

Richard B. Baldauf Jr.
Associate Professor of TESOL, School of Education, University of Queensland, QLD 4072 Australia <rbaldauf@bigpond.com>

Robert B. Kaplan
Professor Emeritus, Applied Linguistics, University of Southern California Mailing address: PO Box 577, Port Angeles, WA 98362 USA <rkaplan@olypen.com>

Introduction

This volume brings together three language policy and planning studies related to the European Union and Eastern and Western Europe.[1] (See the 'Series Overview' in this volume for a more general discussion of the nature of the series, Appendix A for the 22 questions each study set out to address, and Kaplan *et al.* 2000 for a discussion of our underlying concepts for the studies themselves.) In this introductory paper, rather than trying to provide a summary of the material covered in these studies, we draw out and discuss some of the more general issues raised by them.

Except that all three of these polities fall within the broad geopolitical definition of *Europe* (and that the two polity studies are included within the European Union), the three studies included in this volume do not represent any sort of geographic or linguistic coherence. On the contrary, the unifying element in this set of studies is the European Union (hereafter, EU) itself and the language problems and opportunities inherent in that organisation.

The social science research community has been engaged, for nearly three decades, in discussions about the 'correct' role of academic research. In Europe and North America this has lead to the emergence of major theoretical shifts, which, when taken together with the growing number of indigenous voices out of post-colonial societies, have generated new models to reconsider the primacy of positivist and post-positivist research. These discussions, at least to some extent, have sought ways in which positivist and post-positivist methodologies might coexist. Collectively, post-positivist research, phenomenological studies and critical theory have stimulated some contribution to a more precise understanding of language in society and have contributed to the growth of robustness and subtlety applicable to social policy development. This is evident in recent work which has produced an increasing change in focus in the discipline of language planning from an almost exclusive examination of the macro to a greater interest in the micro (see e.g. Canagarajah, 2005). However, as far back as the end of the 70s, some scholars believed that détente was emerging. The question demanding an answer was whether experimentalism was the single best model for providing reliable, valid, and objective knowledge about the role of language in society. Scientists and researchers began to discuss the possible contributions of various models – not exclusively the experimentalist model – to understanding the complexity of differing social and educational structures.

The chapters in this volume show that détente is possible. Indeed, the chapters in this volume demonstrate that positivist and post-positivist models can in fact coexist. *Current Issues in Language Planning,* however, does not favor any particular research model; on the contrary, much of the work on polity studies is descriptive rather than experimental. Some scholars might argue that the description of language situations is not really 'scientific,' but, as we have said elsewhere, thick policy description represents an effort to build a robust data source from which theoretical model building might be approached with greater subtlety. This blending can be seen in the Language Management model which is an outgrowth of structuralism, as embodied in the Prague School linguistics of the earlier part of the last century, but Neustupný and his colleagues have brought the model into the post-positivist world. On the other hand, Chriost's study, though representing the struggles to preserve a language threatened with extinction, employs a more traditional research approach. The discussion of the language problems in the EU is also primarily descriptive. Thus, *Current Issues in Language Planning* is not a repository of research in a traditional experimentalist sense, but represents, rather, a structure in which the ends justify the means.

The European Union

Van Els' study looks at the language situation in the EU itself. It is important to note that, at the time of the original study, the EU consisted of 15 member states and boasted eleven official and working languages. As Van Els notes in his addendum, 'On May 1, 2004 ten new Member States joined the European Union' (this volume). Van Els originally raised the question whether the number of official and working languages needed to be limited; language has explicitly been a topic on which discrimination has been forbidden throughout the brief history of the EU. Apparently this concept is to be preserved despite the increase in the size and diversity of the EU. In preparation for the expansion of the EU, the *European Convention on the Future of Europe* was created by the *European Council* (the Assembly of the Prime Ministers of the Member State) at the end of 2001. The convention produced a draft *Constitution for Europe,* in which Article II-21 specifies 'The Union shall respect cultural, religious and linguistic diversity' (European Convention, 2003: 65, cited in Van Els addendum). While the precise manner in which that respect is to be achieved is not developed in detail, the Constitution does specify that every citizen of the EU 'has the right to address the institutions or advisory bodies . . . and to have an answer' in any of the official and working languages (European Convention, 2003:84, cited in Van Els addendum). The 'languages of the Constitution' are specified in Article IV–10 (cited in Van Els addendum). Rather than deal explicitly with the potential tangle of languages, the Constitution specifies that 'The Council of Ministers shall adopt unanimously a European regulation laying down the rules governing the languages of the Union's institutions . . .' (Article III–339, European Convention, 2003: 259, cited in Van Els addendum). Thus, the EU must develop some means to deal with the twenty or so languages in play. Van Els has argued, both in the initial study and in his addendum, that the EU needs to articulate a coherent language policy to deal with the communication problems in the EU.

It is important to point out that, in June 2005, voters in France and the Netherlands have rejected the proposed EU constitution which brought together in one document many of the understandings, including those related to language, developed within the EU; it is at this moment unclear what that rejection will mean for the future of the EU and for the proposed constitution itself.

The Czech Republic

In the study of the Czech Republic, the authors adopt a 'language management' perspective. In their introduction, they identify the situation of the Czech language, saying that it can be briefly characterised by a number of features:

(1) With over 9 million native speakers, Czech is a relatively small language, although well over the mark at which languages are immediately endangered. Its situation clearly differs from European languages such as Basque, Welsh or Catalan.

(2) It serves a society that is one of the old industrial societies of Europe, and it serves it well, being the medium of communication from the workplace to the highest levels of tertiary education and science. In this point it differs from some much larger languages of Asia and Africa, which are not used as a tool of economic activities or intellectual inquiry.

(3) Contemporary Czech draws on resources of other European languages but it has not been unilaterally dependent on any one of them. It is not characterised by strong purism. In its relationship with other languages it differs, for example, from Ukrainian which has been marked by a strong and often unwelcome relationship with Russian.

(4) The history of the second half of the 20th century, when the whole territory of the then Czechoslovakia was under Soviet domination and strongly influenced by communist ideology, left somewhat underdeveloped certain attitudes to language that are typical for the United States, Canada, Australia and some Western European societies. This includes in particular attitudes to language discrimination. An international comparative study will be needed to establish how individual issues of language discrimination are treated in other European and non-European languages.

(5) Similar to many other Continental languages, corpus policies have traditionally been strongly developed at the governmental level, and this feature keeps Czech at variance with English, where corpus policies have remained at the outskirts of public concern with language.

Some other features of the Czech situation, for example, are the fact that some aspects of language management have for decades been supported by the theory of language problems emanating from the Prague School, which has represented the only well developed approach to language management in structural linguistics. Here, as elsewhere, 'our attitude will be in favor of learning from history, without accepting its limitations and failings' (Neustupný & Nekvapil, this volume).

In Table 1, they provide a summary of the numbers of members of ethnic groups in the Republic, based on 1991 and 2001 census data.

Table 1 Responses to ethnicity in the Czech Republic (1991 and 2001 census data) (*CILP* 4 (3&4), 190)

	1991		2001	
Czech	8,363,768	81.2%	9,249,777	90.4%
Moravian	1,362,313	13.2%	380,474	3.7%
Slovak	314,877	3.1%	193,190	1.9%
Polish	59,383	0.6%	51,968	0.5%
German	48,556	0.5%	39,106	0.4%
Silesian	44,446	0.4%	10,878	0.1%
Romany	32,903	0.3%	11,746	0.1%
Hungarian	19,932	0.2%	14,672	0.1%
Ukrainian	8,220	0.1%	22,112	0.2%
Russian	5,062	0.1%	1,369	0.1%
Bulgarian	3,487	0.0%	4,363	0.0%
Greek	3,379	0.0%	3,219	0.0%
Ruthenian	1,926	0.0%	1,106	0.0%
Rumanian	1,034	0.0%	1,238	0.0%
Vietnamese	421	0.0%	17,462	0.2%
Austrian	413	0.0%	–	–
Jewish	218	0.0%	–	–
Serbian	–	–	1,801	0.0%
Croatian	–	–	1,585	0.0%
Albanian	–	–	690	0.0%
Other	9,860	0.1%	26,499	0.3%
Undeclared	22,017	0.2%	172,827	1.7%
In total	10,302,215		10,230,060	

While ethnicity in Table 1 is not the same as language spoken (e.g. there is no Moravian language), the majority of these ethnic groups and their languages spill over into neighboring or proximal polities and any language planning must involve some recognition of the desires regarding language of those neighboring polities.

From a 'language management perspective', the authors also note that it is necessary to realise that different degrees of sociocultural distance obtain between these various communities. Basically, the authors observe, four groups may be distinguished:

(a) The Western group characterised by higher incomes and managerial status, reflect small numbers that do not appear prominently in Table 1.
(b) The Central European group – the Czech speaking communities, Germans (the local community), Poles, Slovaks, and Hungarians – show little sociocultural difference among these groups.
(c) The Peripheral group – the Ukrainians, Russians, Armenians, and communities originating in the Balkans – again show small numbers and also do not demonstrate great sociocultural differences.

(d)   The Outer group – the Roma, the Vietnamese, the Chinese, etc. – show considerable sociocultural differences.

These sociocultural differences translate into status and other power relations among the several communities and, in view of this phenomenon, the differences may project into language management and must be taken into consideration. (See Neustupný, forthcoming.)

At considerable length, in terms of simple management vs. organised management (terms taken from Language Management theory), the authors examine in detail the historical and contemporary situation of Czech (standard and common as well as dialects and slang among Czech citizens and Czech returnees from other regions), Slovak, Romani, Polish, German, Ruthenian, Ukrainian, Russian, Vietnamese, in terms of language-in-education practices and literacy.

Northern Ireland

Mac Goilla Chriost, in his study, offers an overview of the background of, and current language policy and planning matters related to, the language situation in Northern Ireland. The Irish language receives special attention due to the size of the Irish-speaking community in the region and the historical and political profile of the language. The current policy and planning framework for Irish is analysed, and recommendations are provided on how effective progress in this area might be made in the short to medium term. The development of a local, community-based approach is suggested.

The situation in Northern Ireland is closer to those in Wales or in New Zealand than it is to the more common language situation in which a major national or official language dominates, thereby creating difficulties for minority languages and foreign languages. It emphasises the sorts of language-in-education models designed to strengthen the national or official language at the expense of other varieties while delivering through the education system opportunities for students to learn other languages that are or might be economically important. The language situation is quite different from that in Canada, where French as a second official language is mandated by law. This language situation also differs from those in Belgium or Switzerland where languages have a regional basis.

Whether the attempt to preserve Irish has been as successful in Northern Ireland (or in Ireland – see Ó Laoire, 2005) as it has been in Wales is difficult to judge. The position of Northern Ireland is somewhat anomalous, since the polity is not an autonomous state, but rather is included within the UK, and since it has been characterised by internal strife over the recent past. Like Ireland, the supremacy of English is not a recent phenomenon (as it is in many post-colonial polities) but rather stretches back over 400 years. Furthermore, Northern Ireland shows nothing like the diversity of indigenous languages as appear in the Czech Republic.

Summary Comments

Thus, the discourse represented in these three studies varies from the more traditional descriptive to the more post-modern, and from the macro to issues of more micro consequence. Table 2 suggests the diversity of the polities

Table 2 Basic facts pertaining to the polities (Expanded from Europe I, 2005)

Country Name	Population	Area in Sq. Km.	GDP* in billions US$	Type of Govern- ment
Finland	c. 5,000,000	337,000	$103.6	Republic
Hungary	c. 10,000,000	93,000	$75.4	Republic
Sweden	c. 9,000,000	449,000	$175.0	Constitutional Monarchy
Czech Republic	c. 10,272,179	78,866	$116.7	Parliamentary Democracy
Northern Ireland	c. 1,688,600	14,121	NA	Part of UK

*GDP = Gross Domestic Product

represented in the two areal volumes on Europe along virtually any scale one wishes to apply. The emergence of the EU has created a platform from which the diversity of Europe can confront some common problems, but, as Van Els suggests, the EU has done relatively little about the language diversity among its member states, perhaps precisely because the organisation has insisted on the sanctity of its linguistic diversity. If, as the guiding documents of the EU suggest, 'The Union shall respect cultural, religious and linguistic diversity,' that diversity, now locked into policy, creates both great expense (in the form of translation[2] into and out of all of the languages of the member states), and the impossibility of a solution both to the expense and the administrative complexity.

It is interesting to note the extent to which the respective Ministries of Education are basically responsible for language policy. In both polities, it is the Ministry of Education that is responsible for first language education. It is also of interest that the number of the minority languages is defined by the Ministries of Education. It is apparent that smaller communities (basically those of 'new' immigrant populations; e.g., the Vietnamese in the Czech Republic) do not have the resources for extensive language education. Thus, there is a need to provide language support for both traditional minorities and recent immigrant communities (particularly in accord with the provisions of various recent EU treaties) and the difficulties this need poses for all members of the EU, for both of the polities under discussion here, and for the increasing membership of the EU.

Both polities report extremely high rates of literacy. However, the meaning of literacy is not uniform. The expansion of the EU has had some impact on language education/ preservation, but these developments are too recent to have had any measurable effect. In sum, in both polities, basic long-term policies have been directed toward assimilation. While these polities share a number of common educational, social and economic problems, the approach to problem solution tends to be largely restricted within the polity; there is relatively little evidence of broader – European-wide – solutions. But the development of the EU holds great promise for more effective recognition of multilingualism and multiculturalism and for the development of more effective remedies in first and second language education and literacy.

At the same time, the expansion of the EU has exacerbated problems relating to the role and reach of English as a language of wider communication within the European context. The language situation in the operations of the EU is extremely complex (see, e.g. van Els in this volume; van Els & Extra, 1987), but there is no question that English has assumed an important role. Not only has the role of English changed, but the operations of the EU have also created a significant terminological issue, since it is desirable that terminology should be consistent across all the members of the EU. These matters have placed great pressure on language policy practitioners with respect to language maintenance in the context of both inter-polity and intra-polity use.

We hope that this areal volume will better serve the needs of specialists. It is our intent to publish other areal volumes subsequently. We will do so in the hope that such volumes will be of interest to areal scholars and others interested in language policies and language planning in geographically coherent regions. (See the Series Overview elsewhere in this volume for more detail on our future plans.)

Notes

1. The studies in this volume were previously published as follows: **European Union**: *Current Issues in Language Planning* 2(4): 311–360; **Northern Ireland:** *Current Issues in Language Planning* 3 (4): 426–476; and **The Czech Republic:** *Current Issues in Language Planning* 4 (3&4), 181–366. Authors' updates to their studies – taking into account major changes in the language planning and policy situations relevant to the subject of the study – follow each article as an addendum to the original article.
2. The problem of translation is not just one of expense, but is also related to the fact that it is so massive an exercise because of the number of languages involved that translation into lesser used languages is often done via one of the major languages – often English. Tosi (2004) argues that this process, along with the use of language workbenches, translation tools which draw on already translated stock phrases, means that translations into, e.g., Italian, may often be hard to recognise as standard Italian, and may in some cases not actually be comprehensible. Eventually such translation problems will need to be addressed if the EU equality-of-languages policy is going to be anything more than symbolic.

References

Canagarajah, A.S. (2005) *Reclaiming the Local in Language Policy and Practice.* Mahwah, NJ: Lawrence Erlbaum.

van Els, T.J.M. and Extra, G. (1987) Foreign and second language teaching in Western Europe: A comparative overview of needs, objectives and policies. *Sociolinguistica* 1, 100–125.

Kaplan, R.B., Baldauf, R.B., Jr, Liddicoat, A.J., Bryant, P., Barbaux, M.-T. and Pütz, M. (2000) Current issues in language planning. *Current Issues in Language Planning* 1, 135–44.

Neustupný, J.V. (forthcoming) Language and power into the 21st century. Paper presented at the conference Language and Empowerment, organised by the Malaysian Association of Modern Languages, Petaling Jaya Hilton, Kuala Lumpur, 11–13 April 2002.

Ó Laoire, M. (2005) The language planning situation in Ireland. *Current Issues in Language Planning* 6.

Tosi, A. (2004) The language situation in Italy. *Current Issues in Language Planning* 5.

Further Reading

The Czech Republic

Auty, R. (1973) The role of poetry in the early nineteenth-century Slavonic language revivals. *Revue des Etudes Sud Est Europeennes* 11 (1), 31–7.

Bosak, J. (1988) Vztahy slovenciny a češtiny a ich vyskum v novej etape [Relationships between the Czech and Slovak Languages at the New Stage of their development and perspectives of study]. *Jazykovědny Časopis* 39 (2), 113–19.

Chloupek, J. (1986) Čeština a slovenstina z hlediska jazykové politiky [Czech and Slovak languages from the perspective of language policy]. *Sbornik Praci Filosoficke Fakulty Brnenske University, A: Rada Jazykovědna* A34, 55–9.

Drozd, L. and Roudny, M. (1980) Language planning and standardization of terminology in Czechoslovakia. *International Journal of the Sociology of Language* 23, 29–41.

Filipec, J. (1978) Die tschechische Sprachwissenschaft und Sprachpflege: ein Uberblick [Czech linguistics and language protection: An overview]. *Muttersprache* 88 (6), 363–7.

Fodor, F. and Peluau, S. (2003) Language geostrategies in eastern and central Europe: Assessment and perspectives. In J. Maurais and M.A. Morris (eds) *Languages in a Globalising World* (pp. 85–98). Cambridge: Cambridge University Press.

Gladrow, A. (1989) Aktuelle Fragen der Sprachkultur in der CSSR [The topical questions of language culture in the Czechoslovak Socialist Republic]. *Zeitschrift fur Slawistik* 34 (6), 888–92.

Himmel, B. (1996) Fremdsprachenunterricht in Tschechien und der Slowakei-Das Erbe und die Reformen [Foreign language education in the Czech Republic and Slovakia-heritage and reform]. *Zeitschrift fur Fremdsprachenforschung* 7 (1), 1–14.

Hubschmannová, M. (1995) Trial and error in written Romani on the pages of Romani periodicals. In Y. Matras (ed.) *Romani in Contact: The History, Structure and Sociology of a Language* (pp. 189–205). Amsterdam: Benjamins.

Hubschmannová, M. and Neustupný, J.V. (2004) 'Terminological' processes in North-Central Romani. *Current Issues in Language Planning* 5 (2), 83–108.

Jedlicka, A. and Gutschmidt, K. (1988) Probleme der tschechischen Schriftsprache wahrend der Wiedergeburt und ihre Losung [Problems of written Czech during national rebirth and their solution]. *Zeitschrift fur Slawistik* 33 (5), 645–56.

Kavka, S. and Skacel, J. (1987) Language planning implications in a socialist society. In J. Chloupek and J. Nekvapil (eds) *Reader in Czech Sociolinguistics* (pp. 257–73). Amsterdam: Benjamins.

Kraus, J. (1990) Do pitannya pro dinamiku komponentiv ches'koi movnoi situatsii [On the problem of component dynamics in the Czech language situation]. *Movoznavstvo* 24 (2(140)), 11–16.

Kraus, J. (1995) Sprachkultur und Sprachpolitik in der Tschechischen Republik der 90er Jahre. [Language culture and language planning in the Republic of Czechoslovakia in the 1990s]. In J. Scharnhorst and E. Ising (eds) *Sprachsituation und Sprachkultur im internationalen Vergleich: Aktuelle Sprachprobleme in Europa* [*The Language Situation and Language Culture in International Comparison: Topical Language Problems in Europe*] (pp. 83–90). Frankfurt: Peter Lang.

Krupa, V. (1987) K otazke jazykovej situacie a jazykovej politiky [On the problem of language situation and language policy. *Jazykovedny Časopis* 38 (2), 137–42.

Mainz, R. (1981) Fesselnd wie ein Polyp: Betrachtungen zur Parteisprache im Ostblock [Gripping like a polyp: Reflections on the party language in the Eastern Bloc]. *Muttersprache* 91 (3–4), 178–84.

Meyerstein, Z.P. (1973) Language planning and lexical change in Czech through the Centuries. *Pacific Coast Philology* 8, 42–4.

Millet, Y. (1983) Continuite et discontinuite: Cas du tcheque. [Continuality and discontinuality: The case of Czech]. In I. Fodor and C. Hagège (eds) *Language Reform: History and Future* (vol 2) (pp. 479–504). Hamburg: Buske.

Salzmann, Z. (1980) Language standardization in a bilingual state: The case of Czech and

Slovak, two closely cognate languages. *Language Problems & Language Planning* 4 (1), 38–54.

Saskova Pierce, M. (1987) A reanalysis of the concept of colloquial Czech and its use in the Prague Linguistic Circle Language model. *Dissertation Abstracts International, A: The Humanities and Social Sciences* 48 (2), 381-A.

Stich, A. (1994) Prezivetje jezikovné dominacije: Primer cescine [Surviving domination: The case of the Czech language]. *Javnost/Public* 1 (3), 11–21.

Thomas, G. (1996) The Prague School theory of language cultivation or purism by the backdoor. *Canadian Slavonic Papers / Revue Canadienne des Slavistes* 38 (1–2), 195–204.

The European Union

Anonymous (1994) Sprachen in der Europaischen Union [Languages in the European Union]. *Zielsprache Englisch* 24 (4), 42–3.

Anonymous. (1999) Mise en oeuvre du multilinguisme dans l'Union Europeenne [The implementation of multilingualism in the European Union]. *Traduire* 181, 27–35.

Anonymous. (2000) Homburger Empfehlungen zur Forderung der europaischen Hochsprachen [The Homburg recommendations for the cultivation of standard European languages]. *Sprachreport* 16 (4), 20–21.

Ammon, U. (1996) German attitudes to European language policy. In B. Bakmand, R. Phillipson and T. Skutnabb-Kangas (eds) *Papers in Language Policy* (pp. 11–14). Roskilde: Lingvistgruppen Roskilde Universitetscenter.

Arcaini, E. (2001) Prospettive linguistiche della Nuova Europa. Il ruolo della traduzione [The linguistic prospects of the new Europe. The role of translation]. *Studi Italiani di Linguistica Teorica e Applicata* 30 (3), 425–34.

Baetens Beardsmore, H. (1994) Language policy and planning in Western European countries. In W. Grabe and *et al.* (eds) *Annual Review of Applied Linguistics* 14 (pp. 93–110). Cambridge: Cambridge University Press.

Bellier, I. (2002) European identity, institutions and languages in the context of the enlargement. *Journal of Language and Politics* 1 (1), 85–114.

Bister Broosen, H. and Willemyns, R. (1999) Europe's linguistic diversity and the language policy of the European Union. In G.F. Carr, W. Harbert and L. Zhang (eds) *Interdigitations: Essays for Irmengard Rauch* (pp. 713–72). New York: Peter Lang.

Christ, W. (1997) Eine Wahrung fur Europa-aber wie viele Sprachen? [One currency for Europe – but how many languages?] *Neusprachliche Mitteilungen aus Wissenschaft und Praxis* 50 (2), 66–7.

Chvátalová, V. (2002) Jazyková politika Evropské unie zevnitr [European Union language policy: A view from within]. *Časopis pro Moderní Filologii* 84 (2), 76–85.

Fischer, K. (1999) Mehrsprachigkeit in Europa [Multilingualism in Europe]. In A. Raasch (ed.) *Deutsch und Andere Fremdsprachen-International LanderBerichte-Sprachenpolitische Analysen-Anregungen [German and Other Foreign Languages-International State Reports-Language Policy Analyses-Suggestions]* (pp. 211–16). Amsterdam: Rodopi.

Freudenstein, R. and Loewenthal, M. (1995) Une nouvelle politique linguistique pour l'Allemagne et l'Europe (resume): Pourquoi avons-nous besoin d'une nouvelle politique linguistique? [A new language policy for Germany and Europe: Why are we in need of a new language policy?]. In G. Dondelinger and A. Wengler (eds) *Plurilinguisme et Identite Culturelle: Actes des Assises Europeennes pour une Education Plurilingue [Pluralism and Cultural Identity]* (pp. 132–7). Luxembourg, 3–6 November 1993). Louvain-la-Neuve: Peeters.

Freudenstein, R. (1999) Bilingualism, language policy, and the European Union. *Georgetown University Round Table on Languages and Linguistics* (pp. 350–55). Washington, DC: Georgetown University Press. [Language in Our Time: Bilingual Education and Official English, Ebonics and Standard English, Immigration and the Unz Initiative.]

Grin, F. (1995) The economics of foreign language competence: A research project of the Swiss National Science Foundation. *Journal of Multilingual and Multicultural Development* 16 (3), 227–31.

Gubbins, P.P. (1996) Sense and pence: An alternative language policy for Europe. In C.

Hoffman (ed.) *Language, Culture and Communication in Contemporary Europe* (pp. 124–31). Clevedon: Multilingual Matters.

Harmond, W.R. (1998) La angla, cu sola lingvo por EU? [English, the EU's only language?] *Esperanto* 91 (7–8 (1105)), 134.

Jucquois, G. (1995) Le Monolinguisme ne couterait-il pas finalement plus cher que le multilinguisme? [In the end won't monolingualism cost more than multilingualism?] *Cahiers de l'Institut de Linguistique de Louvain* 21 (1–2), 61–76.

Jucquois, G. (2002) Dominations culturelles ou solidarites interculturelles? Nouvelles perspectives de l'Union europeenne [Cultural dominations or intercultural solidarities? New Perspectives of the European Union]. *Cahiers de l'Institut de Linguistique de Louvain* 28 (1–2), 227–44.

Jucquois, G. (2002) Des 'grands,' des 'moyens' et des 'petits.' Propositions pour une nouvelle repartition des roles et des langues [The 'big,' the 'average,' and the 'small.' Proposals for a new division of roles and languages]. *Cahiers de l'Institut de Linguistique de Louvain* 28 (1–2), 221–5.

Koskinen, K. (2000) Institutional illusions: Translating in the EU Commission. *Translator* 6 (1), 49–65.

Krausneker, V. (1999) Gebardensprachen, Sprachenpolitik und die Europaische Union [Minority languages, language policy, and the European Union]. *Wiener Linguistische Gazette* 66, 54–72.

Lenaerts, G. (2001) A failure to comply with the EU language policy: A study of the council archives. *Multilingua* 20 (3), 221–44.

Liddicoat, A.J. (2002) Language planning, linguistic diversity and democracy in Europe. In A.J. Liddicoat and K. Muller (eds) *Perspectives on Europe: Language Issues and Language Planning in Europe* (pp. 21–39). Melbourne: Language Australia.

Loos, E. (2000) Language choice, linguistic capital and symbolic domination in the European Union. *Language Problems & Language Planning* 24 (1), 37–53.

May, S. (2002) Developing greater ethnolinguistic democracy in Europe: Minority language policies, nation-states and the question of tolerability. *Sociolinguistica* 16, 1–13.

Muller, K. (2002) Language competition in European Union institutions. In A.J. Liddicoat and K. Muller (eds) *Perspectives on Europe: Language Issues and Language Planning in Europe* (pp. 41–59). Melbourne: Language Australia.

Nelde, P. (2000) Prerequisites for a new European language policy. *Journal of Multilingual and Multicultural Development* 21 (5), 442–50.

O Riagain, D. (1995) Working for Europe's linguistic heritage–The European Bureau for Lesser Used Languages. *Europa Ethnica* 52 (1), 10–14.

Oakes, L. (2002) Multilingualism in Europe: An effective French identity strategy? *Journal of Multilingual and Multicultural Development* 23 (5), 371–87.

Pfeil, W. (1996) Die Sprachenregelung in der Europaischen Union-Eine Frage von Verfassungsrang? Historische Entwicklung und zukunftige Perspektiven [Language regulation in the European Union – A constitutional question? Historical development and future perspectives]. *Lebende Sprachen* 41 (1), 1–5.

Phillipson, R. (1996) On English in Europe. *English Today* 12 (4), 58–9.

Phillipson, R. (2000) European language policy: An unmet sociolinguistic challenge. *Sociolinguistica* 14, 197–204.

Quell, C. (1998) Requirements, dynamics and realities of language use in the EU: A case study of the European Commission. In D.A. Kibbee (ed.) *Language, Legislation and Linguistic Rights* (pp. 288–309). Amsterdam: Benjamins.

Riemersma, A. (2001) Stipe foar minderheidstalen yn Europa noch net wetlik regele [Support for minority languages in Europe not yet legislated]. *Pompebleden* 72 (4), 46–8.

Rindler Schjerve, R. (2002) Minderheiten in der europaischen Sprachpolitik: Perspektiven einer 'neuen' Mehrsprachigkeit [Minorities in European language policy: Prospects of a 'new' multilingualism]. *Sociolinguistica* 16, 23–31.

Rutges, B. (2000) Crise lingual in le Union Europee [The linguistic crisis in the European Union]. *Panorama in Interlingua* 13 (1), 4–6.

Schlossmacher, M. (1995) Official languages and working languages in the political bodies of the European Union. *New Language Planning Newsletter* 9 (4), 1–2.

Smith, R. (1996) Single market, single currency, single language. *English Today* 12 (2), 10–14.
Truchot, C. (2003) Language and supranationality in Europe: The linguistic influence of the European Union. In J. Maurais and M.A. Morris (eds) *Languages in a Globalising World* (pp. 99–110). Cambridge: Cambridge University Press.
Verdoodt, A. (2002) Du principe de territorialite a la Convention-cadre pour la protection des minorites nationales [Territoriality and the proposed directive on the protection of minorities]. *Recherches Sociologiques* 33 (3), 111–16.
Vogel, J. (1995) Mit dem Sprachverband in die Jahre gekommen. Oder: Sprachkursforderung aus der Sicht eines Tragers-Wunsche und Hoffnungen [Growing old with the language union. Or: The promotion of language courses from an agent's perspective. Desires and expectations]. *Deutsch lernen* 20 (4), 352–7.
Weydt, H. (1998) Welche Sprachen in den europaischen Institutionen? [Which languages for European institutions?] *Grundlagenstudien aus Kybernetik und Geisteswissenschaft (GrKG / Humankybernetik)* 39 (2), 69–80.
Willemyns, R. and Bister Broosen, H. (1995) Het talenprobleem in de europese unie [The language problem in the European Union]. *Verslagen en Mededelingen van de Koninklije Academie voor Nederlandse Taal en Letterkunde* 1, 77–103.
Witt, J. (2000) Anmerkungen zur zukunftigen Behandlung der Amtssprachen der Europaischen Union auf der Grundlage einer Burgerbefragung [Remarks on the future treatment of official languages of the European Union using a public opinion survey]. *Lebende Sprachen* 45 (3), 101–5.
Woldring, H.E.S. (1995) Political integration and linguistic plurality. *History of European Ideas* 20 (1–3), 109–14.
Wright, S. and Ager, D. (1995) 'Major' and 'minor' languages in Europe: The evolution of practice and policy in the European Union. *European Journal of Intercultural Studies* 5 (3), 44–53.
Zelazny, W. (2003) Wspolnoty Europejskie wobec problemow jezykowych [Addressing language problems in the European communities]. *Language Problems & Language Planning* 27 (1), 27–43.
Zinck, J. (1997) L'Union europeenne et le multilinguisme [The European Union and multilingualism]. *Francais dans le Monde* (supplement) (January), 10–13.

Northern Ireland

Antonini, R., Corrigan, K. and Li, W. (2002) The Irish language in the Republic of Ireland and in Northern Ireland. *Sociolinguistica* 16, 118–28.
Barbour, S. (1996) Language and national identity in Britain and Ireland. *New Language Planning Newsletter* 11 (2), 1–4.
Davis, R.L. (1990) Don't disturb the ancestors. *Teangeolas* 27.
Farren, S. (1991) Culture, curriculum and educational policy in Northern Ireland. *Language, Culture and Curriculum* 4 (1), 43–58.
Farren, S. (1996) Language policy in a divided community. In T. Hickey and J. Williams (eds) *Language, Education and Society in a Changing World* (pp. 54–62). Clevedon: Multilingual Matters. Inter library loans
Mac Donnacha, J. (2003) Ethnicity and language change: English in (London)Derry, Northern Ireland. *Language Problems & Language Planning* 27 (1), 85–90.
McCafferty, K. (2002) Language and politics: Northern Ireland, the Republic of Ireland, and Scotland. *English World Wide* 23 (1), 137–41. (review, available on line
Mac Póilin, A. (ed.) (1997) *The Irish Language in Northern Ireland.* Belfast: Ultach Trust.
Nic Craith, M. (1999) Irish speakers in Northern Ireland, and the Good Friday agreement. *Journal of Multilingual and Multicultural Development* 20 (6), 494–507. 494.2
O'Reilly, C. C. (ed.) (1999) *The Irish Language in Northern Ireland: The Politics of Culture and Identity.* New York: St Martins Press.
Sutherland, M.B. (2000) Problems of diversity in policy and practice: Celtic languages in the United Kingdom. *Comparative Education* 36 (2), 199–209.
Wilson, J. and Stapleton, K. (2003) Nation-state, devolution and the parliamentary discourse of minority languages. *Journal of Language and Politics* 2 (1), 5–30.

Language Management in the Czech Republic

J.V. Neustupný
School of Languages, Cultures and Linguistics, Monash University, Melbourne, Australia

Jiří Nekvapil
Department of Linguistics, Faculty of Arts, Charles University, nám. Jana Palacha 2, CZ-11638 Prague, Czech Republic

This monograph, based on the Language Management model, provides information on both the *simple* (discourse-based) and *organised* modes of attention to language problems in the Czech Republic. This includes but is not limited to the language policy of the State. This approach does not satisfy itself with discussing problems of language varieties but tries also to attend to issues pertaining to situations, functions, and other aspects of communication. While Part I deals with theoretical prerequisites of the study, Part II surveys ethnic communities which are resident in the territory of the Czech Republic, and Part III, the most extensive in the study, provides a description of the current state of the major varieties spoken in the country. It is suggested that a weak form of diglossia (Standard vs. Common Czech) is one of the major areas of problems within the Czech language. Among the other communities the Roma community presents most distinctly interactional as well as narrowly communicative problems. All non-Czech communities seem to be gradually assimilating to the matrix (Czech) community, particularly with regard to language. Part IV is devoted to the survey of language management in different situations. The authors particularly deal with changes that occurred after the Velvet Revolution of 1989 and resulted in intensive management in all domains of interaction. Part V presents individual observations on areas that have so far failed to attract systematic attention. Included are problems of the functions of communication, problems of communicative settings, problems of participants and networks, problems of the communicated content (such as politeness), problems of the message form and of channels of communication. This section also includes a discussion of problems affecting the use of electronic media. Finally, in Part VI attention moves to issues of theories of language management: the renowned Prague School Theory of Language Cultivation, the Communist Party theory of the 1950s to 1980s, and current theoretical stances. A Table of Contents is appended at the end of the monograph.

Keywords: language management, language policy, ethnic minorities, Central Europe, Czech language, Prague School of Linguistics

PART I: LANGUAGE MANAGEMENT IN CZECH SOCIETY: TARGET AND MODELS

The Target Society and Languages

Why Czech?

In this study we wish to present a portrait of language problems in a mature, small-to-medium sized European nation. The nation we have in mind is the Czech Republic. The treatment of language problems in the Czech Republic should be of interest to those who have only come in contact with languages such as English, French or German or with languages of the Third World.

The Czech state has existed for more than a millennium but the 'Czech Republic' is new: it came into existence on 1 January 1993, following the break-up of the former Czechoslovak Republic, which itself was in existence for only seven decades. The Czech Republic lies in central Europe, with Germany to the northwest and west, Austria to the south, Slovakia to the east and Poland to the northeast. It has a territory of 78,866 square km (30,450 square miles) and a population of 10,230,060 (as of the 2001 census). It is only slightly smaller than Austria, Portugal or Hungary, and its population approximately equals that of Belgium, Portugal, Hungary or Greece. Ireland is of comparable size but has only 40% of the Republic's inhabitants.

The situation of the Czech language can be briefly characterised by a number of features:

(1) With over 9 million native speakers, Czech is a relatively small language, although well over the mark at which languages are immediately endangered. Its situation clearly differs from European languages such as Basque, Welsh or Catalan.

(2) It serves a society that is one of the old industrial societies of Europe, and it serves it well, being the medium of communication from the workplace to the highest levels of tertiary education and science. In this respect it differs from some much larger languages of Asia and Africa, which are not used as tools of economic activities or intellectual inquiry.

(3) Contemporary Czech draws on resources of other European languages and, although it has a close relationship with German, it has not been unilaterally dependent on any one of them. It is not characterised by strong purism. In its relationship with other languages it differs, for example, from Ukrainian which has been marked by a strong and often unwelcome relationship with Russian.

(4) The history of the second half of the 20th century, when the whole territory of the then Czechoslovakia was under Soviet domination and strongly influenced by communist ideology, left somewhat underdeveloped certain attitudes to language that are typical for the USA, Canada, Australia and some western European societies. This includes in particular attitudes to language discrimination. An international comparative study will be needed to establish how individual issues of language discrimination are treated in Czech, other European and non-European languages.

(5) Similarly to many other Continental languages, corpus policies have traditionally been strongly developed at the governmental level, and this feature keeps Czech at variance with English, where corpus policies have remained at the outskirts of public concern with language.

Some more features of the Czech situation will be developed in parts of this study. This concerns for example the fact that some aspects of language management have for decades been supported by the theory of language problems of the Prague School (see Part VI), which has represented the only well-developed approach to language management in structural linguistics. Here, as elsewhere, our attitude will be in favour of learning from history, without accepting its limitations and failings.

The neighbourhood

The linguistic neighbourhood of Czech is surprisingly simple. The longest linguistic border is with German, as spoken in Germany and in Austria. In the east there is Slovak and in the northeast Polish. Historically Czech had contacts with Upper and Lower Sorbian (Lusatian), spoken in the territory of former East Germany. Note that there is no common border with Hungarian, and that historically Czech–Hungarian direct contacts were limited, this being further reinforced after the division of Czechoslovakia into the Czech Republic and Slovakia in 1993.

Czechs and the Czech language

The core of the nation consists of the Czech ethnic group. According to the 2001 census, people who declare Czech as their 'mother tongue' (the term used in the census) amount to 9,707,397, that is 94.9% of the population of the Republic. Apart from those who reported as Czechs, this figure includes persons who in the 2001 census claimed other ethnic identity but declared Czech as their mother tongue: for example, Slovaks (32,529), Germans (10,836), Poles (4064) and other ethnic groups that have not been singled out in the census statistics. Also, 4527 Roma reported Czech as their mother tongue, but the real number of those who speak the language natively is probably much higher (cf. also Nekvapil, 2000a for data from Census 1991). Czech belongs to the western branch of the Slavic language family and is a language with a long tradition of literature and scholarship. The territory of the Czech language coincides today with the present-day Czech Republic. Up to the end of World War II extensive border areas were German speaking.

Other ethnic communities

Although border languages are limited to three, the fact that the territory of the Czech language has been located in the western part of what is today often called 'Middle and Eastern Europe' meant that it has always been at the cross-roads. France and Italy were not far away. In the 20th century, migrations from eastern Europe and even from Greece took place. However, the most important neighbour was undoubtedly Germany, which throughout history provided waves of immigrants, bringing with them their language. The maximum extension of the German community was registered in 1910, when there were 3,492,362 ethnic Germans in the country. In the 1991 census the number was 48,556, while in 2001 it had decreased to 39,106. Slovakia was immediately to the east and, although the border between the Czech Republic and Slovakia has always been stable, the fact that the two territories formed a joint state from 1918 to 1939, and then again between 1945 and 1993, brought to the Czech territory large numbers of Slovaks. At present the number is not less than 193,190. Two other communities are large: the Polish community, which occupies, together with members of the Czech community, the northeast corner of the country, and the Roma community, which is dispersed throughout the Republic. In 2001 51,968 people opted for Polish identity, while 11,746 identified themselves as

Roma. However, in the case of the latter the actual numbers are much higher, and we shall deal with this matter in Part II.

In Nekvapil and Neustupný (1998) we had already pointed to the fact that the size of a community carries little importance. In the Czech Republic, at least the following communities must be acknowledged along with those mentioned previously: Albanian, American (USA), Armenian, Austrian, Bulgarian, Chinese, Croatian, Greek, Hungarian, Jewish, Rumanian, Russian, Ruthenian, Ukrainian, Serbian and Vietnamese. However, there are further, even smaller, communities that await recognition and encouragement.

Czechs abroad

Czechs do not only live in the Czech Republic, although it is undoubtedly true that the number of Czechs abroad has been relatively limited. Emigration or exile during the 19th and 20th centuries never reached proportions similar to those of some neighbouring nations. Data about Czechs abroad vary, perhaps because they hardly ever define what the term 'Czech' means. According to Mladá Fronta Dnes (30 December 1993, pp. 1–2) in 1990 there were two or two and a half million 'Czechs' who lived in other countries – more than 205,000 elsewhere in Europe, 1,950,000 in northern and central America, 9,400 in South America, approximately 10,000 in Africa, 6,500 in Asia and 15,000 in Australia. More recent estimates, published by the Czechoslovak Foreign Institute (*Československý ústav zahraniční*) in 1999, give lower figures for some areas (e.g. for North America) and their total is 1,602,000 (for details see Kučera, 2003).

From a historical perspective, there were over two million Czechs (and Slovaks) abroad after WWI, principally in Austria, Hungary and in the territory that became Yugoslavia – but most expatriates lived in the USA (about 600,000 Czechs in 1920). The older emigration numbers suffered through natural attrition but there were new reinforcements: i.e. between 1920 and 1930 approximately 320,000 people emigrated from Czechoslovakia for economic reasons. Many left at the beginning of WWII, but returned to the country after the war. Between 1948 and 1967, and again between 1968 and 1989, a total of approximately half a million people left the country, mainly for political reasons (*Sborník hesel*, 1999/2000: 5). Many of these political emigrants did not return to the Czech Republic, but there were other groups of earlier emigrants who did. We shall report on two such recent groups – Czechs from the Ukraine and from Kazakhstan – in Part II. Although this re-emigration affected only several thousand people, their language behaviour has been the object of study by linguists. However, most attention to date has been paid to the language of Czechs in the USA (cf. Eckert, 2002; Kučera, 1990).

It is unnecessary to emphasise that the number of Czechs abroad does not indicate the number of people who speak Czech. Kučera (2003), who starts with an estimate of 1.6 million Czechs living abroad, assumes that this population only includes two or three hundred thousand Czech speakers.

What is Language Management?

This study is based on Language Management Theory. The theory originates in the 'language correction' theory (published in Neustupný, 1978), developed in the 1970s and 1980s mainly by Neustupný and Jernudd, and it grew as an extension and adjustment of language planning theory. The main features of the Language Management Theory have already been articulated in Neustupný (1983, 1985), but the classical statement, where the new designation 'management' is used, can be found in Jernudd and Neustupný (1987).

In this theory the word *Management* refers to a wide range of acts of attention to 'language problems'. In the language planning theory of the 1960s, 1970s and 1980s 'language problems' were principally problems of language in the narrow sense of the word. Current Language Management Theory aims to incorporate not only the whole of language, defined in the traditional narrow sense, but a wide range of additional problems implicating discourse, politeness, communication in intercultural contact situations, matters arising in proof reading, speech therapy or literary criticism. All these appear on the Czech scene.

Simple and organised management

One of the basic features of the theory is a distinction between *simple* and *organised* management of language (see, e.g. Jernudd & Neustupný, 1987). *Simple management* is management of problems as they appear in individual communication acts; for example, the problem of spelling a particular word, or the problem of how to redress the use of an expression that a speaker has just uttered but now considers as not sufficiently polite. *Organised management* occurs at a different level. The main features are:

- more than one person participates in the management process;
- discourse about management takes place;
- thought and ideology intervene.

Since these features are present to varying degrees, there is a gradual transition between the two extremes: simple and organised. Management within families often relies on simple correction in discourse, but frequently it also incorporates decisions discussed in detail by parents, and may be connected with ideologies of ethnicity. This was the case in some German families during the post-war period in the Czech Republic (Nekvapil, 2003a). An example of a highly organised management process is language reform – a complex process consisting of many components. Management theory maintains that, in principle, language problems originate in simple management, and from there they are transferred to organised management. However, this does not mean that organised management would be merely a summary of simple management acts. There is more (cf. Neustupný, 2002). Finally, the results of organised management are again transferred to discourse: without correcting individual discourse, the whole management process would make little sense.

The management process

A second prominent feature of the Language Management Theory is its processuality. Both simple and organised management is seen as developing in a number of stages (Neustupný, 1985). They commence with the *deviation* from a norm, with different participants often possessing different norms or 'expectations'. Of course, the norm is a flexible entity that is subject to continuous adjustment. However, it would be unrealistic to suggest that norms do not exist at all (Neustupný, forthcoming 2). Following the deviation stage, the deviation may be *noted*, a noted deviation may be *evaluated*, and subsequently an *adjustment plan* selected. In the last stage the plan may be *implemented*. For example, it is important to ask to what extent deviations from norms appear in Czech speech, how they are noted in individual discourse and at what levels of organised management (e.g. by employers); how they are evaluated, what adjustment plans are available and in what way such plans are implemented.

Socioeconomic, communicative and linguistic management

The third feature is the establishment of a hierarchy between language (in the narrow sense), communication and socioeconomic management. Language management alone (e.g. measures taken towards removing gender-loaded forms of language) makes little sense. It is necessary to make sure that such forms are not used in communication. In order to remove them from communication it is necessary to remove them from the socioeconomic structure. The right sequence is:

Socioeconomic Management > Communicative Management > Linguistic Management.

However, communicative management does not automatically follow from socioeconomic management, and linguistic management does not automatically follow from communicative management. Each of them must be pursued in its own right.

Interests, power and management

A fourth feature is the insistence on the recognition of the multiplicity of interests within a community. Language management is not a value-less, objective, 'scientific' process. The interest of the Czech language community and of the Roma, the interests of intellectuals and unqualified workers, differ. Also, the capacity to implement one's interests, in other words *power*, are subject to variation, and no language management system can overlook this fact. While interests have been present in the theory under various names at least since 1983 (Jernudd & Neustupný, 1987; Neustupný, 1983), power was added only later (Jernudd, 1996; Nekvapil, 2003b; Neustupný, 1996).

Levels of management

Finally, while language planning theory turned its attention mostly to society-wide management networks, such as governmental committees or various arms of the government, Language Management Theory emphasises management at a number of levels: the individual, associations, social organisations, media, economic bodies, educational institutions, local government, central government, or international organisations. It is obvious that in the Czech Republic management of language takes place at all these levels (Nekvapil, 2000a, 2000b), although it is not possible to capture the entire configuration of the levels at this stage of development of the theory.

A note should be added on the relationship between Language Management Theory and other theories of language problems. As noted in Neustupný (2002: 433), many existing theories operate in a space akin to the theory of languages management, although they may not use the term *language management* or may work in different social systems (language acquisition, language therapy, literary criticism, critical discourse analysis, etc.). Also, there is no necessary contradiction between the theory of language management and the theory of language planning as displayed, for example, in Kaplan and Baldauf (1997). Language planning is increasingly becoming an enlightened discipline. However, *language management* is a more comprehensive term, and the theory furnishes a wider framework that hopefully can achieve even more.

The Object of Language Management

In order to arrest all communicative problems within a community in a systematic way, one needs a list of rules or strategies that can become the object of language management. The model used in the discussion in this monograph is a 'Hymesian model'. It is based on Dell Hymes' models of speaking of the 1960s and 1970s (see esp. Hymes, 1974) but has been subject to reformulation (cf. Neustupný, 1987, 1993b; Sherzer & Darnell, 1972). Theoretical problems of the model are not discussed here. (For such discussion, see Neustupný, 1997.) The version employed is a relatively 'conservative' one close to Neustupný (1987). It will be assumed that the following types of strategies exist and that they are subject to language management.

- participant strategies;
- variety strategies;
- situational set strategies;
- function strategies;
- setting strategies;
- content strategies;
- frame strategies; and
- channel strategies.

From the point of view of language management, it is essential that all these strategy areas are covered.

Participant strategies

These strategies determine participants and networks in communication processes. When management occurs, these strategies are noted, evaluated, and adjustment may be carried out. In this monograph these strategies are dealt with at two points:

- Part II describes what categories of participants in the language management process within the Czech Republic exist, what problems arise and in what way they are adjusted. Emphasis placed on categorisation according to ethnic criteria, particularly with attention to the problem of assimilation of non-Czech ethnic groups towards the Czech matrix community.
- In Part V (Participants) more detailed problems concerning the categorisation of participants, in particular categorisation according to gender, is discussed.

Language variation strategies

Variation strategies govern the use of language varieties and variables – what languages are spoken and what problems affect these languages and their individual rules. Part III, which focuses on these matters, constitutes the central and most extensive component of this monograph. Problems of Czech, the language of the matrix community, is treated first, followed by problems pertaining to the languages of other communities living in the territory of the Czech Republic.

Situation strategies

Situations are recurring sets of the use of language. Part IV surveys sets of situations called domains (e.g. daily life, family, friendship, education, work, public and culture domains) and examines what problems are characteristic for each domain.

Function strategies

Language fulfils many functions, extensively described in the literature; with regard to these functions problems may occur. For example:

- Is the communicative function of various language varieties spoken in the Czech Republic performed to the satisfaction of participants?
- Are there any problems concerning the symbolic function of language?
- How does language relate to its social functions (e.g. the issue of connecting two different cultures and societies)?
- How and to what extent does language management take place?

These issues, as far as they appear in the Czech Republic, are discussed in Part V (Problems in Functions).

Setting strategies

Setting strategies determine the time and place of communication. When deviations from these strategies occur, management can take place. A few examples are dealt with in Part V (Problems in Settings). Only one example of speech used in a setting for which it is inappropriate are provided.

Content strategies

These strategies are important, because they select the content of communication. When they do not function satisfactorily, problems occur. As in the preceding parts, analysis in Part V (Problems in Content Strategies), concentrates on only a few examples. Focus is on the communication of politeness, problems of public criticism and a few other matters.

Form strategies

These strategies, also sometimes called message form or frame strategies, determine the form of communication, the form of routine components, or the order of components. Problems occur in this area as well; some of them are presented in Part V (Problems in Form Strategies). Some of the problems discussed here concern the form of proper names (i.e. personal or place names).

Channel strategies

Channel strategies govern the various channels through which communication forms are turned into surface structures. There are problems of the spoken and written media that overlap with the problem of varieties (spoken and written); these are discussed in Part III. A new problem occurs in the context of the electronic media; this is discussed in Part V (Problems in Channel Strategies).

From this brief survey, readers will understand that, although the entire framework for the analysis of communication problems is presented, the current state of research on language management in the Czech Republic does not permit complete discussion of all pertinent problems. Future researchers will, hopefully, be able to fill out the whole framework and thus provide a more comprehensive picture of the overall problem that language presents.

Part II: COMMUNITIES

Introduction

This part will introduce ethnic communities which reside in the territory of the Czech Republic and their problems. Two introductory comments may be helpful.

Overall census figures

Figures in Table 1 represent responses to the 1991 and 2001 census questionnaire about the respondents' ethnicity (*národnost*).[2] Table 1 cannot simply be accepted as the 'accurate picture' of the ethnic composition of the population without a commentary. Answers to the census question correspond to the individual's sociocultural management with regard to his/her ethnicity and this management reflects the interests and power relationships within Czech society. For example, respondents themselves evaluate their own ethnic categories negatively or expect that they would be evaluated negatively by others. The result is a process of adjustment during which they change their own categorisation with the expectation that they can, in that way, escape membership in a less powerful social group.

Distance between the communities

It is also necessary to realise that different degrees of sociocultural distance obtain between various communities such as those in Table 1. Basically four groups may be distinguished:

(1) The Western group (e.g. North Americans or Germans newly arrived from Germany) that is characterised by higher incomes and managerial status. Their numbers are small and they do not appear prominently in Table 1.
(2) The central European group: the Czech-speaking communities, Germans (the local community), Poles, Slovaks, and Hungarians. There is little sociocultural difference among these groups.
(3) The Peripheral group, that comprises the Ukrainians, Russians, Armenians, and communities originating in the Balkans.
(4) The Outer group (the Roma, the Vietnamese, the Chinese, etc.). These communities show considerable sociocultural differences.

This distance translates into status and other power relations between the communities, and in view of this the differences may project into language management and must be taken into consideration.

Table 1 Responses to ethnicity from 1991 and 2001 census

Ethnic identity	1991		2001		
	Number	(%)		Number	(%)
Czech	8,363,768	81.2	↑	9,249,777	90.4
Moravian	1,362,313	13.2	↓	380,474	3.7
Slovak	314,877	3.1	↓	193,190	1.9
Polish	59,383	0.6	↓	51,968	0.5
German	48,556	0.5	↓	39,106	0.4
Silesian	44,446	0.4	↓	10,878	0.1
Romany	32,903	0.3	↓	11,746	0.1
Hungarian	19,932	0.2	↓	14,672	0.1
Ukrainian	8,220	0.1	↑	22,112	0.2
Russian	5,062	0.1	↑	12,369	0.1
Bulgarian	3,487	0.0	↑	4,363	0.0
Greek	3,379	0.0	↓	3,219	0.0
Ruthenian	1,926	0.0	↓	1,106	0.0
Rumanian	1,034	0.0	↑	1,238	0.0
Vietnamese	421	0.0	↑	17,462	0.2
Austrian	413	0.0	↓	–	–
Jewish	218	0.0	↓	–	–
Serbian	–	–	↑	1,801	0.0
Croatian	–	–	↑	1,585	0.0
Albanian	–	–	↑	690	0.0
Other	9,860	0.1	↑	39,477	0.4
Undeclared	22,017	0.2	↑	172,827	1.7
Total	10,302,215		↓	10,230,060	

The Czechs

The Czech, Moravian, and Silesian communities

Historically speaking, the territory of the Czech Republic consists of three parts: Bohemia, Moravia and Silesia (see Map 1). However, this division is not merely a matter of history. Although normally speaking and writing the same standard language, Czech, inhabitants of these three parts sometimes possess a different identity. The 1991 census provided, for the first time, the possibility to declare under the heading *národnost* ('ethnicity') not only a Czech ethnic identity but also a Moravian or a Silesian one. There is no doubt that Moravia has always been considered a specific cultural entity not only in Moravia and Silesia, but also in Bohemia. This was less so with regard to Silesia, the substantial part of which has been incorporated in Poland for most of the time. The Czech part of Silesia

Figure 1

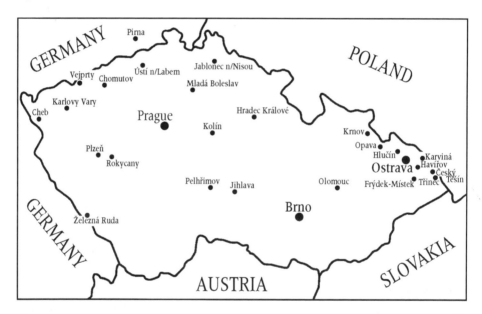

Figure 2

has traditionally been considered in the everyday awareness of inhabitants of Bohemia as a region belonging to Moravia. Throughout its history, Silesia has not only changed its political affiliation; it has also been an ethnically varied territory, and people who identified themselves ethnically as Silesians lived side by side with others who considered themselves Polish, German, Czech, Jewish or more recently also Slovak or Roma. In addition, a large portion of the population was ethnically indifferent, switching its identity depending on the situation.

In the 1991 census 8,363,768 (81.2% of the population) declared Czech,

1,362,313 (13.2%) Moravian and 44,446 (0.4%) Silesian ethnicity. It is important to realise that the distribution of this reporting was geographically uneven. While none of the Bohemian regions reported more than 1.3% Moravians, in the South Moravian Region the number rose to 49.5% and in the other region of Moravia, the North Moravian Region, it represented 15.4% of all inhabitants. It was in North Moravia where virtually all people with Silesian identity resided. Most of them lived in the Opava (see Map 2) District (11.2% of all inhabitants, cf. *Národnostní složení*, 1993, Table 15). The reporting of the Moravian and Silesian identity was thus closely connected with the Moravian and Silesian regions of the Republic. It is highly probable that, in previous censuses, when only the officially approved ethnicities (Czech, Slovak, Polish, German, Hungarian or Ukrainian/Ruthenian) could be reported, most of those who in 1991 declared themselves as Moravians or Silesians had previously reported their ethnicity as Czech or Polish respectively.

The results of the 1991 census with regard to the Moravian and Silesian identity must be taken seriously. Of course, there were special circumstances. Firstly, the census took place not more than 16 months after the Velvet Revolution of 1989. The result of that revolution was that the population felt liberated from any previously dictated social, economic or cultural categories, and plurality and diversity were becoming highly valued. The second, related, circumstance is that the census became a political issue and politically interested groups took up the question of the Moravian and Silesian ethnicity in the media and in the Parliament just before the census day. Therefore the possibility that the reporting was also motivated by momentary political concerns should not be discarded. Note that in the 2001 census, which was conducted in a substantially quieter atmosphere, only 380,474 people (3.7%) declared Moravian, and 10,878 (0.1%) declared Silesian ethnic identity. Within a decade, the number of individuals identifying themselves as Moravian or Silesian has declined by about 75%.

Some analysts conclude that the Moravian or Silesian ethnicity failed to prove its existence (Prokop, 2001). The Report of the Government's Council for Ethnic Minorities also plays down the fact that considerable numbers of people reported as Moravians or Silesians by interpreting it as a sign of special regional (i.e. not ethnic) identity (Zpráva, 2002: 7). However, there is no doubt that this identity is based on cultural and linguistic differences supported by differences in socioeconomic interests and power. Throughout modern history, Moravia and Silesia played a subsidiary role within the western part of the Czechoslovak state, economically and socially, and it is this reality that is being reflected in the consciousness of a part of the Moravian and Silesian population.

The cultural specificity of Moravia and the Czech part of Silesia are evident. However, their special position also manifests itself linguistically. In these regions, local dialects are better preserved than in Bohemia. This fact is connected with less vigorous industrialisation at the outset of the industrialisation process. Common Czech (see Part III) is frequently rejected, and the language spoken in semi-formal situations (and by some speakers on all occasions) is Standard Czech. This fact, as well as the influence of the local dialect (e.g. shortening of vowels in Silesia), distinguishes speakers from Bohemia, Moravia and Silesia on all but very formal occasions. There were some attempts to use Moravian dialectal or dialectally tinted language in written communication. The first grammars of the 'Moravian language' were published at the beginning of the 19th century, when the future shape of Standard Czech was still in its infancy, and somewhat diffident attempts to establish 'Moravian' as a language appear even today (see Part III, 'The Czech Language').

The question of what language was considered as 'mother tongue' (a term used in the census questionnaire) by those who reported as Moravians or Silesians is of interest. Even within the atmosphere of 1991, 1,356,605 of those who claimed Moravian ethnicity (out of the total number 1,362,313) cited Czech as their mother tongue; 2,702 reported Slovak, 794 reported Hungarian, and 422 reported German mother tongue. Surprisingly, only 151 reported Polish. Of those who reported Silesian identity, 43,474 (out of a total of 44,446) gave Czech as their mother tongue. Other mother tongues claimed were: Polish (449), German (237), and Slovak (103).

Since 8,332,500 of those who declared Czech ethnicity (out of a total of 8,363,768) reported their mother tongue as Czech, it can be concluded that a very high proportion of the population of the Czech Republic in 1991 (95.8%) claimed Czech as their native language. The results of the 2001 census confirmed the stability of this picture. However, as far as ethnic identity was concerned, 8,363,768 (81.2% of the population) claimed Czech identity in 1991 as compared to 9,249,777 (90.4%) in 2001.

Czech-speaking and other-speaking communities throughout history

Was there homogeneity?

It is generally assumed that, at the dawn of history (which in the case of Bohemia and Moravia covered the last few centuries of the first millennium), the territory of the present Czech Republic was ethnically Czech. The actual extent is a matter that may never be clearly established. However, it is certain that the country was not closed to the world. Visitors, including of course members of military expeditions, were many, and merchants of various origins travelled through the territory. Ibrahim ibn Jakub reported in the second half of the 10th century that Prague was an important centre 'built of stone' – this obviously in reference only to churches (Turek, 1963: 36). Progressing urbanisation, which started in Prague as well as the development of other trade centres, saw small groups of foreigners settling down. Communities that have stayed permanently included Germans, Jewish groups (reported as early as the 10th century), and some Italians.

The first immigration wave

The development of agriculture in Europe necessarily led to population growth, and uninhabited territories were sought to accommodate the human surplus. It is only natural that the population unwanted in the territory of present-day Germany headed in an eastern direction where the Czech ethnic group had been unable to occupy fully the large territories of Bohemia and Moravia, formerly dominated by Teutonic tribes (Neustupný & Neustupný, 1961). Especially during the second half of the 13th and the first half of the 14th century, German settlers, encouraged by Czech kings, occupied relatively large areas close to the border. In some cases they spread over the original Czech population. However, a territory as large as the pre-WWII Sudetenland should not be considered for this immigration.

At the same time, the 13th century witnessed an increased tempo of urbanisation in Europe, and, particularly during the second half of the century, this trend affected the Czech lands, when a large number of new towns was created to support economic development. Under these circumstances the nobility, and particularly the Czech kings, found it advantageous to invite foreigners to work in the newly founded cities as well as to found new villages. Chronicles have reported that King Přemysl II (reigned 1253–1278) accumulated great wealth through introducing Germans to his territories (Hoffman, 1992). This wave of (principally) German migration resulted in large-scale ethnic variation: the territory of the Czech Republic has never returned to its short-lived ethnic homogeneity.

The presence of Jewish migrants has been confirmed as early as the 10th century; they were settling down in large numbers by the 12th century, bringing to the country another ethnic and religious minority. Ghettoes were not necessarily typical at this stage (Hoffman, 1992).

End of 13th and the 14th century

By the end of the 13th century, migration from the outside decreased, and around the mid-14th century it temporarily stopped entirely. Under the rule of Charles IV Czechisation of towns (of which there was now about 100) continued; even prior to the Hussite revolution, switched on by the burning of the religious reformer John Hus at the stake in 1415, many towns had a Czech majority, while others had Czech minorities of various strength (Hoffman, 1992: 61). Apart from those areas close to the border, the rural population of the countryside was predominantly Czech. Originally, the language used in the German-settled towns was German, but, particularly in the Hussite and post-Hussite period, Czech language was gradually adopted or used along with German.

During the second half of the 14th and into the 15th century, under influence from western Europe, Jewish residents were periodically expelled, especially from the royal towns. In the 15th century they established themselves in towns that belonged to the nobility, but partly also in villages, mainly in trade professions.

From the beginning of 15th century, the Roma became a permanent feature of the Czech scene. Needless to say, the language of religion and science of this period was Latin, which also served as the international *lingua franca* among the educated. The religious leader, John Hus (1371–1415), delivered his sermons in Czech, using Latin notes. He wrote both in Latin and in Czech. Later, so did the educationalist Comenius (1592–1670, died in exile in Holland).

New immigrants

The end of the 15th century again witnessed a population surplus in central Europe which translated itself into a new wave of German immigration into Czech lands in the 16th century. This time the settlers occupied areas of non-agricultural land, particularly in the northern mountains. They engaged in textile industries, production of glass, and other occupations for which the quality of land was irrelevant.

At about the same time, a small group of Valachian shepherds arrived in Northeast Moravia. The migration started in Rumania, but, when it reached Moravia, the population consisted mostly of Slavs, who, in the course of the following centuries, assimilated linguistically (but less so culturally) to the base population (Maur, 1998a). Two more migration waves were directed toward Moravia. One wave consisted of Croats who were seeking refuge from the Turks. In 1945 only three villages retained their Croat identity. The second wave consisted of a large group of Anabaptists (Calvinists) who fled religious persecution in Switzerland. They exercised considerable influence in wine production and pottery making, but had to leave again with the loss of religious freedom in the Czech lands after the battle of the White Mountain in 1620, following the Czech Protestant revolt against the Hapsburgs.

The persecution of Jewish residents continued; however, in the second half of the 16th century the Prague Jewish community experienced a kind of cultural boom. The renaissance court of Emperor Rudolph II (reigned 1576–1611) brought a large number of foreign artists and scientists to Prague. In the society at large, along with Czech, the language of the majority of the emperor's subjects and the nobility, German, was widely used. The importance of Latin as the language of ideology was still paramount, even though German and Czech started making inroads.

The Hapsburg period and the aftermath

The Hapsburg dynasty was on the Czech throne permanently from 1526 till 1918. The Hapsburgs were antagonistic to the reformation, which since the Hussite period was strongly represented in the Czech lands, and it is particularly the period of the Hapsburg rule after the battle of the White Mountain (1620), in which the Czech side was defeated, that is normally associated with the name 'Period of Darkness'. Under the Hapsburgs, the boundaries of the Czech and German ethnic groups moved toward their 1945 position, but there was no large immigration to speak of (Maur, 1998b).

Before and during the first part of the Hapsburg rule, the multi-ethnic character of the country was accepted as a fact of life. Regions or villages spoke different languages, but they were not in competition. There was a relationship of complementarity between the agricultural areas and the towns. Occasionally, ethnic conflict flared up when socioeconomic interests were involved. Within the towns, ethnic origin was one factor in the distribution of power, but even there it was not the only factor, and it should not be perceived through 19th century eyes. After all, the nobility often ruled over a varied collection of fiefdoms, and the Bohemian kings also held other crowns, serving as emperors within the Holy Roman Empire. They married with partners from various ethnic origins. It was only natural, therefore, that they spoke various languages and that their courts harboured people of various provenances. The Czech lands belonged to the medieval Holy Roman Empire within which the German language held the strongest position. Although Latin was the language of culture and ideology, it gradually lost ground to the vernaculars, first of all to German, but also to Czech. The knowledge of both Czech and German was widely distributed, though for no period of Czech history should we imagine a situation approaching perfect bilingualism.

Under Hapsburg rule the position of German was definitely strengthened. However, with the process of the formation of the Modern German and Czech Ethnicities (Hroch, 1999a, 1999b), commencing during the second half of the 18th century, language was increasingly connected with the interests of ethnic groups which started using language as the primary symbol of their identities (Hroch, 1999b). In particular, through the process of industrialisation, the position of the Czech element was reinforced, so that the structure of employment among the Czechs and the Germans in Bohemia and Moravia in 1910 was virtually identical (Horská, 1998). It was on this basis that a relationship of ethnic antagonism developed on both sides (Musil, 1998), leading eventually to the Munich Agreement of 1938, which mandated the incorporation of the Sudetenland into Germany, and which set the stage for the deportation of Germans from Czechoslovakia after WWII. According to the Munich Agreement, Czechoslovakia was required to hand over to Germany, Poland, Hungary and the Soviet Union 37% of its territory together with 37% of its population. There were 855,000 ethnic Czechs in this territory; approximately half of them were forced to, or elected to, leave the territory. After WWII, in accordance with a decision reached at the Potsdam Conference (1945) close to 2.7 million Germans were required to leave Czechoslovakia. Only a small number were permitted to remain.

Returnee communities

This section is devoted to the history of the Czech-speaking communities. It finishes with a brief outline of emigrant communities of Czech origin which eventually returned to the Czech Republic.

As mentioned previously, Czech emigration of the 19th and the first half of the 20th centuries was less extensive than similar phenomena in many other European countries. No doubt this was the consequence of the relative affluence of the Czech lands and the fact that they underwent early industrialisation. Czech immigration headed mostly to the USA, although there was another stream departing to some Balkan countries (cf. Vašek, 1976) as well as in an eastern direction to Czarist Russia. There, following the abolition of serfdom in 1861, opportunities were created for free farmers to acquire land under conditions that seemed to promise prosperity. Conditions for the emigration of Czech farmers were the object of negotiation with the Czar's government by the prominent Czech political figure F. Palacký (1798–1876). Czech politicians were interested in the possibility of retaining the ethnicity of Czech emigrants within a Slavic environment. On the other hand, the Russian side was interested in immigrants with a high level of agricultural skills as well as in stopping the advance of the Polish element. At the time of the first Russian census in 1887 there were approximately 50,000 Czech settlers living in more than 200 villages and hamlets.

However, emigration to the east did not meet with success, at least not in the long run. The emigrants came back from the Ukraine (in two waves) as well as from Kazakhstan.

Czechs from the Ukraine

Most Czech emigrants during the 19th century departed towards Volynh prefecture in the western Ukraine. Between 1868 and 1886 alone approximately 20,000 Czechs settled there. Initially, Czech settlers enjoyed a number of economic, religious and other privileges. They had their own schools, theatres, choirs and public libraries. These privileges were gradually trimmed, and in 1937 the teaching of Czech was entirely abolished. During the course of WWII, the

Czechs actively fought Germans either in the Red Army or in the Czech Army Corps, and this fact became the basis on which their repatriation was negotiated and finally approved. In 1947 alone 37,000 people returned, and the total number of returnees was over 40,000. Original pledges of the Czechoslovak government notwithstanding, they were not able to occupy a compact territory and thus lived dispersed in various regions. Nevertheless, they maintained their networks, including intermarriages (Kastner, 1998).

However, the post-war agreement between Czechoslovakia and the Soviet Union only concerned Volynh, not the Kiev prefecture. In 1989, some 9000 Czechs who retained their ethnic consciousness as well as some knowledge of the Czech language were still resident in the Ukraine. Out of these, some 2000 people returned to Czechoslovakia between 1991 and 1993. These people lived mostly in the villages of Mala Zubovshtina and Malinovka, and in a few adjoining areas of Belarus, all within 80 km of the Chernobyl nuclear plant. They claim that, had there been no nuclear accident in Chernobyl and no humanitarian offer to accept refugees from the area from the Czechoslovak government, they may have remained 'imprisoned' in the territory of the former Soviet Union. Approximately 600 families returned, settling in more than 40 localities in Bohemia and Moravia. The success of the action was guaranteed by a positive response from Czech local governments which provided lodging as well as work for at least one family member.

Although repatriation met with wide-ranging support, there were problems. While Czech settlers in the Ukraine were perceived as aliens because of their actively proclaimed Czech ethnicity, in Czechoslovakia they were marked by their Ukrainian/Russian cultural and linguistic features. Although these people did not classify themselves as Volynh Czechs (_Volyňáci_), this is how the Czech community perceived them, probably in recollection of the first wave of repatriation after WWII. Another problem was that they arrived from the former Soviet Union just at the time of heightened anti-communist feeling as well as the general anti-Soviet and anti-Russian atmosphere that developed following the events of 1989. One of the repatriated people reported: 'In the Ukraine I considered myself Czech. That I am a _"Volyňák"_ (Czech from Volynh) I only learned here. It is still better to be called _Volyňák_ than a _Rusák_ [a Russian, pejorative]' (MFD 30 March 1995: 24). Incidentally, this speaker is one of those who personally consulted with President Havel concerning their return. 'Ten years back "at home". In other words Czechs or Russians?' was the title of a TV programme broadcast in 2001 which showed that negative attitudes were not isolated. Another unfavourable circumstance was that the repatriated Czechs were confused with Ukrainian and Russian guest workers who began to appear at the same time. In the mid-1990s, the Czech community at large was unprepared to accept the rights of people who were different.

Czechs from Kazakhstan

Kazakhstan was not the original destination of Czech emigrants (Valášková, 1998). They proceeded there from the Ukraine and Bessarabia (present Moldova) where they had settled in the mid-19th century. In addition, dozens of people of Czech origin were transferred by force to Kazakhstan as 'kulaks' when Bessarabia was occupied by the Soviet Union in 1940. In 1911, the first Czech colonists arrived in northwestern Kazakhstan, where they purchased land and founded the village Borodinovka approximately 120 km from the city of Akt'ubinsk. As a part of systematic colonisation, further villages with Slavic (Russian, Ukrainian and Bulgarian) farmers were established close to Borodinovka. However, the closest settlement to Borodinovka, only 2 km away, was a Kazakh hamlet. In 1929 a *kolkhoz* (collective farm) was formed in Borodinovka, where Czechs worked together with the Kazakhs. The school, in which the language of instruction was Russian, was also shared. However, this long history of Czech-Kazakh contacts had no influence on the marriage policy of either group – when, after WWII, mixed marriages started appearing, they involved Czech-Russian pairs. In the post-war period, many people from Borodinovka emigrated to cities, mainly to Akt'ubinsk, but they did not lose contact with their native village. Prior to re-migration to the Czech Republic, the Czech population of Borodinovka stood close to 350, and there were approximately 300 Czechs in Akt'ubinsk, including members of other ethnic groups who were related to the Czechs by marriage.

The atmosphere of political liberalisation towards the end of the 1980s and at the beginning of the 1990s resulted in acts of assertion of their ethnicity by the Czech community. In Akt'ubinsk they founded the *Kulturně-osvětové centrum Čechů v Kazachstánu* (Cultural and Educational Czech Centre in Kazakhstan) (1992). The teaching of Czech started both in Akt'ubinsk and Borodinovka with the help of the Czechoslovak Embassy in Moscow. However, this ethnic emancipation of Czechs and other ethnic groups in Kazakhstan met with resistance from the Kazakhs. Following Kazakh independence in 1991, Russian schools were abolished, and the Kazakh language was introduced as the official language. The economic opportunities of the non-Kazakh population diminished as a result of labour market discrimination. The danger of ethnic conflicts increased, and the non-Kazakh population started leaving the country.

In this situation, Czechs in Kazakhstan commenced negotiating with the Czechoslovak government as well as with private institutions regarding a move back to Czechoslovakia. The first such initiative appeared in 1992, but the first Czech families did not arrive in the Czech Republic until 1995. By the beginning of 2000, approximately 150 families (more than 500 people) changed their domicile and found new homes in a number of Czech localities (cf. MFD, 16 July 1999: 1).

The repatriation of Czechs from Kazakhstan did not attract as much attention of the media or of the Czech community as had the repatriation from those areas of the Ukraine and Belarus which had been affected by radioactivity from Chernobyl. Occasionally, those arriving from Kazakhstan were considered foreigners, and discrimination appeared (MFD, 26 October 1998: 3). Although many of them possess secondary or tertiary education, they were still only able to find work as manual labourers.

The Slovaks

The Slovak community, which in the 2001 census consisted of 193,190 people (1.9% of the population of the Czech Republic), has undergone remarkable changes in the course of the 20th century. These changes did not merely affect the size of the community. With respect to the status of the community, during the years of the Republic, Slovaks constituted one of the two principal contributors to the demographic, economic and cultural profile within the society; since the partition of Czechoslovakia in 1993, their status was again relegated to that of a minority.

Czechs and Slovaks have occupied separate territories that do not historically overlap. Slovakia starts where Moravia, the eastern part of the Czech territory, ends. Still, the Czech–Slovak partnership has a long history. The territories are adjacent, and the linguistic and cultural proximity overrode the fact that the Czech–Slovak border was also a political one. While Czechs had had their own strong and independent state and even later, under the Hapsburgs, had retained an independent identity, Slovaks had not enjoyed the same favourable conditions. Throughout the Middle Ages and up to 1918, they lived within a single state with the Hungarians. The close linguistic and cultural relationship between Czechs and Slovaks achieved particular relevance under the conditions of modernisation when the formation of the Czech and Slovak ethnic identity rose to occupy the agenda of the day. Throughout the 19th century, contacts were comprehensive. Many Slovaks studied at Czech schools, and this fact transferred to the relationship between organisations to which former school friends belonged. Apart from students, Slovak labourers, seeking better working and pay conditions, came to the Czech lands. While, towards the end of the 19th century, the current Czech Republic already was an industrial society, Slovakia remained agricultural.

In 1918, on the debris of the Hapsburg monarchy, a new state, Czechoslovakia, was born. Within the state, Czechs and Slovaks were formally equal, but in fact the distribution of power was strongly biased toward the Czechs. Many Slovaks started moving to the Czech 'metropolitan' areas. In 1921 there were 16,000 Slovaks in the Czech lands, in 1930 the number rose to 44,000 and before the outbreak of WWII, in 1937, the census revealed the presence of 65,000 who were dispersed throughout the territory. After 1918, there also was migration from the Czech part of the Czechoslovak Republic to Slovakia. At least some of this migration consisted of intellectuals and public servants (Šrajerová, 1999), a development motivated by the fact that Hungarian rule left the Slovak territory with an extremely limited intellectual class. The movement of Czechs and Slovaks within the territory of the Czechoslovak Republic is not easy to document on the basis of census data, because the censuses worked under the assumption of a single 'Czechoslovak' ethnicity. This assumption, incorporated into the Constitution, was partly pragmatically motivated (to show the strong Czech–Slovak 'majority' within a state which incorporated 23% Germans and almost 6% Hungarians), but it had its ideological roots in the early 19th century belief of a single 'Slavic' ethnicity, which, for many people, was used as a programmatic statement. This programme was more acceptable to the Czechs than to the Slovak intellectuals whose numbers were growing in Slovakia, because the 'Czechoslovak identity' was being formulated at the expense of the specificity of Slovakia (cf. Berger, 2003; Marti, 1993). Between the two world wars, Slovakia became a kind of 'colony' of the Czech component of the state.

The discontent of the Slovaks with the state of affairs within the common Republic was one of the reasons why the independent Slovak State was created, under the sponsorship of the Nazis, in 1939, and which continued its existence throughout the period of WWII. After WWII, Slovakia was 'naturally' reincorporated into the liberated Czechoslovakia, but the experience of independence left a strong mark on the ethnic consciousness of Slovaks.

The deportation of some 2.5 million Germans after the war (mid-1940s) left a vacuum in the formerly German parts of the Czech territory, and this vacuum could not be filled through appeals to the Czech population alone. As early as 1946, the cabinet plan counted on the arrival of Slovaks. Between 1945 and 1947 some 110,300 people migrated from Slovakia. Largely, they settled in western and northern Bohemia; very few went to Southern Bohemia and Moravia (Prokop, 2000; Šrajerová, 1999). However, a continuous Slovak settlement did not eventuate. Slovaks who arrived were primarily motivated by a desire to improve their economic conditions, to acquire land and real estate or to work in industrial enterprises. There were virtually no intellectuals among these people. Nevertheless, they were initially interested in maintaining their Slovak identity, a fact that surfaced in the foundation of local branches of the *Matice slovenská*, an ethnic maintenance-and-development organisation that played an important role in Slovakia. Fifty-three branches of this organisation were created in 1946–1947, engaging in establishing Slovak libraries, extending the distribution of the Slovak press and arranging theatre performances in Slovak. However, in a few years, a trend appeared that gradually strengthened through the end of the 20th century: a shift toward Czech culture and language. This trend developed not only to help simplify interaction within a new environment but also as a shift to a culture that was perceived to be more powerful and desirable. As a consequence, in the course of the 1950s, branches of *Matice slovenská* ceased to exist (Šrajerová, 1999: 144).

The main impulse for the massive migration of Slovaks to the Czech territory in the 1950s and 1960s was the growth of heavy industry. Apart from northern Bohemia, this growth mainly took place in the Ostrava region in northern Moravia, and that is where many Slovaks headed. Again, most of these people were unqualified labourers, but some of them came with the intention to gain qualifications and return to work in similar establishments in Slovakia. In the Ostrava region, workers from Slovakia were given special benefits, in particular in housing. This meant that in some areas of the region, such as in Havířov, Karviná or Petřvald, Slovaks were soon in the majority. In the Karviná district, 3838 Slovaks were resident in 1950, but 30 years later the number had reached 25,558 (Prokop, 2000). In 1970, this district showed the largest concentration of Slovaks in the Czech lands. Karviná City established its first Slovak elementary school in 1956 and its second in 1969. In 1968 the city saw the rebirth of a branch of *Matice slovenská* that continued to be active until the mid-1970s. The introduction of Slovak schools was also considered in Havířov, Třinec and Ostrava, but these plans met with little enthusiasm among the Slovak population. The Karviná schools thus remained the only Slovak schools that ever existed in the territory of the present day Czech Republic. It is paradoxical that, throughout the duration of the Czechoslovak Republic, Slovaks, as one of the basic ethnic groups of the Republic, were legally not a minority, and consequently did not have a right, like the designated 'minorities', to schools in their own language.

Since the 1950s, the number of Slovaks in the Czech lands gradually rose:

258,025 in 1950, 275,997 in 1961, 320,998 in 1970 and 359,370 in 1980. Throughout this period, Slovaks were accepted by the Czech matrix population with a friendly but sometimes patronising attitude, whether they spoke Slovak or Czech. In the 1950s most Slovak students who studied at Czech universities continued speaking Slovak while in the Czech lands. There was social pressure on the side of Slovak society to do so. After the introduction of the federation system in 1968, the Slovak community also included people who went to Prague to represent Slovakia in the federal government and in other institutions; these people, too, continued speaking Slovak. At the same time, Slovak culture, in particular popular music, television and films, as well as science and humanities were happily accepted by the Czech population. Nevertheless, the average level of education within the Slovak community remained at a level lower than that of the average for the Czech community, and this was reflected in the structure of Slovak employment. Davidová (1990), in the course of her research on communi-cation within large enterprises of the Ostrava region, collected useful sociologi-cal data that bear witness to the position of Slovaks compared to that of other ethnic groups. For example, in a coal-mine in Petřvald close to Karviná, which employed 5300 people, 81% were Czechs (today some might categorise them-selves as Moravians or Silesians), 15% Slovaks and 3% Poles. While 3% of the Polish employees were in executive positions, only 1% of Slovaks could be included in the same category. Other enterprises demonstrated a similar power structure (Davidová, 1990: 43).

The 1991 census was the first in the 20th century that registered a decrease in the number of Slovaks in the territory of the present day Czech Republic. The decrease was about 40,000 people. Slovak ethnicity was recorded by 314,877 people – i.e. 3.1% of the overall population. However, this was not the result of the return of Slovaks to the land of their origin. Two other factors were decisive: firstly, a number of people opted for Czech ethnicity both for themselves and for their children; secondly, many Roma, who had previously considered them-selves Slovaks, reported for the first time as Roma. Census questions had not enabled the Roma to identify as Roma between 1930 and 1991. Since the bulk of the original Czech Roma were exterminated in the Nazi concentration camps, and the Roma who resided in the Czech lands were post-war immigrants from Slovakia, it was only natural that in the pre-1991 censuses they declared them-selves as Slovaks. This has to be taken into consideration when evaluating demo-graphic statistics. Šrajerová (1999: 149) assumes that in 1970 the share of the Roma who declared Slovak ethnicity was 13.1%, 10 years later it was 15.6% and in 1991 the number actually grew to 23.5% (i.e. 74,000 individuals), notwithstand-ing that they could (and some did) report as Roma.

Slovak immigration to the Czech Republic of the 1990s was characterised by the fact that all strata of Slovak society were included. The decisive factors were no longer economic but social (e.g. the reunification of families) and, following the birth of an independent Slovakia, also political (dissent from Prime Minister Mečiar's authoritarian political attitudes). At the same time, 'symbolically' speaking, in the 1990s the situation of the Slovak community in a sense deterio-rated. They now became a minority, and many regretted this change of status. According to sociological surveys, their majority disagreed with the partition of the Czechoslovak Republic (Šrajerová, 1999). Since dual citizenship was not allowed by the legislation of the day, they had to opt for one of the two, and on the basis of pragmatic considerations they mostly opted for the Czech one. On the other hand, throughout the decade, politicians on both sides aimed for 'closer-than-standard' relations between the Czech and Slovak Republics and this favourably influenced the position of the Slovak Community in the Czech Republic. For example, on the basis of agreements between the two governments, thousands of Slovak students study free of charge at Czech universities. The freedom of thought characteristic of the 1990s enabled the cultural flourishing of the Slovak community, and its political as well as cultural diversification, especially in Prague (Haluková, 1998; Praha a národnosti, 1998).

The 2001 census showed a substantial decrease in the Slovak community, from 314,877 to 193,190 individuals within a decade. This decrease of more than 120,000 people is not easy to explain by any single factor. Probably the trend of the older residents to declare Czech ethnicity had accelerated. At the same time, the trend for greater intermarriage between young Slovaks and Czechs has intensified, while recent migration from Slovakia that would have increased the numbers of Slovaks has lost momentum. It is also likely that more and more Roma, who formerly registered as Slovaks, opted for Czech ethnicity.

On the whole, one might conclude that the shaping of the Slovak community in the Czech Republic has been determined largely by two factors:

- The low cultural and linguistic distance between Slovakia and the Czech lands which enables successful communication and fast reaction to changes in the labour market and networks of social contacts. The high rate of intermarriage is not surprising.
- The power structure. Since the Czech culture has been perceived as superior, Slovaks, especially those with lower educational levels, showed little inclination to pursue education in Slovak schools and participate in Slovak cultural institutions. The perceived superior status of the Czech culture can be assumed to have contributed substantially to the ethnic shift of the Slovak community in the Czech lands.

The Roma

With the gradual decrease in the Slovak community within the Czech milieu, as described in the previous section, it is almost certain that the Romani community has become the largest non-Czech community in the Czech Republic. This is not a fact that is readily discernible in statistics. In the 2001 census only 11,000 persons admitted Romani ethnicity. In the 1991 census almost 33,000 persons had opted for this alternative, while official records kept by local authorities until 1989 (a tradition established by the Austro-Hungarian Empire) counted 145,000 persons. Today it is generally estimated that, due to a high birth rate and other factors (such as underestimation in previous statistics), the number is between two-hundred- and three-hundred-thousand (Možný, 2002). The Roma live virtually everywhere in the country, but the largest concentration can be found in northern Moravia and north-central Bohemia (Zpráva, 2002). In comparison with the rest of Europe, the number of the Roma is high, following Rumania, Bulgaria, Spain, Hungary, Slovakia, the former Yugoslavia and Turkey.

The basis of the Roma question is not in the physical features of the Roma, which sometimes, though not always, differ from the matrix population. (Dark complexion and certain features of the physique tend to be interpreted as Roma characteristics.) Rather, the Roma question constitutes the most significant ethnic problem of present day Czech Republic because of sociocultural disparity between them and the matrix population. Sociocultural difference leads to differential socioeconomic power, and this projects into all domains of conduct, including linguistic behaviour. It is necessary to realise that the problem is not based only in the Roma population but also in the matrix community. Hence, when policies are formulated, they must address the Czechs as well.

The Roma immigration to the Near East and Europe originated in India. Although the Roma themselves do not possess any memory of their Indian origin (Hancock, 1988), their language and culture point to India in an indisputable way. In the territory of the present Czech Republic, their appearance has been confirmed as early as the end of 14th century, and they have been present ever since. The original Czech Roma were virtually exterminated in the Nazi concentration camps during WWII, while Slovak Roma were not. (During the war the independent Slovak state was not directly governed by Nazi Germany.) The bulk of the contemporary Roma population arrived from Slovakia after WWII, and it is necessary to understand that even at the present time they retain close ties with the Roma in that country, although the links may be waning in the case of the very young. Keeping up family relationships across national boundaries has also been the rule for other smaller Romani groups. While the pre-war Czech Roma maintained the nomadic way of life often associated with the Roma as a whole, the Slovak Roma were basically sedentary.

Although the contemporary Roma community appears to the Czechs to be homogeneous, it is not. Linguistically it can be divided into the original Czech Roma (now a very small group), the Slovak-and-Czech Roma, the Hungarian Roma, the Vlach Roma and various other smaller groups. These groupings, already lacking homogeneity in themselves (Elšík, 2003), live side by side in their Czech environment, rather than in a single social structure. The Roma continue to be a sum of many smaller groups ('clans' based on family ties) which lack cohesiveness, although there are attempts to create the consciousness of a whole.

One of the basic issues involved here is that the sense of Roma ethnicity has not yet been fully established. The political elites within the community have realised this problem and are trying to amend it (Leudar & Nekvapil, 2000). The issue of an underdeveloped ethnicity creates not only inadequacies in the political representation of the Roma but also supports the ongoing loss of the Roma culture and language. Within the younger generation, the traditional value system has been seriously threatened. To many Czechs, the Roma appear to be a community without any culture. However, traditional culture – tales, proverbs or music – is in fact still alive and new culture – poetry, literature or painting – is quickly developing.

In Slovakia and other countries east of the Czech Republic the Roma typically live in settlements at the outskirts of villages or towns of the matrix population, but in the Czech Republic the usual domicile is within towns and cities, where the Roma are concentrated in areas, sometimes very central, which have been abandoned by other dwellers. These areas are normally characterised by low quality slum housing, frequently beyond repair. Prior to 1989, the Communist Party government exercised a policy of dispersing the Roma, but within the more liberal atmosphere of the 1990s the concentration of the Roma in certain areas has continued to be the rule. The traditional occupations have long been lost; men typically work in jobs in the construction industries, and women in cleaning. Their income is at the level of about 60% of the average wage for men and about 25% in the case of women. Additionally, there is a very high rate of unemployment, an amazing 70% in some areas and occasionally even as high as 90% within a society where, in the 1990s, the overall unemployment was under 10% (Možný, 2002). It is not surprising that, under these conditions, delinquency within the community does occur; from the point of view of the matrix population, the Roma more than occasionally are seen as thieves and prostitutes. More recently, drug dependence has also been reported. However, the extent of criminality together with other comparisons across ethnic groups needs more objective assessment than is currently available.

The attitudes of the matrix population toward the Roma community are negative. While the overall indices of xenophobia are not particularly high (Bártová, 2002; Jesenský, 2000), the Roma are more than disliked. The behaviour that is stereotypically the object of criticism includes their lack of interest in children's education, the handling of apartments and other dwellings ('they burn parquets for heating'), the level of hygiene, the erratic attendance at work, etc. The problems, real or assumed, are not seen as a heritage of the past that cannot be overcome in a decade, but as personal deficiencies of individual Roma. Normally, however, such criticism is not based on personal experience. The Roma are not invisible, but few people have had direct interaction with them. Still, when asked in 1999 whether they would like to have a Romani family as their neighbours, more than 40% of respondents in the survey answered univocally 'no'. (Incidentally, this is identical with the European average; cf. Možný, 2002: 134.) In 1991 negative response had still been over 70%. Seen from the Czech Republic point of view, one might reverse the judgment and say 'only 40% said no'. Bártová correctly points to the fact that, west of the Czech Republic, tolerance towards the Roma does not differ from tolerance to foreigners in general because, apart from Spain, the numbers of the Roma are small and the issue does not stand out. Within the Czech Republic, criminality on the Roma side is paralleled by discrimination and brutal attacks from the matrix community. Such attacks are usually performed by extremist right-wing groups, such as Skinheads or their sympathisers, but silently approved by many Czechs. The Roma community is frightened, because they can be killed for no apparent reason, including women and children. The Czech police are sometimes overtly anti-Roma, and Czech courts have so far been lenient towards the killers.

A large comparative study of the presentation of the Roma in Czech, Slovak and Hungarian media was conducted by Nekvapil *et al.* (2000). For the Czech media, analysed by J. Homoláč, four findings were of particular interest:

(1) The comparison of reports on three separate killings of Roma (1991, 1993 and 1995) revealed that newspaper reporting increased in quantity as well as quality.
(2) The killings were not perceived as events in their own right but rather as responses to Romani criminality; they were not seen as racially motivated

unless the victim was classified as a 'decent Romany'. There was a trend to present characteristics stereotypically attributed to the Roma and to employ them as a means of explaining the violence.

(3)   Even when there was a one-sided attack, the situation was explained as a 'skirmish' between the Roma and Skinheads, not an act of the majority community directed towards the minority.

(4)   It was unusual for the Czech media to describe positive actions of the Roma, and when the media did describe positive actions, those actions were presented as exceptional. Negative reporting, based on stereotypes, abounded in the Czech press (see also Homoláč *et al.*, 2003; Nekvapil & Leudar, 2002).

The sociologist Keller (2002) summarises the discrimination against the Roma in the following points:

(1)   A Roma child is discriminated against at the moment he or she enters a Czech school. There are sociocultural as well as linguistic barriers to education. Large numbers of Roma children have been placed in 'special schools', a fact that seriously affects their further education. Only a small number of Roma children complete more than elementary schooling.

(2)   The second level of discrimination occurs in employment. The rate of unemployment is huge. If unqualified work is available, it is often so poorly paid that social welfare benefits constitute the more attractive option. This is not to say that there are not many Roma who would like to work.

(3)   Especially since the beginning of the 1990s, a trend has appeared in the matrix community to assert its 'right to intolerance'. The Roma have often been refused access to restaurants or swimming pools and have been physically attacked, though the agents were not normally typical members of the matrix community (Keller, 2002).

Another point should be added: the Roma have suffered the loss of their language. This matter will be dealt with in Part III.

   This is a very dangerous situation. The political system of Czechoslovakia under the communist government dealt with some of the issues within an assimilationist framework, but failed to resolve them. Towards the end of the 1990s, some Roma attempted to improve their situation by emigrating, for example, to Britain or Canada. However, these avenues have been closed by the governments of the countries in question. Admittedly, some work has been done, and the future is not entirely grim. The government of the Czech Republic is obviously under international pressure, particularly in view of its expected entry into the European Union which requires that all member countries have a clean record on human rights and ethnic relations. Hence, in the 2000s, more and more measures have been taken to improve the situation, including attempts to change the attitudes of the police force (Zpráva, 2002). In 2001, the Government reorganised its interdepartmental Council of the Czech Government for Matters of the Roma Community, to include 14 Roma out of the total membership of 28. The government further approved a *Koncepce politiky vlády vůči příslušníkům romské komunity* 'The Principles of Government's Policy Towards Members of the Roma Community', a document that must be welcome after a decade of a -

laissez-faire policy (see Part II, Communities: A Summary). In 2002 there was one appointed Roma Member of Parliament. A Roma representative is a member of the Czech Radio Consultative Working Party for Ethnic Broadcasting, and the Roma are represented on the government's Council for Ethnic Minorities. The government financially supports the Museum of Roma Culture in Brno as well as a number of Roma periodicals and cultural programmes (Zpráva, 2002).

At present, the Roma are prepared to defend their interests; however, the matrix community often perceives its interests as being opposed to those of the Roma, and it possesses the power to realise its interests. The only power the Roma can exercise is through radical social and political action, and there is no doubt that they are able to do so. A question that is of importance is to what extent the interests of the Roma intellectual elites, which represent the Roma in the community at large, will in the future coincide with the interests of average members of the community. Responsibility lies with the government to show that it is prepared to take further effective measures to alleviate the situation. In 2002, the new Prime Minister, Vladimír Špidla, appealed to the Roma to cooperate with the government on a policy to improve the conditions of the community. As Keller notes (2002), the basic prerequisite is the improvement of the economic performance of the country in general, but much more can be achieved before that happens if the ideology of the matrix community moves towards more ethnic tolerance.

A considerable number of cultural, social and political Roma organisations are oriented not only toward the left but also toward the right (cf. Zpráva, 2002: 71).

The Poles

In the 2001 census, 51,968 people reported Polish ethnicity. In 1991, the number was 59,383. Most of these people live in the Těšín region, a relatively small North Moravian territory which is a component of the Czech part of historical Silesia that borders on Poland. It consists of two districts: Karviná, where, in 2001, 19,040 people (6.8% of the population of the district) registered as Poles, and Frýdek-Místek, 18,077 people (8% of the population). The remaining Poles live dispersed among the Czechs and other ethnic groups, essentially over the whole territory of the Czech Republic – a higher density can be observed only in northern, eastern and central Bohemia. It is necessary also to take into consideration that at present several thousand Poles work on long-term permits in the Republic. In the Škoda-Volkswagen automobile factory in Mladá Boleslav alone, several hundreds were employed in 1996. In the case of Poles in the Czech Republic it is therefore possible to identify at least three categories (Zeman, 1994):

- the Těšín community;
- Poles living in other districts; and
- foreign workers.

However, it is the first category that attracts most attention, and that category will constitute the target of this account.

Maximum size was attained by the Polish community in 1910 when 158,261 people reported Polish as their mother tongue. In the following decade the number dropped to 103,521, a decrease caused partly by a change in patterns of reporting in the Těšín region where many people were ethnically indifferent, and partly by emigration. Since then, the number of people who declared themselves to be Poles has consistently declined to the current level. It seems that, in the years from 1950 to 1980, almost 33,600 Poles (46.2% of the 1950 community) changed their ethnic allegiance, now mostly reporting as Czechs (Srb, 1987).

The Polish minority of the Těšín region originates in the decision of the post-WWI negotiations about central Europe when the region was allotted to the Czechoslovak state. This was an act of management by force, and there was no way of opposing the power of those who made the decision. Many Poles, who in this way found themselves living outside of Poland, considered the decision as unjust. This feeling marked the cohabitation of Poles and Czechs on the territory ever since, and language management within the situation has attracted much attention from Czechoslovak (now Czech) and Polish authorities (Borák, 1999) ever since. At the end of the 1930s, and also immediately following WWII, the incorporation of the region into Czechoslovakia became the object of severe conflict between Czechoslovakia and Poland. The post-war conflict was terminated only following strong pressure from the Soviet Union in 1947.

In the period between the two world wars, the Těšín region witnessed the development of a dense network of Polish schools and a large number of Polish cultural, sports and economic institutions. Initially, there were few Polish intellectuals of local origin, and these were mostly school teachers. The population predominantly found employment in the mining and iron works industries. The process of further industrialisation which followed WWII led to the dissolution of the original ethnic structure. It brought to the Těšín region tens of thousands of Slovaks whose overall percentage in the Karviná district in 1991 was as high as that of Poles. In 2001 Poles (19,040) were, however, again more numerous than Slovaks (15,948). In comparison, the Czech element comprised 229,658 people. Polish ethnicity was also negatively influenced by the disappearance of Polish villages and the movement of the population to urban centres such as Havířov. Under the Communist Party government, Polish associations were reduced to a single organisation, the *Polský kulturně-osvětový svaz*, founded in 1947. This name itself makes it clear that the aim of this organisation was strictly non-political. At the beginning of the 1950s, the network of Polish schools expanded, but subsequently, with the decline in demand, the number of schools also decreased. In 1955, the principle of bilingualism, which guaranteed bilingual signs on buildings, bilingual official notices, etc. in towns and villages with a larger number of Polish inhabitants, was accepted in the region (obviously approved by a top organ of the Communist Party before it was codified in official regulations). The implementation of the principle has been a sensitive issue up to the present time. There are indications that, for the Polish community, it has primarily been understood as a strategy symbolising the equality of Poles and Czechs within the region (Sokolová, 1999b). In daily life most Poles are at least receptively bilingual in Polish and Czech. However, an important non-symbolic role was played by Polish libraries, or the Polish section within local libraries, as well as by the Polish section of the Těšín Theatre. Since 1951, Polish broadcasting is also available on Czech national radio.

Following the changes of 1989, social organisation became freer, and Poles diversified in their allegiances. Apart from the *Polský kulturně-osvětový svaz*, a more ambitious *Rada Poláků* came into being. However, it seems that no major change in the life of the community eventuated (Borák, 1998). Previous trends continue, and the most prominent of these is assimilation. According to the available statistics in 1994, Poles entered into only 27.9% of ethnically homogeneous marriages. One of the factors in the decline of opting for Polish ethnicity has been the emergence of the Silesian ethnic category, which attracted 44,446 people in 1991 and 10,878 in 2001.

The trends mentioned above notwithstanding, Poles in the Těšín region remain the only territorially bound historical ethnic minority in the Czech Republic. Hence they have attracted the attention of a number of specialists, for example from the *Slezský ústav* (Silesian Institute) in Opava. Since the end of the 1980s sociolinguistic work has started to appear. In 1990, Ostrava University established a special *Kabinet pro výzkum polského etnika v České republice* (Unit for Research of the Polish Ethnic Group in the Czech Republic). After the demise of Czechoslovakia in 1993, more attention of the Czech and Polish authorities has concentrated on the Polish minority of the Těšín region than had occurred in the ethnically more varied Czechoslovak state.

At the time work on this monograph ended (February 2003), there were definitely Poles who felt that their interests were being suppressed through the power of the Czech state. The Report of the Government's Council for Ethnic Minorities mentions that its Polish member negatively evaluated the conduct of the 2001 census because, immediately prior to that census, the Czech media reported that the census documents might be misused, thus in fact deterring minority individuals from declaring their true feelings. According to the Polish member of the Council, the actual number of Poles in the territory of the Czech Republic was 70,000. In this figure, he included all those who had declared Silesian ethnicity. In that part of the Report that conveys the views of individual members of the Council, the Polish representative criticised the current situation on many counts, including hidden intolerance and discrimination (Zpráva, 2002: 68). His attitude shows that problems do exist. It is an important question to what extent the joint entry of Poland and the Czech Republic into the European Union in 2004 will change the overall situation.

The Germans

Germans, or German-speaking inhabitants, have lived in the territory of the present Czech Republic for more than 10 centuries. The co-existence of the Czech and German elements has had a special historical significance and has been highlighted earlier in this paper. The current situation will be the focus of the following text.

As mentioned above, the largest number of Germans in the territory of the Czech Republic was attested in 1910, when the population reached 3,492,362 (Srb, 1988). Old continuous settlements could be found, primarily near the borders with Germany and Austria, but there were ethnic islands within areas that were almost totally Czech. The German element was particularly strong in cities and towns, especially in Prague, Brno, and Jihlava. The wide distribution of the German population is attested by the fact that a recent project to produce an

Atlas historických německých nářečí (Historical Atlas of German Dialects) found it necessary to collect data from nearly one-third of the present-day territory of the Czech Republic (Bachmann, 2002). After WWI, large numbers of Germans – e.g. Austrian officials and others who were not native to the country – left; a similar exit of foreign officials, soldiers and others brought in by the occupation during the period between 1939 and 1945 occurred after WWII. Nevertheless, in the middle of 1945 the remaining native German element represented approximately 2,809,000 individuals – i.e. 26.3% of the entire population. Yet, two years later, following the large-scale deportation of Germans to Germany and Austria, only some 180,000 (2.1% of the population) remained (Srb, 1988). This deportation was arranged on the basis of agreements reached at the Potsdam Conference (1945) and the implementation of the agreement was accepted by virtually the entire Czech population which considered the deportation a logical conclusion to WWII, a period marked by atrocities committed by the Nazis who, in their turn, had been enthusiastically supported by the majority of Czech Germans. No major objections were raised abroad either. At present, a number of people, including many Czechs, see the decision in a different light, but both the emotional and ideological atmosphere of the mid-1940s led to virtual universal acceptance of its justification at that time. Deportation did not affect German antifascists (often Social Democrats or communists), some old people, Germans from mixed marriages, and persons who were necessary for the functioning of the economy. These exemptions, of course, did not guarantee that such people would not be discriminated against. Often the decision regarding who should be allowed to stay was a matter of chance. The implementation of the deportation was not always compassionate; on the contrary it was sometimes even brutal – a record that has been reported in biographical research by many participants (see, e.g. Stehlíková, 1997: 70).

Over the course of the following decades, the numbers of Germans decreased further: 159,938 in 1950; 134,143 in 1961; 80,903 in 1970; 58,211 in 1980 and 48,556 in 1991. The most recent figure represented only 0.5% of the population. This decline was partly due to emigration to the German Federal Republic and partly to rapid assimilation. In the period from 1965 to 1969 alone, when emigration procedures were eased, some 48,000 people left. The process of assimilation was aided by territorial dispersion, mixed marriages, the absence of German schools and negative attitudes among the Czech majority to anything German, based on the experience of repression by the Nazis during wartime. Demographic research conducted in the 1980s showed that the German community was characterised by a low percentage of children and a high participation in the economy, mainly in working-class jobs. The majority in the German population consisted of women (a higher ratio than in the matrix population), and 55% of the community was over 50 years of age. The education profile of the community was one of the worst in the country (Srb, 1988).

Assimilation of the German community further deepened in the 1990s. In 1991, within the group up to 35 years of age there were only 9% homogeneous marriages (i.e. both husband and wife German), while a few years later this figure declined to a mere 3%. Sokolová *et al.* (1997: 67) spoke about the dissolution of the community in the Czech matrix community. This view seems to be confirmed by the most recent census (2001), when only 39,106 (0.4% of the population of the country) claimed German ethnicity, 10,000 less than in 1991. This drift occurred notwithstanding the fact that German ethnicity no longer carried any social or political stigma or disadvantage.

Although in the course of the deportation the composition of the remaining German community was selected to suit the world view of the Communist Party, when the Party assumed unlimited political power in 1948, its approach to the community was guided by principles of discrimination rather than 'proletarian internationalism'. It is true that, at the beginning of the 1950s, four persons of German origin were 'elected' (i.e. in fact appointed by the Party) to the Parliament, but it was not until 1953 that all Germans were granted Czech citizenship, and the community did not achieve the legal status of a 'minority' until 1968, eight years after other groups. After the Prague Spring, the first official organisation of the Community, founded in 1969, was the *Kulturní sdružení občanů ČSSR německé národnosti* (The Cultural Association of Citizens of German Ethnicity) which continued to exist through the following decades. Before the Velvet Revolution (1989) it had 8000 members in 60 branches.

After the Velvet Revolution of 1989 a number of changes took place. However, these changes pertained largely to the political rather than to the daily-life domains. The most prominent feature of the change was the appearance of a new organisation, *Shromáždění Němců v Čechách, na Moravě a ve Slezsku* (Assembly of Germans in Bohemia, Moravia and Silesia). This body tries to work within the spirit of the democratic society of the 1990s. However, the survival of the *Kulturní sdružení* shows that not all Germans negatively evaluated their previous form of association. At the beginning of the 1990s, intensive contact took place between the *Shromáždění Němců* and representatives of the *Sudetendeutsche Landsmannschaft* [Sudeten German Welfare and Cultural Association], which represents one segment of the Germans deported to the German Federal Republic. Through this channel, economic aid was directed to Germans in the Czech Republic (Staněk, 1998). Later, however, aid was distributed by official organs of the German government, because the *Landsmannschaft* was viewed with concern not only by the Czech community but also by some members of the *Kulturní sdružení*. The attempt, in 1992, to found a political party called *Demokratická strana Sudety* (Democratic Sudeten Party) in Plzeň, met with considerable resistance not only in the Czech community but even among Czech Germans (Leudar & Nekvapil, 1998). This attempt clearly opposed the interests of the Czech community, being interpreted as an attempt to return to the pre-war period when Henlein's Nazi Sudeten Party pursued a clear policy of attaching the Sudeten region to Germany. Within the Czech community as well as within the German community itself the question appeared regarding what German organisations in the Czech Republic should actually do. Should they concentrate on revitalisation of German culture and language, or should they include political programmes, such as the abolition of the 1945 Beneš Decrees through which German property in Czechoslovakia was confiscated? It is an undisputable fact that the issue of compensation for the deported Germans will remain as an international political issue. However, equally undecided is the question of compensation for Germans who lost their property even though they were permitted to stay in the country. The economic situation of some members of the German community in the Czech Republic is at present satisfactory. Those who possess a knowledge of German often work in foreign (German) companies where pay is much higher than in Czech enterprises. Many others work in Germany. The case of the Hlučín region (cf. MFD 11 May 2000) shows that such arrangements can affect thousands of people.

The German community is not restricted to Germans who were born and educated in the country. A considerable number of German companies are active in the Czech Republic with the consequence that a number of sojourner executives and other employees arrive from Germany. The number is not easy to establish. The 2001 census showed 3438 persons who possessed German citizenship. These Germans, mainly managers, enjoy a high socioeconomic status which is at variance with the Czech Germans. While an average Czech hardly notices that remnants of a formerly huge German community still live in the country, the 'German Germans' are in focus. They are the bearers of foreign capital, which is important to the country, but that foreign capital is also frequently viewed as a risk (Houžvička, 2001). This group of German Germans have tried to prevent resistance due to the fear of German economic dominance by representing their companies as international rather than German (Nekvapil, 1997b).

The long history of Czech-German contact has led to a variety of names for the Germans. Along with the neutral word *Němec*, well documented as early as in the 14th century, there are a number of pejorative denominations such as *Němčour* (a pejorative ending, *–our*, added to the designation *Němec*) or *Skopčák* 'a mouton man' (after the leather trousers German nationalists used to wear) (Skála, 1977), which attest to negative attitudes.

The Ruthenians, Ukrainians and Russians

The arrival of large numbers of Ruthenians (Rusyns), Ukrainians, and Russians in the territory of the present-day Czech Republic occurred after WWI as a consequence of the October Revolution in Russia and, in the case of Ruthenians, the incorporation of Ruthenia (now a part of the Ukraine adjoining eastern Slovakia) into the newly formed Czechoslovakia. In the first days of Czechoslovakia, it was once suggested that the country should be called *Česko-slovenská-rusínská republika* 'Czecho-Slovak-Ruthenian Republic' (Praha: Osobnosti, 2000: 127).

Following the Russian Revolution, a refugee assistance programme resulted in the arrival from former Czarist Russia of a large number of Russians and Ukrainians and a number of members of other ethnic groups (Georgians and Kalmycks for example). This programme was organised by the Czechoslovak government, with the first President, T.G. Masaryk, playing a leading role. It has been estimated that the number of refugees increased from an original 6000 to more than 20,000 in the 1920s and 1930s (Sládek, 1999: 14). Initially, the Soviet regime in Russia was expected to be a temporary phenomenon, and consequently the refugees considered their stay as a temporary one. They did not enter into local networks, living mostly in their closed communities, a lifestyle for which they were provided excellent conditions by the Czechoslovak government which supported their associations and paid for Russian and Ukrainian schools from kindergarten to university. Both a Russian and a Ukrainian university operated in the Republic (for details see Veber *et al.*, 1996; Zilynskij, 1995).

However, the refugee assistance programme was made problematic in the 1930s, when Czechoslovakia, like France, realised that the Soviet Union was both a large export market and politically a potential ally against the German threat. The anti-Soviet émigré community was considered a nuisance and its financial support dried up. Under these conditions, émigrés started leaving the country. On the other hand, Nazi occupation of Czechoslovakia did not result in the demise of the Russian and Ukrainian organisations: for example, the Russian and Ukrainian gymnasia (high schools) as well as the Ukrainian University were active throughout WWII (Kopřivová-Vukolová, 1993; Zilynskij, 1995: 54) – this despite the fact that the operation of the Czech universities was suspended. The end of the 'good old days' arrived with the termination of the war, when the Soviet Army, as it advanced, detained approximately a thousand émigrés, mainly members of the Russian intelligentsia, and hauled them off to concentration camps in the Soviet Union. Only a small number of those people survived and still fewer returned to Czechoslovakia after a long period of forced labour in the camps (Kopřivová-Vukolová, 1993). Many members of the Ukrainian community, seizing the opportunity presented by Hitler's advance into the Soviet Union to further their claims for independence, collaborated with Nazi Germany, but managed to escape to the West before the Red Army arrived.

With the end of WWII, Ruthenia was claimed by the Soviet Union and this resulted in bringing an end to any further reinforcement of the Ruthenian community. New additions could only arrive from eastern Slovakia, but reliable statistics do not exist, because Ruthenians were now identified as a subset of Ukrainians and were registered as such. In eastern Slovakia, a programme of forced Ukrainisation of the Ruthenians started in 1953 and, interestingly, was also directed against their Russification. Under these circumstances, many declared Slovak identity. However, the situation was not completely clear, and the category and term *Ruthenian* did not entirely disappear. The constitutional law of 1968 used a strange formulation to describe one of the officially acknowledged nationalities – 'Ukrainian (Ruthenian)'.

According to the authoritative work about national minorities published in Czechoslovakia before the Velvet Revolution, in the 1950 census 19,384 people resident in the Czech lands registered as being of Ukrainian/Russian ethnicity. Thirty years later the number had decreased to 15,322 (Sokolová *et al.*, 1987: 35). Note that the category used was Ukrainian/Russian and that the term *Ukrainian* was intended to include Ruthenians.

For the first time, the 1991 census allowed individuals to opt freely for either Ruthenian, Ukrainian or Russian ethnicity; 1926 respondents living in the Czech part of the then Czechoslovakia, reported as Ruthenians, but 10 years later, in the 2001 census, the number had decreased to 1106. The community itself claims 10,000 individuals (Zpráva, 2002: 74). Although their number is small, they are well organised (see, particularly, the *Společnost přátel Podkarpatské Rusi* 'The Society of Friends of Ruthenia'), and they have developed wide-ranging publication activities. Thanks to their long-term status, their importance has been acknowledged in the fact that they are represented on the government's Council for Ethnic Minorities and in organs of the Prague City office.

As for Ukrainians, the 1991 census registered 8220 individuals, while 10 years later the number had increased to 22,112. In the contemporary Czech Republic,

Ukrainians represent the largest group of foreign workers; it is assumed that the 2001 census captured only part of them.[3] Whether university graduates or individuals with only basic education, they are mostly active as manual workers. Attitudes of the matrix community are more often negative than positive (Zilynskij, 1996) because, for an average Czech, they are not easily distinguished from Russians, and the media often refer to 'Russian-speaking gangs and mafia'. Ukrainians, like other ethnic groups, receive financial support from the government for their social, cultural and publication activities. The most active organisation is *Ukrajinská iniciativa v ČR* 'Ukrainian Initiative in the Czech Republic'.

Russian ethnicity was declared in 1991 by 5062 people, but in 2001 the number rose to 12,369. This increase is no doubt partly due to Russian foreign workers who are active in the Czech Republic under conditions similar to those of the Ukrainians. However, not a negligible segment of the new arrivals consists of well-to-do Russians who own shops and real estate. Among Czechs, the view – not quite without substance – prevails that this segment of the Russian community has established itself particularly well in the internationally well-known resort, Karlovy Vary (Karlsbad). The social life of the Russian community has only commenced – the Czech population still vividly remembers the Soviet invasion of 1968 and the ensuing occupation, and these memories do not favour the existence of organised elements of Russian society in their midst.

The Vietnamese

The first groups of Vietnamese arrived in the Czech Republic as a consequence of the 1955 agreement on economic, scientific and technical cooperation between Czechoslovakia and the Vietnamese Democratic Republic. The Vietnamese came to Czechoslovakia to obtain practical qualifications in mechanical engineering, metallurgy and other areas; indeed, some of them were sent to study in high schools and universities. Their numbers gradually increased, and the peak was reached at the beginning of the 1980s when approximately 30,000 resided in the territory of Czechoslovakia. Because the aim of their stay was apprenticeship in a profession, they were mainly young people. Some of them came for a few years of practice in industrial organisations, having first obtained basic qualifications in their own country. Two Czech enterprises, ČKD Praha and Tatra Kopřivnice, alone offered placement for more than 500 Vietnamese sojourners. Admittedly, many of them were not exclusively concentrating on their work – they had families to look after in their home country and earning money as well as purchasing goods not available in Vietnam were important side purposes of their stay. In this respect they were perhaps not very different from the category of foreign workers, except that their selection and arrival were strictly regulated by the state and both governments perceived their stay as having ideological significance. In the first two decades of this program, the Czech population maintained a positive attitude, but in the 1980s the atmosphere changed somewhat because the Vietnamese sojourners were allegedly buying large quantities of merchandise that were in short supply (motorcycles, bicycles, sewing machines, etc.). In mid-1980s intermarriages appeared. Following the demise of the Communist Party regime in 1989 the new Czechoslovak government cancelled the agreement with Vietnam which resulted in a radical decrease in the size of the Vietnamese community. In the 1991 census, only 421 people reported Vietnamese ethnic identity, but the demography later changed again. In the 2001 census, 17,462 persons claimed Vietnamese ethnicity. It is not entirely clear how to explain this discrepancy; at least four factors must be considered:

- In the 1991 census some Vietnamese did not declare their ethnicity because they were frightened of being deported.
- The 2001 census included residents with a long-term visa (over 90 days), while the 1991 census only registered people with permanent permits.
- On the basis of a new intergovernmental agreement with Vietnam, new young Vietnamese commenced arriving to obtain work practice in the industrial sector.
- As Müllerová (1998) noted, there was a massive influx of Vietnamese who arrived from former East Germany.

The Vietnamese from East Germany deserve special mention. Their entrance was principally caused by the liberal rules for conducting commercial activities in the Czech Republic; e.g. foreigners were allowed to open commercial enterprises without having a permanent visa. It is not surprising that relatively large Vietnamese communities are located in areas bordering Germany, the former GDR (Köppen, 2000) or what used to be West Germany. For example in Cheb, with 33,000 inhabitants, there were, in 2001, 1488 Vietnamese who thus represented the leading non-Czech community (4.5%). The largest concentration of Vietnamese seems to be the border community of Hřensko, where, out of a population of 247, 43 people (17.4%) are Vietnamese. In the somewhat larger township of Železná Ruda (approximately 2000 inhabitants), 11.8% are Vietnamese. When interpreting these figures, it is necessary to realise that ethnological research conducted by Jitka Slezáková in Jihlava (Slezáková, n.d.) showed that the Vietnamese community residing in that city was in fact just double the 2001 census numbers.

The Vietnamese belong to the most visible communities in the Czech Republic. Not only is their physical appearance different from that of the matrix community, but the matrix community is in frequent contact with them. The Vietnamese are venders in local markets, or failing the opportunity to sell in local markets, their stalls flank a number of highways and some city streets. Czechs often purchase merchandise at these stalls, because the goods are cheap. However, the attitude towards the Vietnamese community is basically hesitant. Pejorative descriptors such as *rákosníci* 'cane people / reed warblers' are sometimes used in reference to them.

However, in fact the power relationship between the matrix and Vietnamese community is sometimes reversed. A Nova TV programme (7th February 1996) demonstrated that in Železná Ruda, previously mentioned, Vietnamese enterprises constitute the main economic support of the township, Czechs are employed by Vietnamese shop keepers (for example as cleaners) and little Vietnamese children are looked after by Czech nannies.

The Vietnamese do not necessarily trade only in street stalls. Some sell through normal shops, in which they often employ Czech assistants. The birth of the *Svaz vietnamských podnikatelů*, 'Association of Vietnamese Entrepreneurs', occurred in 1992; the organisation participates in the publication of the magazine

Que Huong/ Domov (Slezáková, n.d.). In 1999 a *Svaz Vietnamců* 'Vietnamese Association' was formed in Prague to protect the interests of the community. There is a branch in Ostrava. A new magazine *Bambus* was founded in 2003.

The Vietnamese presence in areas that immediately border Germany has a special character. Consider the township of Vejprty (population of 3336), where only 60 Vietnamese were recorded in the 2001 census, but the activities of these 60 are easily visible. They engage in the sale of goods in street stalls, in shops and in the town market hall. The town is located very close to the border control point. The shops are clearly oriented toward German, not Czech, customers: the German proficiency of the Vietnamese is reportedly better than their Czech, and they have erected a large advertisement on the roadside which reads, in German, *Sparen, sparen, nach Vejprty fahren* 'Save, save, come to Vejprty'. A negative attitude toward the Vietnamese also characterises people on the German side of the border, because these activities harm German retailers. The Vietnamese exploit the economic asymmetry between Germany and the Czech Republic. Given the enlargement of the European Union, they will lose the opportunities for their business operation.

The Hungarians

Hungarian ethnicity was claimed in 2001 by 14,672 inhabitants. Ten years earlier the number was 19,932. It is necessary to realise that the character of the Hungarian community radically differs from that of the Hungarian minority in Slovakia (see e.g. Lanstyák, 2002) or Rumania. They are a small group with an opaque history having always lived dispersed rather than in a single coherent settlement. Also, there is no common border between Hungary and the Czech lands; apart from some memories of WWI, when Czech soldiers, drafted into the Austrian Army, passed through Hungary and a later limited experience with Hungarians from Slovakia, for Czechs Hungary has never been a country on which they focused much attention. In 1921 the number of Hungarians in the Czech lands was 7049 – mostly people who migrated from Slovakia or Ruthenia during the Hapsburg era, but from that time up to 1991 the community experienced a continuous, though limited, increase. Most of these people came because of work opportunities. A sharp and sudden increase occurred in 1945 and 1946 when approximately 45,000 thousand Hungarians were deported from Southern Slovakia to the Bohemian border zone with Germany. This was a phenomenon similar to the deportation of Germans. (Hungary was an ally of Germany throughout WWII and occupied parts of Slovakia during the war.) However, this was not a case of deportation to the 'home' country, and it did not last. When it was cancelled in 1948, most of those concerned returned to the place of their origin. Statistics from 1950 showed only 13,201 people. Hungarians have lived dispersed in all regions of the present-day Republic, especially in the industrial areas of northern and western Bohemia, in Silesia (the Karviná district) and in Prague, which is the cultural centre of Czech Hungarians. Between 1954 and 1989 Hungarians living in the Czech lands did not have an independent cultural organisation. Only after the political changes of 1989 was the *Svaz Maďarů žijících v českých zemích* (The Association of Hungarians Living in the Czech Lands) formed. This organisation engages in publication activities (e.g. in publishing the cultural revue *Prágai tükör* 'The Prague Mirror'), among other activities, i.e. it cooperates in broadcasting Hungarian programmes on radio. (For more details see Praha a národnosti, 1998: 34–49.)

The decrease in the number of people who declared Hungarian ethnicity in the 1991–2001 decade was more than 25%. On the one hand, this change can be explained by deepening assimilation; on the other, by the fact that replacement of natural decreases by new immigrants became difficult, because what was now involved was migration from abroad rather than from other areas of the same state.

Although the Hungarian community is not one of the smallest, apart from the activities of Hungarian intellectuals (who, however, are often not identified as such, because many Slovaks also have Hungarian names), it is one of those which is least visible. A sociological survey conducted in 1992 showed that many Hungarians did not wish others to know about their ethnicity (Sadílek & Csémy, 1993: 17).

The Greeks and Macedonians

Greeks

Greeks appeared in the territory of the Czech Republic as a consequence of the Greek civil war between 1946 and 1949. As a result, approximately 12,500 refugees arrived, and this first wave included 3500 children. In 1950 there were 5200 Greek children of whom 4000 had arrived without their parents. Subsequently, the size of the Greek community fluctuated due to family reunions and increased somewhat in 1956 as a result of an influx of Greeks from Hungary, where refugees were afraid that the Hungarian uprising might lead to the persecution of people with left-wing political views. Left-oriented ideologies were typical for the majority of the Greek community (Otčenášek, 1998).

Greek refugees were assigned domicile in border areas sparsely populated after the deportation of Germans, in particular in northern Moravia. Purely Greek villages came into being, and there was a high concentration of Greeks in some towns; for example, in the mid-1950s, Krnov had a Greek population of 2500, approximately 12% of the total population. The Greeks worked principally in the textile and machine manufacturing industries. The information given so far is valid not only for Greeks but also for Macedonians. Since both groups arrived from Greece under the same circumstances, the numerical relationship between them is difficult to establish and has been the object of debate (cf. Dorovský, 1998; Sloboda, 2000/2001; Sloboda, 2003); however, since the sociocultural and communicative behaviour of the two groups shows differences, it is necessary to deal with them separately.

Members of the Greek ethnic community hoped that they would soon be able to return to their country and did not, therefore, make any effort to adapt themselves to their Czech environment, except in the most basic respects. Children were initially educated as Greek children in Greece. However, it soon became obvious that return to Greece would not be a matter of months or years, and in the 1951–52 school year children started attending Czech schools.

A Greek newspaper *Agonistis* (Fighter), among other periodicals, was published from 1950, and up to 1969 it included a Macedonian page. There was also radio broadcasting in Greek. However, the community was still oriented towards returning to Greece, a fact clearly visible in marriage preferences, the range of which was restricted to the community. When return became possible, approximately three-quarters of the Greeks opted to go back; this happened in three waves between 1975 and the end of the 1980s. In the 1990s, the number of Greeks stabilised at approximately 3300 individuals (3379 in the 1991 census and 3219 in 2001). However, representatives of the community itself estimate the number of individuals of Greek origin at 7000 (Zpráva, 2002). Greeks who remained in the Czech Republic and those who returned to Greece developed an active relationship, often of a commercial nature. Slovaks apart, Greeks still represent the largest single non-Czech group of students enrolled at Czech universities (500 in 2000).

Greeks living in the Czech Republic have formed a number of associations, the strongest of which is the *Asociace řeckých obcí v České republice* (Association of Greek Communities in the Czech Republic) which concentrates on such tasks as maintenance of the Greek language, Greek dances, festivals, and the local Greek press. In 2002 a representative of the community was a member of the *Rada vlády pro národnostní menšiny* (Governmental Council for Ethnic Minorities).

Macedonians

Macedonians emerged as an ethnic community in the Czech lands under historical circumstances analogous to those affecting the Greeks – i.e. as a consequence of the civil war in Greece. They represented approximately a third of the arrivals from Greece. Their reception paralleled that of the Greeks in that they received schooling in Macedonian (textbooks were provided from abroad), broadcasting in Macedonian was instituted, and there was a Macedonian press. Exact numbers are difficult to establish because the emergence of the Macedonian ethnicity was still recent, and because some speakers of Macedonian considered themselves to be Greeks or Bulgarians (Sloboda, 2003). A basic difference between them and the Greeks was that they were not able to return to their homes in northern Greece even after the end of the dictatorship in 1974, because Greek authorities continued to refuse their applications, unless they declared Greek nationality and ethnicity and changed their names. This practice resulted in a higher degree of assimilation of Macedonians to Czech society which was linguistically facilitated by the fact that, unlike Greek, Macedonian is a Slavic language. Being barred from Greece, the only possibility for them, if they wanted to move closer to their homeland, was to resettle in the Yugoslav republic of Macedonia, which welcomed them. Many, indeed, left for that destination. Among those who remained in the Czech lands, some assimilated to the matrix population while others opted for Greek ethnicity. It is interesting that the Macedonian ethnicity was not reported at all in either the 1991 or the 2001 censuses, although some other very small groups (413 Austrians in 1991 or 690 Albanians in 2001) were. Some of them may have been included in the category *Others*. There were new Macedonian arrivals in the 1990s. A Macedonian periodical, *Makedonska misla* (Macedonian Thought), is currently being published in Prague.

Other Communities

In this section, some other smaller communities residing in the territory of the Czech Republic will be mentioned. Nekvapil and Neustupný (1998) speak of the smaller communities as groups characterised not only by their size, but also by their relatively 'limited visibility'. This is still true of some of those groups, although others, such as the Vietnamese group, do attract considerable attention from the matrix community. They have been discussed separately in a previous section. In Nekvapil and Neustupný (1998: 126) it was pointed out that 'no community is too small to be ignored', and this point of view has recently been endorsed by others within the Czech Republic (Šatava, 2001).

Some of those communities are known to the authors from personal experience, while the presence of others is also attested in the existing literature. However, such information is rarely sufficient to provide a clear picture of the present state of their range of interaction within the Czech Republic. In preparing the 2001 census, the Czech authorities anticipated the existence of some of these smaller communities when they prepared their questionnaires not only in Czech, Polish, German, Romani, Ukrainian and Russian, but also in English, French, Arabic, Vietnamese and Chinese. But even this linguistic diversity did not cater for the whole range of ethnic diversity in the country.

The 2001 census documented the presence of 690 Albanians, 1801 Serbs and 1585 Croats. These numbers may underestimate the real strength of those communities. The numbers reflect the unrest of the 1990s in the Balkan peninsula. Nevertheless, the unrest is not the only factor, at least not in the case of the Croats whose presence in the Czech territory has a long history. As mentioned previously, since the 16th century, several Croat villages have existed in southern Moravia. In view of the support by the Croatian government of Nazi Germany during WWII and in view of the alleged collaboration with the Nazis by the Croat community in Moravia, the then over 2000 Croats were forcibly dispersed into more than a hundred Moravian towns and villages where they were soon assimilated. Only after 1989 could those who still possessed their former identity form an association. From 2001 their representative is a member of the government's Council for Ethnic Minorities. Apart from concern about the maintenance of their folkloristic traditions, they have also declared an interest in the maintenance of their *čakavian* dialect of what used to be called *Serbo-Croatian*. The community had never had the opportunity to receive education in their own language. Before and during the war they attended German schools; then Czech schools became the only option. A brief account of their language was written 70 years ago (Vážný, 1934) but no further research has been published to date.

Bulgarians and Rumanians (4363 and 1238 persons respectively in the 2001 census) are more recent, though not very recent, arrivals. Both groups participated in the resettlement of the border areas vacated after the original German population was deported. Members of the Bulgarian community are currently organised in a number of associations, publish periodicals and have a representative on the government's Council for Ethnic Minorities. There is an elementary and a middle school bearing the name of Petr Beron collectively accommodating 120 students. These schools were established by the Bulgarian Embassy in Prague (Zpráva, 2002). There is little information available concerning the language behaviour of the Bulgarians; however, some are known to use Russian, which is linguistically close to Bulgarian, a feature which has sometimes elicited negative comment. In the Report of the government's Council for Ethnic Minorities, the representative of the Bulgarian

community was critical of some attitudes of the administration, but he anticipated that improvement would be imminent due to the adoption of the new
Law (see Ethnic Policy of the Czech State below). The Rumanian community
has always been much smaller than the Bulgarian community, and information
on its behaviour is scarce.

A post-1989 community that cannot be ignored originates from North America. Sometimes it is claimed that in the 1990s Prague became for the 'Americans'
what Paris was for them in the 1920s. Some 20,000 of them are estimated to live in
Prague alone, although the census recorded no more than 3000 people with US
nationality. Sherman (2001) noted that this group of foreigners, who come for
other than economic or political reasons, find it difficult to integrate into Czech
society. The grounds for this behaviour should be looked for both on the side of
the North American citizens, who sometimes lack willingness to give up their
expatriate status, and Czechs who do not easily admit foreigners of this type into
their networks. Sherman also claims that, in the case of mixed American-Czech
marriages, while the couples often live in the territory of the Czech Republic, the
language used is English and socioculturally US patterns dominate. In the same
study, Sherman points out that in communicative situations massive language
management takes place, with misunderstanding being common on both the US
and Czech side. In the following extract from her data B (male, US citizen)
describes how, in conversation with Czechs, he used compliments in the belief
that this practice would improve communication:

(Translated from Czech; E = researcher, P = Czech wife of B)

B: I tried it, like, about ten times or so.
E: And they didn't, they didn't react to it?
B: It was almost like for nothing, it was (they were) like 'Oh come on!', they
         were like that, a typical Czech reaction, that is.
E: Yeah.
B: Yeah it's like 'Hey, that was, like, good food' or (they reacted) like 'Noooo!'.
P: Compliments make people nervous, those simple ones.
B: Or it was only so-so or I don't know what, what, like 'That's a nice suit
         you're wearing' and so (they say) 'It's so, so, it isn't true.' (laughter)
         (from Sherman, 2001: 271)

B refers to the presence of communication problems due to differences in the use
of compliments.

In the most recent census (2001), no respondents reported Jewish ethnicity
(národnost), although 218 individuals claimed being ethnically Jewish in 1991.
There is a private elementary school (serving about 100 students) as well as a
Jewish high school (a four year gymnázium with approximately 80 students),
which teach Hebrew as part of their curricula. These institutions receive a
governmental grant (Zpráva, 2002: 34). In the government's Council for Ethnic
Minorities there is an active Jewish observer. However, it is apparent that at present members of the Jewish community in the Czech Republic consider themselves as a religious rather than an ethnic group. The history of the Czech Jews
may provide an explanation. Unlike in eastern Europe, in the Czech territory

they had begun to migrate from the country into towns and cities in the 19th century. They became merchants, industrialists, lawyers, doctors or intellectuals and this change contributed both to their loss of religiosity and to their linguistic assimilation (Kieval, 1988). At the beginning of WWII, many emigrated and during the war most of those who did not, perished in German concentration camps. There was another wave of emigration when the Communist Party took power in 1948, and these population movements left only some 3500 people to enter the 1990s (Pěkný, 1993).

This brief survey of 'other communities' does not mention many other groups. There are, for example, refugees from various parts of the world, e.g. Armenia. The study of Turks and Arabs has only begun. There are quite a few individuals from societies which were a part of the Soviet Union, such as the countries of the Caucasus, or which maintained friendly relations with the Soviet bloc, such as Cubans or Africans, who settled in the Czech Republic after WWII. Kalmycks, discussed in Nekvapil and Neustupný (1998), have not been included here, because fresh information about this population was simply not available. There is a Chinese community (more than 1500 people with Chinese citizenship (PRC)). The 1991 census registered 413 people with Austrian ethnicity, while the 2001 census does not speak of this group at all; however, the most recent census noted 1000 people with Austrian citizenship. Furthermore, there are student communities that deserve special treatment. Neustupný (2003) reports on communication problems of Japanese students in Prague, but his paper represents only a limited contribution to a vast area. Tourists have not been mentioned at all.[4]

Communities: A Summary

The Czech Republic, as already discussed, is by no means a homogeneous society. Even at the present time, having been given the opportunity to identify their preferred ethnic association in the census, close to 10% of the population select a category other than 'Czech'. This survey has, however, demonstrated that, had the count been taken a few decades earlier when the process of assimilation was relatively undeveloped, the heterogeneity of the country would have been significantly higher than it currently is. This original situation still survives in the memory of the older members of the communities.

Types and size of the communities

The largest community is, of course, the Czech one, with its Moravian and Silesian branches which, while not accounting for the whole population of Moravia and Silesia, do in many respects claim a somewhat separate identity. Furthermore, the figures often given for the Czech community include a number of less than whole-hearted members: those who were afraid (socially, not politically) to declare other membership, those who changed their declaration recently and those who hesitated because of mixed allegiance. Not many (altogether 12,978) used the opportunity, given in the census, to claim plural ethnicity. Since membership is always a matter of degree and situation (see Nekvapil, 2000c), the Czech community, in particular, cannot be seen as entirely homogeneous. Moreover, there are differences of interests and power within the community.

Some communities can be designated as historical (Neustupný, 1997). The

German community is the most representative of these, although its numbers have definitely been declining. Discrimination lasted for decades, and it seems too late now to restore the community at least to its post-WWII structure. The only historical community that is continuing its efforts for maintenance is the Polish community in the Těšín region; but its numbers are declining as well. The Roma were a historical community before the extermination of the Czech Roma in concentration camps; the contemporary Roma are immigrants from Slovakia. So are the Slovaks. Other groups are immigrant as well, except for the Germans-from-Germany, Anglo-Americans and some other expatriate communities whose members are sojourners.

One of the specific features of the Czech situation seems to be that, apart from the Roma and the Slovaks, there are no really large communities. There is no clear boundary between middle sized and small communities and for some of them virtually no reliable data are available.

The phenomenon of assimilation

The most prominent feature of the non-Czech communities is their high degree of assimilation. There was political and social pressure in the case of Germans and, no doubt, social pressure in the case of others. The ideology of the Communist Party expected assimilation (see Part VI). However, there is no evidence of strong overt pressure toward giving up one's ethnic identity in recent history. This fact notwithstanding, major communities in the Czech Republic do assimilate.

The basic factor in assimilation seems to be the fact that Czech society, until the political changes of 1989 and beyond, has been a Modern, rather than a Post-Modern society. Unlike an Early-Modern society, such as that of 19th century Europe, Modern society is deeply assimilative without exerting much overt pressure (Neustupný, forthcoming 2). Assimilation is expected – both by the matrix community and by other, minority, communities. It is not necessarily viewed as a tragic event. Members of many communities in the Czech Republic assimilate silently and, so to speak, 'voluntarily'.

The wave of the Post-Modern multiculturalist ideology arrived only in the 1990s and, in our view, has not yet fully established itself. The European Union requires that candidates for membership subscribe to it. In the Czech Republic, a new Minority Act was adopted in 2001 and active policy-making both preceded and followed it (see next section). An inspection of the relevant documents reveals a willingness to comply. On the other hand, there is some doubt whether this willingness is genuine – (is it in other countries?) – and whether it is matched by changes in the consciousness of the general population. If the figures cited in an earlier section can be believed, they seem to indicate that opposition to Roma neighbours has declined over the last decade; it is, consequently, necessary to accept the fact that change does occur.

Interests and power

When observed historically, the questions of interests and of power vary extensively. In relation to the German community, it is notable that in some periods the power of the Czech majority asserted itself, but there were long historical stretches, such as that of the Hapsburg rule (mainly from the 17th century to

1918) and of the wartime occupation of Czechoslovakia (1939–1945) when the interests of the German community, with the active assistance of external German states, absolutely prevailed. It is necessary to realise that, in the mid-20th century, people still remembered the Austro-Hungarian Empire not as a fairy tale kingdom under a benevolent Kaiser but as a stage for the struggle among ethnic interests and the struggle for power. It was obvious that the Czechs were the underdogs, with the German element retaining its privileges by using the support of the economic establishment and the Vienna dominated state. The first period of the Czechoslovak Republic (1918–1939) reversed the situation to some extent. However, the interests of the German community and of other minorities were safeguarded through international pressure. Nevertheless, the situation did not appear to the German community as satisfying its interests, which were seen in the context of the Modern paradigm as unification with bordering Germany and Austria. This unification was achieved through the Munich Agreement of 1938 which dictated that large territories be handed over by Czechoslovakia to Germany. The occupation of the remaining part of Czechoslovakia by Germany followed in 1939, and the ensuing period of terror is still vividly remembered by many Czechs.

The post-war period saw the reversal of the power relationship when, in the interest of removing the ethnic problem, Czechoslovakia deported over 2.5 million Germans. In the immediate post-war period, the memory of the war led to social stigmatisation of those Germans who were not deported and of the German language. However, owing to the deportation of the Germans, the German interests within the society became indistinct. The fact that two German states existed and that one of them was in very friendly relations with the communist government of Czechoslovakia made the exercise of overt political power against the Germans and German difficult. It remains to be ascertained whether the assimilation of the Germans in the 1970s and 1980s was still due to the negative attitudes of the matrix society. At present, the prestige of Germany is high, and discrimination hardly exists. Still, the community continues shrinking.

The problem of the interests of the Těšín Polish community has also been connected with international relations. While Czechoslovakia was strong, the power of the Czechoslovak state prevailed. With its weakening in the wake of WWII, Poland occupied the Těšín region, but the situation returned to the domination of Czech interests after WWII. Since then, the Czech state has been careful not to initiate assimilative measures, but assimilation proceeded automatically as a process characteristic for a Modern society.

In the case of the Slovak community, Slovak interests were not safeguarded before WWII. This was one of the reasons why the Slovaks established their own state in 1939 which, however, had a short duration. Under the cover of communist state control, ethnic problems appeared to be basically solved, although from time to time voices of protest were heard from the Slovak side. When that cover was lifted, Slovak politicians decided, during 1992, that their interests were not adequately served within the power structure of Czechoslovakia, and, in 1993, opted out. Czech politicians were happy to assist. There was no referendum. At present, the situation of the Slovak community in the Czech Republic seems to be satisfactory, although continuing assimilation requires detailed analysis of the underlying power relationships.

The Roma have been the most strongly affected population. Their interests have been neglected. The matrix community is gradually realising that the Roma community is acquiring the power to speak and act for itself. While it is unlikely that other communities might assume a strong antagonistic position against the Czechs, it is possible that the Roma will.

What to do?

On the surface, the ethnic situation in the Czech Republic seems to be well managed, with the exception of the Roma and some parts of the Polish community. There is no overt ethnic conflict. In fact, however, antagonism does exist, and may intensify, especially as Czech society immerges further into the Post-Modern era. For example, the question of schooling in native languages is likely to emerge. It is important not to succumb to the view that social problems can be totally eliminated through the action of a benevolent state. On the other hand, there is a need for the state to improve its management tools and for the subjects of those policies to exert pressure within the state.

Ethnic Policy of the Czech State

This section will supplement information included in previous sections by providing a systematic account of the structure of contemporary governmental management of ethnic policy. (For the history in the second half of the previous century see Nekvapil, 2003c.) The problems of ethnic communities were not given adequate attention in the 1990s, but the situation has changed since the beginning of the present century. As already mentioned, it is in particular the question of the entry of the Czech Republic into the EU that has played a key role in the change of heart of the Czech government. However, the change of the government, from conservative to social democratic, may also have contributed to the transformation in the atmosphere.

Legal norms: The ethnic minority law

The *Zákon ze dne 10.července 2001 o právech příslušníků národnostních menšin a o změně některých zákonů* (Law on the Rights of Ethnic Minorities and Amendment of Some Laws made on 10th July 2001) (No. 273/2001) is the basic legal instrument of this period. It should be noted that a distinction is made between the majority and the minorities: the law does not employ the concept of community, an idea which would imply that the majority is also a community and thus also subject to particular rights (Clyne, 1991). A *národnostní menšina* (ethnic minority) is defined with reference to its ethnic origin, language, culture and traditions, its size and its will to be considered a minority. This definition is in agreement with the concept held by the Council of Europe (Zpráva, 2002: 12). A *příslušník* (member) of a minority is a citizen of the Republic who wants to be considered as a member of a minority. This citizenship condition on ethnicity rights is old-fashioned. It is also important to note that the law accepts the existence of minority groups as primary and derives the concept of its members from there. This is in opposition to the way of thinking of the previous conservative government which claimed that all rights were rights of the individual and not group rights (Frištenská & Sulitka, 1995). Administration authorities do not keep evidence about ethnic membership. Such membership is established on the basis of rules not provided in this law.

Members of ethnic minorities are guaranteed the rights of:

- assemblage;
- participation in decision making about their minority;
- use of personal name in the minority language form;
- multilingual names of companies and other institutions, street and other signs;
- use of the minority language in contact with authorities, in the courts, and at elections;
- education in the minority language, development of their own culture, and
- diffusion as well as reception of information in their own language.

Five important laws have been revised as a part of this new law.

With regard to the participation in decision making, the law stipulates that it should be implemented through committees established in separate regulations and through the *Rada vlády pro národnostní menšiny* (government's Council for Ethnic Minorities; see following discussion), of which it gives limited details. The law also says that the integration of the Roma community will be coordinated by regional and local government. All articles specify that details will be decided in separate legal documents. The right to the use of one's personal name is unlimited, but the right to use other proper names, and to use a language in administration, in the courts, in elections and in education only applies to minorities *které tradičně a dlouhodobě žijí na území České republiky* 'which traditionally and over a long period of time live in the territory of the Czech Republic'. However, any minority is free to establish private schools where the ethnic language is taught as a subject. State funding for culture and media is also limited to the 'traditional and long-term' resident communities. This funding is, of course, available on the basis of application. No community has the right to receive a subsidy.

Some participants from the ethnic communities expressed hesitation and regret during the language management processes that preceded the adoption of this law. They sought the establishment of ethnic minority government and ethnic minority elections, and they proposed that articles concerning rules about minority matters, which are at present dispersed in a large number of legal acts, be collected and incorporated into the law. These proposals were, however, rejected by the government (Zpráva, 2002: 13).

In practice, the right to use minority languages in contact with administration authorities and in the courts, specified in the law, has failed to acquire backing through additional legislation, and, in 2002, it was not implemented (Zpráva, 2002: 10).

Management agencies

The agencies and agents involved in the management of ethnic relations are listed in Zpráva (2002). They are:

(1) The Parliament (in particular, its Petition Committee).
(2) The Government's Council for Ethnic Minorities.

The Council consists of 18 representatives of ethnic communities (one to three members for each, depending on community size) and 11 members representing the government. The membership formula does not allow for the membership of academics or of any other specialists. The Council discusses proposals put before the government, presents recommendations about grants, etc.

(3) Governmental Council for Matters concerning the Romani Community. This Council consists of 14 representatives of the Romani community and 14 representatives of the government. Again, there is no place for academics or other specialists. A major task of the Council is to oversee the implementation of the *Principles of Policy of the Government toward Members of the Roma Community.*

(4) Ministerial committees.
Consultative committees have been established in the Ministries of Culture and of Education, Youth and Physical Training. There is a Consultative Committee of the Minister of Education for Questions of Ethnic Schools, which in 2001 included members of the Polish, German, Roma, Slovak, Hungarian and Ukrainian communities (Zpráva, 2002: 28). There is also a consultative committee in the (state) Czech Radio, but no similar structure in the Czech Television exists, a fact that has been criticised by members of the ethnic communities.

(5) Public Defender of Rights (Ombudsman).

(6) Commissioner for Human Rights.
This office was occupied by Petr Uhl who prepared both the *Ethnic Minorities Law* and *the Principles of the Government's Policy towards Members of the Roma Community.* However, the progressive character of his proposals has frequently been watered down in the subsequent process of political decision making (cf. Uhl, 2000).

(7) President of the Republic.
Václav Havel and his office actively established contacts with members of the ethnic communities and supported their activities. Particularly important was his endorsement of some attitudes and projects of the Roma community.

(8) Local Government.
Legal regulations prescribe that villages or towns in which more than 10% of inhabitants are of other than Czech ethnicity (in Prague and in the regions, more than 5%) must establish Ethnic Minority Committees. In 2001, such committees existed in 32 villages or towns, 4 regions and 2 cities. Where the statutory conditions have not been fulfilled but a need exists (as in Prague), special committees may be established. (Zpráva, 2002: 14).

Management acts

As an example of a management act that emanates from the agencies mentioned above, attention is called to the *Principles of the Government's Policy towards Members of the Roma Community, Assisting in their Integration to Society* (see www.vlada.cz/IS02/vrk/komise/krp/dokumenty/navrhk.il2.htm). Prepared by the networks listed above, it was adopted by the Cabinet under number 279 on 7 April 1999. The title of the policy may appear assimilationist, but in fact it is an enlightened document which states that the loss of the Roma culture would be a serious cultural loss, and that integration must proceed while at the same time respecting Roma culture. The policy establishes the principle of legally guided positive discrimination. The government also requires a policy towards Czechs: preventing racial discrimination, popularisation of Roma culture and teaching about the Roma in schools. This policy is being implemented by branches of the government – it is too early to say what results may ensue. The government's target for achieving the conditions which will make the Roma equal to those of the matrix community is the year 2020.

Part III: MANAGEMENT OF LANGUAGE VARIETIES

The Czech Language

The Czech language: A brief history of its management

Czech before the Hapsburgs

With the ascent of the Czech lands into history, the Czech language, one of the western Slavic dialects, underwent extensive language management. From a purely spoken variety it developed into a language of considerable sophistication.

Christianity, the ideology of the European Middle Ages, was embraced in the 9th century. It came from two sources: initially from the Western Church, based in Rome, and later from the Byzantine Empire. The Western Church established itself firmly in Bohemia and Moravia, and it was one of the factors that led the country not only into the domain of the Holy Roman Empire of the medieval period, but linguistically into the sphere of influence of Latin. Latin served as the first written language of the country not only in religion but in historiography, law and administration.

The Byzantine connection was initiated in the 860s (CE) by the ruler of Great Moravia as a means of political support against the expansive West. It was short-lived in the Czech lands. For a religious mission to materialise, it was necessary to prepare liturgical texts, for which a language had to be found and a script created or adapted. The resulting acts of language management gave rise to the language called Old Church Slavonic, derived from a Bulgarian dialect, and two scripts: the Glagolitic and later the Cyrillic alphabet. This process of language management was implemented by two Greeks from Salonika, Constantine and Method, prior to their departure for Moravia. The tradition of Old Church Slavonic and the script was transferred from Moravia to the East where it was used in the formation of the East European Orthodox Church and the East Slavic civilisation.

Graphisation of Czech, the management process from which Czech emerged as a written language, occurred on the basis of the Latin alphabet. It took the form of simple management, solving the problem of writing individual proper names first, moving to the use of other words (such as Old Czech legal terms) in Latin documents, and finally to the writing of individual sentences and subsequently whole texts. The first continuous texts are dated from the 13th century. By the end of the 14th century, Czech was a stylistically highly elaborated language which had penetrated to the domains of administration and ideology. Spelling was relatively fixed. At the same time, as norms were being established, management appears in the form of commentaries on texts (Šlosar & Večerka, 1979). The religious reformer John Hus (1371–1415) was not only a theologian but was also actively involved in language management. He is known for having spoken out against loans from German and is supposed to be the author of the book *De orthographia bohemica*, which proposed that cluster spelling, used up to that time, be replaced by a diacritical system, which would employ the signs ´ and · (later changed into ˇ). So, *chzezzt* 'honour' would be written *čest*. This proposal was not immediately implemented, but it eventually led to contemporary Czech spelling, which has influenced the spelling of a number of other languages.

In the following period, Renaissance humanism, the Czech language was the object of further management and was developed to serve in all domains of communication. This is sometimes designated the 'Golden Age' of the language. As far as management is concerned, the following points must be mentioned:

(1) Czech received and accepted influences from Latin (including syntax), German and other languages.
(2) Language received ample attention in various grammars, dictionaries or stylistic handbooks.
(3) Spelling was further systematised, applying most principles of the diacritic system.
(4) The requirement that foreigners learn Czech was enacted, and the extensive implementation of that Parliamentary Act was only arrested by political developments at the beginning of the 17th century (Šlosar & Večerka, 1979).

The 'Period of Darkness'

The development of the Czech language received a serious blow in the 17th century. In 1620 Czech nobility lost the decisive battle at White Mountain to the Hapsburgs. Many people were executed or lost their property, and those who did not agree to convert to Catholicism, the religion of the Hapsburgs, were required to emigrate including, for example, the educationalist Comenius (1592–1670). The country was ruled from Vienna, and that situation was not to change for 300 years. The new order not only meant that the administration of the country in principle passed over to German hands, it also meant that the social and communication networks which supported the 'Golden Age' of Czech civilisation were fatally disrupted. Protestant scholars, authors and readers had to leave the country. Legally, according to the *Obnovené zřízení zemské 'The Reinstated Constitution of the Land'* of 1627, Czech and German were equal, but in fact they were not. The range of the functional use of the Czech language was narrowed. Czech needed to be retained, of course, to preach religion to the peasants to keep them obedient. Literature was limited to works with religious or practical content. In the end, the language found itself largely removed from schools, the sciences, the humanities, law and administration. Norms of language suffered. Although some emperors, such as Joseph II (1741–1790), were clearly in favour of German only, these changes were not necessarily the result of a centrally organised management, but rather were a process originating at lower levels (see Berger, 1999). This era of the deconstruction of Czech has, in the nationalistic idiom of Czech historiography, been designated as the 'Period of Darkness'.

At the present time everything is not seen as black and white. As far as the Czech language is concerned, there was a reduction in its functional use but, as Stich (1993) has stressed, it is difficult to speak of overall decay. The language, used with a different audience, admitted novelties, but these cannot be said to be outside the normal course of development of a language. The influence of dialects on the written language was not as marked as is sometimes claimed. The language should not be judged by comparing it with the grammars and dictionaries of the period which, admittedly, were not always successful in managing lexical development (Stich, 1993). Moreover, Newerkla (1999, 2000) notes that, although the situation of Czech was deteriorating, Czech was taught at three high schools (gymnázium) until 1779. As already shown by Havránek (1980: 72) and confirmed by recent research (Berger, 1999), Czech was even used, to a certain extent, in written documents within the administrative domain.

Nevertheless, the nearly two centuries of this development meant that written Czech diverged widely from the language of the previous period; it was underdeveloped in many respects and could not easily serve either as a national symbol or as the tool of communication in a society aspiring to enter the age of modernisation. The language of the nobility and of many cities and towns was German, without reference to whether the people concerned were of German or of Czech origin.

The 'Revival Period'

The negative evaluation of the linguistic situation of the 'Period of Darkness' crystallised towards the end of the 18th century – the period when modernisation commenced in Europe. In Austria, of which the Czech lands then formed a part, the new management processes manifested themselves as a 'National Revival'. Adapting to a certain extent the periodisation scheme suggested by Hroch (1999a, 1999b), this National Revival can be divided into three periods.

The First Revival period: Language as a symbol

At the beginning of the process, the atmosphere of the ongoing economic, social and cultural changes was reflected in the need to identify the boundaries of the new society. A set of symbols was needed: common history, literature, religion and language. Language normally becomes one of the most important components of the set, because it symbolises not only the exchange-of-information networks, but also networks of the aesthetic and of emotional life of the population. Since, in the case of Czech society, the language of the day was held in little esteem, a necessity arose to find a language that would serve as a more effective symbol.

Hroch (1999a) describes this period as the time of scholars. It is the scholars who pursued language management by creating a symbol through the act of describing it. In the case of the Czech lands of the end of the18th century, much of the work in language management was undertaken by Josef Dobrovský (1753–1829) or under his influence. The language he selected as that symbol, not against the will of others around him, was the Renaissance Czech of the 16th century. There was no doubt that this was a highly sophisticated language and that it made an excellent symbol. It did not coincide with the language of the day, so it was difficult to master for those who did not possess necessary resources. In this and the following periods one may often read about Czechs who had to learn their own language. Of course, there were people from Germanised environments whose spoken Czech was imperfect, but these remarks probably mostly relate to the need to learn the written language which, in Dobrovský's codification, was a language substantially different from the spoken Czech of the time.

Apart from codifying the norm, important for the establishment of the symbol were pamphlets called the 'defense (*obrana*) of the Czech language'. Between 1773 and 1793 at least ten such texts were published (Hroch, 1999b: 64). Another management act was the establishment, in 1791, of a Chair of the Czech language at the university in Prague, but since this was the only place in the country where written Czech could be acquired in an organised way, the Czech language programme also performed an important practical role. On the whole, participants in this series of management acts were not aware of the historical significance of their acts. They were in fact sceptical about the future of the Czech language.

Aside of this elitist management one can identify the more spontaneous activity of the publisher V.M. Kramerius, whose work affected a large number of readers, as well as the development of the Czech theatre (Hroch, 1999b).

The Second Revival period: The period of national propaganda

This period commences in the first decade of the 19th century. Its principal actors were the members of the younger generation – the 'patriots' – a group of individuals who assembled in various groups. The most important of them was Josef Jungmann (1773–1847) and his associates. There were attempts at organised language management in many areas. New grammars were published and Jungmann edited a voluminous dictionary of the Czech language. Wide use of the language was promoted, and attempts were made gradually to broaden its application as the language of instruction.

It would be wrong to assume that, in the previous period or in the time before it, the coexistence of the Czechs and the Germans was always without problems. However, on the whole, there was coexistence. During this second Revival period, the patriots appeared to be in quite obvious confrontation with the German element (Cuřín, 1985: 88). Even at the beginning of the 19th century one should not think that the Czech lands were actually bilingual. The population of the Czech towns or villages was monolingual in Czech, and the problem of communication was thus considerable for those who wanted to climb the social ladder. Even if the study of German was initiated early in life, Czech speakers did not achieve native-like competence (Hroch, 1999b) – a situation that marked the experience of the new generation of the 'patriots' and on which their language management attitudes were based.

One important area of management concerned the teaching of Czech and the place of Czech as the language of instruction. Apart from the 'trivial' (elementary) schools, all other schools used German as the language of instruction. Czech was taught as a subject at Prague University, and in theological seminaries. In general, the Catholic Church, for pragmatic reasons, played a very positive role in Czech language management. As early as 1818, an article appeared in one of the Czech periodicals, recommending that the language of instruction in all middle schools for Czech pupils should be Czech. Subsequently an attempt was made, in 1820, to introduce Czech as the language of instruction at one school in

Prague, but without success. At the high schools (gymnázium), Czech first appeared only occasionally and as a selective subject, but gradually it was accepted (Hroch, 1999b). Translation into Czech was another important vehicle of language management, as was original writing (initially mainly poetry) and non-fiction writing.

Another language management act that took place in this period was spelling reform undertaken by a group of patriots. The spelling that was adopted, against the wishes of conservative members of the Czech community, was basically identical with the spelling used at the present time (see below). Considerable attention was devoted to word formation and lexicographical work, normally undertaken by individuals, for example natural scientists, who created the entire terminology of their disciplines. These examples point to the importance of simple management and to lower levels of organised management by individuals or by small groups of individuals. Many inadequacies of Czech perceptible at the beginning of the period were largely resolved by the middle of the century, without any intervention of community-wide agencies. The only agency that could be mentioned was the *Matice česká*, founded in 1831 as a branch of the Museum of the Czech Kingdom, which was particularly active in publishing. However, even this was a private initiative, without the sponsorship of the state.

The Third Revival period: Ethnic identity established

According to Hroch (1999a), this period was characterised by a complete social structure of the ethnic group, from top to bottom. It was not individual patriots but the full community which took part in the management process, and the management process thus acquired national political significance; consequently, there could be coordinated action, and normal political processes could apply. In Hroch's view, this phase commenced in the Czech lands around the middle of the 19th century, in particular at the time when Austria changed over to a constitutional system.

Under repeated pressure from the Czech community, radical changes occurred. In March 1848, the Emperor confirmed, in his own hand, the equality of the Germans and the Czechs and of their languages. This act resulted in Czech versions of all laws being promulgated in parallel with German versions, and it also resulted in Czech being widely introduced in the high schools (gymnázium). There were additional complications and transformations. Since 1867, the principle prevailed that, depending on the native language of the population, only one language was to be used as the language of instruction so that no one would be forced to study in a language they did not choose. Thus, the language of instruction in all schools for Czechs was now Czech (Newerkla, 1999, 2000). Prague University was split into separate German and Czech institutions in 1882 and the Czech university was teaching entirely in Czech (Havránek, 2002).

The clause in the 1867 law that forbid making any language compulsory in fact served the language interests of the Czech Germans. Since German continued to be the language of internal administration at the level of the empire, all Czechs had to study it anyway. There was no problem there. However, for Germans, the learning of Czech was not only tedious; any acknowledgement that a knowledge of Czech was necessary would endanger their privileged position in state administration. Since the mid-1800s, Czechs continued their attempts to secure a greater share of such positions, and such interests can be understood to underlie the background of contemporary writings about language policy (such as Pacák, 1896).

At the beginning of the third period, many other problems still remained unresolved. Yet, the Standard language, as codified by Dobrovský and further developed by Jungmann and others, was generally accepted and tested in literary work. From the 1830s, the first lasting literary achievements appeared from the pen of Mácha, Němcová, or later of Neruda.

In the 1870s, anti-German purism was embodied in the *Brus Matice české* (1877, 1881, 1894) and other handbooks of correct Czech usage. However, the anti-German character of these publications was not obvious on the surface and, in any case, the *Brus*, its backing by prestigious personalities notwithstanding, had little effect on actual usage. The recommended pedantic adjustments did not gain the support of speakers/writers in their daily simple management. The first *Rules of Czech Spelling* (*Pravidla českého pravopisu*), a generally binding handbook of spelling and morphology, was authored by Gebauer *et al.* in 1902 (see more in a later section). *Kallilogie čili O výslovnosti* (1873), by Durdík, represented the first attempt to codify the pronunciation of the Standard.

Management of Czech in Czechoslovakia

The state of Czechoslovakia was established in 1918 out of the debris of the Austrian-Hungarian monarchy. The official ideology claimed that there was one Czechoslovak language, with two branches, Czech and Slovak. Within the Czech part of the territory, Czech became not only the universal language of education (apart from schools of the German and Polish minorities, see Nekvapil, 1997d) – that had already been achieved in the years of the monarchy – but it also became the language of law and administration at all levels. There was initially a feeling that Czech was not yet sufficiently elaborated to fulfil all of these tasks. Many areas of usage had to be newly developed; e.g. diplomacy, finance, defence, and some areas of law. The problems did not lie only in the lexicon but also in the style.

Owing to the democratic character of the new state, the use of the Standard was required from a wide range of citizens in a number of public situations. Since the native language of the population was so-called *Common Czech*, or a dialect (see sections that follow), the Standard sometimes created obstacles for speakers with lower levels of education. However, this matter was never raised as an issue of organised management. The puristic attitude of the *Brus* type was defeated by speakers in their refusal to apply it in simple management. It was attacked theoretically and destroyed by the Prague Linguistic Circle in the 1930s. Czech is not a language that easily accepts loan words, but this is a consequence of its typological profile (Neustupný, 1989a), not of a policy of purism. There are many loans and, in particular, there is no hesitation to accept them if they are based in the Greek or Latin lexical tradition.

To a large extent, literature ceased to be perceived as a form of organised language management, a method of developing the community language. However, it continued to be a locus of simple management, when authors encountered problems in coding their thought in already existing language. One of those who approached the task of coding his modern thought in modern language with considerable success was Karel Čapek (1890–1938), who, in the 1920s, used colloquial Czech in his writings.

After the Munich Agreement of 1938, areas close to borders were incorporated into surrounding states (i.e. Germany and Poland); the remaining territory was occupied by Germany in March 1939. By this time, the Czech language was already fully developed and codified, so that it was both structurally and attitudinally resistant to German. Also, the occupation was relatively short (1939–1945). Linguistically there was no impact extending beyond the period itself. However, for at least two decades, Czechs developed a distaste for German even in simple management (Cizí slova, 1971: 14).

After WWII, the Institute of the Czech Language (*Ústav pro jazyk český*) was created in 1946 as the first institution in the country to monitor Czech and to contribute to its management. The Institute operates a language consulting service (Uhlířová, 1998).

Language management in Czechoslovakia under Communist Party rule

The rule of the Communist Party extended from 1948 to 1989. Throughout this period, especially after the unsuccessful attempt in 1968 to liberate the country from Soviet influence, the Communist government emphasised the necessity 'to learn' from the Soviet Union. Principles of status management directed to ethnic community languages were strongly influenced by Soviet models. It might be expected that a similar situation obtained with regard to corpus management and that loans from Russian would be welcome. However, the contribution of Russian has been meagre (Daneš, 1997a) even in areas such as military terminology, where more loanwords might be expected. On the contrary, although the official attitude was hostile, as early as the 1960s one could see many loans from English, in particular in the registers of pop-music, sport, and (later) computing. After 1989, Russian loan words that referred to Soviet institutions and life (and sometimes also to similar phenomena as introduced to Czechoslovakia) have been relegated to the lexicon of historiography. The same is true about the stylistic features of the language of political propaganda.

However, it cannot be denied that the destruction of the class structure of the previous society resulted in certain informality of speech. In many situations of informal communication, particularly in the territory of Bohemia, the use of the Standard was negatively evaluated and Common Czech (see the following section) was used. This contributed to rapprochement between the Standard and the Common language, a fact that was sometimes described under the heading 'democratisation of Standard Czech' (Cuřín, 1985: 123; Havránek, 1947).

At the level of organised management, an act of importance was the review of the Rules of Czech Spelling (*Pravidla*), conducted in 1957, which brought the spelling of foreign words closer to their pronunciation.

The Institute of the Czech Language completed nine volumes of the *Příruční slovník jazyka českého* (Reference Dictionary of the Czech Language, completed 1957), and four volumes of *Slovník spisovného jazyka českého* (Dictionary of Standard Czech, 1971), an extensive grammar of Czech *Mluvnice češtiny* (A Grammar of Czech, 3 vols, 1986, 1987), and an officially sanctioned codification of Standard pronunciation (*Výslovnost spisovné češtiny* I, Pronunciation of Standard Czech, 1954 and II, 1978). A *Český jazykový atlas*, Czech Linguistic Atlas, commenced in the 1960s, and is now close to completion. After 1968, the Party required that the Institute concentrate on large prestigious projects of 'national' importance, such as the Dictionary of Old Czech, rather than pursuing theoretical work, where connections with Western linguistics would be necessary. There was an emphasis on the study of the Standard language. After 1968, a narrow stratum of linguists attempted to support the government, which had been installed by the Soviet occupation authorities, by creating 'Marxist linguistics', but in actual research most linguists continued working in a framework which was an extension of prewar structuralism.

There was no major positive initiative to manage the situation of ethnic community languages. Some more information on this issue will be presented in sections devoted to individual community languages.

The problem of Standard and Common Czech

The problem

One of the issues that leads to both simple and organised management, and possibly the most serious problem of variation within contemporary Czech, is the difference between the Standard and the Common language (*spisovná* vs. *obecná čeština*). This difference affects the daily linguistic practices of all native speakers of the language. In the 1990s, the term '*substandard*' was used by Mattheier and others (cf. Mattheier, 1997; Daneš, forthcoming) to refer to varieties (such as Common Czech) which are situated between the Standard and the dialects[5]. They share some properties of the Standard, mainly the fact that they are supra-regional, but they are situated below the Standard (hence *sub*), between it and the dialects. Thus, there are three different points on the scale of Standardness:

Standard Czech
↓
'*Substandard*'
(Common Czech)
↓
Dialects

The Standard and Common Czech seem to be at first sight two strictly separated varieties of language. This is not so. There is a continuum between an extreme form of the Standard (such as that used in writing), the Common language and a dialect. Speakers select forms from this range depending on the situation and on their regional background. A strong management process is involved, in the course of which certain forms are evaluated negatively if they are too Standard and others if they are too '*substandard*' or dialectal. All regions of the country participate in the three-level variation. However, in Bohemia and Western Moravia (zone 1) the dialects are weak (have in fact been largely 'lost'), while Common Czech is very strong. The impression is that there is a dichotomy of the Standard and the Common language. On the other hand, in most of Moravia (zone 2) it is Common Czech that is weak, with the dialects being strong. The impression in zone 2 is of a dichotomy between the Standard and dialects.

Although formality is not the only feature that selects between the three types of language, it can be used as the initial approach in characterising the usage. The following can be said:

- Formal situations require the Standard in both zone 1 and 2. This covers the language of written documents, most TV and radio media, newspapers and most public speaking. Some shopping situations are included, especially with regard to the language of shop attendants. The Standard is the sole object of instruction in schools. In other words, it is the language of power.
- Semi-formal situations in zone 1 admit a considerable number of Common Czech forms in the case of zone 1 speakers. These may be negatively evaluated by speakers of zone 2. Zone 2 speakers communicating in semi-formal situations use Standard forms but may mix in some features of their local dialects, and such features are open to negative evaluation. These situations include the language of instruction in schools and universities that may, in zone 1, include a considerable number of Common Czech features.
- In informal situations a strong admixture of Common Czech in zone 1 and of dialects in zone 2 may occur. The percentage normally varies depending on the norms of social strata and individuals.

The extreme form of the Standard is codified, and in written language (except for some literary works) it appears in its pure form. Common Czech is not codified, but the boundary between it and the Standard is relatively clear. So too normally is the boundary between Common Czech and the dialects (the features of which are marked as dialectal by speakers of other regions, e.g. the masculine ending *–ovo* of possessive adjectives , as in *tátovo bratr* 'father's brother', which is marked as western Bohemian if used in semi-formal situations). Common Czech differs from the Standard not only in its lexicon but also in the morphological system where some areas (such as the declension of adjectives) diverge quite radically.

	Standard Czech	Common Czech
Sg. Nom./Acc.	velké město	velký město
Gen.	velkého města	velkýho města
Dat.	velkému městu	velkýmu městu
Abl.	velkém městu	velkym městu
Instr.	velkým městem	velkym městem
Pl.Nom./Acc.	velká města	velký města
Gen.	velkých měst	velkejch měst
Dat.	velkým městům	velkejm městum
Abl.	velkých městech	velkejch městech
Instr.	velkými městy	velkejma městama

Some of the forms can be explained by sound change (e.g. é > ý) but some cannot. However, there are no differences in the inventory of phonemes.

On the whole, discourse studies of the opposition of Standard and Common Czech have been rare, and linguists and others still base their considerations on personal experience rather than on discourse data (Uličný, 1998/1999). This is not a situation peculiar to this problem, or to the management of Czech. Discourse data will be particularly vital to establish in what way one can conceptualise the dichotomy in terms of individual variables that do not allow a clear boundary between the two opposites.

A note concerning the origin of the Standard/Common Czech dichotomy may be useful. As mentioned in a previous section, Standard Czech is a language artificially established (or 'revived') in the course of the 19th century on the basis of certain varieties of Renaissance Czech of the 16th and 17th centuries. Between the Renaissance period and the 19th century, the spoken language underwent changes, and the changed language has survived as Common Czech. However, the Standard has basically retained the Renaissance form. Sometimes Standard and Common Czech are supposed to be in a relationship similar to diglossia, the Standard being the High and the Common language the Low variety in the sense given to these terms by Ferguson (1959; Neustupný, 1989b).

Simple management

The distinction leads to problems in discourse in five areas. The first is noting Common Czech forms or marking them negatively by speakers in zone 2. To what extent this happens in discourse is a matter to be established in empirical research. The second area occurs within zone 1. There may be an indecision as to which of the two sets should be used. This indecision often results in the use of the lower forms (Common Czech), which subsequently may be upgraded to the higher variety (the Standard). This is what happens in the following TV conversation.

> **M:** *Komu zavoláme?* 'Whom should we call?'
> **S :** *Jendovi Šuranskýmu.* 'Jenda Šuranskej.'
> **M:** *Jendovi Šuranskému?* 'Jenda Šuranský?'
> **S :** *Jendovi Šuranskému.* 'Jenda Šuranský.'

M is the moderator of a TV programme and S is a participant. In the second line S uses a Common Czech form *Šuranskýmu* 'Šuranský (Dat.)', but after the moderator utters the Standard form in a confirmation move, S too switches to the Standard form in the fourth line. Similar adjustments, including the language of TV moderators (Nekvapil, 2000b: 174), abound. Another interesting case of simple management has appeared in our data containing train conversations. The conductor enters the train compartment saying *dobré/ý ráno* 'good morning' and leaves with *děkuju/i* 'thank you'. This is a case of avoidance of the difference by pronouncing the endings between the Standard (*dobré* and *děkuji*) and the Common form (*dobrý* and *děkuju*) indistinctly (see Nekvapil & Neustupný, forthcoming). The third problem is the lack of competence of some native speakers of Common Czech to use the Standard in speaking, or to use individual Standard forms together with Common Czech forms as expected. Fourthly, there is occasionally the feeling that speakers would like to adhere to their first language (Common Czech) rather than to employ the 'artificial and stiff' forms of the Standard. This is sometimes felt with regard to the written medium as well. Finally, some Common Czech lexicon and phraseology is stylistically perceived as substandard or vulgar even by native speakers of Common Czech. Nekvapil

(2000b: 173) gives an example of a sentence from a private letter that commences with:

> *Píšu asi krávovinky, ale aspoň si počteš. Zrovna se rozmejšlím dát to naší malý*
> *zkonzultovat, ale radši ne, vona by mne nadávala . . .*
> 'I guess I am writing stupid things, but at least you'll have a good read. Right
> now I'm considering whether to ask our "little one" to check it for me, but
> no, she would blast me . . .' [6]

It is not so much the Common Czech forms *rozmejšlím* 'considering' (for Standard *rozmýšlím*) or *vona* 'she' (for *ona*) that attracts attention. The passage is filled with emotion-loaded expressions such as *krávovinky* 'stupid things', *si počteš* 'you'll have a read', *naší malý* 'to our little one', or *nadávala by* 'would blast', out of which some are just informal (*si počteš, nadávala*), but some are on the verge of being vulgar (*krávovinky, naší malý*). The question is whether or not it is the use of Common Czech that not only tolerates but directly invites the vulgar expression. Some speakers feel that Common Czech does invite such modes of language.

Organised management

Organised management over the last decades has reflected these discourse problems when in several cases it re-codified Standard Czech to a position close to the Common language. For example, for the 1st person present tense of certain verbs, the Standard (as codified in the Rules of Czech Spelling) has accepted the Common form ending in *–ju*, e.g. *kupuju* 'I buy' along with the original Standard form *kupuji* 'I buy'.

However, on the whole, in organised management the attention given to the existence of Common Czech is limited. Perhaps the modern Standard norms have been too strongly established; perhaps it is felt that a far-reaching reform implicating a switch to a new Standard is not warranted. There is a pro-Common Czech camp among Czech linguists headed by Petr Sgall (Sgall, 1999; Sgall & Hronek, 1992; Sgall *et al.*, 1992) which has pointed to such facts as the need of speakers to concentrate on formal features of discourse (its Standard-ness) at the expense of content. They also point to the fact that, while some Standard forms are too bookish (e.g. *lidmi* 'people [Instr. Case]') the corresponding Common forms (*lidma*) remain outside the codified Standard, resulting in problems concerning the expression of certain contents. Members of this group, particularly Petr Sgall, have made suggestions about gradual acceptance of some Common forms into the Standard, but their suggestions have failed to convince the majority of participants in the management process. In the view of many linguists, the difference can be evaluated as one of style; it has been suggested that the selection of one form over another should be guided by the relative formality of the situation. Yet, it must be admitted that the situation does not fully resemble stylistic selection: the difference lies between arbitrarily diverging varieties, and is not merely a matter of stylistic choice. The Common language form *dobrej* 'good' as a form has nothing to do with the informality of the situation in which it replaces the Standard form *dobrý*. Most other languages of Europe use, for different degrees of formality, different styles (where the form of expression reflects the characteristics of the situation), but not devices that resemble differences between separate varieties of a language.

However, within the atmosphere of the Czech Republic at the end of the 20th century, the strengthening of middle-class norms, not the democratisation of language, was the program of the day. Although the new political leaders (who came out of the underground after the disintegration of the socialist world in 1989) in public speaking initially used a variety that contained an admixture of a number of Common language elements, soon switched to the Standard. A similar leaning towards traditional norms could be observed throughout the nation. In this situation it would be unrealistic to expect that the diglottic situation of zone 1 would soon change.

In any case, as already noted in Nekvapil (2000b), no organised management should take place before a systematic inquiry is conducted to establish how the use of the Standard and the Common Czech forms is in fact managed in discourse. There should be no compulsion to use the Standard in informal contexts (Čechová, 1996), but in any case this is not happening at present to any significant degree.

The problem of dialects

The situation

Whereas Common Czech can be defined as a supra-regional koine, there are dialects, specific to a particular region or locality both in zone 1 and zone 2, as noted in the preceding section. While features of the Common language in principle do not bear any specific local markers within zone 1, dialectal features are perceived as such. Dialectal marking of speech is a different problem.

The dialectal differentiation of contemporary Czech territory is not sharp in Bohemia. In west and southwest Bohemia, a 'sing-song intonation' is the most prominent feature, but there are other features in the lexicon and morphology. Compared to this situation, the north of Bohemia (resettled in the 1940s and 1950s after the forced evacuation of the German population) developed into a basically dialect-free zone where Common Czech is spoken. Remnants of the original dialects exist in eastern and southeastern Bohemia and, surprisingly, even in some parts of central Bohemia (Jančáková, 1997a). Moravia shows much more extensive survival of dialects, with three dialectal zones: Haná dialects, with a centre around Olomouc and covering the area of Brno; the Silesian dialects of the north; and the Moravian-Slovak dialects of the southeast. In Moravia, although some morphological features support the Standard rather than the Common language, other features are specific to the dialects.

Simple management

Where dialects exist, they constitute the native languages of the population. When communication in the public domain occurs, dialectal features are in general adjusted. Such adjustment, connected with the belief that dialects are the language of the less educated and less prestigious countryside (Krčmová, 1997), is accepted as natural. A different attitude can be observed when a speaker returns to his/her own dialectal community; in such cases, switching to the dialect and management of deviations from norms of the dialect can be observed. In this way speakers communicate solidarity with their original community (Krčmová, 1997). This much can be said in the absence of discourse data that would show details of the processes involved.

Organised management

In some societies, such as Britain, local (and ethnic) accents have been accepted through organised management within the media as the language of announcers on the radio and TV. No such positive management measures have been recorded for the Czech situation, although strong noting (in the sense of the Management Theory, see Part I), negative evaluation and adjustment to the Standard are evident. Of course, admixture of the dialect appears in the speech of other than radio/TV personnel, either because of their inability to adjust, or because of individual's policies. Incidentally, this is also true of the intrusion of the Common language.

There is no evidence of large-scale management resulting from the positive evaluation of dialects. However, it was noted earlier that the profound linguistic and sociocultural differences between Bohemia and Moravia have led to the idea of recognising a separate Moravian language, an idea which first appeared at the beginning of the 19th century and which has mainly been defended by authors and politicians rather than by linguists. The last contribution to a series of attempts at codification of such language was published in 1998 (see Berger, 2000). It is doubtful that the establishment of another Standard, which would necessarily oppress dialects existing under its umbrella, is the best contemporary answer to the problem of the dialect.

Slang

The situation

The meaning of the term *slang* is subject to considerable variation in English (Chapman, 1986) as well as in Czech. In Czech the following understanding of the term is common:

> Slang is an integral part of the national language; it is a substandard stratum of specific naming units which is adopted in day-to-day (most often semi-offical or unoffical) communication among people who interact in the same working environment or in the same sphere of interest; it serves partly the specific needs of language communication, and partly as a means of expressing affiliation to a certain social environment. (Hubáček, 1979: 17)

This definition includes not only so-called group or interest slangs but also professional jargons (Nekvapil, 1993). It is obvious that language problems relating to slang mostly concern lexical variation.

The main differences between the Standard and slang can be characterised in the following way:

- frequent employment of certain word-forming procedures, of which some suffixes are especially typical of slang (*-ák, -ař, -ka*);
- frequent employment of metaphoric and metonymic transpositions;
- a general tendency towards shorting, manifesting itself through univerbalisation of naming units and abbreviation of Standard words.

In Czech linguistics *slang* is not used to denote a substandard linguistic stratum distributed in principle over the whole community, as is Common Czech. Nevertheless, slang shows a strong tendency to co-occur with Common Czech. Slang expressions are difficult to apply in combination with Standard grammar and the Standard lexicon, whereas Common Czech grammar seems to invite (though not require) slang expressions. This relationship gives the slang-related variation a particularly strong position within the system of the Czech language.

The possibility of using a slang expression only exists in languages in which the process of standardisation has advanced. It is only against the background of the Standard that a slang expression is recognised as such. Normally this happens in the period of a large-scale build-up of languages for special purposes (Nekvapil, 2002). It is not a mere coincidence that, in Czech, slang begins to be discussed only after the formation of Czechoslovakia in 1918. In the Austro-Hungarian Empire, German was the dominant language and it was not until after 1918 that Czech started being extensively used in such communicative domains as the army, governmental offices and the railways. Terminological committees were formed, and they produced sets of Standard terms. Under these conditions, the function of slang started being fulfilled by German terminology that sometimes continued to be used against the background of the newly formed Czech Standard lexicon. By that time, loans from German in general had acquired a non-Standard accent. This was not understood by the German Army when it occupied the Czech lands in 1939 and issued ordinances in Czech that were full of Germanism: these were accepted with ironic smiles by the Czech population as inappropriate to the serious intention the occupiers wanted to communicate.

At present in Czech linguistic literature about 70 different slang strata (Klimeš, 1997) are normally mentioned: students' slang, railway slang, miners' slang, musicians' slang and sports slang are among those that seem to be best developed and that have received most attention. An extensive expansion is taking place in the case of computer slang.

Simple management

Problems that occur in discourse and are connected with slang are of two types: first, the speaker may be unable to distinguish a slang expression from a Standard term and may use the slang expression in a formal situation or, conversely, may use a Standard expression in an informal situation where slang would be expected. Management (including negative evaluation) by other participants may then follow. This closely connects with the second problem: an individual may not possess slang competence characteristic for the situation in which he or she interacts. The latter is typical for people who are not yet fully incorporated into a new environment, e.g. apprentices or new army conscripts. Normally, speakers realise that the knowledge of a slang and its correct application serve as proof of membership in a certain social group. This function is, of course, also fulfilled by Standard specialised terminology adequate to the situation, but the impact of the slang is much more forceful.

Organised management

Since organised management has normally been dedicated to the cultivation of the Standard language, it considers the existence of slang as a menace. Slang develops in a spontaneous way and its originators frequently, and sometimes intentionally, violate the structural patterns of the Standard lexicon. The traditional management strategy is not to mention slang at all. Even at the level of description ('noting' within the management theory), it receives little attention by language managers. In Czech linguistics, it has never been a well established object of research, although since the 1960s a considerable number of short papers have been published, mainly in non-centrist periodicals, pointing to the importance of this aspect of social variation in Czech. At central institutions, such as the Institute of the Czech Language, some slang expressions (especially in the case of components of so-called 'professional jargons') were noted, evaluated and incorporated into the Standard norm. At school and in apprentice schools the use of the slang continued to be considered 'vulgarisation of language', and the schools made an attempt to eradicate it. At present, attitudes toward slang are more relaxed, and this is connected, among other things, with a more frequent use of slang expressions within the language of the mass media.

A large number of words that are presently borrowed from English (e.g. in computing, popular music or sports) are felt to be slang. A new feature in this case can be seen in the relatively rapid loss of their slang character. A number of such expressions are accepted into special usage dictionaries, which fulfil the codifying role. When these expressions leave the specialised networks, they easily become a component of the Standard. There is not much resistance from other areas of organised management devoted to codification, such as the journal *Naše řeč.*

Language of returnees

Speech of Czechs from the Ukraine

Situation, problems

Little attention has been accorded to the language management of Czech repatriates from the Ukraine after WWII. In contrast, the language of the returnees of the 1990s was subjected to systematic research because the settlements Mala Zubovshtina and Malinovka, from which 1990s returnees arrived, represented a Czech language island; the data from these isolates made possible the study of older or dialectal stages of the Czech language (Jančáková, 1997b). Use of that data for language management was a secondary consideration. However, relatively early researchers pointed to the deficiencies of this approach: the influence of Ukrainian and Russian could not be ignored. This resulted in the involvement of sociolinguists, who investigated the situation both before and after repatriation (Pišlová, 2002). In summary, one can claim that, in the pre-repatriation language, typically an archaic dialect of Czech (of the Northeastern group) was in contact with Ukrainian and Russian (Čmejrková, 2003). Interestingly, through contact with Ukrainian, Czech dialectal features were reinforced (e.g. the bilabial pronunciation of *v*, word-final *u* instead of *l*, or the loss of hiatus and prothetic *j*). It became apparent that a number of originally assumed Ukrainian influences cannot be separated from the influence of Russian, especially when, in the lexicon or in the inflection of the numerals, the rules of these two languages coincide. This point is important with regard to the noting and evaluation of non-Czech elements in the speech of these speakers. Czechs from the matrix community perceive a 'Russian accent' where the phenomenon may actually be of Ukrainian origin. This management cannot easily be eliminated because little knowledge of Ukrainian is distributed in the Czech community, while Russian was the object of systematic compulsory instruction until 1989. The perception as 'Russian' cannot be challenged on the basis of other typically Ukrainian features (*h* instead of *g*, etc.), because competence in Russian reaches only a limited level and many non-Russian features are covert for Czech speakers.

After repatriation some specific features of the speech of Ukrainian Czech started subsiding. This change occurred faster in the lexicon but was relatively slower in the prosody. It is clear that, although matrix Czech norms are accepted, noting of deviations from them is stronger in some parts of language (the lexicon) than in others (phonemics). The speed of adjustment differs according to the generation of the speaker, with younger speakers proceeding more rapidly, because for them the degree of incorporation into local networks seems to be of great importance (Pišlová, 2002). Since the socioeconomic position of the returnee community (including some active businessmen, doctors and academics) was at the centre of attention, it can be assumed that their sociocultural, non-grammatical as well as grammatical communicative competence already has approached, or soon will approach, that of the matrix community.

Simple management
A.N., born 1924, says:

> *Ptali sme se tudletech teda, tech mistňich Čechu, teda řikáme. Co že vi ináč, inádž hovoříte. Přidu do opchodu, a voňi řikaj drožďi. Já poudám drožďi, co to je? Poudám, proč neřikáte kvasňice. A proč neřikáte vjedro a řikáte kíbl. A voňi se smejou.*

> We asked then those people, those local Czechs, we say, how come that you speak differently. I come to the shop and they say *drožďi* ('yeast'). I say *drožďi*, what is that. I say why don't you say *kvasnice*. And why don't you say *vědro* and say *kýbl* ('bucket'). And they laugh. (Jančáková, 1997b: 53)

In this example, A.N., a member of the oldest generation of returnees, notes certain lexical features in the speech of matrix Czechs and evaluates them negatively. Adjustment is suggested, but this is laughed at. The words proposed as adjustment are not actively used in the younger generation of many matrix community speakers but they are fully comprehensible. *Vědro* 'bucket' tends to be made of wood (as it was when the emigrants were leaving the Czech lands) – *kýbl*, made of other materials, is strongly non-Standard. However, linguistic discrimination would hardly be based on these examples.

Otherwise the speech of A.N. more or less agrees with the norm of northeastern Bohemian dialects. Some of the features may be archaic (*smejou se* for *smějou se* 'they laugh'), but there are no obvious 'mistakes'. Again, the archaic features are not enough for a strong negative evaluation. Discrimination is most likely to be based on prosodic features of returnee speakers, which are not only deviant but also carry, for many Czechs, the negatively evaluated meaning 'Russian'.

The following excerpt from an Introduction to the Master's thesis of Alena Pišlová, herself a member of the youngest generation of the returnees, documents a decision at the 'individual level' of management to further adjust her own Czech in courses of Czech for foreign speakers. The writer hints at the number of individual management processes on which the decision was based.

Narodila jsem se ještě na území bývalého Sovětského Svazu českým rodičům, jejichž prarodiče byli potomky českých kolonistů nebo sami přišli na Ukrajinu jako malé děti. Od své matky a otce jsem zdědila vědomí vlastní národnosti a ruku v ruce i vědomí českých tradic a mateřského jazyka. Je třeba samozřejmě brát v úvahu relativnost míry a úrovně získaných poznatků. Jazyk, kterému jsem se naučila, jsem považovala za český a jasně jej oddělovala od jazyka společnosti, ve které jsem vyrůstala. Po přesídlení do České republiky bylo zajímavým zjištěním, že podoba mé mateřštiny je jiná než ostatních lidí kolem mne, i když jde o stejný jazyk. Tak se projevil zájem o hlubší poznání češtiny . . . Tehdy ((tj. v r. 1996)) jsem si podala žádost na FF UK obor čeština pro cizince . . .

I was born in the territory of the former Soviet Union to Czech parents, whose grandparents were off-spring of Czech colonists or themselves came to the Ukraine as little children. From my mother and father I inherited my ethnic awareness and with it the awareness of Czech traditions and our mother tongue. It is necessary, of course, to take into consideration the relativity of measure and level of the knowledge I gained. The language I learned I considered as Czech and divided it clearly from the language of the society in which I was growing up. After moving to the Czech Republic it was an interesting realisation that the form of my mother tongue is different from that of other people around me, even though it is the same language. In this way an interest in a deeper understanding of Czech appeared . . . Then [in 1996] I applied for admission to the Faculty of Arts at Charles University, with specialisation in teaching Czech to foreigners . . . (Pišlová, 2002: 2, 9).

Organised management

Prior to their return to the Czech Republic, the Czech Ministry of Education organised a two-month course (in the Bohemian city of Pelhřimov) for students from Czech villages in the Ukraine to smooth out their further studies at Czech schools on their final arrival in the Republic. This is where Czech linguists commenced their research. On their return, these students were integrated into the Czech education system, commencing with kindergarten and continuing up to university.

Speech of Czechs from Kazakhstan

No linguistic accounts concerning the language behaviour of the Czechs from Kazakhstan exist. This account is, therefore, based on the observations of journalists and ethnographers (in particular Valášková, 1998). There seems to be no doubt that competence in Czech is scanty among this population. Czech stopped being used in the local school at the end of 1920s and its place was taken by Russian. This fact notwithstanding, the older generation possesses knowledge of Czech, though influenced by Russian. Valášková (1998: 164) reports that even younger women are able to pray in Czech and possess an active knowledge of a number of folk songs. Some repatriates brought with them the knowledge of Kazakh (and left behind some knowledge of Czech). The younger generation could hardly do more than acquire elementary Czech, taught in courses organised in Kazakhstan at the beginning of the 1990s. Young families apparently still use Russian in the family domain, especially when the partner is ethnically

Russian or Ukrainian. Those concerned with the re-emigration stress the point that a 'language barrier' exists. This barrier is probably higher in the case of the written language, where a transition from azbuka to the Latin alphabet is needed and where stronger language norms are in place than in spoken contact. Although Czechs are often willing to act as language teaching volunteers (MFD, 26 August 1998: 3), it remains a fact that repatriates from Kazakhstan experience negative attitudes common in dealing with 'Russian-speaking foreigners'.

Written language and spelling

Orthography is a system of strategies and rules that allow us to switch from speaking to writing at the phonemic/graphemic level. As pointed out early in the Prague School (Vachek, 1939), the difference between spoken and written language cannot be reduced to questions of orthography, a fact that has continued attracting attention ever since. There are important and inescapable differences in the lexicon and grammar of spoken and written texts, and in the case of Czech these differences have attracted the attention of language management activities. Yet, the question of correspondence at the phonemic level has always maintained its position as the most important issue of language management. In this sense, the situation in Czech has not differed from language cultivation in other languages. Both in schools and in the community at large the problem of orthography has attracted attention at the expense of other problems. However, as in other languages, the weight of orthography within language management is gradually diminishing at present.

The principles of Czech orthography

The Czech language uses the Latin alphabet, augmented by three diacritics as in letters á, ř and ů. Orthographical systems use various principles which determine what elements of the spoken language are represented by a single sign (grapheme) in the written language.

(1) The distinctive feature principle: individual distinctive features of phonemes are represented by single signs. Many languages use this strategy, but in no language does it become the governing principle. In Czech, vocalic length is represented by the diacritic called *čárka* 'accent' a/á, i/í, u/ú (however, most long u are written as ů), e/é, o/ó. This sign is not used in any other role. On the other hand the Czech *háček* 'hook' does not represent any single phonemic feature. In each of the pairs t/ť (in printing after t and d the *háček* is normally represented by an apostrophe), c/č and r/ř it represents a different phonemic distinction.

(2) The phonemic principle: phonemes are represented by single graphemes. This is the leading strategy in the Czech system of spelling. However, there are a number of exceptions, due to the application of the 'morphological principle' (see below). Phonemically conditioned exceptions are:

  (a) The representation of the phonemes ť, ď and ň. They are written t, d, n before i and ť, ď, ň elsewhere. (However, in foreign words t, d, n before i retain their normal value.)

  (b) The grapheme ě basically corresponds to the phoneme e. However, additionally it also marks other phonemic distinctions. After t, d, n it means that the preceding consonant is 'softened' to *t'*, *ď*, *ň*. After p, b, v it means that j must be inserted between the consonant and the vowel e. And after m, it marks the insertion of ň.

(c) In foreign words the grapheme s can represent the phoneme z.

In principle each phoneme occupies the space of one letter. Some phonemes have their own graphemes (*a*, *t*, *r*, etc.) while other phonemes are represented by a letter plus a diacritics (*á*, *ř*, *t'*, etc.). However, this principle is violated in two cases:

(a) The combination of graphemes *c* and *h* represents a single phoneme χ (as in Scottish *Loch* or German *Bach*).

(b) The grapheme x represents two phonemes: *ks*.

(3) The morphemic principle: this principle means that the same morpheme is represented in the same way (whatever the pronunciation may be) and different morphemes are represented differently (even if their pronunciation is identical). There are several types of application of this principle:

(a) Final unvoiced consonants are written as voiced consonants if in other forms of the word the consonant is voiced (e.g. *dup* 'oak' is written *dub*, because the genitive case is *dubu*). Here writers must realise what the 'basic' form of the morpheme is.

(b) The vowel i / í is written y / ý in the stem of some morphemes (e.g. *být* 'to be'). (This spelling mostly reflects the historical pronunciation; at the present time, there is no difference in pronunciation.) Writers must know which morpheme has *i* and which has *y*. Primary school children memorise a list of words which contain the y-morphemes, and must judge for themselves which other words contain the same morpheme.

(c) In endings, the phoneme *i* is also represented differently, depending on the morpheme: for example if it represents 'past+male+plural+3rd person' it is written i, but if its represents 'past+female+plural+3rd person', the correct spelling is *y*. Writers must be able to analyse the morphemes in question.

(d) For the long *u* there are two graphemes (*ú* and *ů*) that are differentiated by their position vis-à-vis the boundary between morphemes.

(e) The phonemic sequence *mně* is written *mně* if it is related to a morpheme which includes both *m* and *n / ň* (e.g. *vzpomněl* 'remembered' because of *vzpomenout si* 'to remember'), otherwise it is written *mě* (*město* 'a town'). Writers must be able to analyse words morphemically.

(f) Apart from this, the phonemic sequence *mně* is written *mě* in the accusative case of *já* 'I', but *mně* in the dative and locative cases. Writers must understand the grammatical character of these words.

(g) Some morphemes use voiced graphemes for unvoiced phonemes without any particular reason: *ž* in *až* 'when', or z in *způsob* 'mode'. The morpheme pronounced *gdyš* 'when' is written *když*; there are only historical reasons for this. (Similarly, *kdy* 'when', *kde* 'where', etc.) In this case, writers must remember how each of these morphemes is written.

(h) In numerals, the stem is written with a numerical symbol, while the ending is indicated either by a dot (*v 9. století*, pronounce: 'v devátém století'), or the ending is directly added (*v 9tém století*, pronounce: 'v devátém století').

(4) The lexical principle. One or several words are written in a particular way. This happens only in the following cases:

(a) Cardinal numerals and signs: 3 (pronounce *tři*), 21 (pronounce *dvacet jedna*), 1/6 (pronounce *jedna šestina*), signs in scientific language, etc.

(b) Abbreviations: ČTK (pronounce *čétéká*), UK (pronounce *univerzita karlova*).

(c) Foreign words: *management* (pronounce *menedžment*).

This tedious list of principles and rules has been given in full, except for some equally difficult rules of punctuation, in order to illustrate the size of the spelling problem native speakers face.

These principles of spelling have been influenced by the typological profile of the Czech language. As Skalička (1979: 309–10) has shown, the inflectional type, which is strongly represented in that profile, can lead to a larger than average number of consonants. This problem of too many consonants (compared with the limited number of Latin script graphemes) has been solved in Czech by using the diacritics. At the same time, the language uses the morphological principle, which is also important for inflection. The lexical principle is well established for numerals, but abbreviations have never been popular and the spelling of foreign words has gradually been more and more adapted to Czech spelling, although in proper names and recent borrowings the foreign graphemic form persists.

As a result of the application of these principles, correct spelling presupposes a knowledge of a number of lexical and grammatical rules. For example, the spelling of the word *výmyk* 'upward circle (in gymnastics)' with y requires its morphological analysis and the recognition of the morpheme *–myk–* as identical with *–myk–* in more common words such as *zamykat* 'to lock up'. In addition it is necessary to possess the knowledge that the morpheme *–myk–* is one of the morphemes using y (not i). Or, in order to determine whether the phonemic sequence *mně* in *nebaví mě to* 'it doesn't amuse me' should be spelt as *mě* or as *mně*, the writer requires the knowledge that it is an accusative, not a dative. Of course the use of such rules is automatised in the case of frequent active users of the written language, but those who only write occasionally have to manage (in the sense of the management theory) their spelling in each case. In the course of compulsory school education, the basic rules of Czech spelling are acquired by nearly all native speakers, but the active use of some rules is socially limited, particularly in reference to the use of capitals and the writing of foreign words. The spelling system is normally very difficult for members of communities other than Czech communities. This was, for example, true of Germans who remained in Czechoslovakia after WWII. In biographical research (Nekvapil, 2001) they claimed that mastering Czech spelling was the most difficult task in their linguistic adaptation to the new environment.

As in all societies of the Modern stage of development, correct spelling has been considered the first requirement of education. In Czech, the inability to distinguish between *i* and *y*, in particular has been looked upon as a sign of intellectual primitivity. In the eyes of the public, spelling has often been seen as logical, and deviations from it as evidence of the lack of the ability to think logically. In passing, it must be noted that the division of the former Czechoslovakia was, at one stage, closely connected with a spelling problem. The political representatives of Slovakia (correctly) pointed to the fact that the component *–slovensko* in *Československo* was not transparent and required the form *Česko-Slovensko*. Linguists were summoned when the matter was discussed in the cabinet.

Simple management

Simple management of spelling is widely distributed within the community whenever the written language is used. One of the authors of this paper (JVN) has written Czech frequently, but he has always 'noted' the problem of *mě* or *mně* and sometimes selected the correct spelling only after a complicated adjustment process. He believes that his use of the *i/y* is automatised and correct. He does not 'note' the problem. He occasionally 'notes' other problems, such as capital letters, or the spelling of foreign words, but in these cases the sanctions are weak, and in his manuscripts he relegates the problem to professional proofreaders.

In general we can say that simple management of spelling has gradually been decreasing. This decrease is the result of changes in educational philosophy which have tended to emphasise content over form. To some extent, the influence of electronic mail can also be perceived. Since some users cannot use (or elect not to use) specific Czech graphemes (with accents and hooks), e-mail can differ to a considerable extent from normal Czech texts. For example, the sentence

> *Jiří slíbil, že mně to dá včas* 'George promised that he would give it to me in time'

is transformed into

> *Jiri slibil, ze mne to da vcas.*

These pseudo-Czech texts contain so many deviations from normal Czech that a few additional deviations due to spelling problems may remain unnoticed.

However, the extent of simple correction still remains vast. Although studies of adult spelling processes are rare – if they exist at all – the extent of confusion is revealed by the number and range of questions addressed to the Language Advisory Unit of the Academy of Sciences (Uhlířová, 2002). Questions frequently address the i/y problem, capital letters and loan-words. The fact that most of those addressing the Advisory Unit are people who write for the public (journalists, editors, proofreaders, authors of official and legal documents, etc.), as well as teachers of the Czech language, shows that the extent of uncertainty within the community is considerable and that, unlike in English speaking communities, the questions involved often cannot be easily resolved by reference to dictionaries or standard manuals.

Organised management

Organised management begins at school, where considerable emphasis is placed on correct spelling. Much of the training in spelling is through the use of 'dictation' exercises in which the teacher reads individual sentences containing difficult points of spelling and subsequently corrects the students' mistakes.

The following examples are from a dictation presented in 1999 to students in Year 9 at a public school in eastern Bohemia. The student whose work is considered here in the meantime went on to high school (gymnázium), and can minimally be considered average, but most likely he is an above-average performer.

> *Zbyla nám milá vzpomýnka* [the grapheme *ý* has been underlined twice in red by the teacher]. *Masitá strava je sytá. Psík se svynul do klubíčka* [the syllable *svy* has been crossed out by the student and replaced by *svi*]. 'We have been left with a pleasant memory. Meat dishes are nourishing. A dog curled up.'

In this extract we can see a case of simple post-management by the student (*svy→svi*). The teacher's correction (*vzpomýnka→vzpomínka*) is a part of organised management within the education system. The double underlining shows that the mistake is considered to be serious. In a follow-up interview, the student explained his spelling of *vzpomínka* 'memory' with *ý* by (a false) morphemic association of the word with the word *myslet* 'to think'.

At the level of the mass media, the state television TV1 in 1998 introduced a programme called *Diktát* 'Dictation' within the busy evening primetime zone. The teacher (originally Zdeněk Svěrák, otherwise known as the leading actor in the Oscar-winning film *Kolya*) dictates a text which is being taken down by 'students' in the studio and by many people throughout the country. The prestige of the programme is enhanced by the fact that the final evaluator is the Director of the Institute of the Czech Language of the Academy of Sciences of the Czech Republic. The programme is still very popular.

Rules of Czech Spelling

By far the most influential instrument of language management with regard to spelling is the publication called *The Rules of Czech Spelling* (*Pravidla českého pravopisu*) which has a history stretching back for more than 100 years. The beginning of a system which is on the whole identical with current spelling can be identified in the first half of the 19th century. However, there were differences, and considerable variation still existed, although the system was accepted by the community as 'natural' (Sedláček, 1993). The situation rapidly changed in the second half of the century, when schooling in Czech developed in an unprecedented way, making a further codification of the spelling system necessary. At the same time, new Czech literature, which liberated itself from the provincialism of the previous period, was heading in a direction towards further unification of the usage in a way different from the tradition of the first half of the century. The association *Matice česká* published a handbook called *A Sharpener of the Czech Tongue* (*Brus jazyka českého*) in 1877 which, in a way, was a predecessor of the *Rules*. Furthermore, textbooks for all schools had to be approved by the authorities and as a consequence, in fact, had a codifying effect. Nevertheless, the situation was opaque, and the government asked a leading linguist, Josef Gebauer (1838–1907), to head a committee that would compile a handbook for high schools, presenting a comprehensive picture of the problem. The result of the work of the committee, published in 1902, created the tradition of the *Rules* that has lasted to this day. The *Rules* handbook is revised from time to time, sometimes after a long interval. The dates of the more substantial revisions were:

1913, 1941, 1957 and 1993. However, small individual changes in codification occurred in between these dates.

The 1902 first edition of the *Rules of Czech Spelling* emphasised on its title page that it was 'the only edition approved by the Ministry of Culture and Education'. The full title which was 'Rules Directed to Czech Orthography and Morphology, Accompanied by an Alphabetic List of Words and Forms' points to the fact that: (1) the *Rules* consisted both of a set of rules and an alphabetically arranged glossary, and (2) the *Rules* contained not only an orthographic but also a morphological part.

At the beginning of the 20th century, Czech society was sufficiently modernised to be sure that no radical reform would be forthcoming. Gebauer and his Committee were conservative. They referred to Jungmann (1773–1847) and Palacký (1798–1876), and even older literature, as the source of models for correct language, notwithstanding the fact that these possible models were the sources of variation the handbook intended to overcome. However, the members of the committee admitted that there was a need for a more efficient way of finding out and, in fact, the handbook demonstrated at least two relatively progressive features. Firstly, as concerns morphology, the members of the committee took a stand against arbitrarily changing language, and they accepted only those forms that had actually existed in language (even though they often preferred older forms to more contemporary ones). Secondly, Gebauer's Introduction (Gebauer, 1902) mentioned the requirement of uniformity, but also accepted some of the existing variation; for example, both *dveře* and *dvéře* 'door' were accepted.

Even this degree of liberalism was unacceptable to many established language teachers who required strict codification. As early as the 1903 printing, the number of alternative forms was reduced. The preference for a 'straightforward regularity' (*přímočará pravidelnost,* Vilém Mathesius' later term) became still more pronounced in the 1913 edition which was criticised, in the 1930s, on behalf of writers and journalists, by the Prague Linguistic Circle (Sedláček, 1993: 69).

The *Rules* established themselves within the Czechoslovak Republic as the arbiter of usage, particularly in education and official work. Although the use of the *Rules* was not legally binding until recently (see the following discussion), they have been widely accepted as the norm for all written language. Publishers required authors to comply with the *Rules*. Except for the 1902 edition, the authors of the *Rules* remained anonymous, although it was well known that leading linguists, such as Bohuslav Havránek or František Daneš took part in the compilation of the post-war editions.

After 1948 (the year when the Communist Party assumed power), the changed political situation brought new factors into play. The functionalist attitude, established by the Prague Linguistic Circle before WWII – an attitude which considered language and its parts, such as the orthography, as tools – was on the whole accepted, and no major reforms of the spelling system were forthcoming. No need was seen for major changes in the name of democratisation of language (Havránek, 1947). For instance, the distinction between *i* and *y* has never been seriously considered as an object of reform (Sedláček, 1998: 156). The lack of reformist thought was in line with the Communist Party's self-image as a defender of national traditions. On the other hand, a few areas of the *Rules* were considered to have ideological implications. One such area was the use of capital letters. Capital letters were always considered honorific (cf. the traditional – now somewhat obsolete – honorific singular-address *Vy* against the non-honorific singular address *ty*). It is interesting that immediately after WWII, when anti-German emotions were fed by the fresh memory of war-time atrocities, the word *Němec* 'a German' was often written (against the codified norm) as *němec*. In the 1957 edition of the *Rules* (the first edition to be approved by the Central Committee of the Communist Party), the names of established institution such as *ministerstvo zahraničí* 'Foreign Ministry' continued to be written with lower case letters, while new socialist institutions, such as *Pohraniční stráž* 'State Border Guard', were capitalised. The February 1948 communist takeover was designated as *Únor* 'February'. Even if the words concerned were not necessarily mentioned in the glossary part, the honorific meaning of capitalisation was obvious in the first (*Rules*) part, where these words were given as examples.

Another ideologically sensitive point of the 1957 *Rules* was the attitude to foreign words, in particular the differentiation of *s* and *z* in some particular words. The integration of foreign words into the Czech spelling system began as early as the 1913 *Rules*. The 1957 edition further extended the range of words in which pronounced *z* was written as *z*; for example, the word previously written *analysa*, was hereafter to be written *analýza* 'analysis'. However, the Central Committee did not approve the words *prezident* and *socializmus*, because it was afraid that the untraditional spelling with *z* might lessen the authority of these institutions, notwithstanding the fact that the pronunciation *president* or *socialismus* (with *s*) did not occur at all. 'Museum' became *muzeum*, except that in the case of the historically important *Národní museum* 'National Museum' the Minister of Education (formerly a history professor) pushed through an exceptional spelling with s.

A change that was not ideologically tinted concerned the unification of vocalic length in foreign words. In view of considerable variation in Common Czech and in different areas of the Czech territory, the authors of the 1957 edition attempted not simply to reflect the usage but to present codification rules that would guide and influence Standard pronunciation.

The first post-Communist *Rules* of 1993 proposed only a few changes, but these were welcomed in a very critical fashion. This critical tone was partly the consequence of the fact that this was the first time in the second half of the century when the public could freely express their opinions. Nothing was considered 'obvious' (cf. Ajvaz' title *Proti samozřejmosti* 'Against obviousness'; Ajvaz, 1994). Nevertheless, at least two important themes surfaced in the discussion. First, the principle of integration of loans into the Czech phonemic system was attacked. The reason was the newly perceived need to retain uniformity with western European languages. The author Josef Vaculík wrote about a 'barbaric plan to erase in the graphical picture the pedigree of words, and to obscure in the general graphical consciousness of history Romance, Germanic and Celtic influences', while the linguist Marvan spoke about 'a distinct boundary between the orthographic spirit of the West and the East' (see Marvan, 1993). The second theme in the discussion concerned the attempt of the authors of the 1993 *Rules* to make the handbook easier to use for the 'average user' by excluding some more difficult alternative spellings. After the fall of the communist system in 1989 there was no space left for defending the position of the socially weak, who preferred more regularity. The public required more freedom for the strong, in this case the middle class, and defended variation against uniformity. The stand was further influenced by the penetration of new postmodern attitudes that placed variation at the top of sociocultural values.

The Ministry of Education, which approves each new edition of the *Rules* for use in schools, reacted by refusing an immediate endorsement. The handbook was actually introduced into schools in 1994, with the proviso that alternative spellings were allowed. The acceptance of alternatives is now characteristic for magazines and journals within various special fields, which give authors the opportunity to decide which alternatives to employ. This postmodern spirit contrasts with the previous situation, when the *Rules* had to be followed and the publisher decided in case the handbook allowed more than one choice. The principle of accepting alternatives has also been endorsed in later publications based on the 1993 *Rules*: the *Akademický slovník cizích slov* (Academic Dictionary of Foreign Words) (1994), or *Slovník spisovné češtiny pro školu a veřejnost* (Dictionary of Standard Czech for the School and the Public) (1995). The current situation thus reflects the overall decline in normativism and the creation of conditions for differentiated norms. The target does not any longer seem to be 'spelling for the Standard language', but rather 'spelling for everyday life', 'spelling for specialised communication', or 'spelling for literary works'.

Interestingly, it is difficult to identify Russian influences during the period of Communist Party rule, except that some authors (see Sedláček, 1998: 157) consider the 'phonetic' writing of foreign words as an influence of Russian. However, it has had a long tradition in Czech extending back before WWII. At present, the influence of English has not penetrated into the codification, but is felt in practice, particularly in the case of capital letters or punctuation.

With regard to spelling, Czech organised management has thus remained the 'property' of the middle class. The difference between the 1902 *Rules of Czech Spelling* and the 1993 handbook is vast, but most of the changes occurred at the beginning of the century; in fact, the second half of the century brought few changes (Sedláček, 1998: 163). The strategies that guided the development were modernisation strategies, principally of the Modern stage. This implied changes toward the spoken language. However, the spoken language involved was a variety of the Standard, not Common Czech. Little intentional democratisation can be detected, although it is true that the current form of the spelling is easier to apply for an average user.

Literacy

Literacy refers to the ability to use the written language. However, to read and write is not identical with the ability to use the script. We can divide the related problems into three large areas:

(1) Problems of 'grammatical' competence; i.e. the knowledge of the script, orthography and punctuation (in the case of Czech, the knowledge of the strict rules of spelling).

(2) Problems of non-grammatical communicative competence; i.e. the selection of the suitable variety of language (in Czech, the Standard), special

functional features of language, the selection out of a range of texts to read, the establishment of settings for reading and writing, etc.

(3)   Problems of sociocultural competence; i.e. the social needs and rewards for reading/writing or sufficient funding for the time spent on the use of the written language.

As in the case of other language problems, the solution of sociocultural problems precedes problems of non-grammatical communicative competence, and these again precede those of grammatical competence. At present it is widely accepted that literacy is not primarily a problem of script and orthography.

The Czech lands have always belonged to those parts of Europe with the highest rates of literacy. In the 15th century, Aeneas Sylvius (later Pius II) commented that Hussite women knew the Scriptures better than Italian bishops (Polišenský, 1991: 46). In the 19th century, Bohemia, together with areas such as Scotland or the Nordic countries, belonged to the most literate countries in Europe (Cipolla, 1969). This should not be taken to imply that the problem of literacy was solved. Before World War II, full literacy was restricted to the middle and upper classes. Even if in full command of the skill of reading, perfection in writing was difficult to achieve for those who had not completed secondary school education. One mistake in a letter (e.g. 'y' instead of 'i' or a hypercorrect lexical item) was sufficient to declass the writer. The fact that the morphology of Standard rather than of Common Czech was required exacerbated the problem.

Under the communist government, problems of literacy did not receive serious attention. The attitude of the Modern society, which assumed that the problem of literacy had been solved (Neustupný, 1984), was compounded by Communist Party ideology which claimed that the principle of free education for all was the universal answer to the problems of the past. This view was partly correct, because class distinctions were largely removed from the education system, and the system itself stopped reproducing inequality. However, in the second half of the 20th century the problem of literacy in advanced countries had already moved to functional literacy (cf. Verhoeven, 1994). Mere equalisation of educational opportunities can solve differentials with regard to the grammatical components of literacy but it does not automatically solve problems in the use of written language and in social needs for it. However, it must be admitted that the second half of the 20th century also brought changes in the teaching of the Czech language which, under the influence of B. Havránek, F. Daneš and other members of the former Prague School of Linguistics, was thoroughly modernised; there was also considerable expansion of publishing and development of public libraries. Books were cheap and the quality high, with many titles also being translated and marketed abroad. However, from the histories of countries of similar socioeconomic profile, it is clear that the rate of functional illiteracy often exceeds 10%. For example, research conducted in Holland demonstrated that 11 to 17% of Dutch adults experienced problems in writing within the range of their daily life and/or work situations (Doets, 1994). Similarly, the final report of IALS (Literacy, 2000: xiii) illustrates that even in countries with very high literacy profile, 8 to 15% of the adult population encountered severe literacy deficits in everyday life and in work situations. It would therefore be misleading to imagine that in the Czech Republic the literacy problem was solved.

Moreover, in the Czech situation the Communist Party's claim that all children had equal access to education was partly but not entirely true. Children from some 'bourgeois' families or from families of dissidents (including a large number of children of those who were expelled from the Communist Party after 1968) were refused higher education which resulted in limiting the range of functional literacy they could achieve. Problems in completing their education affected the children of the German ethnic group after 1945, when education in German suddenly became unavailable (see the section on German that follows). In view of the Czechoslovak government's attitude towards literacy prior to 1989 and its negative attitude to social surveys that would reveal deficiencies, and in view of the right-leaning policies of the first post-Communist governments, little statistical data on the Czech situation within the last 20 years exists. However, there are certain expectations based on participant observation within the communities involved.

Firstly, there is only one large group that is affected widely and seriously – the Roma community. Most of the Roma migrated from Slovakia after World War II, where they had not normally achieved literacy in Slovak or any other language. Still, there were no attempts to provide them with literacy in Czech. This observation is probably also true of some others who arrived in the Czech lands from Slovakia. The use of Romani in print has so far been restricted to the Roma intellectual elites, and as such it could not become a vehicle for building literacy. Of course, one should not presume that the whole Roma community is (functionally) illiterate. However, with the rate of unemployment close to 80%, the effects of (functional) illiteracy make themselves felt while, on the other hand, unemployment further reinforces (functional) illiteracy. The situation is serious. Illiteracy is not only affecting the old. Some Roma children placed in special schools never achieve a base on which their literacy could later develop. A similar situation has been noted in the case of some other foreign groups (e.g. the Vietnamese community), although there child illiteracy in Czech does not emerge as a serious menace. Obviously, functional literacy in Czech among most other recent immigrant communities must also be considerably low, but this situation remains covert. Secondly, there is the problem of mentally or aurally handicapped children. Their literacy needs have remained largely unmet. Thirdly, there is the problem of functional illiteracy among native speakers of Czech who are not handicapped but who, for social reasons, missed some stages of their schooling or lost literacy skills later. Evidence from other countries suggests that the number of such individuals can be surprisingly high. The Czech Army is one of the institutions that had first hand experience with such illiteracy. However, due to the reorganisation and reduction of the Army, this situation has now changed.

Although, by international comparison, literacy in the Czech Republic may be high, similarly to many other societies with the same degree of development, the need for full literacy is restricted. This restriction, together with the need to employ a Standard (i.e. Standard Czech) that is no one's native language, as well as the difficulty of Czech orthography, leads to a situation in which literacy appears to be a matter that should be closely monitored by language managers.

The IALS Project

The issue of functional literacy has been raised in the context of economic rationalism in the International Adult Literacy Survey, launched in 1994. The Czech Republic participated in its second phase (SIALS), conducted in 1998 (Human Resources, 2000; Literacy, 2000). Functional literacy was defined as 'the capacity to participate in the world of information' and was considered, in the tradition of 'economic rationalism', primarily a problem in the employment domain of communication. The problem was divided into five levels, from level 1, which was elementary, to levels 4 and 5 that required complex processing of incoming information. Level 3 was the first level considered to be a suitable minimum for coping with the demands of everyday life and work. Furthermore, three types of literacy were in focus:

(1) 'Prose literacy' was the competence needed to understand texts (e.g. newspaper texts, brochures, etc.).
(2) 'Document literacy' refers to the competence necessary to use information from formats (e.g. application forms, transportation schedules, tables, etc.).
(3) 'Quantitative literacy' designates so-called numeracy (i.e. the competence to deal with numbers and numerical functions).

Among 20 participating countries, two groups of countries performed, respectively, exceptionally well or exceptionally poorly. The former group included Sweden, Finland and Norway (and to a lesser extent Denmark and The Netherlands), while the latter group included Hungary, Slovenia, Poland, Portugal and Chile. The results for these two groups are not difficult to explain. The Czech Republic is in the same group with Belgium, The United Kingdom and Ireland (ranks 11–14) for prose literacy. In the case of document literacy it rises to the group that includes Germany, Canada and Belgium (ranks 6–9), and for quantitative literacy it appears close to the top of the scale – in the same group as Denmark and Norway (ranks 2–4), second only to Sweden.

One of the special features of literacy in the Czech Republic is its relatively equal distribution across groups with different educational levels (tertiary, completed upper secondary, less than that). These results seem to indicate that working environment, rather than education, plays a decisive role. However, since in the Czech sample young graduates showed exceptionally good results, there is hope for further improvement, given improved access to higher education.

Nevertheless, the Czech results are relatively weak in the case of prose literacy in general, as well as in its composition: the Czech ranking falls to rank 14 when compared with the number of respondents on level 3 or above. This again points to the need for improved access to higher education.

However, the difference in ranking between the three types of literacy has not yet been fully explained. Why are Czechs good on numeracy and looking at documents, but not equally good at reading newspapers? The answer probably cannot be given before the actual instruments used in the survey become readily available. The only example of the instrument given in the Report (Literacy, 2000: 108) is hopelessly North American in orientation; should it have remained in questionnaires in languages other than English without a profound rewriting, it could not have yielded valid results. (What does it mean 'to swim three laps around Manhattan' for someone who has never heard of long-distance swimming? What is Manhattan anyway?) We would be sympathetic to France, which withdrew from the project partly because 'test items were biased in favour of "Anglo-Saxon" cultures' (Report, p.123).

Further clarification of the issue can be provided by adding the rankings for four non-European, English speaking countries (US, Canada, Australia, NZ) on one hand and for four European countries of the 'middle zone' (Germany, Belgium, Switzerland, ČR) on the other (cf. Figure 2.3 of the Report). The results are in the following table.

	Prose literacy	*Document literacy*	*Quantitative literacy*
4 Overseas English speaking countries	34	48	49
4 Continental European countries	45	34	28

The figures are added ranks of the four countries. The lower the figure, the better relative competence.

These figures seem to show that the English speaking countries perform significantly better on Prose literacy. With decreasing importance of language expression in Document and Quantitative literacy tests, their performance deteriorates. On the other hand, the Continental countries of the middle zone lag behind on Prose literacy but when language expression becomes less important, they outperform the English speaking countries in a significant way. Should these considerations be correct, how can they be explained? One factor seems to be that language is not simply 'grammatical competence'. It does not suffice, when setting questions, to translate sentences, if the settings, topics and other components of non-grammatical ('sociolinguistic') competence are left unchanged. Should the questions have simply been translated from English into the other languages they still may have retained a sizable advantage for English speakers. The second reason may be in the language of testing/interviewing, i.e. the way questions are formulated and answers required. The only example in the Report reveals a typical English language testing pattern. We are not experts on this matter, but this pattern may certainly be unfamiliar at least to Czech respondents.

Simple management

Literacy is accessible to acquisition through simple management processes if:

- a sufficient base for further acquisition has already been built through learning the script and some basic strategies of orthography;
- settings for acquisition are available; and
- there are sufficient needs and rewards for becoming literate.

Under these circumstances, learners acquire not only grammatical, but also non-grammatical communicative and sociocultural competence necessary for literacy. There is no doubt that many of the IALS indicators are acquired in this way.

Czech parents, like parents in many other societies, are eager to support their children's acquisition of literacy by providing them with a selection of reading materials and with access to the internet. This practice is particularly true for middle-class parents, but in Czech society this support involves a much wider scope. The internet as a means of supporting literacy, among other skills, has also been highlighted in the decision of the Ministry of Education to provide internet facilities to each school. Schools guide parents in supporting their children's literacy acquisition by checking their reading. However, such guidance is normally unavailable in Roma households (Hübschmannová, personal communication).

Organised management

The school system is the main place where organised management leading to literacy takes place. However, there is also adult education. Although the OECD report for the Czech Republic (Literacy, 2000: 42) showed that the mean hours of participation in adult education were quite low (ranking 4th from the bottom of the list of 20 countries), in fact opportunities exist even in this area. There is also the possibility to participate in distance education. A number of courses aiming at requalification can include the Czech language as one of the subjects. However, all these courses presuppose completed compulsory education and are, therefore, not available to many Roma applicants. No tuition specifically dealing with the literacy problems of adults could be identified.

An important role has been played by the so called 'special schools' (*zvláštní školy*). Under this system, children who, for various reasons, do not perform well are transferred to 'special schools' where the teaching process is slowed down; as a consequence, lower levels of literacy are achieved. For many years this was the only procedure to deal with the needs of Roma children. Positive evaluation of this system lies in the assumption that children who underachieve should be given the opportunity to proceed at their own pace; conversely, children who show special talent should be enabled to develop their talent further. Negative evaluation of the 'special schools' is represented, for example, by the attitude of Roma activists, who have opposed placing their children in ghettos which only result in the reality that normal employment channels will be closed to them. These activists have, partly through judicial channels, achieved the decision that, from the 2000/2001 school year, the transfer of children to 'special schools' can be effectuated only on the basis of a special test independent of the child's competence in the Czech language (MFD, 16th June 2000). With regard to selective schools for especially talented children, the opposition argues that, through the transfer of talented children, the normal schools are impoverished and their levels are diminished.

Within the current ideological situation in the Czech Republic, equalisation of access to literacy is perceived as a 'return to communism'; any policy proposing such a practice is likely to face strong criticism from right wing and centrist politicians. No clear drive towards radical increases in functional literacy across the board can be identified. The interests of the middle classes are well served: the SIALS survey has surprisingly shown that in the Czech Republic higher levels of education are more open to children of educated parents than in the developed EU countries (Human Resources, 2000: 102). After decades of Communist Party rule, this phenomenon is seen by many as a way to raise the economic condition of the whole nation to a higher level.

The Slovak Language

Situation, problems

Language shift that characterises the communicative attitudes of the Slovak community in the Czech Republic should be seen in the light of the economic, social and political power relationships within Czechoslovakia, where the Czech element was definitely the stronger partner. However, it should also be related to the close relationship between the two languages. Slovak and Czech historically belong to the same group of western Slavic languages which, among living languages, also includes Polish and Sorbian (Upper and Lower). However, within this group, Slovak and Czech share a particularly close relationship. Degrees of agreement between the two languages exceed differences. Even though the phonological systems are not identical (Standard Slovak has an additional vowel *ä* and a range of *r/l*-like sounds, while Czech has the special consonant *ř*), most of the divergence falls within the range of differences usual between dialects of the same language. In the morphological system, nominal as well as verbal endings definitely differ, but these differences, although extensive, are systematic and easy to comprehend. Both languages possess basically the same lexicon. Zeman (1997a: 1653) notes that 'among the 500 most frequent words in both languages, 230 (46%) are the same and 154 (30.8%) are in partial coincidence.' A Slovak easily becomes a receptive bilingual in Czech and a Czech in Slovak (cf. Kořenský, 1998b). However, active use of the other language is not automatic and must be specifically acquired. Since there are 'false friends' in the lexicon, 100% competence is not guaranteed.

Of course, there was a question whether a 100% understanding was taking place when Czechs and Slovaks still lived in the same state. Lexical items that are completely different are rare but sometimes puzzling. Slovak [Sl.]*raňajky* against Czech [Cz.] *snídaně* 'breakfast' is difficult to interpret unless the speaker has acquired the item. Sl. *t'ava* corresponds to Cz. *velbloud* 'camel', Sl. *pivnica* means 'cellar' while Cz. *pivnice* designates a 'beer hall'. Words that sound the same and have a similar meaning can have very different stylistic values. The sociolinguistic profile of the two languages is also different. In Slovak, the Standard is directly opposed to the dialects (i.e. there is no Common Slovak), and the dialects are vigorous. There are differences in sociolinguistic rules of address and there are other rules that have not been sufficiently examined.

Prior to the division of Czechoslovakia, some authors had argued that assuming complete mutual understanding would be naive. In this sense, one can, with justification, use the term *semicommunication*, coined by Haugen (1966), who used the term to describe the uses of Danish, Norwegian and Swedish in situations in which each speaker continued speaking his/her own language. He described *semicommunication* as 'the trickle of messages through a rather high level of "code noise"' (Haugen, 1966). On the other hand, he also emphasised the idea that what was necessary was the goodwill to understand each other. Apart from the Nordic languages, Haugen referred to the case of Czech and Polish and, of course, Czech and Slovak. Budovičová (1987a, 1987b), who introduced Haugen's term to Czechoslovak linguistics, emphasised the existence of language problems. This orientation towards the negative aspects of Czech/ Slovak *semicommunication* was fresh and useful in the 1980s when the establishment, by definition, saw all social problems as having been solved. Now the phenomenon can be seen in a more positive way.

It is doubtful whether the Czech/Slovak *semicommunication* during the time of the Czechoslovak Republic was equally developed in both directions. Czech was the language with more prestige and more power. On the whole, the receptive competence of Slovaks in Czech was superior to that of Czechs in Slovak. Slovaks read in Czech, while Czechs rarely touched a Slovak book. Since in the 1960s, the publication policy of the Slovaks was more flexible than that of the Czechs, the translation of *One Day in the Life of Ivan Denisovich* by Solzhenitsin first appeared in Slovak, and Czechs who acquired it as their first-ever Slovak book were surprised that their competence was not adequate to understand more than the bare story. Incidentally, no Czech-Slovak or Slovak-Czech dictionary was on the market until 1967 when Gašparíková and A. Kamiš published their *Slovensko-český slovník*. One of the authors of this monograph used the combination of a Slovak-Hungarian and subsequently Hungarian-Czech dictionary (because he did not know Hungarian) when reading the Slovak translation of Solzhenitsin's novel.

The hierarchical relationship between Czech and Slovak has a long history. In Slovakia, Czech fulfilled the role of the written language as early as the 15th century, and continued its supremacy until Standard Slovak was established in the first half of 19th century. Czech remained the written language of Slovak Protestants (Nábělková, 2002a) longer than it did in the case of Catholics, who had switched to a variety of Slovak earlier. It was the Protestants who, in the 17th century, formulated the idea of Czechoslovak unity (Pauliny, 1983: 112). At that time, the linguistic relationship was not paralleled by differential power: if anything, it supported the case for the liberation of Slovaks from Hungarian rule. The relationship changed, however, when the Czechoslovak Republic was born and Slovakia assumed second position in the new State. Czech intellectuals and public servants held the power, and this was reflected in the power relationship between the languages. Even contemporarily, the presence of Czech in Slovakia is conspicuous. Bookshops keep Czech literature and even Czech translations from other languages. In 1999 the largest Slovak television channel, Markíza, broadcast more than one-sixth of its programmes in Czech. This programming comprised mainly television serials and films (Kompasová, 1999/2000). The privileged position of Czech seems to have been retained even among the youngest generation of Slovaks (Ivaňová, 2002).

Problems of communication are not exhausted by issues of grammatical competence. An important role is played by sociocultural competence. In this respect, Zeman (1997b) points to two circumstances: Firstly, prior to the division of Czechoslovakia, the federal media, accessible to the average listener/viewer emphasised the overall Czechoslovak context, rather than the specifically Slovak or Czech context. Secondly, after the division, the unfamiliarity of the specifically Slovak context may present a more serious hindrance to communication than do grammatical and lexical differences between Slovak and Czech. Needless to say, the lack of sociocultural knowledge of the other society negatively affects daily life communication as well.

The linguistic behaviour of the Slovak community in the Czech Republic is strongly influenced by the attitudes of the Czech community. Therefore, it will be necessary in the future to watch carefully the behaviour of both sides in actual discourse situations between Czechs and Slovaks. No management recommendations can be formulated without an understanding of simple management.

Simple management

Never in the history of the Czechoslovak Republic have the modes of actual communication between Czechs and Slovaks become an object of linguistic research. Any understanding of simple language management throughout this period must therefore derive from data other than discourse interaction. Informal evidence must be considered, and more recent studies must be used for extrapolation of results in the direction to the past.

Eva Vrbová, a Slovak researcher who is a member of the Slovak community in Prague, has pointed out that in discourse between Slovaks and Czechs receptive bilingualism was not expected to function equally for all speakers (Vrbová, 1993). In the case of small children and also of old people there was automatic switching to the code of these addressees or at least presumably difficult features were transposed to the other code. These discourse management strategies, which remind one of Ferguson's 'simplified registers' (Ferguson, 1981), were applied as pre-adjustment, before any communicative inadequacy occurred. Two conclusions can be derived from this fact:

(1)   Czech-Slovak receptive bilingualism was not a 'natural' phenomenon that developed out of the similarity of two systems of grammatical competence, but was rather a management strategy that was tailored to the needs of particular speech situations;
(2)   Such discourse management strategy was capable of growing into active bilingualism, particularly in the case of Slovaks.

Except for small children and old people, Czechs and Slovaks applied their own system of grammatical competence, especially if they did not know each other well. However, according to Vrbová's observations, adjustment to the language system of the addressee was not unusual even in other situations. It occurred in the language of those who knew each other and were assured that the addressee lived on the territory of the other language on a long-term basis (Vrbová, 1993).

In discourse, Czechs have certainly not remained unaffected by Slovak. For example, in the following conversation, which took place in Prague in the 1990s, a Slovak female speaker SF1 speaks with a Czech female speaker CF1. SF1 speaks Slovak and CF1 Czech. However, CF1 takes over the word *korčul'ovat'* from Slovak for Czech *bruslit* 'to skate', giving it a Czech pronunciation *korčulovat* and dropping the reflexive particle *se/sa*. She also uses the Czech past tense of the verb (*korčulovala*); in this case the ending happens to coincide with the Slovak one.

SF1: *My sme sa boli korčul'ova☐v ňeďeľu.* 'We went skating this Sunday.'
CF1:*Já neumím korčulovat, ja sem korčulovala naposledy, když mi bylo dvanáct. Pak sem jezdila na kolečkovejch teda.* 'I cannot skate, I skated for the last time when I was twelve. Then I used roller (skates), you know.' (from Ivaňová, 2002: 37).

In this example, CF1 probably uses the Slovak word for 'skating' for complex discourse reasons. However, in the past, many Czechs used Slovak expressions in their conversation, even in the absence of Slovak speakers, as word play. Nábělková (2002b) reports that Slovaks, in pub conversation, also use Czech as word play.

Within contemporary Czech-Slovak communication, there are a number of communication problems that originate in 'semicommunication'; i.e. noting of problems, evaluation and adjustments. One example occurs across the two following conversational turns:

CF2: *Sem dostala dneska takovej imejl, že se nemůžou dovolat a věčně se dovolaj k těm Moravákům.* 'I got today such an e-mail, that they cannot get us on the telephone, and all the time they can get the Moravians.'
SF2: *Pretože si im dala <u>zlou zlú</u> linku.* 'Because you gave them the wrong line.'

CF2 is a Czech woman who claims to always speak with Slovaks in Czech. SF2, a Slovak woman, answers in Slovak, originally mixing into her Slovak a Czech form *zlou* for Slovak *zlú* 'wrong'. She notes, evaluates her usage negatively and immediately implements an adjustment. This example shows that communication problems are not always the result of misunderstandings. In this case no misunderstanding occurs: there is only a negative evaluation of SF2's own grammatical choice in discourse.

Another discourse strategy is to pre-adjust individual items that might cause communication problems. This can be performed in three ways:

(1)   As noted already by Budovičová (1986) for the situation of former Czechoslovakia, speakers avoided differing elements and selected elements that were shared by both languages. For example, a Slovak speaker may use the Slovak word *tužka* for Czech *tužka* 'pencil' rather than the synonym *ceruzka* which may be incomprehensible to his Czech interlocutor.
(2)   Slovak speakers employ basically Slovak, but when a Slovak expression differs from its Czech counterpart, they use the Czech word (Ivaňová, 2002). The reverse is also true. As documented by Zeman (1988), Czech speakers who speak to Slovaks in Czech select Slovak alternatives for differing lexical items, e.g. Slovak *pečeň* for Czech *játra* 'liver'.
(3)   Speakers may pronounce endings indistinctly in order to cover the difference between Slovak and Czech; for example *počk*[]*j* to minimise the difference between Czech *počkej* and Slovak *počkaj* 'wait' (Hoffmannová & Müllerová, 1993: 316).

The most recent research is that by Ivaňová (2002), who studied the interaction patterns of Czech and Slovak university students in Prague and formulated the following conclusions.

(1)   Czech speakers are not bilingual; their competence in Slovak remains at the level of receptive bilingualism. However, on the basis of the knowledge of a few structural differences between the two languages, they modify their Czech structures in discourse and present them as Slovak. As they use, or attempt to use, Slovak, they try to oblige, convey their liking of the other side, to use humour and language play. They do not expect the use of Czech from their partners; on the contrary, they encourage them to use Slovak. In the opinion of the present authors, one can observe a friendly attitude on the Czech side, but it might be a patronising attitude.

(2) Slovak speakers, on the other hand, are not merely receptively, but also actively, bilingual, and they use their active competence in communicating with some Czech interlocutors. There is shifting depending on their relationship to their partners and on the domain of communication (public or private). The closer the partner, the more Slovak will be used by the Slovak interlocutor.

Large-scale sociological investigations in the *Slezský ústav* (Silesian Institute) in Opava have been mainly directed towards the ethnic situation in northern Moravia and partly also towards that in northeastern Bohemia in the 1980s. These investigations demonstrated that the shift of the Slovak community toward Czech is intensive in a number of situations and that it is continuing to intensify. There was a lack of agreement between declared ethnic membership (which remained Slovak) and declared language use (that was biased towards Czech). The last extensive research, conducted in 1994, showed that, according to their parents, only 5% of ethnically Slovak children spoke predominantly Slovak while 68.5% of children spoke predominantly Czech (Sokolová *et al.*, 1997: 84). The number of mixed marriages is increasing: according to marriage statistics, Slovaks in 1994 reported only 16.2% of ethnically homogeneous marriages. Nevertheless, Sokolová *et al.* (1997) claimed that their Slovak respondents were not as much oriented to the use of Czech as respondents were in previous decades; it is possible to identify a more bilingual and bicultural orientation – as opposed to the Czech monolingual and Czech monocultural orientation of past decades. For language management, this means that, since all cases of shift start in discourse, it will be important to understand its mechanism if there is an intent to arrest this shift. Moreover, if some Slovaks assume more positive attitudes to the maintenance of Slovak, are such attitudes reflected in discourse, or are they rather a part of the ideological structure of the communities? If the latter, how can they be transferred to discourse, the only location in which maintenance can take place?

There are definitely changes in the behaviour of Czechs and Slovaks in contact situations. A Slovak woman (T), who is a student and simultaneously works in an office in Prague (Ivaňová, 2002), can serve as an example. In communication with her company's clients, who are mostly Czech, Czech is spoken and written. In communicating with her Czech colleagues of the same age she uses Slovak. However in discourse with a female colleague, who is her senior by age, she uses Czech in order 'to be polite'. This happens notwithstanding the fact that the older woman possesses considerable experience of being exposed to Slovak during the period of the Czechoslovak Republic. In this case, the atmosphere of the former Czechoslovak Republic, which would lead one to expect a 100% Slovak from T, is gone. T's usage resembles that of Czechs in the office. They would speak Standard Czech to their clients and to an older woman, and Common Czech to their peers. This new pattern does not place Czech and Slovak into a hierarchical relationship. The ideal relationship between Czech and Slovak probably lies in the retention of the Czech-Slovak 'semicommunication' devoid of any emotive management and accompanied by switching to the other language as the domain of communication and the situation require.

This attitude can be seen in the following testimony, where it seems to be conscious. For X, an author, the Czech Republic is just another foreign country.

Why should one declare one's ethnic specificity and symbolise, through the use of Slovak, a non-existent past? In an internet magazine X formulated this view in the following way:

> ... *ked som predtym par rokov hovoril v anglosaskom prostredi po anglicky, v cesku teraz hovorim cesky. ked na to pride, som slovak, ale nepotrebujem to neustale demonstrovat a riesit narodnostne vztahy* ... (Slovak, the writer does not use diacritics)
>
> ... since I spoke in an Anglo-Saxon environment over a few years English, in Czechia now I speak Czech, when it matters I am Slovak, but there is no need to constantly reassert that and try to solve ethnic relations ...

Nevertheless, the inequality problem persists. From the internet magazine *Inzine*, Ivaňová (2002) selected a number of strategies which Slovak contributors employ to legitimise the reason they select Czech in discourse in Czech environments. Several of these legitimisations claim that Czech is richer in expressive power than Slovak. Czech is presented as a language in which all problems have been solved. Slovak intellectuals, rather than creating their own expressive means, just employ Czech. This practice provides a prerequisite for a massive influx of Czech elements into Slovak and creates problems for Slovak organised management.

Organised management

In the first constitution of Czechoslovakia (1920), the national language, called the 'Czechoslovak' language, had two forms: Czech and Slovak. This was a legal construct. In fact it was assumed that the 'forms' were two national languages which were equal in law. However, Slovak occupied the position of the weaker partner. Since it had fewer speakers and was considered less developed than Czech, it could not in fact assume a position equal to Czech (Marti, 1998). The inequality of Slovak surfaced in the fact that Czech started being widely used in Slovakia, serving partly, for example, as the language of instruction at the university in Bratislava. As late as the 1930, discussions were held as to whether it was feasible to develop Slovak as a language of science and technology, or whether it would not be more rational to use Czech in such contexts. In view of this situation, it is not surprising that Czech influence on Slovak was massive. While the existence of Czech elements in Slovak has persisted as a problem in organised language management in Slovakia up to the present, the influence of Slovak on Czech has been minimal, and when it occurred, it was not considered a threat but rather an enrichment. This situation is typical for partnerships of unequal power. Towards the end of the second decade of the existence of Czechoslovakia, Slovak intellectuals, who were leaders in introducing Slovak to all registers of social life, were already emancipated and linguistically mature leaders in language management. However, there was no organised management with regard to Slovaks who resided in the Czech lands during the time of the inter-war Czechoslovak Republic.

Following the end of WWII, the situation changed. The concept of a 'Czechoslovak language' was abandoned, and Slovak intellectuals began to mount resistance to all forms of Czech domination. As massive emigration to the Czech lands proceeded, some weak attempts at organised language management also appeared. Šrajerová (1999: 144) mentions a Cabinet decision according to which, in the 1952/1953 school year, 'Slovak language circles' were to be established. The decision required that 279 such circles were to be established in the Karlovy Vary region and 38 in the Plzeň region. A provision for the training of 160 teachers was approved. There are no reports to assess to what extent these circles were successful, but it is evident that in the course of time they met the same fate as the local branches of *Matice slovenská*, mentioned in the earlier section on the Slovak Community; that is, they ceased to exist.

The equal rights of the Czech and Slovak languages were explicitly formulated in the 1968 Constitution that established the Czech-Slovak federal system. Both languages were supposed to be different from minority languages. These were the only languages in which laws were published and which were the official languages of the national administration. The state administration (within the Czech and the Slovak part of the Federation) could be addressed in either language, but the administration was not obliged to respond in other than the local language. The conviction that receptive bilingualism should be promoted was thus actively supported by organised language management. The idea of full bilingualism was still missing.

Budovičová (1987a, 1987b) noted that the negative aspects of semi-communication were strongest in the language of literature (where understanding was most difficult), less pronounced in the language of the media and daily life, and least serious in specialised forms of language. This hierarchy can, in fact, be observed in acts of organised language management. Even prior to the division of Czechoslovakia, it was common for poetry and prose to be translated from one language to the other. In order to coordinate terminological work, joint terminological committees for individual disciplines worked to achieve parallel development of special terminologies. School curricula included teaching about the other language and specified that examples of texts had to be studied. The alternation of Czech and Slovak announcers on television and radio news and sports and in other programs was very effective.

After the division of Czechoslovakia in 1993, Slovak disappeared from school curricula. The situation at the universities was chaotic. Some institutions in the Czech lands continued teaching Slovak within the framework of Slavic or Czech studies; others discontinued it. However, towards the end of the 1990s, it was felt that systematic attention to Slovak was necessary. This impetus appeared in a most vocal way at a National Seminar on Teaching Slovak and Slovak Literature at Czech Universities, organised in 2000 by the University of Hradec Králové (Zeman, 1999/2000). Among the conclusions and recommendations of the Seminar the following should be mentioned:

(1) The Ministry of Education lacks a comprehensive policy concerning the teaching of Slovak.
(2) In view of the current estrangement of Czech and Slovak and the two nations, it is essential that at least some universities establish a Czech-Slovak major.
(3) It will be necessary to posit at least three aims for the teaching of Slovak:
  (a) the education of Bohemists with a wide background of the knowledge of Slavic languages;

(b)   the education of teachers of Slovak to Czechs;
(c)   the education of Bohemists with a very high command of Slovak who could teach Slovak children in the Czech Republic;
(4)   It is desirable to incorporate the teaching of Slovak and Slovak literature in primary and secondary schools within the fund allocation for multicultural education. This process has already begun.

The interest in reintroducing Slovak into Czech schools has also been confirmed in public opinion surveys. In an extensive survey carried out by Musilová and her colleagues in 1998, 53% of Czech respondents agreed with the suggestion to reintroduce Slovak. Among those who disagreed, one fourth claimed that this was unnecessary because 'everyone understands Slovak' (Musilová, 2000). Hence, even after the division of Czechoslovakia, the perception of receptive bilingualism appears to have been widespread.

A similar attitude exists at the highest level of the government. In a meeting held in 2002 between Czech Prime Minister Zeman and Slovak Prime Minister Dzurinda, the incorporation of Czech texts in textbooks of the national language and the showing of Slovak programmes on the Czech TV were emphasised (Mlčoch, 2002). A significant language management act at the level of publishing is demonstrated in the publication of a new textbook authored by M. Sokolová, K. Musilová, D. Slančová and J. Dršatová (forthcoming): *Renovovaný kurz jazyka slovenského pro Čechy – Renovovaný kurz českého jazyka pre Slovákov* (A Revised Course of Slovak for Czechs – A Revised Course of Czech for Slovaks).

What is the situation in Czech television? It has frequently been suggested that TV played a decisive role in the development of receptive bilingualism in the past. The media claim, with obvious partiality, that young Czechs no longer understand Slovak because of its disappearance from TV. This view can be only partly supported. While the Slovak cultural programme that used to be scheduled every Monday on Czech television disappeared, it would be an exaggeration to claim that most viewers were waiting for it with bated breath. It is certainly more significant that the alternation of announcers in news and sports programmes disappeared. However, it is important to realise that, in socialist Czechoslovakia, there was in principle only one TV programme, and the share of it that Slovak got was overall limited. At present there are four channels and, although the occurrence of Slovak is not 'planned', much Slovak can be heard in the speech of Slovak artists and other personalities who live in the Czech Republic and who are interviewed on Czech TV. Slovak sports personalities often speak, and they are the ones who are noticed by young people. Until empirical surveys become available, it will be necessary to listen with a grain of salt to arguments about the disappearance of Slovak from Czech TV. Such arguments may constitute one of the components of an overall myth about Czech and Slovak growing further and further apart. (Concerning the deconstruction of the myth see Nábělková, 2000, 2002b.)

On a number of occasions, it has been noted that organised management grows from the platform of simpler forms of management; e.g. management within families. This point can also be claimed in the case of Slovak in the Czech Republic. Maintenance within families has been minimal, and little interest has been shown in Slovak schools. The lack of interest in simple management has contributed to the scarcity of organised management. In Prague, where about 20,000 Slovaks live, there has never been a single Slovak school. In the mid-1990s, the association *Obec Slovákov v Českej republike*, organised a project, approved by the Education Ministry, to establish a Slovak High School (gymnázium) in Prague; however, that experiment failed because only eight applicants turned up, while the minimum target was 20 (Praha a národnosti, 1998: 96). The only primary Slovak school in the territory of the Czech Republic, in Karviná, ceased to exist at the end of the millennium.

It has been argued that the old conception of the linguistic life of the Slovak community within the Czech Republic, based on the model of post-war Czechoslovakia, has been overtaken by time. Although a power relationship between the two societies and the two languages still partly exists, it is giving way to arrangements common in international society. There may be inequality, but it is covered under the ideology claiming that all states are equal. It is natural that more and more Slovaks in the Czech Republic speak Czech at work, in education, or in the public domain. However, there is no reason to use Czech in the family or in the friendship domain. Using Slovak in these latter domains will occur more and more frequently. On the other hand, there will be Slovaks who want to assimilate, and language managers have no right to prevent this.

Semicommunication is not a vice. It will be used more and more within international society, and it would be absurd to claim otherwise. One can assume that, in view of the linguistic closeness of Czech and Slovak, semicommunication will flourish. Perhaps a different name for the phenomenon should be created; one that would not suggest that something has gone wrong.

The Romani Language

Situation, problems

Romani is structurally and lexically an Indian language, closely related to the languages of present-day northwestern India. A large number of grammatical features and common lexical items can easily be identified. On the other hand, Romani dialects also contain a number of lexical features borrowed from the languages with which its speakers have historically come in contact and, primarily, from the languages of the matrix societies in which the Roma have lived. These borrowings also include some grammatical words (e.g. in the Czech-Slovak dialect *al'e* 'but'). Romani is divided into a number of dialects. The original Czech dialect and the Sinti (German) dialects spoken in pre-war Bohemia and Moravia have become virtually extinct since the holocaust (Elšík, 2000/2001), and continue to be used only in individual families (M. Hübschmannová, personal communication). Present-day Romani as spoken in the Czech Republic derives mostly from Slovakia. The dialects are:

(1) Slovak-and-Czech Romani (Elšík, 2003, aptly calls it the 'Central' group) is the majority dialect, which further splits into an Eastern and a Western variety.

(2) Hungarian Romani is a grammatically conservative dialect, mostly spoken in Hungary and adjoining countries. It came to the Czech Republic from Slovakia.

(3)   Vlach (Wallach) group. The particular dialect which is present in the Czech Republic is Lovari. Members of the Vlach group were itinerant until a strict law was adopted and enforced in 1958.

The dialects are distinct but there is at least basic inter-intelligibility among them (Hübschmannová & Neustupný, 1996: 104).

Multilingualism of the Roma

While speaking about language management of the Roma, it is necessary to realise that many of the middle and older generation are bilingual or multilingual. Apart from their dialect of Romani, they also use Czech, often Slovak, and sometimes Hungarian. The knowledge of Slovak and Hungarian is required to maintain personal networks abroad. The Czech they speak may be pidginised in the case of communication with other Roma, and it will be necessary to determine whether they distinguish between a variety of Czech spoken among themselves and another variety spoken to the *gajo* (non-Roma people). Similarly, their Romani may be characterised by a smaller or larger admixture of the matrix language, and their Czech and Slovak may combine into a single variety. This situation resembles the relaxed strategies of language use described by Khubchandani (1981) for India, with the proviso that one cannot assume that the pattern is in any way necessarily connected to the Indian origin of the language. For many of the younger generation, a variety, or varieties, of Czech become the only language available for active use. The government's Council for Ethnic Minorities estimates that approximately one half of the Czech Roma uses Romani (Zpráva, 2002: 4), but the use of a language is a complicated phenomenon, and experts assume that, even in the case of those who do not actually conduct daily conversation in the language, sometimes amazing degrees of competence still remain.

Simple management

There is evidence that native speakers of Romani note and evaluate dialectal difference in discourse. In Hübschmannová and Neustupný (1996), apart from individual examples (p. 97), three speakers of the eastern dialect of Romani were asked to comment on a text written in the western dialect of Slovak-and-Czech Romani. Certain, though not all, differing features were noted and some were evaluated by the judges. It was interesting that the word *mamuj* 'against' (*prociv* in the eastern dialect) was evaluated once negatively and once positively. On the whole, the management was not strong, with one of the three speakers, in particular, noting differences but refusing to evaluate. A stereotypic evaluation appeared in one case when the word *čulo* 'a little' was marked as belonging to a *degeša* (unclean, language of dog and horse flesh eaters) dialect despised by the *žuže* (clean) Roma. There is, in fact, no linguistic difference between the *degeša* and *žuže* communities, and the word *čulo* is simply a regional variant.

While Romani shows a relatively high degree of maintenance in the settlements of the Slovak type, within the Czech urban setting, shift is rapid and, unless the trend can be reversed, there may be nothing to maintain within 10 or 20 years. One should realise that, not unlike many other communities, a number of Romani intellectuals do not support the maintenance of the language, rather claiming that their *romipen* 'Roma-ness' does not depend on the language. Ironically, the writer Dezider Banga (Hübschmannová, personal communication), who himself also publishes in Romani, is among such individuals.

There does not appear to be any study of Romani discourse that demonstrates how management takes place when the spoken language is used. Informal observations confirm that there is much switching at lexical level between Romani and Czech, and such switching testifies to problems in communication that are solved through switching. Of course, this is not the case when a Czech word is already a component of the Romani lexicon. When it is not, there is a possibility that switching will become automatised at the level of the speaker in question. This illustrates how language loss proceeds: from individual utterance, to the language of an individual, and then to the language of the whole community. In formal contexts, for example, when a Roma speaks at a conference, his/her Romani can be completely free of switching, but the language expression, in this case, is of course managed: within a very formal context such as this, problems are noted, and adjustment is implemented so that no switching takes place.

Hübschmannová (1979) showed another important phenomenon connected with management of language by the Roma in discourse. The Czech of Romani children at Rokycany (western Bohemia), where 82% of the children included in her study reported using Romani at home, was ungrammatical. However, the Czech of Romani children in a Prague sample, where only 6% of children used Romani at home, was equally ungrammatical. This example shows the lack of management of the children's Czech. A pidgin or a creole was being born. This process, typical for a situation of limited networks between native and non-native speakers (Hymes, 1971), still continues at the present time.

On the other hand, as the formation of ethnic awareness proceeds, more and more individuals try to speak and learn Romani. In some families, children are systematically addressed in the language. However, there is little opportunity to develop and reinforce this knowledge further in classroom situations.

Organised management

While the Romani language is still in use, attempts at its management appear at higher levels of organisation as well. Although practically all political programmes produced by Romani groups, and recently also by governmental organisations, praise the language as a symbol of the existence of the Roma, little management is conducted. Most of the following management acts have been pursued with the strong assistance of agents who are not themselves Roma.

Romani at primary level

There is no primary, or other, education that uses Romani as the vehicle of instruction, although there are Romani children who arrive at school with a mixture of Romani and Czech, or with Czech that is lexically (and grammatically) pidginised. Nevertheless, the question of Roma education has been discussed intensively, and certain steps have been taken towards improving its level. For example, the establishment of preparatory classes has contributed to the improvement of the education of Roma children. Such classes were originally designed for Roma children, but they are now open to all 'socio-culturally disadvantaged children' (Praha a národnosti, 1998: 25). In 1998, the Ministry of Education approved the employment of Roma assistants whose task is to make it easier for Roma children, using their own language, to start school attendance at Czech primary schools. In the school year 1999/2000, there were 114 preparatory classes operating at kindergartens (11), primary schools (62) and special schools (41) (Statistická ročenka školství, 2000). Towards the end of 2001, the Ministry employed 264 Roma assistants; however, there were large districts with dense Roma populations that had no assistants (Zpráva, 2002: 33).

Because of different linguistic and social background, Roma children experience considerable communication difficulty, even if, on the surface, their Czech reveals no major problems. A standard adjustment measure has consisted of transfer to 'special schools' which were basically designed for mentally retarded children. Formally, a psychological test for retardation must be conducted, but cases have been recorded in which children were moved solely on the basis of an interview with their parents. Teachers schedule appointments for the tests, but parents do not take their children to be tested, and the special school does not refuse the children. Parents endorse, or even initiate, the transfer if they know that the child is unhappy at the normal school. Roma children themselves mostly enjoy the special school where requirements are grossly reduced and where most children come from Roma families. Teachers in normal classes are glad to get rid of underachievers. None of the participants in this adjustment process worry about the fact that the children will be unable to proceed to higher education (graduates of the special schools cannot enter secondary education) and that they are for life excluded from jobs that require anything more than the very elementary education level. A new generation of the unemployed is in the making (Wilková, 1999). Czech authorities and teachers take the special schools and the treatment of the Roma children to be natural and unavoidable. The self-assured tone of their statements is frightening (cf. the daily MF Dnes, 16 June 1999).

Roma activists and foreign experts have pointed to the fact that the psychological tests are culturally biased. For example, Roma children arrive at school without control of such concepts as 'first name' or 'surname'. At home they are called by nick-names. Many other speech patterns are different. The children lack the support of tutoring by parents, because in families of unemployed manual workers such a pattern does not usually occur. Regular attendance at school is not enforced by parents, especially if they find that the children are unhappy about their classes. The negative attitude of many parents to schooling is soon transmitted to the children. Under these circumstances it is difficult to speak of objective psychological testing.

Secondary and adult education

The Roma Social Secondary School (*Romská střední škola sociální*) at Kolín, approximately 50 km east of Prague, was founded in 1998. This school provides full secondary level training in the area of social care for Roma ethnic communities. Graduates are expected to find employment in national or local government or in other social work institutions. The curricula include classes in Romani, a survey of the history and culture of the Roma and Roma literature (Praha a národnosti, 1998: 75). There is also a Protestant Academy (*Evangelická akademie*) in Prague which, since 1997, also includes a *Roma Academy*. This institution trains adult students of Roma extraction for social work as advisers in Roma problems in local government. The curricula also include Romani (Praha a národnosti, 1998: 73). Both schools receive financial support from the government. In Brno, classes of Romani are available at the Cultural and Educational Centre for Roma Children and the Young (*Kulturní a vzdělávací centrum pro romské děti a mládež*). These courses also accommodate teachers, public servants and police officers (Lidové noviny, 27 January 1999). A television course of Romani entitled *Amare Roma* was broadcast, by Czech TV, from 2000 to 2001 (Elšík, 2000/2001).

University courses

The fullest and most rigorous tertiary programme is available in the Faculty of Arts at Charles University in Prague – a five-year course, developed in 1991 by the specialist in Romani language and culture, Professor Milena Hübschmannová, in which 20 students devote themselves fully to the study of the Romani language and culture or the study of Romani together with another discipline. The students are partly of Czech, partly of Romani origin. Graduates of the programme normally become teachers, public servants or work in other positions connected with the Roma issue.

The Romani language is also available in the Education Faculty of Charles University, where teachers are trained, and in the Education Faculty of the J.E. Purkyně University at Ústí nad Labem, in an area characterised by a high density of Roma population. Many students are connected with the Special Schools where Roma children form a majority. Teachers are non-native graduates of the Charles University programme (Elšík, 2000/2001).

Overall, the programmes described constitute a very limited range for a country in which the Roma community is the second or third largest community.

Textbooks

The compilation of textbooks is an important act of language management. Antonín Puchmajer's *Románi Čib*, published posthumously in 1821, was the first textbook of the language ever written. There were no other textbooks until *Cikánsky snadno a rychle* was launched in a popular series of textbooks in 1900. These books were based on the Czech variety of Romani, which has since become extinct. The first modern textbook was Jiří Lípa's *Příručka cikánštiny* (Prague: Státní pedagogické nakladatelství, 1963); this was followed by two short books authored by Milena Hübschmannová: *Základy romštiny* (Prague: Academia, 1973) and *Cikánština* (Ústí nad Labem: Krajský pedagogický ústav, 1976). The most recent textbook is *Romaňi čhib*, published in 1999 by Hana Šebková and Edita Žlnayová by the Fortuna publishing house. This was the first 'full' textbook of the language. All texts published after Lípa's present the Slovak-and-Czech variety of the language (Elšík, 2000/2001).

Of great importance is the *Romsko-český a česko-romský kapesní slovník* by Hübschmannová, Šebková and Žigová, published in 1991 (Prague: Státní pedagogické nakladatelství), one of the most rigorous dictionaries of Romani that has ever been published.

Standardisation and elaboration

No attempts at standardisation have been made, except for the standardisation of spelling. The spelling rules were developed at the end of the 1960s by the

Linguistic Commission of the Union of Gypsies-Roma, and they have been adhered to with relative consistency (cf. Hübschmannová & Neustupný, 1996).

Elaboration of Romani takes place in individuals´ efforts on the pages of Romani journals such as *Romano džaniben* (published in Prague, 1994 to date). No systematic attempts at elaboration of the lexicon or the grammar are known, although Hübschmannová *et al.* (1991) in fact has developed the language in many respects.

Governmental level management

The Czech government has always featured Romani on its list for potential language management action. One reason for this was the pressure from the USA to keep the Roma problem under control. However, under the new-liberalism philosophy of the Klaus government, the *status quo* was to be preserved. In the eyes of the government, ethnic issues were sufficiently attended to, and positive discrimination with regard to any group was out of the question. The following Social Democratic government of Miloš Zeman appointed Petr Uhl as a Cabinet Commissioner for Human Rights. Uhl submitted a number of proposals to solve the Roma question, including special provisions within the proposed Ethnic Minorities Act.

It was only in the late 1990s that the attitude of Czech politicians changed. The Czech Republic ratified the Framework Convention for the Protection of National Minorities and signed the Charter of European Regional or Minority Languages; the Ethnic Minorities Law was accepted in 2001. A number of special measures which also affect the Roma have been adopted (see previous sections on the Roma). Of basic importance for future language policy is the establishment of the government's Council for Matters of the Roma Community.

Further management?

One of the basic problems unlikely to be attended to at the educational or governmental level is the issue of networks. One branch of this problem consists of networks between the Roma and the matrix population. Only such networks can contribute to arresting the pidginisation of Czech spoken by the Roma and open the way to wide-ranged acquisition of the matrix system of communication. At the same time, such networks will, without necessarily wiping out their specificity, help to integrate the Roma into the matrix community from the point of view of their sociocultural behaviour. The second branch of the issue consists of networks within the Roma community – networks that will reinforce the process of formation of Roma ethnicity and that will make it possible for the Roma to join forces in order to maintain their language – should this be their wish.

Another issue that may appear on the program of the day is standardisation. In Hübschmannová and Neustupný (1996), the authors argued that old (modern) models of standardisation should not be used for Romani. Whether or not to standardise, and in what way, should be a choice for the community as it achieves maturity and as it faces the issue.

Whatever language management at whatever level may take place, one thing is certain: language management will not succeed unless it is preceded by empowering the Roma through socioeconomic and communicative management (Neustupný, 1993a). Perhaps it is possible to exterminate the language without socioeconomic planning, because maintaining the current socioeconomic regime is in fact a policy. However, to solve existing problems, to maintain the language and to develop it requires the strengthening of the socioeconomic position of the Roma.

The Polish Language

Situation, problems

Polish shares with Czech, Slovak and Sorbian membership in the group of Western Slavic languages. This fact alone indicates the closeness of the two languages. Though at present Czech and Polish show a number of structural differences (see Lotko, 1998), the comprehensibility of speech in the other language is relatively high. Haugen (1966) correctly included Czech and Polish among his examples of the phenomenon he called *semicommunication* (see section on Slovak language). The best conditions for receptive Czech–Polish bilingualism no doubt exist in the Těšín region, but it could become a wider phenomenon in other Czech territories as well. For example, when, in the 1970s and 1980s, Polish TV was more attractive than Czech TV, many television antennas in Czechoslovakia were set to receive Polish signals. This was true not only of the Czech-Polish border areas but also of some large east Bohemian towns such as Hradec Králové, and the occurrence was not limited to intellectuals. It seems that between Poles, Czechs and Slovaks potentially a similar communicative relationship can obtain as between Danes, Norwegians and Swedes. This fact awaits the attention of language managers, especially in view of the expected entry of the three central European nations into the European Union.

In the Těšín region, the Polish community, in daily communication, employs three different varieties of language: their Těšín region mother dialect, a locally influenced variety of Standard Czech and an equally locally affected variety of Standard Polish (cf. Bogoczová, 1994). More than half of the Poles have been reported to use these three varieties in the family domain as well (Bogoczová, 1994: 24). The most extensive use is made of the Těšín dialect. This phenomenon is connected with the fact that Standard Polish is seen as a hard variety, used principally in official Polish schools. A sophisticated form of conversational Standard Polish could not develop in the region, due to politically induced isolation from the Polish spoken in Poland, since contacts were limited. In view of this, Poles from the Těšín region experience difficulty in everyday conversation with Poles from Poland: the amount of discourse management in which they must engage is excessive. The prestige of the Těšín dialect is increased by the fact that it is also used by a population that reports Czech ethnicity. For such speakers, it may be either the native dialect or a form of speech they acquired through long residence in the region. The dialect stands linguistically half way between Polish and Czech. Ironically, the variety which enjoys the highest prestige in the Polish community is Standard Czech which connects with the power of the state and of the Czech matrix community in general. Czech is also the language offered by Poles in communication in first encounters with strangers. The degree of Standardness of the Czech used by members of the Polish community is often higher than in the case of Czech speakers of the same region. (An illustrative example is provided below.) Hence, one cannot easily derive conclusions about ethnicity on the basis of speech behaviour alone. Bogoczová (1997) showed that, in the language of the youngest generation of Poles, it is the influence of Czech, not of Polish, which asserts itself strongly in the lexicon and with regard to prepositions, conjunctions and particles. Less influence of Czech is noticeable in pronunciation, and still less in inflection.

A note on the attitudes of the Czech population to Polish seems useful. This attitude largely reflects their relationship with the Poles and with Poland. Bogoczová (2002) claims that when the Polish economy began to prosper during 1990s, Czech attitudes to Poles and Polish improved. The current interest in Polish has partly been invoked by the demise of the linguistic monopoly formerly held by Russian. Polish is becoming the leading Slavic language studied by Czechs studying in departments of Slavic Studies at Czech universities.

Investigations by the *Slezský ústav* confirm that the language shift of Poles towards Czech is not as extensive as it is in the case of Slovaks, but it does reach high levels. The most recent extensive research conducted in 1994 revealed that, according to the opinions of parents, only 24.1% of children spoke (given no specification of a domain) predominantly Polish, 40% spoke Polish and Czech, and 31.9% predominantly used Czech (Sokolová *et al.*, 1997: 84). However, considering long-term trends, it seems that there is an accompanying increase in the orientation of the Polish community towards bilingualism and biculturalism (Sokolová *et al.*, 1997: 88). This trend is less evident among Slovaks in the Těšín region, and the bilingualism of the Czechs clearly lags behind both groups. Two languages are spoken by only 16% of Těšín Czechs, and those languages are Czech and Polish (Sokolová, 1999b: 130). Incidentally, it is necessary to add that figures from the investigations just quoted, as well as from the 1991 and 2001 censuses, must be interpreted with care, because the Těšín dialect used by both Poles and Czechs is often taken for Polish by Poles and for Czech by Czechs (Bogoczová, 2000: 28; Sokolová, 1999a; cf. also Lotko, 1994: 15).

Simple management

In the work domain, the selection of varieties is normally determined by the variety preferred by the superior. Bogoczová (2000: 21) notes that, when the superior is oriented towards the use of Czech, Czech is used. On the other hand, if the code preferred by the superior is the Těšín dialect, subordinate employees use the dialect or Czech. It is not unusual that subordinates have a better command of the variety than their superior. In the following conversation, which is a fragment of a meeting in the Třinec Iron Works, A is the superior (over 50, local origin, Czech), while B is a female employee within his section (37, local origin, ethnically Polish, graduate of a Polish primary and high school).

A: *É tady mi řikate konkretňi vjeci, ale vysledeg je takovy, že komunykace vazne . . .* 'Well, here you tell me concrete results, but the result is that communication comes to a deadlock . . . '

B: *Já jesli dovolíte, doplňím, doplňím trošku šéfa . . .* 'If you allow me, I'll supplement, supplement the chief's . . . '

It seems clear that A is oriented towards the use of Czech, but his management of Standard Czech is limited. B, who uses the Těšín dialect in her daily life, adjusts her language to the choice of her superior. Her Czech, unlike the Czech of her superior, is managed and void of the influence of the dialect. In the language of A, there is a shortening of long vowels (*řikate* instead of *říkáte* 'you say', *takovy* instead of *takový* 'such') and an assimilation of voiceless consonants before voiced ones (*vysledeg je* instead of *výsledek je* 'the result is') (from Bogoczová, 2000, abbreviated).

Organised management

Reference to organised language management has been made throughout this section; at this point, a more detailed note on Polish schools should suffice to complete the review. The Polish community has at its disposal a relatively extensive network of kindergartens and primary schools, a high school (gymnázium) and Polish classes at a number of other secondary schools. In the Polish primary schools, the language of instruction is Polish but, starting from Year 2, pupils must attend the subject 'Czech language' which has been allocated the same number of hours as Polish. There has been a decrease in the number of students (in 1950: 81 Polish primary schools with 8176 pupils; in 1995: 29 schools with 2617 pupils), but this decrease is not only caused by the decrease in the number of Poles but also by smaller families. In families of those who reported as Poles in 1991 only 142 children (out of the total number of 3279) in the Těšín region attended Czech primary schools. More recent data show that interest in Polish schools is increasing (Sokolová *et al.*, 1997: 110). It appears that problems are caused not so much by a lower number of schools as by their location (Sokolová, 1999b). A matter that is being discussed is the minimum number of children per class.

Language management for Polish has as its target the language of the only historically established and geographically specific minority in the Czech Republic. Historically, there has been a power element, accompanied throughout the Soviet period by the 'friendly' relations between Poland and Czechoslovakia. Unlike the case of German, management has not been affected by memories of WWII. However, there are few indications so far that the management would be moving over into a 'postmodern' system. If this trend actually exists (see, e.g. remarks on mutual receptive bilingualism between Czech, Polish and Slovak in previous sections), it may be more characteristic for regions other than the Těšín region, where older patterns of relationship seem to survive.

The Slovak community in the Těšín region has already been mentioned. Its position can be characterised in the following way: Slovaks have lost the character of one of the constituent ethnic groups of the state, but they have not yet accustomed themselves to the position of a minority. Hence, they are not sure how to use their minority rights. However, many of them feel that the authorities in the Těšín region should not limit their attention in language management to the relationship between Czechs and Poles. Statements by the only two Slovak respondents who evaluated the language management principles as currently practiced in the Těšín region negatively are provided.

> [The first comment is] Why Polish only? All citizens of the Republic know Czech. If more than Czech, then Polish *and* Slovak should be acknowledged as equal. [The second respondent commented:] This region is settled not merely by Czechs and Poles but by other ethnic groups as well. Bilingualism is discriminating against other groups. (Sokolová, 1999b)

The German Language

Situation, problems

As early as the 9th century, some, though limited, strata of the population were bilingual in Czech and German (Skála, 1977). In the course of the following centuries, the relative status and the function of these two languages varied depending on the political and economic situation. It should be mentioned that German, as it was used in Prague, was considered in some periods (e.g. the period of the rule of Charles IV (1346–1378)) as highly cultivated and was sometimes called the precursor of later Standard German (Povejšil, 1980). While this interpretation was later corrected and relegated to the list of myths about Prague German (cf. Trost, 1995), it remains a fact that Prague German occupied an important position in the development of the German language. The literary production of the late 19th and early 20th centuries (e.g. the poetry and prose of Rilke, Kafka or Werfel) should also be noted. Admittedly, German was used in Bohemia and Moravia, and not only by German intellectual elites. Apart from cultivated German there was also macaronic German (Kauderwelsch) and kitchen German (Kücheldeutsch), based on various regional koine (especially Austrian) and on dialects. Incidentally, there was also kitchen Czech (Küchelböhmisch). Czech–German bilingualism thus operated on a number of sociocultural levels and, depending on its location, on a number of regional varieties of language (Nekula, 2002b; Trost, 1995).

The boundaries between the two languages, as they are attested from the first half of the 20th century, had stabilised at the roll over from the 18th to the 19th century. One of the extreme positions of the German isogloss was situated only 40 km north of Prague (Skála, 1977). Although most of the population was monolingual in either Czech or German, up to the end of the 18th century the use of one language or the other did not constitute uncontrovertibly testimony of ethnic membership. The belief that Czechs speak Czech and Germans German was the result of sociopolitical polarisation that took place in the 19th century. Even then it was possible to witness a numerous group of speakers who were bilingual and in principle ethnically uncommitted (Trost, 1995).

The long-term intensive contact between Czech and German on various sociocultural levels leads to the question to what extent and in what ways did these languages influence each other. On the whole, one can say that their coexistence has not led to any far-reaching changes in their structure or identity. However, although historically they belong to two different branches of the Indo-European family, Czech and German share a number of features that are due to their areal proximity. The study of such management phenomena, known as the Sprachbund (language union), only gained momentum towards the end of the 20th century. The shared features are numerous, although they do not necessarily affect central areas of language. Some of them are due to the authority of Latin, which influenced both languages independently; others are the consequence of direct contact on the Czech territory, in which case German mostly had the upper hand. Although the outward shapes of words are different (except for international words of Latin and Greek origin) the structure of the lexicon and phraseology is very similar.

The number of words directly borrowed from German was considerable in

Renaissance Czech, but most of such words were replaced by Czech words due to a wave of purism in the 19th century. Words which remain can be divided into three strata:

(1) First, there are some old borrowings, for which awareness of their origin has been completely lost (Cz. *muset* from Gm. *müssen* 'must', Cz. *hřbitov* from Gm. *Friedhof* 'cemetery').

(2) Second, Czech contains a number of substandard words, sometimes used as slang (see section on Czech language), which are not restricted to particular generations of speakers (Cz. *cálovat* from Gm. *zahlen* 'to pay', Cz. *kumšt* from Gm. *Kunst* 'art'). Many of these words are limited to specific professions (Cz. *hytlák* from Gm. *Hüttelwagen* 'railway van').

(3) Finally, some words are limited only to the oldest generation of speakers, sometimes to speakers of a dialect: the authors of this monograph only know them from lexicographical manuals (Cz. *búny* from Gm. *Bohnen* 'beans', Cz. *firhank* from Gm. *Vorhang* 'curtain').

The words listed above show that loans from German have been morphologically adapted to suit the system of Czech phonology and grammar. For example, the substandard word *cálovat* derived from German *zahlen* 'to pay', receives Czech verbal ending –*ovat*, and in a sentence undergoes morphological changes as any other Czech verb (*cáluji, cáluješ, . . . cáloval, zacálovat*, etc.). They can also become the base for further word derivation (*hytlák* 'railway van', diminutive *hytláček*).

However, as far as lexicon is concerned, the physical proximity of German as well as direct contact led to a large number of calques, especially in compounds; for example, in Cz. *hanopis*, Gm. *Schmähschrift* 'slanderous writing', Cz. *chvályhodný*, Gm. *lobenswert* 'praiseworthy', Cz. *vlastnoručně*, Gm. *eigenhändig* 'by own hand'. Incidentally, Czech loans in German have been recognised in Gm. *Peitsche* from Cz. (or West Slavic) *bič* 'a whip', Gm. *Grenze* from Old Cz. *granicě* 'border' and a number of words in German dialects spoken in border areas (such as Gm. *Brewenze* from Cz. *mravenec* 'ant' or Gm. *Schischka* from Cz. *šiška* '(pine) cone'; cf. Skála, 1977). The lexicon of German spoken in Bohemian towns was probably more substantially affected by borrowing from Czech than assumed so far (Jodas, 2001; Krčmová, 1993).

An areal relationship between Czech and German also obtains in the case of phrases such as Cz. *to je k dostání*, Gm.*das ist zu bekommen* 'it is available', Cz. *dělat kyselý obličej*, Gm. *ein saures Gesicht machen* 'to make a sour face' (Šlosar, 2002). The fact that some of these expressions occur in Austrian but not German German makes linguists wonder about the direction of the borrowing process (e.g. Newerkla, 2002, referring to the work of Kurzová and others).

The relationship on other than the lexical level is less perspicuous. Some features of Czech that have been mentioned include diphthongisation (Berger, 1998); also, loss of the genitive of negation, of the instrumental of predication and of certain kinds of participles may be due to the influence of German (Berger, 1998; Trost, 1995). On the other hand, management does not seem to have worked only in a single direction. Consider, for example, grammatical gender in European languages. While only a few remnants of the original three genders characterise English, French has retained two, and German three. The vicinity of the Slavic languages (Czech more than others), which have three genders, cannot be omitted from the consideration of this phenomenon, or from the consideration of the maintenance of other historical features in German. On a more particular level, it has been argued that the German periphrastic future (*ich werde sprechen* 'I'll speak') was influenced by Czech (Leiss, 1985).

In the second half of the 19th century, Czech–German bilingualism received a strong blow from the nationalistic feeling, developed on both the Czech and German side, that language and ethnic loyalty are inevitably connected. German still remained the language of the top levels of the society, intertwined with foreign elites, but, following the inauguration of Czech as the language of instruction at the university level (1882), it became possible to achieve the highest level of education in that language. This development further decreased the need for bilingualism. Fewer and fewer Czech pupils enrolled in German middle schools (Nekula, 2002b). The foundation of Czechoslovakia in 1918 resulted in a language law, adopted in 1920 (amended in 1926) that required, of public servants and employees in the public sector, knowledge of Czech or Slovak (Staněk, 1999: 98). This requirement meant that, among other things, Czech officials took over positions in the Sudeten areas close to the border, because there were few local German speakers who possessed a sufficient knowledge of the new official language (cf. Povejšil, 1997).

The occupation of Czechoslovakia by Germany at the beginning of WWII brought a complete reversal of the relative weight of the two languages. Within the remaining Czech territory of the *Protektorat Böhmen-Mähren*, German was the language of the masters. On the other hand, after WWII German became a despised language, and a trend appeared to discourage Germans who were not deported from speaking their language (Nekvapil, 2000c). The negative attitudes toward the Germans extended to attitudes toward the German language, including words of German origin (Tejnor *et al.*, 1982). The pragmatic decision at the end of 1947 to reintroduce German as an elective subject in schools was commented on in the press in the following way: 'all right, let's learn the language, but let's not speak it, especially not with the Germans!' (from Staněk, 1993: 52). More than half a decade of terror, with daily executions, mass murders, and concentration camps, all associated with the German language, were not easily forgotten. In the 1960s, a revival of interest in learning German first appeared, but it was not until the 1990s that a more tolerant attitude to borrowings and calques from German emerged (Nekula, 1997).

Germans who were not deported gradually altered their language behaviour. Owing to the fear of discrimination and the complete absence of German schools, Germans oriented their language management toward the use of Czech. Sociological research demonstrated that, within a single generation after WWII, the role of German as an ethnic symbol substantially declined. While in 1970 only 7.2% of Germans considered Czech to be their native tongue, by 1987 the figure had risen to 33%. In the same year, from among those who considered German their native language, 8% used Czech predominantly at home, and 79.8% used Czech and German; only 5percent used German alone (Sokolová, 1991). Linguistic studies, which employ more detailed scales (minimally, German dialect, Standard German, Czech), confirm the importance of generational classification. For example, these studies have revealed that, in the 1960s in the Cheb region, the oldest generation of Germans used their native dialect together with dialectally influenced Standard German, while the middle generation added Czech, and the youngest generation retained only the German dialect and Czech (Povejšil, 1975). Research conducted in the town of Jablonec and its surroundings 20 years later showed a definite decline in bilingualism in the middle generation and a substantial decline in the youngest generation, which tended to be monolingual in Czech. The oldest generation still retained German within the family domain but spoke Czech in public (Bezděková, 1988). These studies demonstrate a significant assimilation trend in all generations of the German population. These results are supported by additional evidence arising from qualitative methodology using biographical research (Nekvapil, 2001, 2003a). Biographies of Germans who were approximately 20 years old in 1945, confirmed that their grand-children first started acquiring German at school – if they started learning it at all.

Nevertheless, the German community has not completely lost its language. Dialectologists who work on the Atlas of Historical German Dialects discovered, to their surprise, that competent informants could be found in all the main centres of their research (Bachmann, 2002). Admittedly, it is a different matter to provide responses to a dialectological questionnaire and to use the language proficiently as a means of daily communication. Leaving the ongoing work on the Atlas aside, the German of the original German population has not yet been subjected to systematic description. That variety seems to be strongly dialectal; there is a lack of labialisation of vowels (*ö, ü* are replaced by *é, í*; cf. Krčmová, 1993), and the phraseology is influenced by Czech (e.g. *ich habe keine tschechische Schulen* modelled after *nemám žádné české školy*). Many Czech Germans are ashamed to use their German in communication with Germans from Germany.

What is the Czech of the German population of the Czech Republic? In the case of the middle and young generation it is undistinguishable from the Czech of other native speakers. The Czech of the oldest and older generations of speakers shows specific features: replacement of voiced by unvoiced consonants (*tobytek* for *dobytek* 'cattle'), lack of palatalisation of dental plosives (*nedelal* for *nedělal* 'he didn't do'), replacement of ř by other consonants (*žeknu* for *řeknu* 'I'll say'), and displacement of the accent connected with lengthening (*vychovála* for *vychovala* 'she educated') (Hašová, 2000); there are also problems with the Czech aspectual system and with gender (Skála, 1977), as well as with nominal and adjectival declension (Hašová, 1996).

In the context of German expatriate managers' use of Czech, research conducted in the Škoda-Volkswagen joint venture company at the beginning of the 1990s showed that the initial enthusiasm to learn Czech was soon replaced by the realisation that the language is not easy to acquire, and active competence stopped at a few greetings such as *dobrý den* 'hello' and a few other words such as *porada* 'meeting'.

Language biography of Mr S

Socioeconomic and sociolinguistic problems of the original German community throughout the 20th century are well illustrated through biographical research. The following example from Nekvapil (2003a) will serve as a suitable closing to this section of the monograph.

Mr S was born in 1926 in the family of a village cobbler. His father and mother were Germans. The family lived in a village in east Bohemia, near the Czech-German language boundary. German was the only language spoken in the family. The father of Mr S could speak a little Czech, his mother none at all. The most important contacts of Mr S with Czech during his childhood occurred on the following occasions:

(1) In 1937/1938 he learned Czech at primary school for two hours a week (this lasted for only one year, till the occupation of Czechoslovakia by Hitler);
(2) For a short time, a Czech boy lived in the family to learn German;
(3) Several Czech children attended the same school as Mr S for a longer time to learn German.

Apart from Czech, Mr S did not learn any foreign language at school. Originally, Mr S wanted to become a farmer. However, when he was 17 (in 1943), he was drafted into the German army. As a German soldier, he went to Hungary where he learned a little Hungarian. He can still remember some Hungarian words. Immediately after the end of World War II, he was sent to work in the interior by the Czech authorities. His family was deported to Germany.

Living in an exclusively Czech environment in the interior, he had to learn Czech. In 1948 he met his future wife – a German, born in 1928. She did not live in a purely Czech environment after 1945 which was why she did not master Czech as well as Mr S. Being a Czech citizen, Mr S had to serve in the Czechoslovak army in the early 1950s (for three years, followed by three years' work in the mines); he started learning Russian there. However, he took only the first steps. During this period, he constantly improved his Czech. He also devoted himself to learning written Czech systematically.

When he finished working in the mines, he was (together with his wife) employed as a worker in a textile factory in east Bohemia up to his retirement, i.e. for 34 years. He and his wife lived in the nearby village K. In 1958, he was nominated by the local council officials to become a representative of the German minority in the council, as a consequence of his good knowledge of Czech. Mr S accepted the offer and held the office till 1974.

Mr and Mrs S have always spoken German to each other, as well as to their sons. Two varieties of German, however, were used in the family. Mr and Mrs S spoke a dialect to each other, and standard German to their sons. The sons of Mr and Mrs S, Horst and Kurt, have actively learned Standard German, which made it possible for them to become representatives of foreign companies in the Czech Republic after 1989. They have a passive knowledge of the local German dialect, their parents' basic means of communication. Both mastered Czech perfectly. Both married Czechs. Their wives have only a passive command of German. Czech is spoken in Horst's and Kurt's families. The first language of their children – i.e. the grandchildren of Mr and Mrs S – is Czech. German (and English) is a foreign language for them. They learn it at school in the county town where both the families live. When the children visit their grandparents in the village K., Mr and Mrs S try to modify the children's behaviour, and talk to them in German – the grandchildren understand, yet reply in Czech. (Nekvapil, 2003a: 70, 71)

Simple management

Thanks to language biographical research, a number of narratives in which members of the German community reflect on their language management are available. Such reflections show that, on occasion, the subjects immediately react to language problems as those problems appear in discourse. This practice is demonstrated in the following extract from the narration of Mr S whose story has been presented.

S: . . . now look, the fact that I learned Czech, I moved only among Czechs. There was nothing else I could do but learn the language.

Well and I was lucky, for I always bumped into people who were willing to help me. When I asked, when I say something wrong, correct me, and the same goes for grammar too. When I began to write in Czech, I was working in the mine and there we had boys, down from South Bohemia or some such place, so we became friends and Peter in particular, you know, any time when I began to write Czech, he'd say write something, and I'll correct it for you, and so I did. Well, at first he explained this and that and then he says, you know what, to hell with you, you're you're pretty good now, us having Czech schooling, unlike you, but we make mistakes the same as you do. (translated from Czech, Nekvapil, 2001: 83, abbreviated)

This passage directly refers to processes of simple management, particularly in the case of written Czech. Correction in discourse by native Czechs was a necessary prerequisite for integration of the German community into mainstream society. For the older generation, no opportunity for organised management existed.

When the Czech society implemented the strategy that Germans should not use German, a crucial decision for each German family arose about how to conduct language management of their children. This problem is well illustrated in a fragment from Mr S's narrative (translated from Czech in Nekvapil, 2001, abbreviated).

S: We were, when eh the children came, the first-born was Horst, so we were telling ourselves, well eh to teach him bad Czech, that would be a bad thing. He'd better speak proper German, 'cos he'll learn Czech among children in no time at all. And that's what happened. There was this kindergarten teacher, I went to see her when he was old enough to go to the kindergarten, and I said: Look here. That's the way it is with him, he doesn't speak Czech too well yet, and she says: Mr S don't you worry, I'll teach him and so she did.

The passage indirectly refers to simple management of German within family situations that led to the acquisition of the German. At the same time simple management of Czech within the kindergarten situation is also described.

Another strategy that has been attested in more than one family concerns the functional distribution of a dialect and the Standard in the case of German. Parents who spoke a dialect to each other reported that they intentionally selected Standard German when speaking to their children. This was a consequence of the fact that, after 1945, no German schools existed, and any variety of German could only be transmitted to the next generation within the family domain. The important point is that the informants themselves selected speaking the Standard as a management strategy.

However, anti-assimilationist management was not as widely practised as the examples given so far might indicate. On the contrary, a large proportion of the Germans who escaped deportation selected pro-assimilation management. No doubt, this management performed a social function: assimilation was socially advisable. At the same time, the energy needed for simple management in discourse is considerable, and simple management was no doubt also avoided on this account. At the present time, the attitude of those concerned is different. Here is what Mr S reports.

S: Many regret today that they put aside German then, after forty five, so that today they don't speak German any more. Many regret it. And they almost envy us now that our two sons speak perfect German. (translated from German, abbreviated, the original in Nekvapil, 2000d: 42)

Organised management

Czech language policy in relation to German passed through several stages. In the 1920s and 1930s, Germans, like other minorities within Czechoslovakia, enjoyed a number of linguistic and cultural privileges. Special rights could be claimed in districts where a minority represented more than 20% of all inhabitants. The German minority was granted an extensive system of primary, secondary and specialised schools, and a German university continued operating in Prague.

During the occupation of Czechoslovakia, from 1939 to 1945, Czech language policy was in fact suspended: German was the language of the masters, and it was Czech that had to defend itself. However, formally, the state was a 'protectorate', and since Czech-German bilingualism was rare by then, an immediate removal of Czech was impracticable. However, a strong programme of Germanisation was mounted; the overall aim of Germany was a complete liquidation of Czech and the Czech nation (Malý, 1991). All public announcements and radio broadcasting were in German, followed by Czech; public notices and signs were in German (large) with Czech translations (small); publication in Czech was restricted; secondary schools were only allowed a limited intake, and Czech universities were closed.

Language policy with regard to those Germans who were allowed to remain in the country after WWII reflected the wartime experience of the Czechs and was in accordance with discriminatory state policies in other respects. An important role in the policy was played by the school system. Compare the experience of Mr P who described the interrelation of the family, individual and organised management in the following way:

P: . . . my wife, she spoke German also, she was from a mixed marriage. From the very beginning we spoke German with our children. Well, right, it worked till a certain point, until they went to school. And then the children came home and said: We don't want to speak German any longer, because they keep telling us we are fascists. Right, in the books it was simply so, Germans and so on they were fascists. (from Nekvapil, 2000c, translated from German, abbreviated)

Only after 1968 were Germans granted a constitutionally guaranteed right to education in their first language. However, no German schools were opened. The main argument of the government was the high dispersion of the German population and its progressive assimilation, especially in the youngest generation. According to statistics, in 1990 only 585 ethnically German children attended primary schools in the territory of present-day Czech Republic.

Commencing in mid-1950s, German children could improve the knowledge of their mother tongue in elective 'language circles'. This, however, did not contribute much to their competence. On the other hand, the 1950s witnessed the introduction of some other elements into the life of the German community. From 1951, a weekly magazine in German, *Aufbau und Frieden*, was published. In court proceedings, the use of German was allowed. In the case of contact with state and local authorities, the practice was uneven. It was recommended that, where the community was large, German should be used both in written and oral contact, even should such a practice entail the use of translators or interpreters, but such practices were not common. German broadcasting, to a limited extent, commenced in 1957. The *Kulturní sdružení*, mentioned in Part II, was founded in 1969, with one of its aims being the support of the knowledge and use of German in the community. However, such support only became operative with the help of the German Federal Republic after the Velvet revolution in 1989. It should be mentioned that, on the basis of the Czechoslovak–German treaty of 1992, a number of Czech-German Encounter Centres sprang up. In 2001 there were 14 such Centres, especially in localities with a higher density of German population. German schools are still difficult to establish because of the high degree of dispersion of the German element, and also because of a lack of demand. A viable project proved to be the establishment of a private German primary school and a high school (gymnázium) in Prague; these are open not only to ethnic Germans but to all interested parties. This project was initiated and implemented by the Association of Germans in Prague and Central Bohemia. The languages of instruction are German and Czech. German has been given the role of a means for the creation of a multicultural identity as well as the re-creation of the lost ethnic identity of the German students. The question remains whether such a re-creation is in fact possible. The last census figures do not seem to give much hope, and specialists who compare the situation of the German element in the Czech Republic and in Hungary have assumed a sceptical attitude (cf. Stevenson, 2000).

It is true that the German community can profit from a considerable interest in German as a foreign language. The support of German as a foreign language is unusually high, and not all of that support is due to foreign encouragement (cf. *Deutsch in der Tschechischen Republik*, 2000/2001). Learning German shows almost the same range of extension as learning English. In 1995, over 700,000 young people studied the German language (see Staněk, 1998: 97). The study of German is supported by the interests of Czechs who work in Germany as well as by those employed in Czech–German joint ventures operating in the territory of the Czech Republic (Zich, 2001). However, so far there are no indications that this instrumental role of German will influence the revitalisation processes within the German community.

Ruthenian, Ukrainian and Russian

Situation, problems

The three languages discussed in this section belong to the eastern group of Slavic languages. (Concerning the linguistic features of Ruthenian see Jabur, 2000; Vaňko, 2000.) While mutual comprehension is relatively easy within the western group (Czech, Slovak, Polish), the case of Czech and the languages of the eastern group requires some previous study, experience and effort. However, the closeness of the languages assists acquisition, to a considerable degree proceeding much faster than in the case of unrelated languages. With regard to Czechs the position of the three languages is very different. Russian was an obligatory school language between 1945 and 1989; consequently, its existence is well known, and it is seen as a language having international status. The existence of Ukrainian is recognised, but it remains vague in the consciousness of most people. On the other hand, very few people know the term *rusínština* (Ruthenian), to say nothing of possessing the information that the status of the language is rising. It has recently been codified, and it is now being taught in some schools in Slovakia (Magocsi,1996). Hence, in the awareness of the people, all three groups are thought to 'speak Russian'. Incidentally, the view that all languages east of the Czech Republic (including Slovak!) are Russian appears occasionally among poorly educated people (Nábělková, 2000). The identification of Ruthenian and Ukrainian with Russian does not favour speakers of these languages, because, due to the occupation of Czechoslovakia by the Soviet Union in the immediate past, many Czechs still maintain a negative attitude to Russian-speaking foreigners and to the Russian language itself.

So far the language of Ruthenians, Ukrainians and Russians who live in the territory of the Czech Republic has not been subjected to study. Those who have lived in the country for a long time, as well as their children, have been linguistically assimilated, except that first generation immigrants usually speak with a 'Russian' accent. Integration seems to be thorough in the case of Ruthenians who do not have a program for the maintenance of their language, an aim that would be difficult in view of the fact that Standard Ruthenian has only recently been introduced in Slovakia, where the number of Ruthenians is much higher (Zimek, 1999/2000), and in view of the fact that many Ruthenians abroad use Ukrainian or Russian as their written language. On the other hand, Ukrainian associations strongly support the introduction of at least basic forms of Ukrainian schooling (Praha a národnosti, 1998: 113) and over a number of years have operated a 'Sunday school', in the framework of which Ukrainian children learn Ukrainian and take other subjects taught in that language. This school is not a part of the normal school system; rather, the practice resembles the 'Saturday School' pattern widely employed in such places as Australia, Canada, and the USA for the support of minority languages.

The situation of Russian is quite different. Russian is still being taught at a number of primary and high schools (see the section on Foreign Languages that follows). As a result, the Russian community can mount more ambitious plans, such as the reopening of the bilingual Czech–Russian high school (gymnázium), scheduled for 2004 (Vesti, 2002: 2).

Foreign workers from eastern Europe communicate with each other in Ukrainian or Russian, while in relation to the matrix community they often use pidginised Czech or a foreigner-talk variety of their own language.

The Vietnamese Language

Situation, problems

Vietnamese is a language that differs completely from Czech both genetically and typologically. Since working knowledge of the language is limited to only a few individuals in the Czech Republic, the Vietnamese who reside in the country must learn Czech if they wish to communicate with the matrix community. Learning Czech is a difficult task, and not all Vietnamese successfully achieve fluency. In interviews conducted by Jitka Slezáková, one Vietnamese respondent says that learning Czech is the most difficult task for these people:

V: *Jazyk, ten nejhorší pro nás. Já něco umím, ale třeba starší lidi to těžký, oni nebudou učit. Třeba moje mamka tady taky byla už sedm let a taky blbý. To těžký, pro ní strašně těžký. No tak ona nemůže.* 'Language, it worst for us. I know something, but for example older people, that difficult, they will not learn. For example my mum was here already seven years and it also silly. It difficult, for her terribly difficult.' (Slezáková, mimeo)

Slezáková (mimeo) characterises in the following way the language of a Vietnamese retailer who has been in the Czech Republic for one year: 'In view of the shortness of his sojourn in this country he failed to understand questions and was totally unable to answer when they were more complicated.'

The pronunciation of the Vietnamese often renders Czech sentences incomprehensible, their morphology is simplified, and syntactically the language (as spoken by Vietnamese) consists of short sentences piled one on another. As would be expected, Vietnamese children who attend Czech schools often speak Czech better than Vietnamese adults, using Czech not only with Czechs but also with their siblings and cousins, irrespective of the insistence of their parents that they speak Vietnamese. Vietnamese adults often use their children as interpreters.

The typical network existing between Vietnamese and Czechs is a commercial transaction. Apart from this, the two communities also interact in official contacts with Czech authorities. Official interpreters and unofficial interpreters (such as children) are sometimes used, but the Vietnamese community has already acquired knowledge of the typical content of negotiation, and it is not unusual for individuals to be able to manage on their own. Other networks were infrequent during the 1980s (Heroldová & Matějová, 1987), and there is no reason to think that the situation will have changed in the intervening time. It is no wonder that the mother of the retailer quoted above mastered no Czech during the seven years of her residence. Similar conditions obtain in the case of immigrants in many countries, particularly when older women are involved. Conversation with customers, beyond the commercial transaction itself, is difficult, not only because of the immigrant's limited grammatical competence, but also because of the differences that obtain in the non-linguistic communication system, such as topics that are constrained in Czech (e.g. the marital status of customers, their financial situation, the age of female speakers, etc.). For the factory work environment in Australia, Clyne (1994: 153) has identified a number of such barriers for the Vietnamese. No doubt further research will identify even more communication problems, similar to those common between speakers of other European and Asian languages (cf. Neustupný, 1987).

Although in Czech the use of the familiar second person pronoun *ty* 'you' is subject to a number of constraints (Nekvapil & Neustupný, forthcoming), it often happens that Czech customers use this pronoun, rather than the more 'polite' *vy* to adult Vietnamese speakers. The reason for this behaviour is undoubtedly complicated: e.g., problems in judging the age of the interlocutor, the use of foreigner talk, or a feeling of superiority. Some Vietnamese whose sociolinguistic competence in Czech is sufficiently developed evaluate such usage negatively. Slezáková (mimeo) has recorded the following exchange with a Czech interviewer:

I: *Měl jste někdy problémy s Čechy? Třeba s policií . . .* 'Have you ever had problems with the Czechs, for example with the police . . . '
V: *Na to domluvit, to pro mě ne. Já vím, to některý viděj tvář jako Vietnamci, jsou cizí, tak oni mluví jako ty, tykat jako. Některý policie nebo některý člověk, tak oni mluví se mnou jako tykat. Ale oni musí se mnou mluvit jako vykat.* 'To make myself understood, (as) for me no. I know, some fellows see a face like the Vietnamese, they are foreign, so they speak as *ty*, to use *ty*. Someone police, or some man, so they speak with me as to use *ty*. But they must speak with me to use *vy*.'

It is necessary to note that some Vietnamese also use *ty* in first-encounters with Czechs, but in this case the reason seems to be that the Vietnamese are not (yet) familiar with the *vy* forms. In the following example, a Czech policeman asks a Vietnamese vendor for his documents:

P: *Dejte nám tu občanku.* 'Please give us (a *vy* form) your identity card.'
V: *Poškej.* 'Wait (a *ty* form).'

Simple management

As already mentioned, problems in discourse between Czechs and Vietnamese are of considerable magnitude, resulting not only from the lack of grammatical competence but also from non-grammatical strategies of communication and from violations of the sociocultural rules of conduct. Frequently, differences in the duration, frequency, and 'form' of smiling are mentioned. Müllerová (1998: 123) recalls the following event:

In 1983, two groups of Vietnamese workers, approximately 60 persons, got jobs at the steelworks in Kladno. These Vietnamese had poor knowledge of the Czech language, but Czech workers did not pay attention to this fact at all: 'The Vietnamese are here, they want to be here, so they have to understand everything.' [note the feeling of superiority of the Czechs, JVN/ JN] Whenever the Vietnamese did not understand Czech, they always nodded and smiled. The Czech workers thought: 'The Vietnamese understand and they do not want us to explain anything to them – that is the reason why they are always smiling.' In fact, the situation was quite different: the Vietnamese did not understand Czech and, in accordance with their national habit they nodded, smiled and repeated 'yes, yes'. This reaction of the Vietnamese meant: 'I am sorry, I do not understand, but I am trying to cooperate as much as possible.' At the steelworks a Czech foreman tried very hard to explain to a Vietnamese worker what he had to do immediately, but the Vietnamese behaved as already mentioned: he nodded and smiled. In a few minutes the Czech foreman got nervous, slapped the Vietnamese in the face and shouted at him: 'I'm trying to tell you over and over again what you have to do and you are smiling, you do not respect me as your boss. What are you so proud of?' In a minute nearly all the Vietnamese and Czech workers had arrived and wanted to solve the problem with a fight. Fortunately the leader of the Vietnamese and the interpreter realised what had happened and started to explain the misunderstanding immediately.

The happy ending of this story, probably genuine, is not typical for everyday interaction between Czechs and Vietnamese. In this case, the presence of an interpreter, an agent of organised management, had a decisive impact on the situation. This incident reminds us of Clyne's observation that, in Australian factories, central and southern European workers doubt the integrity and trustworthiness of their Vietnamese co-workers who 'say yes and then they don't do it' (Clyne, 1994: 151).

The following fragment recorded by Slezáková (mimeo) refers to a textile shop where both Czech and Vietnamese shop assistants work.

I: (to the Czech) *Jak vy se tady s nimi domluvíte?* 'How do you communicate with them?'

Č: *Ale jo, tak co potřebujem, se domluvíme. Kvůli práci. Když je něco potřeba, taky. To my se domluvíme. Že se domluvíme dobře?* 'Well yes, what we need, we communicate. Because of our work. When there is a need, also. We communicate. Don't we communicate well?'

V: *Ano. Něco já ptám zboží a vy . . .* 'Yes, something I ask goods and you . . .'

Č: *O zboží ví, ale takhle holt něco – buď rukama nebo různě, jak nám to jde. Ale moc ne, no.* 'They know about goods, but otherwise – either with hands, or variously, as we can. But not much, yes.'

I: *A jinak vycházíte spolu dobře až na tu řeč?* 'And otherwise, apart from language, do you have good relations?'

Č: *No, tak voni nám rozumí přece jenom. Ale my jim vůbec.* 'Well, they after all understand us, but we (don't understand them) at all.'

The last sentence of this conversation illustrates that communication problems are not easy to examine in standard interviews.

An interesting adjustment strategy, also occurring in intercultural situations in other communities, is illustrated by the fact that the Vietnamese make address easier for their Czech interlocutors by asking to be addressed by Czech names, e.g. *Antonín*.

Individual language management occurs, and the proof is that the Vietnamese sometimes keep a Czech textbook or a Vietnamese–Czech conversation book under the counter.

Organised management

In Communist Czechoslovakia, the Vietnamese were, on arrival, channelled through intensive three-month long courses of Czech (or Slovak), and these courses were concluded by an examination (Heroldová & Matějová, 1987). Actually, some of the Vietnamese had gone through similar courses in Vietnam, before their departure for Czechoslovakia. In such cases, their teachers were Vietnamese; as a consequence, the students acquired reasonable competence in grammar and in the written language, though little competence in comprehension or in speaking (Müllerová, 1998). In the case of some undergraduate and postgraduate students, one-year intensive courses in Czech were organised in the 1980s. Such programmes produced people with a good knowledge not only of Czech grammar, but also of communicative and sociocultural strategies which, to a considerable extent, prevented the occurrence of interaction problems (Müllerová, 1998). It seems that Vietnamese who were active in the Czech territory before 1989 possessed interactive competence much superior to that of their countrymen who came to the Czech Republic later. The new arrivals have no language education at their disposal. They acquire their competence through unorganised 'natural' acquisition processes in the marketplace; first generation speakers are hardly able to communicate about anything other than prices and types of merchandise.

At present, organised management only affects some children. In our field work conducted at Vejprty in 2002, there were only two Vietnamese children in the local school, one in the 1st and one in the 4th form. These two are children of parents who arrived in Czechoslovakia before 1989. (The number of Vietnamese in the 2001 census in Vejprty was 60; in this number, which no doubt underestimates the total number, there must have been more than two children of school age.) The field work revealed that formerly five other children had attended, but these had either left for another location with their parents or had completed compulsory education. In 1995, four children had arrived from Germany and had attended a special school because they possessed no Czech at all. Additionally, there are Vietnamese children in a nearby high school (gymnázium) in Chomutov. The experience of teachers with these children has been very positive. They are talented and eager to learn. Some of them are offspring of parents who possess university degrees but work in retail because such employment is more lucrative. The Vietnamese only send their children to school when they have been granted permanent residence. While, under such circumstances, school attendance is free, before securing permanent residence, parents would be obliged to pay for their children's school attendance. Thus, organised language management benefits the Vietnamese only when they have obtained permanent residence status, and even then, it only benefits the second generation.

The Vietnamese case shows a number of weaknesses in contemporary Czech language management. Materials on linguistic minorities in the Czech Republic, published by the central or local governments, pay minimal attention to the Vietnamese. One of the reasons for this neglect presumably stems from the fact that, as a rule, they do not possess Czech citizenship. However, dividing residents, whether short or long term, according to their citizenship is an outdated principle. Here is a large community, probably between 20–30,000 people, who actively contribute to the economic life of the Czech Republic. The public, though not openly hostile, is not always friendly to this community, not because it creates socioeconomic problems, but simply because of its foreignness and its inability to communicate. Huge numbers of communication problems are not attended to at all in the system of organised management. The report of the government's Council for Ethnic Minorities (Zpráva, 2002) only mentions this community because the 2001 census questionnaires were also printed in Vietnamese (p. 2), a measure that was the result of pragmatic considerations, and in connection with the Vietnamese programme on radio (pp. 15, 23). A Vietnamese representative was not nominated to be a member of the Consultative Group for ethnic radio programmes but was invited to participate by the Director of Czech Radio.

The Hungarian Language

Situation, problems

Hungarian belongs to the Finno-Ugric language family which is usually supposed to be unrelated to Indo-European languages (such as English, French, the Slavic languages or most Indian languages including Romani); Hungarian also possesses a grammatical structure different from that of the Indo-European languages. This lack of affiliation means that no 'natural' receptive bilingualism between the languages is likely. Additionally, while in the case of other European languages (including Czech), extensive lexical similarities exist, resulting from the shared interference of Latin and Greek and mutual borrowing, no such similarity exists in the case of Hungarian, which has applied strict puristic attitudes. A number of pages of a Hungarian book must be inspected before a single familiar word can be identified. Since the knowledge of Hungarian has always been close to zero in the Czech lands, communication between Czechs and Hungarians required the use of an intermediate language such as German (or more recently English) or quick linguistic adaptation to Czech. Adaptation was facilitated in the case of those who were coming from Slovakia and possessed the knowledge of Slovak which could easily be transformed into competence in Czech. Unfortunately, this aspect of communication cannot be ascertained from the sociological and sociolinguistic surveys of the 1990s carried out in the Czech Republic because Czech researchers did not consider the issue of the knowledge of Slovak in the case of Czech Hungarians as worthy of attention.

The statistically representative sociological survey of the Hungarian community conducted in 1992, in which more than 1000 Hungarians took part, showed that 66.3% of the respondents predominantly spoke Czech at home, 18.3% spoke

Hungarian and Czech, and only 12.9% principally spoke Hungarian (Sadílek & Csémy, 1993: 29). Note that this distribution occurs in spite of the fact that Czech is not a language easily acquired by Hungarians (unless they already know Slovak) and that the family domain is the only one in which there is any chance that Hungarian could be maintained. A more recent survey, conducted in 1997–98 (Eőry & Hašová, 2003) was oriented qualitatively. Its authors summarised the results as follows:

> The process of language loss is fast among Hungarians; in general it is completed by the second generation, but invariably by the third. This is proved by the fact that among 32 informants there was not a single third-generation speaker of Hungarian, and they could not even mention such a person in their families. (Eőry & Hašová, 2003: 99)

This process may be difficult to alter, even though some Hungarian intellectuals have produced a program to reverse it. However, it appears that, in families of Hungarians with tertiary education, the language shift in the second generation is most pronounced (Sadílek & Csémy, 1993: 29).

Simple management

Simple management processes are, to a large extent, reflected in the results of surveys that investigate competence in Hungarian. In the Sadílek and Csémy's (1993: 26) survey, 45.5% of members of the Hungarian community evaluated their knowledge of Hungarian as very good, 31.8% as good, 19.2% as poor, while 3.5% declared no knowledge of the language. The strictest self-evaluation appeared, as could be expected, in the case of the youngest group (18–29 years of age) which assessed its knowledge as poor in 25.7%, and as zero in 13.1%. On the other hand, irrespective of their generational membership, the respondents evaluated their Czech as very good in 53.1% of cases; 40.9% of them assessed it as good, and only 6% assessed it as poor or nil. On the basis of these results, the authors concluded that Hungarians in the Czech Republic were more competent in Czech than in Hungarian (Sadílek & Csémy, 1993). This conclusion may be questioned because the evaluation of the non-native language (Czech) may be more positive than that of the native Hungarian. These figures, however, are most obviously valid for the youngest generation which, not surprisingly, seems to be most strongly assimilated. Results of the assimilation process have also been reflected in the 2001 census (see Part II on Hungarians). The survey reported in Sadílek and Csémy bears witness to extensive communication problems experienced by speakers in discourse, in their use of both Hungarian and Czech.

It is remarkable that, in the same survey, 41.7% of respondents reported that they were not interested in teaching their children Hungarian, while 32.3% were undecided. Women were twice as interested as men.

There is still too little data derived directly from discourse. From the data available, it can be assumed that speakers frequently do not notice interference. In the following conversation, the Hungarian speaker of Czech omits the reflexive particle *se*, probably because in Hungarian it often corresponds to a suffix that cannot be separated from the word.

P: . . . *aby mě zabrzdil prostě, tak já jsem už ty věci z lavice naházela. A vrhla jsem* *k tomu oknu . . . ' . . .* so he puts on the break for me, so I throw away things from the bench. And I threw (myself) to the window . . . '

The unnoted deviation is in the form *vrhla jsem* that, according to Czech norms, should be *vrhla jsem se* (from Hašová, 2001: 53, simplified).

In the following example, P incorporates the Czech word *podpora* 'subsidy' into his Hungarian utterance. The Czech element is given the Hungarian accusative ending *–t*, and the final vowel is lengthened.

P: *Én is nyugdíjas én is podporát kapok mondom magamnak semmi baj.* 'I am also retired, I am getting a subsidy, I tell myself it doesn't matter' (Hašová, 1996: 90)

Adjustment drawing material from the other language is common in contact discourse for items with culturally specific meaning. Neither in this nor in the preceding discourse samples is there any evidence of noting of the deviation by participants in the encounter.

Organised management

In the case of Hungarian, no organised management at the governmental level could be discovered. However, financial support for Hungarian press and organisations (Zpráva, 2002) should be mentioned here.

At the level of education, Charles University has been teaching Hungarian philology for more than a century. The programme is significant, but its motivation is not primarily language management for the Hungarian community. One of the aims of the *Svaz Maďarů žijících v českých zemích* (Association of Hungarians in the Czech Lands) is 'to develop the cultivation of the mother tongue and support its natural link with Hungarian culture' (Praha a národnosti, 1998: 43). The *Svaz*, in cooperation with the *Maďarské kulturní středisko* (Hungarian Cultural Centre in Prague, founded in 1977), offers courses in Hungarian for children from Hungarian families. The problem is that these courses are limited to Prague. Also, it seems to be difficult for the Centre to obtain information from schools that would indicate interest in courses in Hungarian. This may be a problem common to a number of minority languages: as long as such basic information is missing, mounting a course is difficult.

The picture of language management by the Hungarian community in the Czech Republic is at a considerable distance from the situation evident in some other countries. There is little sense of patriotism. Evaluation of inadequate language maintenance is not necessarily negative, and adjustment that would lead to maintenance is weak. A similar situation obtains with regard to Hungarian in such other countries as Australia, where Hungarian belongs to the group of low-maintenance languages (Clyne, 1991). Although the overall power of the Czech community is paramount, its impact does not take the form of forced assimilation. On the other hand, there is no evidence that, in deciding not to maintain their language, Hungarians in the Czech Republic act without expecting that such maintenance might be negatively evaluated by Czech speakers. There is a need for work at the discourse level of management which should show where the sources of evaluative attitudes within the community can be identified.

Greek and Macedonian

Greek

Greek immigrants arrived mostly from economically underdeveloped moun-
tainous regions. They typically spoke only Greek, and only a few possessed any
knowledge of another language (Sloboda, 2000/2001). Many refugees originally
restricted their contact with the matrix community to the bare minimum,
because they hoped for a speedy return to their homeland. Czech was not in
focus; this attitude also occurred among children who were initially provided
with schooling in which Greek was taught on the basis of materials imported by
international support groups from Rumania and later from Poland. However,
starting in 1951, the children were enrolled in Czech schools, and it was then that
the lack of knowledge of the Czech language emerged as a problem. Intensive
courses were provided and extended through the summer vacations. The curricula were adapted, with some subjects being dropped to make space for extra
Greek tuition. Greek was a compulsory subject until 1956, and some other
subjects (such as social studies and history) were taught in the language. Thus,
the children were acquiring both languages, and in view of the fact that they
attended classes with Macedonian children, or lived with them in the same children's dormitories, they also acquired some knowledge of Macedonian.
So-called *Greek Schools* began to disappear as a consequence of the return of a
large number of families with children, as well as teachers, to Greece. However,
the teaching of Greek as a subject was still being practised in 2001/2002 in seven
cities of Northern Moravia, in Brno and in Prague, involving a total of 190
students. Tuition is normally provided in two competence grades (beginners and
advanced), and classes are held after class hours. There are also classes for
pre-school children (Zpráva, 2002). The oldest generation of Greeks, separated
from the homeland to which they were not allowed to return, gradually lost
fluency in their language and had no choice but to assume a positive attitude to
Czech. However, their competence was not always sufficient, and they needed
interpreters when in contact with the authorities (Zpráva, 2002). For those who
were born in the 1960s and 1970s, Czech became the first language, even though
Greek was maintained because of the need to preserve ties with the older generation and with relatives in Greece.

Macedonian

Macedonian refugees who arrived from Greece were mostly bilingual in a
Macedonian dialect and a northern dialect of Greek. However, some of them
were only competent in the former (Sloboda, 2000/2001). At the end of the
1940s, the process of the formation of Standard Macedonian had not yet been
completed. The first Macedonian school was established in Greece in 1947
(Dorovský, 1998: 210), and this fact alone indicated that the knowledge of written Macedonian was close to zero both for the emigrants and for their children
(Sloboda, 2000/2001). Competence in Standard Greek, with its diglottic
pattern, was unlikely to be much better. The structure of school education for
Greek and Macedonian children when they arrived was probably almost identical, the main difference being that Macedonian children were given a few
hours of tuition through the medium of Macedonian. Such children thus

received bilingual education, and when Czech was added later as the principal medium of instruction, trilingual education. It can be assumed that, owing to the features shared by Macedonian and Czech, their competence in Czech developed faster than in the case of children with a pure Greek background. Hence, it is not surprising that the community 'dissolved' within the Czech matrix society – unless individuals identified with the Greeks and accepted their identity. After the 1960s, the teaching of Macedonian gradually disappeared (Sloboda, 2000/2001).

Foreign Languages in the Czech Republic

Competence in foreign languages

The phrase foreign languages designates languages when they are not used by a community living in the territory of the Czech Republic. A language can be both a community language and a foreign language. For example, German is a community language in the Czech Republic, but it is also a foreign language.

There is no simple way to assess competence in foreign languages, and subjective perceptions are historically conditioned. In a 1999 survey (Lidové noviny 27/1/99: p. 3), 57% of Czechs claimed they could communicate in Russian, 51% in German, and 21% in English. However, when asked whether they could read newspapers in that language, only 26% of respondents reported reading competence in Russian, 13% in German, and 8% in English. All these figures seem to be unrealistically high. It is questionable whether such a high percentage of speakers would have had an opportunity to test their ability to communicate with Russians, Germans or foreigners who spoke English. Neither did they have the chance to read newspapers in these languages. In particular, in the case of Russian, contacts at personal level were always limited during the period of Communist Party rule, and did not increase later. However, the survey gives some indication of the upper limit: it is probably true that all the effort of the communist government over 40 years and the relative closeness of the languages notwithstanding, not more than half of all Czechs felt they could communicate even at a limited level in Russian. Similarly not more than half of all Czechs believed that they could do the same in German; the expectation of success in communication through the medium of English remained unshared by more than four-fifths of the population.

Nevertheless, an overall assessment of the competence of Czechs cannot be very negative. One must take into consideration that for over 40 years very few were allowed to leave the country – at best only occasional trips to other countries of the former Soviet bloc were permitted – and it was often dangerous to speak to the few so-called Western foreigners who visited Czechoslovakia. However, even if active competence to communicate in Russian was achieved only by a fraction of the population, many acquired information about the Russian communicative style along with a few basic expressions, which enabled them to use these elements in word play and to orient themselves in the Russian-spoken parts of the Oscar-winning Czech film Kolya. The study of other languages has been intensive during the 1990s, and the competence gained is sometime impressive. However, it should be borne in mind that much of this competence has been achieved in classrooms and is mostly limited to grammar, lexicon and the written language – leaving aside non-grammatical and sociocultural components that are normally acquired through sojourn in the target society.

Simple management in the use of foreign languages

When faced with the need to communicate with a foreigner, Czechs, even if addressed in Czech, show a tendency to answer in a foreign language. This strategy is also known from research in other languages. The language selected is the 'foreign language' of the speaker; even if addressed in English, a shop attendant may answer in German. In the case of speakers with a low level of competence, pidginisation occurs at many levels. It may manifest itself in a real or apparent refusal to interact; a less drastic form affects the facial expression (a 'stern' face) and non-verbal behaviour (vehement gesticulation); and pidginisation often shows at the sentence level where simplification occurs. Transfer from Czech through direct translation of Czech communication means is common. For example, the question *yes?* can be heard as a tag question for English *isn't it* or *OK?* In the case of speakers with a higher level of knowledge of foreign languages, the lack of routinisation and attempts to generate each utterance anew are symptomatic. This is the consequence of a limited exposure to foreign languages through study abroad or extended periods of stay.

The number of problems Czech speakers experience in contact with foreigners leads many to a decision to initiate a management process directed at the entire system of a foreign language – in other words to enrol in a course. In such a case, the speaker may turn to a state school, but private schools, which mushroomed in the 1990s, are likely to be more flexible in providing adjustment in the direction actually needed. For example, a wide range of courses in some languages, such as Spanish, are not offered within the state system.

Organised management: The teaching of foreign languages at primary schools

As a means of management of language problems in contact with foreigners, languages are taught at various levels of the public education process. Within the process we can distinguish the following stages:

(1) Kindergarten (*mateřská škola*, age 3–6).
(2) Primary School (*základní škola*, age 6–15).
(3) Secondary level: high school (*gymnázium*, age 15–19; however, there are also 8 year and 6 year high schools which start at age 11 or 13 respectively), Secondary Technical Schools and Secondary Vocational Schools (15–19, 15–18 respectively).
(4) Tertiary level (*vysoká škola*, courses of varying extension are available at universities and other institutions).

The system was highly centralised until 1989. Since then, it has passed through a period of decentralisation (until 1995) after which a new era of weak centralisation commenced. At present, a foreign language is introduced as a compulsory subject at Year 4 (or in some schools at Year 3) of primary school and is allocated

Table 2 Pupils learning foreign languages at primary schools between 1991/92 and 1998/99 (Vývojová ročenka, 1999)

	1991/92	*1992/93*	*1993/94*	*1994/95*	*1995/96*	*1996/97*	*1997/98*	*1998/99*
English	263,180	261,400	254,211	251,144	267,270	341,586	370,744	390,518
German	356,738	349,982	334,181	315,632	307,378	374,502	366,050	344,247
French	8,607	9,993	9,066	8,281	8,187	8,113	7,539	8,744
Russian	30,599	11,457	3,891	1,484	1,267	816	753	993
Spanish	–	611	385	384	325	283	363	486
Italian	–	11	21	22	38	25	–	–
Other European languages	–	12	251	114	170	13	20	–
Other languages	392	152	23	72	–	539	4	14
Total						700,864	726,526	723,992

400 teaching hours over Years 4–9. In the last four years of high school, the First Foreign Language is also allocated 400 hours. A high school graduate has thus received 800 hours of tuition in the First Foreign Language. The Second Foreign Language is added in the first year of high school and is allocated three hours per week. The Ministry of Education's Course of Studies speaks about the need to deepen 'linguistic, sociolinguistic, sociocultural and study-technique competence' of high school students. Unfortunately, the objectives of language teachers are frequently limited to linguistic competence alone. At the secondary technical and vocational schools, only one foreign language is required, and it is allocated three and two hours per week respectively. The Ministry of Education expects that, in future, English will be compulsory, starting at Year 3 of the primary school, and that a Second Foreign Language will be added at Year 6.

Table 2 shows that the range of languages taught at the primary school level has been extremely limited. In 1998/99, English was the top language with 390,000 students, closely followed by German, which was studied by 344,000 students. French managed to attract 8744 students, while Russian stood at a mere 993 and Spanish at 486. The category 'other languages' accommodated 14 students (for details see Nekvapil, 2003c).

Among language teachers, the limited range of languages available in the primary schools, in particular the 'marginalisation' of French, Russian and Spanish, are watched with concern. In 1989, compulsory enrolment in Russian was abolished, and students were given the freedom to select the language they wanted to study. Now it has been noted that the freedom of choice does not necessarily lead to a plurality of choice (Fenclová, 1998/1999b). Warnings that English may soon monopolise language teaching have appeared (Keliš, 1998/1999). Teachers point to the forthcoming entry into the EU and require from the state a clear policy as well as an increased investment in foreign language teaching (Musil, 2000/2001).

The question of pluralism is difficult. One basic stumbling block is the idea that such pluralism can be achieved with a single foreign language in the curriculum. One could argue that, with English having in fact achieved the status of the international language as such, students who do not study English do in fact relegate themselves to the status of less than world citizenship. English is and will continue to be needed. Plurality can only be a problem of the Second or Third Foreign Language. Another stumbling block is that many teachers envisage plurality as a matter of adding French, Spanish or Russian to English and German. However, one has to proceed far beyond the 'old school languages'. In Europe, languages of the immediate neighbourhood and the EU nations, as well as other European, languages need consideration. From the point of view of a nation such as the Czech Republic that was barred by its history from participation in European affairs for half a century, Europe may seem to be everything. However, the world looms large and African and Asian languages should not be omitted from consideration even at this level.

One of the basic issues in language teaching after 1989 was the shortage of teachers, in particular qualified teachers for the lower levels of the primary schools. The issue still remains unresolved. Although Czech universities started producing considerable numbers of graduates in English and German, the low level of school teacher salaries means that only 10 to 15% of such graduates enter language teaching (Nekvapil, 2003c). After 1989, in-service training for language teachers was assisted by British, German or French specialists, often in cooperation with the British Council and the Goethe-Institut. One of the by-products of these courses was the strengthening of the direct method or communicative language teaching. In-service training is still not mandatory, but the Education Ministry is working on a scheme for further enhancement of the qualification of teachers. Since 1997, the Czech Republic has also participated in the project SOCRATES, and large numbers of teachers have taken part in its Activity B (teacher training). As far as textbooks are concerned, the initial enthusiasm for foreign-produced textbooks has waned. It is now accepted that texts appropriate to the Czech linguistic and sociocultural situation are needed (Fenclová, 1998/1999a). Some such textbooks have been produced, and many are in production.

Organised management: The teaching of foreign languages at the secondary level

Statistics concerning the teaching of languages at the secondary level (Tables 3 and 4) show that English and German are in the same position as at the primary schools. However, there is a difference between high schools (gymnázium) and the more vocationally oriented schools. At the former, English leads German by a large margin, while at the vocationally oriented schools the relationship is reversed. In the gymnázium, French, Spanish and Russian get a larger piece of the cake. It seems that the downward trend in Russian has been arrested. Between 1993 and 1995, enrolments in 'other languages' were relatively high, but it is not easy to explain why they have diminished again. The difference between Tables 3 and 4 seems to be a function of the job market. More vocationally oriented students expect that they may in the future obtain employment in German-speaking countries or in the tourist industry in areas adjoining Germany or Austria.

Table 3 Students learning foreign languages at high schools ('gymnázia') between 1991/92 and 1998/99 (Vývojová ročenka, 1999)

	1991/92	1992/93	1993/94	1994/95	1995/96	1996/97	1997/98	1998/99
English	91,324	101,339	107,664	107,726	118,966	112,301	111,474	112,008
German	68,958	76,364	82,176	84,232	92,698	85,220	84,871	84,536
French	11,477	12,408	13,809	14,610	16,325	15,722	15,476	16,451
Russian	36,150	17,924	8,324	2,911	1,792	1,418	1,500	2,937
Spanish	–	6,145	2,610	2,956	3,314	3,029	2,851	3,160
Italian	–	108	286	627	746	790	700	707
Latin	–	–	–	–	12,197	15,519	12,439	11,945
Classic Greek	–	–	–	–	84	53	123	124
Other European languages	4,418	2,320	9,778	8,648	36	29	5	4
Other languages	–	251	249	63	120	24	31	33
Total						125,534	125,885	125,023

Table 4 Students learning foreign languages at secondary vocational and technical schools between 1992/93 and 1998/99 (Vývojová ročenka, 1999)

	1992/93	1993/94	1994/95	1995/96	1996/97	1997/98	1998/99
English	158,117	195,153	230,895	242,872	193,136	181,641	172,818
German	258,002	295,325	326,450	330,635	251,434	229,207	209,631
French	10,451	15,360	15,942	14,781	12,723	11,312	9,779
Russian	42,041	14,566	7,685	4,969	3,918	3,958	3,590
Spanish	217	2,199	2,942	3,127	2,382	2,371	2,108
Italian	81	557	911	1,132	871	751	902
Latin	–	–	–	3,392	2,194	3,957	3,881
Classic Greek	–	–	–	43	42	59	–
Other European languages	1,781	1,328	2,928	–	50	39	73
Other languages	389	203	180	231	329	115	71
Total					377,378	343,774	312,297

Prognosis

Should English become compulsory and another compulsory foreign language be added at the primary school level, the situation of Russian is likely to improve. Russian will be selected as the Second Foreign Language for at least three reasons:

(1) As a Slavic language it will be easy for students to learn.
(2) There are still large numbers of teachers who can teach the classes.
(3) Ideological opposition to Russian is slowly disappearing while economic relations with Russia and other countries of the former Soviet Union are increasing.

Russian will also reinforce the possibility of *semicommunication* with speakers of other Slavic languages. It can be assumed that the position of Russian will move closer to that of French. Owing to close economic cooperation with Germany and Austria, and also in view of the geographic proximity of the two countries, the position of German will remain strong. Two groups of languages are at present strongly under-represented. First, there are the languages of near neighbours or almost neighbours: Poland, Slovakia and Hungary, and other members or potential members of the EU. Second, there are the languages of Asia and Africa.

This is not to suggest that certain languages should be made compulsory. However, a clear language policy from the Education Ministry taking into account the present deficiencies will be needed. Such a policy should take account of education systems in which a plurality of languages offered at this level is a reality.

Languages at the tertiary level

All tertiary institutions require passing examinations in one or two foreign languages and offer programmes to this effect. Courses are usually of two semesters duration but, if a language for special purposes is included, students may take as many as four semesters. Students usually take languages they have already studied at the high school level. (Further information is available in Nekvapil, 2003c.)

Specialised degree courses in foreign languages and philology are offered at most universities. The range of languages available is sometimes impressive. Charles University (Universita Karlova) claims to be the only university in Europe that offers almost all the Romance languages including such languages as Friulian.

Languages and Czech Entry to the European Union

European Union languages for the Czech Republic

The entry of the Czech Republic and other east and central European nations to the European Union (EU) is expected to occur in 2004 and will no doubt lead to a number of language management processes.

Prior to the expected expansion, the Union employed 11 languages of the 15 members as official and working languages (because some countries use the same language and Ireland does not require that Irish become one of the official languages). About 1300 full-time translators and 800 interpreters (McCluskey, 2001) have already been employed by the Union, and the translation/interpreting operation has placed considerable burden on the organisation, with €685 million being spent in 1999. The annual cost to each citizen has only been about €2 and this figure is not expected to change much after the expansion, since there will be a commensurate increase in population (Cunningham, 2001). However, the operation will grow substantially. There will be at least 19, and probably more, languages after the expansion. The EU has estimated that adding a new official language will require a minimum of 200 translators for the headquarters alone (McCluskey, 2001). It is unthinkable that the Czech Republic (or any of the other newly accepted members) would give up its right to translation or interpreting because this would result in considerable impediment to the democratic process: the majority of the population would be *de facto* excluded from participation in the EU matters (Van Els, 2001).

Prior to joining the EU, the Czech Republic was required to translate into Czech all EU legislation in force. Obrová and Pelka (2001) report on some issues connected with this task. Although versions in all 11 official languages are considered authentic, the Czech team found it necessary to employ three versions (English, French and German) for its work and, on this basis, created a unified system of Czech terminology. The translation of this legislation, called *acquis communautaire*, represents a major language management act. However, in the day-to-day operation of the Union, further translation and interpreting is required. As Johnston (2000) notes, there is a legal position and a *de facto* situation with regard to translations. Although legally all languages are and will continue to be 'official and working' languages, in fact individual organs of the Union decide which languages to use in internal communication (procedural languages). It would therefore be naive to assume that the proceedings of all meetings and all documents produced by the EU would be translated into Czech (or the languages of the other new members); yet, as many will, there will be a need for a continuous supply of interpreters and translators, many of whom will be native speakers of Czech.

As a result of the policy of procedural languages, it cannot be expected that Czech participation would be equal to that of participants who are native speakers of the procedural languages. The Czech government, as well as the governments of other countries whose languages are unlikely ever to become procedural languages, must carefully watch the situation. The Czech government already possesses some negative experience in negotiating with the EU (Chvátalová, 2002).

In view of the enlargement, the EU is considering a number of measures to cope with the increased volume of translation and interpreting work. One of these involves abandoning the principle that a translator can only translate into his/her native language. Translators have been encouraged to learn new languages, and Czech, in fact, has already been studied by a number of incumbent EU translators. Some other strategies include appeals to the document drafters to produce texts that are short and simple. It is also considered necessary to limit the categories of documents that are translated (Cunningham, 2001). It will be essential to adapt existing computer and internet software to handle Czech (and the other new EU languages, all of which use the Latin alphabet with added diacritics). This condition is not met at present (see Part V, Electronic media).

In order to ensure the supply of translators and interpreters, the EU has supported a number of language programmes at Czech universities. One of the issues is that not only will competence in English, French or German be required, but competence will also be required in such languages as Danish, Finnish, Greek or Portuguese. It is unlikely that translation of large numbers of official documents into and from these languages will be needed at the national level. However, the Czech Republic will share the 'backyard' with a number of other nations and much more communication will be needed at that level than has been required so far. The provision of adequate tools of language management, including various language services, is likely to lag behind the commencement of political and economic membership. It is true that the languages of all EU members or prospective members can be studied in the Czech Republic at university level, but it is doubtful that the existing programmes will suffice to cover the increased and diversified needs after the onset of EU membership. Incidentally, it can be expected that the procedural language used in internal organs of the Union by Czech representatives will be English rather than French or German, and this will no doubt further reinforce the position of that language in those organisations.

Czech for other EU countries

The issue, not yet fully realised by the Czechs, is that competence in the Czech language will become one of the language problems of other countries of the Union (Nekvapil, 2003c). The issue does not only involve translation and interpreting at the governmental level. With increased contacts and personal mobility the problem of competence will transgress into other areas, particularly in the economic and cultural domains.

A problem of this kind cannot be served by simple management. A need for organised management at many levels can be expected. At present, Czech is being taught in a number of countries, and the Czech government has actively supported a number of programmes through the provision of lecturers. Out of the contemporary 40 teaching fellowships ('lectorships') for teaching Czech abroad, some countries host more than one (with the largest numbers in France and Poland), but Czech courses taught with the help of Czech lecturers are not available in a number of EU countries (Denmark, Greece, Holland, Ireland, Luxemburg and Portugal), at least partly because of the unwillingness of the Czech government to provide the necessary funding. Recently a Centre of Czech Studies has been established in Brussels under the full sponsorship of the Czech Republic. Among the more recent phenomena is also the teaching of Czech in those parts of Germany that adjoin the Czech Republic where the teaching of Czech sometimes commences at the level of compulsory education. As noted by Cink (1999: 37), in Saxony the offering of Czech goes hand in hand with the active support the public gives to the Czech entry into the EU. At Pirna in Saxony, a bilingual German-Czech high school has been established, and Czech is used in selected subjects as the medium of instruction. Saxony may thus become a model for other parts of the EU.

In the case of Slovakia, the communication problem may be solved through avenues other than the teaching of Czech. As noted earlier, the two ethnic groups have practised what Haugen (1966) called *semicommunication* – the mutual use of each speaker's language. To a lesser extent, this is also true for Polish and for Sorbian. There will be a need to continue providing Slovaks with a sufficient amount of Czech linguistic input as well as to make sure that radically more Slovak input is received in the Czech Republic. The joint entry into the EU provides applied linguists with an opportunity to test the power of *semi-communication* as a language management device in more than one group of languages, such as the Romance languages, the Scandinavian languages or some of the Slavic languages.

Languages of Instruction

The language of instruction at all 'normal' schools in the country is, of course, Czech. However, in the school year 1999/2000 there were 18 bilingual high schools (*gymnázium*) in the Czech Republic – with a focus on German (5), French (5), English (4), Spanish (2) and Italian (2). (See Statistická ročenka školství 2000.) As mentioned earlier, in the mid-1990s an attempt was made to establish a Slovak high school in Prague, but the project failed because of the small number of applicants. There is a Polish high school in Český Těšín and other high school level classes in the same region; other ethnic high schools (e.g. Bulgarian) have been mentioned in passing.

The small representation of English among the bilingual high schools should not be interpreted as a sign of attributing English a low level of importance. There were eight monolingual English high schools, five of them in Prague (Nekovářová, 1999). Since some of these schools are not officially registered with the Ministry of Education, their graduates must have their degrees 'notarised' if they want to use them in the same way as local qualifications. (Such 'notarisation' is also required in the case of qualifications gained abroad.) These schools use British or American curricula. The Ministry of Education only has the right to oversee the teaching of Czech, which is taught as the second language or not taught at all. Some of these schools offer the International Baccalaureate.

In the winter semester 1999, there were 30 Czech tertiary institutions and in these the language of instruction was basically Czech. If other languages were used as a medium of instruction, they were used for the teaching of individual subjects by foreign lecturers or in programmes designated for foreign students. Out of 198,961 tertiary students there were 5468 foreign students, some of them studying in Czech but others taking courses in other languages. Among the 30 institutions, 25 offered programmes in English, 16 in German and three in French. There were no programmes offered in Russian. Courses offered in foreign languages varied according to the field of study. For example, all seven faculties of medicine in the Czech Republic offered at least some of their courses programmes in Czech and English (but not in German), while natural science faculties tended to teach courses in Czech, English, and German. Such courses were relatively rare at the Bachelor level, but the number increased in Masters and particularly in doctoral programmes. (For details see Ammon & McConnell, 2002; Nekvapil, 2003c.)

A number of foreign tertiary institutions were active in the country (Nekovářová, 1999). They offered programmes in the language of the country of their origin, but sometimes also in Czech. These programmes were frequently summer schools or specialised programmes. Twelve of these institutions were British or American, two German, one French and one Spanish.

Language Varieties: A Summary

Languages other than Czech

The survey conducted in Part III has demonstrated that the Czech Republic is not only a multicultural but also a multilingual country. Although figures available from the 2001 census (Table 5) reflect only the declared 'mother tongue', not the languages actually used in daily communication, there can be no doubt concerning this claim. Table 5 indicates that, in the 2001 census, 522,663 people reported a 'mother tongue' other than Czech. This represents 5.1% of the target population. However, if we accept that some respondents failed to report their real 'mother tongue', it is probable that more than 6% of the inhabitants possess a close relationship with a language other than Czech.

Types of languages

The largest non-Czech 'mother tongue' declared in the census was Slovak. Romani probably comes second, followed by Polish and German which were declared as 'mother tongue' by 51,000 and 41,000 people respectively. Other languages are represented by smaller populations.

With regard to their provenance, two languages have been at home in the Czech lands for centuries: German and Polish. Romani is a special case in that the Roma have lived in the territory since the 15th century, but the bulk of the Roma who live in the Republic now are migrants from the East. The other languages also arrived recently. Hungarian, Ruthenian, Russian, Slovak and Ukrainian came from the East; Croatian (in the 16th century), Albanian, Bulgarian, Greek, Macedonian and Serbian came from the South. From still further East, the territory experienced the Kalmyck impact after World War I (Nekvapil & Neustupný, 1998), and in the second half of the century the arrival of the Vietnamese and Chinese languages (the latter unaccounted for in this study). A language that came from the West is English. This range of languages includes many Slavic languages which provide the challenge of the possible use of Haugen's *semicommunication* as a means of language management. This point has been emphasised in this paper. The rich linguistic variety in the territory is further enriched by languages such as Hungarian, Greek or Vietnamese – languages that are linguistically very distant from Czech and pose a question about the ways in which they can be developed as a resource by their hosts: will they be lost or will they be retained, both for their value as human experience and for their future economic potential (Clyne, 1991)? It is recommended that the latter path be selected, to prevent the need to build up the competence *de novo* at considerable cost.

Almost all of the languages represented in the territory of the Czech Republic have their centre of gravity abroad. However, there are at least two that do not serve as national languages in other countries. One of them is Romani, which is not a national language anywhere. No one seems to care about Romani. The other language is Ruthenian, which has only just started to appear as a codified minority language in Slovakia.

Maintenance and shift

Throughout this paper, it has been shown that language shift towards Czech is on the move. While communities may still retain their sense of ethnic identity

Table 5 Ethnic background and mother tongue in the 2001 census (Český statistický úřad, January 2003)

Mother tongue	Population according to mother tongue	Ethnic background									
		Czech, Moravian Silesian	Slovak	Hungarian	Roma	Polish	German	Ruthenian	Ukrainian	Other	Not declared
Czech	9,707,397	9,525,265	32,529	2,196	4,527	4,064	10,836	560	2,385	16,605	108,430
Slovak	208,723	48,877	153,284	448	402	54	81	30	163	1,571	3,813
Romani	23,209	12,289	2,992	66	6,672	6	10	1	8	317	848
Polish	50,740	5,029	144	18	6	44,825	43	0	44	186	445
German	41,328	11,138	245	30	5	104	27,682	2	27	1,339	756
Other	121,795	17,526	3,276	11,844	65	2,815	308	507	19,336	61,681	4,437
Not declared	76,868	21,005	720	70	69	100	146	6	149	505	54,098
Total	10,230,060	9,641,129	193,190	14,672	11,746	51,968	39,106	1,106	22,112	82,204	172,827

(although there is a shift there as well), linguistically they assimilate at a high rate. This is a shame – both because the cultural and linguistic variety is impoverished, and because functional resources are lost. It is the Czech society that should stand up and try to stop the deprivation of its own linguistic environment.

However, communities and individuals who wish to assimilate should be given the right to pursue their intent. Language is not only a symbol of ethnic identity; it is also a symbol of social stability, cultured living and relative economic prosperity. While for many immigrants from the East and South their language represents their ethnic identity, Czech is a symbol of stability, culture and prosperity for them. Language managers should be prepared to provide advice to the communities and individuals about the deep motives for their language management decisions. When a community or an individual decides not to maintain its language, do they simply support the interests of the Czech matrix community, or do they act in their own interest? And how can they empower themselves to carry through what they decide to do?

Language management in the European Community

It is likely that the Czech Republic will enter the EU shortly and this will have an impact on what has been said in this paper. The configuration of interest and power in that larger society will be different. It is possible that the ethnic composition of the Czech Republic and its individual communities will undergo substantial changes. It is too early to predict what may occur.

Language Policy of the Czech State

The Czech state exerts influence on the language situation in the Czech Republic in several ways. One is through its education policy; the other is through the cultivation of language.

Education policy

Language-in-education policy is directed towards Czech as well, but this aspect has not been subjected to analysis. Other languages are attended to in several respects:

(1) Education in community languages is proclaimed as state policy, but in fact it only occurs in the case of Polish. Some modest approaches have begun to appear in the case of Romani. The Ministry of Education guarantees to support courses of an ethnic group language if there is a group of at least three to four children interested; yet it is often impossible to find a competent teacher at the school or in the local community.
(2) Language-in-education policy is also directed towards the acquisition of foreign languages. At the level of the state, the obligatory choice of Russian has been abolished, and free selection permitted. This 'liberalism' has, in fact, only reinforced the selection of English and German.

Language cultivation

There is no evidence of language cultivation activities for any language other than Czech. This is not detrimental to the languages if they have a centre abroad which supports such cultivation. In fact, most community languages in the

Czech Republic are branches of languages that are national languages in other states. However, since these languages are 'isolated' (Vašek, 1976) branches in the Czech Republic, there is a need to give thought to the special features that arise under the conditions of such isolation. At present, this problem is no one's responsibility. Moreover, in many instances, the community languages and their uses have not been given attention even at the level of description (noting).

A language that is in urgent need of elaboration, not through committees but in actual use, is Romani. But apart from supporting the modest literary production of the community, the state has done nothing to activate networks in which such elaboration (as well as maintenance) could take place.

As far as Czech is concerned, the Modern system of language cultivation, often based on the pre-war Prague School approach, is practised. This means that there has been little change for a Standard language that is basically oriented towards the middle class. The recent memory of transition from a 'socialist' to a 'capitalist' socioeconomic system renders inapplicable any policy that would defend the interests of the weak. Problems of variation, some of which have been outlined, still await some change in the socioeconomic paradigm to be noted, evaluated and adjusted.

The usual forms of support, in the form of publication subsidies (Zpráva, 2002) are available for a variety of community languages.

PART IV: MANAGEMENT OF SITUATIONS

The Framework

Part III has examined the ways in which interaction is managed with regard to the selection and use of language varieties. In this section, the management of interaction in individual 'situations' will be discussed. Situations are relatively stable sets (configurations) of interaction strategies. They are stable because they re-occur and because such re-occurrence leads to automation. Since re-occurrence differs in different communities, the range of situations is subject to variation. For example, in Japan, where taxis are widely used, there are relatively fixed 'ways of speaking' within the taxi (greetings, levels of honorific speech, directions to the driver, asking for a receipt, etc.). Using the taxi is a specific situation. In the Czech Republic, taxis are not used extensively, and the way of speaking is not fixed to the same extent. If there is routinisation, it derives from other situations. One often speaks of 'defining' a situation, meaning that speakers assign a particular set of strategies to particular recurring and recognisable sequences of behaviour. Situations of daily life are usually strongly defined (Neustupný, 1993b); in other words, there are multiple strategies that generate their specific recurring features. This phenomenon is emphasised by Müllerová *et al.* (1992: 108) when they analyse, for example, shopping situations or interaction between doctors and their patients.

The existence of situations has considerable relevance for language management. The selection of a particular situation in the process of communication can become an object of management. The acquisition of strategies for situational sets and the ability to 'correctly' participate in them is not automatic. Kraus (1997b: 291) refers to this fact when he speaks of ' . . . the need to master some specialized communicative activities (debates, public appearances, the stylization of special-ized and academic discourses, drafting of legal texts and use manuals) . . . ' In the Czech Republic, the automation of interaction within some situations of use has remained underdeveloped. While much of this ability is gained through simple management in discourse, there can be organised management (for example in schools, companies or offices) to create and use automated situational sets of interactional means. In this and the following sections, examples are taken from transcripts provided by (Müllerová *et al.*, 1992), that cover a considerable range of spoken language situations.

Situations cluster in domains. The importance of domains for sociolinguistics has been emphasised by Fishman (1972). In the following survey, Fishman's concept that domains are *emic* sets varying across different societies is applied. For example, while under other circumstances religion may figure as a major domain, its importance in Czech society is diminished and can better be under-stood as a subdivision within the culture domain. Understandably, domains overlap. A list of domains used in this paper includes:

- daily life domain;
- family domain;
- friendship domain;
- education domain;
- work domain;
- public domain; and
- culture domain.

Situational sets include the distribution of power. In each situation, partici-pants are specified and represent differing interests (Jernudd & Neustupný, 1987) and differing distribution of power (Fairclough, 1989). The issue of power is important for the assessment of problems that occur in situations.

Attention given in linguistics to the distribution of language problems in domains and situations is still limited, and occasionally discussion is restricted to providing questions based on personal experience. Problems listed in this paper are not exhaustive.

Management in the Daily Life Domain

The daily life domain contains such situations as in individuals' daily physical maintenance, in eating and in daily behaviour at home, in transportation, in shopping, in receiving services (at post office, banks, medical services), in eating out, etc.

Among these situations, the language of services has been the object of rela-tively severe management throughout the 1990s, after the return of the Czech Republic to a market economy. The problem was that language usage was auto-mated at a level that did not agree with the new relationship between the customer and the attendant. The management processes, which introduced more polite attitude on the side of the attendant, were largely successful, but they have not yet been completed. At the beginning of the last decade of the millennium, shop attendants still occupied the position of superior partici-pants (see Nekvapil & Neustupný, 2005; Slavíčková, 1993), and they generated expressions of indifference, ennui, and rejection, occasionally even of aggressiveness; a similar set sometimes characterised the communication of the customers (Müllerová *et al.*, 1992). These sets were never accepted as natural; they became objects of negative evaluation and of further management. Frequently curt replies such as *ne* 'no', *není* 'not available' or *nemáme* 'we haven't got any' occurred without any apology. For example:

Cust.   *Teplý jenom, ty normální nemáte.*
          'Warm ones only? Haven't you got the normal ones?'
Att.   *Ne.*
          'No.' (Müllerová *et al.*, 1992: 71, transcription simplified)

However, as Müllerová *et al.* (1992: 84) note, there were attendants who maintained the norm. They apologised for not being able to provide the goods (*opravdu nemáme* 'really (unfortunately) we haven't got them'); they apologised for the time they would take (*hned to bude* 'I'll be there soon'), and they used polite intonation and a lively tone of speech.

At the present time, the situational set for most situations of the daily life domain has reallocated the position of power to the customer, as usual in the 'Western' countries. Even in the case of medical services, the previously unquestioned superiority of the doctor has eased. All these adjustments have been reflected in communication in patterns that do not result in the overt assignment of power or, on the contrary, overt solidarity (such as camaraderie) – the contemporary solution is more subtle.

Another management process that stands out in Müllerová *et al.*'s (1992) data is negotiation about the object of purchase. In view of the lack of advertising, customers did not possess sufficient vocabulary to describe merchandise, and it was the role of the attendant, after a process of negotiation, to provide adjustment on the basis of their own experience:

Att.   *Ňákej, vy chcete ňákej malinkej stan.*
          'Some, you want some small tent?'
Cust.   *Nó, takovej, no nemusí bejt úplně malej, no ale -*
          'Well, such a, well not necessarily very small, well but'
Att.   *Takovejdle ňákej,*
          'Something like this.'
Cust.   *Spíš hlavně co nejlehčí, no*
          'Rather mainly as light as possible, well'
Att.   *Ten vůbec neni.*
          'That one is not available at all.'
Cust.   *Vůbec neni, a dostáváte někdy -*
          'Not available at all, but do you sometimes get (it)'
Att.   *Málokdy, vy myslíte ten silonovej stan.*
          'Rarely, you are thinking of the nylon tent.'
Cust.   *No, no, no.*
          'Yes, yes, yes.' (Müllerová *et al.*, 1992: 70, transcription simplified)

In this extract, the customer attempts to describe the type of tent she wants to purchase. After negotiation, it becomes clear that the object of her inquiry was a tent made of nylon. The pattern of negotiation appears in almost all examples quoted in Müllerová *et al*. (1992). This management strategy is applied because of a particular language problem: the inability of the customer to specify exactly the type of goods wanted.

Management in the Family Domain

The Czech family of the 1990s was moving towards the postmodern pattern. On one hand, sexual behaviour was relatively free while conception and birth were limited. Also, home catering used the possibilities provided by pre-processed or fully processed foods. On the other hand, formal marriages, although greatly decreased, were still the often unquestioned norm (Možný, 2002).

Within this pattern there is room for more conversation, which requires the development of conversational routines beyond what Bernstein (1964) once called 'restricted speech'. Family conversation is widely developed, irrespective of the family's social standing (Hoffmannová *et al*., 1999). Within the modernisation and postmodernisation process, terms of address in the family domain are continuously reallocated, and new terms are born. This management process often remains largely unconscious, except for noting in individual situations, and its results are strongly automated. In Czech, the reciprocal *ty* 'you' address within families has long been the norm. However, in direct address to parents (and grandparents), the usual terms used are kinship terms (*tati!* 'dad', *babičko!* 'grandma', etc.), not pronouns (*'ty!'*) or first names (*'Jirko!'*). Address/reference by first name is rare, though its occurrence is increasing, but it is managed (noted, and evaluated). This seems to be an incoming usage. Also managed (noted and evaluated) is address to members of the family from the point of view of a child (*maminko!* 'mother' in address to one's wife, even when children are not present). These forms are in the process of being abandoned, at least in the urban sector – they represent an outgoing usage.

Problems of intergenerational usage

There is a problem of intergenerational understanding, but it does not reach major proportions. The slang of the younger generation is often derived from English, and it is difficult for the older generation to understand. The younger generation is interested in computers both in word processing and in other functions. The time the youngsters use at the computer is deducted from the time that, in the situational norms of the parents, should be used for communication with other members of the family. While this is one problem, another problem is the 'excessive use' (i.e. use that does not agree with the parents' situational norms) of computer terminology.

Yet another language problem noticeable in family situations is the vulgarisation of language of the children. This is connected with de-tabooisation of the language of the media, which is more typically used by the younger rather than by the older generation as a source of new linguistic expression. However, this phenomenon can also be considered as a consequence of the final breakdown of the traditional family situation in which parents were superior participants and children were obliged to eschew 'impolite' language in front of them. For parents, the older norms apply, while the children's norms belong to a more recent norm set.

'Indeterminacy of expression'

Müllerová *et al.* (1992) include a transcript of a situation in which a grandmother (age 57) and her granddaughter (age 20) participate. The granddaughter occasionally asks a question or comments, but on the whole this is a monologue in which the grandmother talks about her youth. There is one feature that invites attention because it seems to be a problem characteristic for the family domain that reoccurs in other transcripts in the same collection, including the otherwise cultivated exchanges within a radio discussion (1992: 223). It is the high degree of what Müllerová *et al.* (1992: 29) call 'indeterminacy of expression' (see also Hoffmannová, 1994). This includes incomplete sentences, shortcuts, a high frequency of demonstratives (*ten, takovej, takle*, etc.), connectors (*a, no, tak, nebo,* etc.), semantically blurred words (*ňák, ňákej,* etc.) and fillers (*prostě, jako, dyš,* etc.). In the same group, a large number of corrections and rephrasings may be included. A keyword quotation from the transcript is:

> *Ted' sou všude silnice, no tak to už nikdo nemuže . . . tak ňák kam by se šel čvachtat do bláta.* 'Now there are paved roads everywhere, well so, that, nobody can any more . . . so you know where one could go to walk in the mud' [meaning:'now there are paved roads everywhere, nobody can/has to walk any more in the mud'] (Müllerová *et al.*, 1992: 15, transcription simplified)

In this sentence, the underlined words are 'superfluous', they mark hesitation and problems with sentence planning. There is a change of syntactic planning after *nemuže.* All this testifies to the expression problems faced by the speaker. Is this indeterminacy of expression a feature of Czech conversational situations, and if it is, can one attribute it to the account of the grammatical type of Czech? Or is it the relative absence of cultivated models of speech (salons, formal parties, sermons, traditional narratives, etc.) that is responsible for its pervasiveness in spoken Czech? At least in the family or friendship domains, this phenomenon is probably rarely noted or evaluated; of course, it does receive negative evaluation in more formal speech contexts.

Management in the Friendship Domain

Parties

In the 1990s, individualism was apparent in surveys. Only 24% of Czechs responded negatively to the suggestion that 'one can never be sufficiently careful in dealing with others'; the European average was 31% (Možný, 2002). Large-scale 'parties', which to some extent took over from the highbrow salons, were not the general pattern for socialisation with others. (This phenomenon was at least partly the consequence of the occupation during WWII and the following 'socialist' period when meetings in private houses were considered politically suspicious.) With regard to language, this fact implies that management of language (i.e. topics, variety used, etc.) lacks networks in which it could develop.

Whenever such language management is needed, it is left to isolated individuals to develop. Automation of communication does not take place easily.

In the two-couple party recorded in Müllerová *et al.* (1992), (but not reproduced here because of its length), the lack of management of topics and networks is apparent. E1 is unrestricted in dominating the floor in the first part of the recording. Other participants only gloss on her topics. The theme of the second part of the recording (food) is introduced by E1's husband S. The part commences with a little bit of a dialogue, but subsequently the floor is taken by H who presents a story. Both E1's and H's topics go unchallenged for long periods of time. There are few questions and little exchange of information or opinion. Müllerová *et al.* (1992: 44) explain the lack of interruption and response as an attempt to maintain harmony within the group; hence, a management device. There is enough humour in the conversation, which can be considered a part of the Czech conversation set, again a management strategy – positive politeness strategy (Brown & Levinson, 1987) – to maintain the smooth relationship of the participants. As in the grandmother's narrative referred to earlier, there is a large amount of indeterminacy of expression, proof that expression problems are present at the discourse level.

Without further empirical work, it is difficult to generalise about the power relationships in the friendship domain. However, it seems that on the whole participants are equal. The domination of the floor by E1 and H in the conversation just cited is unlikely to have been affected by their social status. The friendship situational set seems to require in Czech that solidarity with equal status is applied, a condition that leads to the use of the *ty* address.

The '*ty*' ritual

An interesting instance of management in friendship discourse is the ritual through which speakers shift their *vy* ('you', corresponding to French *vous*) usage to *ty* ('you', corresponding to French *tu*) (see Skwarska, 2001, mainly for Polish, but also mentioning Czech). A ritual is needed because the change affects an important strategy within a situational set. The ritual is usually initiated by a senior or superior, and probably male in relation to female. Power is needed to achieve this important task. Our field notes contain the following example:

J (male, approx. 45), L (female, approx. 30, co-worker)
J: *Netykáme my si už?* 'Don't we use *ty* yet?'
L: *Ne.* (smiles, looks embarrassed) 'No.'
J: *Tak já jsem Jirka.* (offers his handshake) 'Well, I am Jirka.'
L: *Lenka.* (accepts the handshake) 'Lenka.'
J: *Tak ahoj.* 'So, hi.'
L: *Ahoj.* 'Hi.'
     (The conversation proceeds, *ty* is used hereafter.)

The ritual consists of giving one's first name, a handshake and an informal greeting *ahoj*, which is incompatible with *vy* but compatible with *ty*. What appears to be a matter of momentary decision is often a result of careful consideration, which may include all pre-implementation stages of the management process.

Management in the Education Domain

Communication in school situations has been at the centre of attention of Czech social psychologists, and in connection with the advent of communicatively oriented linguistics (Helbig, 1991) it began to be studied also by Czech linguists and educationalists. Svobodová (2000) writes about a number of problems she noted in the interaction of teachers and pupils in primary schools (particularly in Years 1–4). Her list of 'retarding and blocking factors' of school communication is comprehensive (pp. 90–92). It is particularly remarkable that the participant responsible for most problems seems to be the teacher, who holds a considerable amount of power. Teachers introduce the following problems:

(1) Often they act in an excessively dynamic way, changing the stimuli addressed to the pupils too quickly, while sometimes remaining too slow and dull to raise the pupils' interest.
(2) They talk too much and consequently move the pupil into the role of a passive observer. The pupil's speech is interrupted, with the teacher's talk sometimes overlapping with the pupil's.
(3) The communicative attitude of the teacher is too emotional.
(4) The teacher uses constructions unfamiliar to the pupil, constructions such as *dám si to do tašky* 'I'll put it to the bag' instead of 'put it in your bag', infinitive constructions such as *psát a nemluvit* 'to write, and not to talk' instead of the daily-life 'write and don't talk' or the elliptical *sešity na kraj* 'note books to the side (of your desks)'.
(5) There is much formal and unnatural language, and of hypercorrection in the speech of the teachers. The use of the Standard in the classroom is a question much debated among educationalists (cf. Brabcová, 1996; Čechová, 1996).
(6) One of the most important problems cited by Svobodová is the 'highlighting of the status of the teacher and her controlling role (prohibitions and commands)'. A typical feature is the high frequency of the word *já* 'I'.

The rules that govern the teacher's behaviour are rules of the normal classroom situational set. Svobodová claims that they present problems for the pupils and this may well be so. In any case, as the pupils advance through their educational career, they become acquainted with this set. In Years 1–4, they are still unaccustomed to them.

Changes in educational situation sets

In postmodern societies, interaction in classrooms is being managed to remove from the situational sets the emphasis on the power of the teacher and of the teaching institution. The teacher's desk grows smaller. Student's desks and chairs can move freely within the classroom, and there is no fixed seating order. Teachers (usually at upper levels) can emphasise their closeness to the students by initiating reciprocal address (in English by using first names). The beginnings of this process are only being experienced in the Czech Republic in a few private 'experimental' schools. The arrangement of the classroom space is traditional. The distance between teachers and pupils is considerable; at primary schools pupils are addressed with the *ty* forms, while they are expected to respond with the polite *vy*. However, at the secondary school level, some teachers combine the first name of the student with the *vy* forms (*Viktore, pojďte k tabuli*. 'Victor, come (a *vy* form) to the blackboard'). Unlike Patočka (2000: 81), who considers this pattern as recent, the authors have registered it as early as the beginning of the 1970s.

The situational set of communication at Czech universities is also distant from the postmodern pattern. The students may be seated around a single table if the class is small; however, the teacher may occupy any place according to his or her liking, and address is reciprocal at the *vy* level. Cases have been recorded when young tutors exchanged *ty* forms with their students, but this behaviour has been overtly noted and adjustment required by the head of department. This process demonstrates that change in the situational sets is imminent. However, at present it is expected that students communicate the higher status of the teacher through topical, non-verbal, and other means, even if, in this practice, they are normally allowed a considerable degree of latitude. Teachers teaching within the same department exchange *vy* forms unless they have already established the *ty* usage in other situations. University students have used reciprocal *ty* to each other since the 1950s. The teacher/student power relationship clearly favours the teachers, and the linguistic reciprocity (the use of *vy* forms) is not sufficient to disguise this fact.

Children of refugees

The normal communicative routines at schools have recently been disrupted by the arrival of people from the Afganistan, Armenia, Belarus, Georgia, India, Moldova, Romania, Ukraine, or Vietnam who were applying for refugee status or work visas. While only 1500 applied for residence in 1995, in 2001 the number exceeded 15,000. This increase also implies an influx of foreign children into Czech schools, which are communicatively unprepared for it. Neither are the Czech children who are expected to accept these children into their friendship networks. The Ministry of Education did not start thinking about the problems involved until the end of the 1990s. However, the government is mainly concerned with the socioeconomic aspects of this type of migration and pays minimal attention to its communicative impact. A positive development is that linguists have started to be interested in intercultural communication problems within the education domain. (For details see Zimová, 2001.)

Management in the Work Domain

In the 1990s, the concept of 'economic management' replaced other leading concepts in Czech companies (Bozděchová, 1997), and this change entailed changes in modes of communication. The communication situational set changed. Managers at various levels now had to defend their views. They had to speak to people and had to be able to 'sell' what they have brought with them to meetings. Communication problems within companies have become one of the most important issues at the present time.

Example of a meeting

A meeting within a company has been presented in Müllerová *et al.* (1992). The company was a large enterprise that engaged in engineering and consultation assistance to other companies, and the subject of the meeting was a nuclear electricity plant. There were seven men, aged between 40 and 60, with a 57-year-old chairman. The set included informal speech, all participants exchanging *ty* and first names, and using a great quantity of specialised terminology. The chairman exercised clear leadership, due to his expertise in the subject matter. His authoritativeness sometimes verged on criticism, as when he rebuffed one of his colleagues by saying:

A: *Hele Pavle. Tady se, ty se musíš na to, ty se musíš zase trochu jaksi voprostit . . .*
'Look, Pavel, here, you must in that regard, you must again somehow liberate yourself from . . .' (Müllerová *et al.*, 1992: 158, transcription simplified)

As noted by Müllerová *et al.* (1992), these and other problems probably went unnoticed. Due to the complicated syntax and terminology, as well as the routinised semantics, little of the conversation can be understood by outsiders without translation. However, the authors correctly conclude that such apparent problems should not necessarily lead to language management from the outside. Currently, there is much talk of placing language consultants in large companies: such a staff addition may be beneficial in considering the style of forms and correspondence, of manuals, of public relations and of many other aspects of communication. However, language management need not meddle with those areas of communication which function in a satisfactory way without the intrusion of the linguist (Müllerová *et al.*, 1992: 171); in other words, when no problems are decoded by participants in the situations.

Communication in joint ventures

The period after 1989 was marked by the appearance of a number of joint ventures – mostly German–Czech, but sometimes also American–Czech or French–Czech – in the economy of the Czech Republic. Some of these ventures have been controlled by foreign companies. Even though the economic contributions of these enterprises have been substantial, their day-to-day operation is not without problems and some of these problems concern communication. Normally, these enterprises are managed by foreign managers, but the majority of employees at all levels are Czechs. Problems that appear in these companies are often interpreted as originating in different cultural standards, but many of them are connected with the use of language in intra-company communication (Nekula, 2002a). The socioeconomic dominance of foreign managers is reinforced by their communicative dominance. Managers normally communicate with their subordinates in their own first language and expect acknowledgement of this pattern from their subordinates. Subordinate managers and others do accept the situational pattern imposed on them by the foreign managers, but they are not always able to comply satisfactorily with the imposed set in interaction. The resulting avoidance and interactional errors are sometimes interpreted by foreign managers as passivity, lack of talent, submissiveness or other similar behaviour. Even though large companies such as Škoda-Volkswagen (15,000 employees) arrange courses in Czech for their 'visiting' managers, such courses are not welcome. Language has not merely a practical but also a symbolic value.

German (or English) symbolise management, in other words power, while Czech is symbolic of the actual manufacturing work. Since foreign managers cannot speak Czech, and their Czech subordinates possess only little or no knowledge of the foreign language involved, interpreters are used. Apart from being expensive, this mode of communication further confirms the differential status of the languages used (Nekula, 2002a).

Needless to say, no one is interested in the production of problems or in the construction of a long-term boundary between foreign and Czech employees. In the Škoda-Volkswagen plant, it is apparent that foreign as well as local employees systematically avoid the use of ethnic categories such as 'German' or 'Czech' in conversation, while emphasising their professional identity and association with a 'supranational' enterprise (Nekvapil, 1997b).

Management in Public Domain

Language of politics

As Hlavsová (1997) points out, within the political system of the pre-Velvet Revolution period, most speeches were recitations of scripted texts. On-the-spot public speaking was virtually unknown; after 1989, this practice resulted in the lack of preparation to engage in public speaking among politicians. In a survey cited by Hlavsová (1997), close to 50% of respondents claimed that they would refuse a public position in view of their inability to appear in the public and formulate their thoughts on the spot. The ability to structure a situation cannot easily be transferred from other situations. Hlavsová quotes an actress turned member of Parliament who could hardly control nervousness when she spoke on the floor of the Parliament. Of course, many politicians, such as the later Prime Minister Miloš Zeman, were 'born' speakers from the outset. One of the components of the situational set that was difficult to master was the use of Standard (as opposed to Common) Czech.

The situational set has been noted and negatively evaluated by some sensitive speakers. President Havel claimed that he was astonished to find how television forced him to embody thought into short sentences, into *bons mots*, slogans and exclamations, and 'how easily my television image differs from my real self' (Hlavsová, 1997).

Obviously, not all features of linguistic behaviour in the political domain are evaluated negatively. Some vocabulary of Havel's discourse, such as *smysluplný* 'meaningful' or *sebestřednost* 'self-centredness' have become fashionable words.

Language of law and administration

Language in situations that belong to this area shares the problem of many other languages: the problem that has been referred to when 'plain language movements' (Kaplan & Baldauf, 1997: 74) are discussed. This is at least partly a new issue. Before the 1990s, in Czechoslovakia law was an area of little importance and government required less elaboration. Kraus (1997b) refers to the recent fear of bureaucracy and the disrespect for legal regulations; there is a fear of problems originating in the new complicated language of law and administration. The quality of legal language, he claims, is low; texts are difficult to understand and ambiguous (p. 292). The problem is not one deriving from the reader.

In 1996 the ambiguity of legal texts was defended by Judge Varvařovský of the Constitutional Court, who emphasised the overall sense and purpose of each act against the meaning of individual words or sentences. As Kraus (1997a) observes, this principle, while being unable to disambiguate particular documents, can lead to complete disregard for the quality of administrative and legal texts.

Kraus (1997a) has also noted that, among those who discussed the problem, too much attention was being paid to problems of orthography. He emphasised that in agreement with discussions in other countries, the problem of legal language should be conceived widely, including semantic issues and issues of the structuring of content in general, rather than simple attention to problems of language in the narrow sense of the word.

Management in the Cultural Domain

Science and humanities

This subdivision of the cultural domain contains both written language (papers, reports, etc.) and spoken language (lectures, conferences, discussions, teaching, etc.) situations. According to Daneš (1997b), two features have characterised the structuring of such situations so far:

(1)   a high level of modal expressions, and
(2)   the laxness of composition patterns (an essay type prevails).

In other words, Czech science communication has so far belonged to the 'Teutonic intellectual style' as defined by Galtung (1981). This state of affairs is currently changing with the operation of adjustment strategies that are converting the system to approximate the Anglo-American style, and this leads to the emergence of communication problems.

There have been suggestions by individual scientists that, within the situational set for Czech academic life, English entirely replace Czech. As Daneš argues (1997b), this is not a realistic proposition. Czech, at present, serves as a tool within academic situations perfectly well. While there are contact situations in which English or other languages have traditionally been used, there are others, such as local conferences or publications for wider readership, as well as tertiary education situations, where the use of Czech is natural. No doubt, the mastering of Anglo–American situational sets (including, e.g. the spoken language, immediate and idiomatic reaction to others in discussion, formulae for chairing academic meetings, etc.), in which Czechs lag behind academics from systems where the English situational set is used, remains on the program of the day. However, such patterns should not necessarily *replace* the Czech ones.

It is interesting to note that during the 40 years when Czechoslovakia belonged to the Soviet camp, the language of Czech science has held the fort against a possible invasion of Russian. As in the language at large, no major influence has taken place in this register.

Literature

Literature represents an important set of language acts. Existing situational sets – ways of approaching the creation and consumption of literary works – are changing constantly, and these changes belong to the most important management processes. Literature is the laboratory of language. Čmejrková (1997a) has accounted for one of the recent changes, the change towards postmodern literature. She outlines the strategies of heterogeneity, fragmentation, interruption, conflict of elements, orientation toward detail, variation, paraphrase and many others. These are initially management strategies that create new literature. As they become the standard fare in Czech literature, their status as management strategies weakens, eventually to disappear completely.

Media

Behaviour in media situations is subject to a number of clusters of strategies. With a radical change in the political system after 1989, the system was altered and it was often felt that anarchy prevailed – that journalists were unable to work with the sources of information and in the process of formatting them for transmission to the public (Bartošek, 1997). The newly established tabloid press and private television channels seemed to give unlimited freedom to journalists. This situation, to a large extent, still survives. In language matters, the norm has been relaxed, both with regard to the type of variety (Common Czech elements are frequently used) and spelling.

However, not all changes that followed 1989 should be evaluated negatively. The media have become interconnected and assumed the form of dialogical networks (Leudar & Nekvapil, 2004). Television discusses what has been reported in the press and vice versa. The media began to be used for 'discussions' between politicians who had never met. In this way, a politician can express his views without actually having acknowledged his opponents as valid communicative partners. It is also necessary to concede what has already been accepted as obvious – the new post-communist political discourse. This discourse had to be introduced, and in the process the media had the lion's share. One can easily observe how this change from the old to the new discourse proceeded through a complex and extended series of acts of language management (Nekvapil, 1997c). Not only did journalists stop using expressions embedded in communist ideology, but they also began to use the language of new ideologies. In the following example, the journalist works on a change in attitude to the word *kapitalismus* which, prior to 1989, had an utterly negative connotation shared by communists and most other intellectuals. It was difficult to use the word in reference to a positively evaluated social formation immediately after the Velvet Revolution.

> *Z toho marasmu, kam nás komunisté zatáhli, nás může dostat jen systém, který je sice nedokonalý, ale nejlepší, který známe. Systém, který za léta dokázal svoji životaschopnost, který zaručuje občanům svobody, dodržování jejich práv i prosperitu. Má takové ošklivé jméno – kapitalismus.*
> There is only one system which can extricate us from the mess the communists got us into, a system that may be imperfect, but is the best one we know. A system which throughout the years of its existence has proved its vitality, and which guarantees freedom to the citizens, the observance of their rights, and prosperity. It has an ugly name – capitalism. (Lidové noviny, 28 November 1990)

Book/periodicals reading situations

According to the OECD Adult Literacy Survey (Literacy, 2000), more than 70% of Czech adults claimed that they read one or more books monthly. In this respect, the Czech Republic was second after New Zealand, in the same over 70% group as Ireland, Germany and Australia. In the 1990s, the number of titles published in Czech increased from 3767 to 12,551; and book loans in libraries also increased (Možný, 2002). The growth was paralleled in the publication of periodicals. This trend means that written language was well represented, and the situations of its use in reading provided management models for both writing and for the use of the Standard in speaking (see Standard and Common language in Part III). Since the Standard has remained unsupported by religious situations (see the following section) or by formal communication at parties (see previous section), this modelling probably played an important role in management towards the use of the Standard in general. The high viewing rate of television (the Czech Republic ranked 4th out of 18 OECD countries, Literacy, 2000), which on the whole uses the Standard, further reinforced the same trend. An analogous support of the Standard can be seen in the recovery of the Czech theatre after 1993 (Možný, 2002).

Religion

Sociological surveys conducted during the 1990s confirmed that Czech society was the most secular in contemporary Europe. Only 39% of respondents in surveys claimed belief in God; no other European country showed figures below 50%, with the European average being 77%. Similarly, only 6.6% of Czechs belonged to a religious association as against 71.5% of Swedes (Možný, 2002). This pattern leads to the low functional load of religious situations with the result that religious discourse was a very marginal phenomenon. On this ground, the remaining role of the language of the religious canon (the Bible) as a model for individual or social language management was lost. Religious language has not served as a management model, either in its individual lexical features or in the stylistic values it carries.

Management in Contact Situations

A distinction that cuts across all domains is that of native and contact situations. Contact situations are situations in which contact between different cultures takes place. This contact can be between different varieties within the same culture (as in the case of the culture associated with different genders, regional groups or social strata), but normally the term is reserved for ethnically different culture. Problems in contact situation do not affect problems of grammatical competence (traditional 'language') alone; they extend to non-grammatical communicative competence (such as selection of content or non-verbal communication) and sociocultural competence (what people think or actually do). Although interaction problems also occur in native situations, contact situation are characterised by their special density (Neustupný, 1985).

In the Czech Republic there are internal ethnic groups in the case of which we do not expect other problems than problems of grammatical competence (e.g.

the German community). In communication with members of the Slovak community, non-verbal communication problems may occasionally appear, although they may be covert for most participants. Non-grammatical communication problems among the Vietnamese in contact with the matrix community have been extensively discussed in Part III. However, the most difficult problems are encountered in communication with the Roma; owing to visibility of these problems, the matter is serious. This fact notwithstanding, no research has been conducted on such issues to date. Nevertheless, it is obvious that the Roma follow different sociocultural behaviour, communicate differently, and demonstrate considerable differences in their use of grammatical competence as well.

Although there is variation with some Roma operating at a very small distance from the matrix community, many do engage in sociocultural behaviour that greatly diverges from the matrix norms. This sociocultural behaviour is connected by Czech participants with their non-grammatical communicative behaviour: the Roma form networks differently, they raise different topics and engage in different non-verbal behaviour. Many Czechs believe that the Roma do not smile or laugh, and possess no sense of humour. However, anyone who knows the Roma culture through their narratives or proverbs will disagree. Of course, laughter is a component of non-verbal communication that is most easily affected in contact situations. These differences in sociocultural and non-grammatical communicative behaviour create serious barriers between the Roma and the matrix community.

Czechs and foreigners in external contact situations

Not all Czechs possess the competence to communicate in foreign languages (see Part III). Among those who do, many command the knowledge of more than one. Some foreigners are surprised that, apart from English, Czechs are also relatively competent in German. Since the memory of WWII has not been completely erased, many Czechs of the older generation react more favourably to being addressed in English than German, which was the symbol of political domination and is currently a function of the German economic expansion in the Czech Republic. However, German tourists are of great importance for the country, and it is probably the current tourist situation, rather than the past contact with the Germans, that contributes to Czech competence in the language.

At the present time, quite a few foreigners, mainly North Americans and Germans who are resident in the country, try to communicate in Czech. However, Czechs are still unused to others speaking Czech and tend to respond in their English or German that may be at a level lower than the Czech of the foreigner (see Crown, 1996). This is one of the reasons why foreigners mark Czechs as communicatively arrogant.

In contact situations that employ English, the use of first names in English conversation according to the strategies common in English is monitored, if not avoided. This fact has also been confirmed by Sherman (2001). In Czech-German enterprises directed by German managers, Czech speakers have reported that it is difficult to switch to *du*-forms (German equivalents of the Czech *ty* forms). Furthermore, if the switch to *du*-forms is executed, it has fewer communicative and sociocultural concomitants than the use of *ty* forms in native Czech situations (Nekula, 2002a).

Problems of Situations: A Summary

The use of language in individual communicative situations involves language problems. Such language problems certainly occur in the Czech Republic. What is problematic in the case of situations is not only the selection of a particular variety of language. There are many other rules that occur in clusters – each cluster being symptomatic of a situation.

While we reviewed individual situations, it has been repeatedly confirmed that the world of Czech communication changed radically in the 1990s, when the domination of the Communist Party and the Soviet Union came to an end. Many problems have been solved, and many have persisted. Of course, new problems appeared that are unconnected to the past.

Within the daily life domain, in particular in the context of services, there has been a change from the power of the distributors of services and goods to the power of the consumer. This change required an additional change in the whole structure of politeness, of topics, of non-verbal communication and of other strategies inherent in the situational set. Not all problems have been managed to the satisfaction of all participants; one of the tasks for future research will be to determine in what direction and how the power-oriented changes should proceed further.

In the family domain, new problems stand out. It will be necessary to watch in what way the situational set will stabilise in communication between members of various generations.

In education, it is obvious that some teachers and other participants are unhappy about the teacher-authority-guided situational set; in other words, participants in the educational process note, evaluate and suggest adjustment. This is not unlike the process that can be observed in other societies. A number of communication strategies are likely to change, and the educational situation will never be the same again. Among the other problems within this domain, the need to adjust education in the case of children of refugees and other foreigners has been noted. To what extent will the expansion of the EU affect this issue? After many years of seclusion, the Czech Republic has opened itself to the world, and situations of contact are not only characteristic for the service sector but also for all other domains of communication.

The work domain is not without problems. The problem of the shift of power between superiors and subordinates is prominent here as well. Situations involving joint ventures, where a number of issues are awaiting solution, have been explored. What matters there is not only the language used as the vehicle of communication but the full set of communicative strategies used in individual situations of contact.

The language of politics satisfies few people. One additional problem not mentioned in the previous discussion is the problem of how to speak about the preceding political system, 'communism' – a task in which few people can manage to the satisfaction of many others. The same applies to the political events of November 1989 – was it 'revolution', 'coup' or something else? Problems are also legion in legal and administrative situations. Nevertheless, this is not to suggest that the situation in the Czech Republic is particularly grave. Similar issues exist everywhere. And in many countries of the former Soviet bloc, including Russia, the situation is not much different.

One intriguing question is what has previously been called the indeterminacy of expression. If the existence of this phenomenon is confirmed in further studies that employ a comparative background, this phenomenon should become an area of active management. However, as in other cases, there should be no intervention of organised management except when it supports simple management that grows from a grass roots setting.

PART V: MANAGEMENT OF FUNCTIONS, SETTING, PARTICIPANTS, CONTENT, FORM AND CHANNELS

Problems in Functions

How are problems concerning functions of interaction managed in the Czech Republic? Traditionally speech was supposed to possess only a single function: communicative. Roman Jakobson, on the basis of his Prague School experience, went far beyond this simple view of language (Jakobson, 1960). However, there are more functions, of which Peter Robinson listed an impressive range (Robinson, 1972). Obviously, any classification of functions can be further detailed and reformulated, but language management theory is interested in functions, or whole groups of functions, that have not previously been considered. Only a few of these functions can be mentioned in this monograph.

The communicative function

The communicative function of speech is one that has received much attention. In a way this is only natural. Language is a tool of communication and, if it does not fulfil its function to transfer messages, management takes place. It must be emphasised that the communicative function of language is the basic one. In the 19th century, the Czech Revival movement (see Part III) instituted a language management process that, among other aims, served the purpose of facilitating communication. Adjustment was sought in two basic directions: one represented status management (the effort to elevate Czech to the status of a 'national' language) while the other lay in the sphere of corpus management, the development and elaboration of the Czech language. The first adjustment was necessary because there were too many Czechs for whom German, the language of the Viennese state, was not a satisfactory tool to convey messages: they lacked sufficient competence in the language. The second adjustment arose from the fact that Czech was not a multifunctional language at that time, lacking the means for communicating a number of contexts. Of course, other functions played an important role in the Revival; e.g. the function of symbolising the quality of Czech culture or the function of creating networks for developing Czech industrial production. Any language management fulfils a plurality of functions rather than a single function at a time.

When the communicative function of speech is not fulfilled, miscommunication occurs. In Czech (as well as in other languages), claims of miscommunication resulting from speech variation – e.g. dialectal variation –

occur but are frequently exaggerated. In reality, native speakers do not note most of the potential problems because they use guessing strategies, or because they supplement meaning from the situation; they do not necessarily expect perfect comprehension. Miscommunication does take place in the case of communication between Czechs and members of other communities. As noted in Part III, in listening to Slovak, lack of effective communication can take place, but how often such lack of communication actually occurs is not known. Discourse examples of Vietnamese speakers with poor linguistic competence in the matrix language were cited. In the case of Vietnamese vendors, adjustment takes place in the form of negotiation of meaning, but such negotiation only happens when it is indispensable to the transaction. Otherwise, the communicative function is not perceived as threatened. In the description of the German community, examples were cited of individuals who clearly perceived the problem of the communicative function and implemented adjustment.

In the Czech situation, the communicative function is frequently discussed as the object of management in the case of foreign languages. The study of foreign languages, which is an important form of language management, has primarily been based on communicative needs. A relatively small community such as the Czech Republic cannot survive without a knowledge of foreign languages.

In Part IV, in the section concerning contact situations with foreigners, it was pointed out that frequently the bare message was at stake (communicative function); however, together with the content that was endangered there were also covert messages about the speaker (presentation of self) as well as messages about his/her intentions and attitudes which were negatively evaluated. This information is important not only for communication with short-term visitors but also for communication with members of other communities within the Czech Republic. This is particularly true of members of communities classified, at the beginning of Part II, as the 'Outer group' (i.e. Roma, Vietnamese, Chinese, etc.). In the case of Romani speakers, the problems of understanding are affected by switch-on of communication, by topics, by communicated intent, and by other non-grammatical rules of communicative competence.

The symbolic function

Not all functions of speech can be discussed here; however, among the remaining functions at least the 'symbolic' and the 'bridging' functions require a comment. Czech acquired the symbolic function early in its history, as the Czech community struggled for leadership against the newly arriving German element. Czech was a particularly important symbol of Czech ethnicity throughout the 19th century (and again during WWII). Emotional attachment to fixed language creations, such as works of literature or folk songs, provides proof of ongoing management.

The symbolic function frequently appears as an object of management in connection with purism. In Czech, management based on purism was strong during the 19th century, and it survived into the 20th century until it was overturned by the work of the Prague Linguistic Circle (see Part VI). This purism was of course perceived broadly as strengthening the 'Czechness' of the language, rather than as being simply a quest to eliminate German and other loans (Neustupný, 1989a). A weak form of purism existed under Communist Party rule, not only with respect to the possible influence of English, but in relation to any other foreign elements. This puristic view was also supported by the social function of language: language should be comprehensible to all social strata, but loans from other languages favoured the intellectual class. Any kind of this remaining weak purism disappeared as early as the 1980s and certainly after 1989. It is necessary to point out this fact, since some proximate languages – in particular Hungarian – retain strong puristic management strategies up to the present time (see Medgyes & Miklósy, 2000).

Standard Czech, as opposed to Common Czech, has not only become a vehicle of communication (communicative function) but has also become a symbol of social status. It was a language best acquired by the upper and middle classes, and it symbolised class membership at least until 1948, when the takeover of the state by the Communist Party destroyed the existing class structure. In this sense, a revival of the pre-1948 situation took place after 1989. In Part III, the example was cited of politicians, such as Václav Havel, who switched from a style leaning toward Common Czech to one leaning toward the Standard language. This switch was not undertaken because the morphological elements of Common Czech in his speech were unsuitable to carry the meaning he wanted to convey, but because of the higher status of the Standard.

Regional varieties of language can fulfil a symbolic function in that they provide speakers with a symbol of belonging to a particular community; however, in Czech, the function is not very strong. As noted in Part III, in the section on Dialects, regional accent is expected in internal networks, for example in the family (where it becomes the symbol of unity), and perhaps in the friendship domain. It does not appear to be widely used as a symbol in external networks. On the contrary, management works towards purging regional accent from one's speech.

Although the need to communicate has provided a very strong motivation for the study of foreign languages, there have also been other motivations. After the Velvet Revolution, English was perceived as a symbol of the 'free world'. This function supported the teaching and use of English. On the other hand, in the case of Russian there was a negative motivation: Russian was the language of the former oppressors, and studying it served as a symbol of a wish to return to the Soviet dominated society. A similar fate had, of course, afflicted German in the years immediately following WWII.

The bridging function

Language is a 'bridge' that connects the nodes of various networks. Language management in the Czech Republic does perform this social function. For non-Czech communities, Czech serves as the link to the matrix society, its culture and ideology. Czech, even if not the native language, thus becomes the vehicle of sociocultural assimilation. The ongoing process of assimilation in the Czech Republic is due exactly to this function. It cannot be neutralised unless bridges are established through community languages to other centres. Except for a narrow bridge to Poland and recently to Germany, at the present moment no such connections have been in operation.

Among foreign languages, English serves as a highway along which not only neutral messages but also thought, ideology, and social attitudes are transferred.

English thus serves as a vehicle of what Phillipson (1992) called linguistic imperialism. Admittedly, there is a possibility that English will, for the Czech Republic, become just an uncommitted international language, but at present its presence does favour the creation of networks with the USA, Britain and the world of globalisation that is controlled by those societies. French might become a counterweight, but it does not receive much attention in the Czech Republic. Perhaps the fact that German is presently highly valued should be positively evaluated; however, those who remember the past domination by Germany hesitate to reinforce the language precisely because they feel that connections with German networks should not constitute a preferred option. Admittedly, German also builds bridges to countries such as Switzerland, and this aspect is evaluated positively in the Czech Republic. Communication highways do not only favour the transport of culture and ideology; they also serve as a very active means for the transport of economic relations. This fact provides another reason why the 'bridging function' of language needs proper attention in language management.

Problems in Settings

Settings implicate time and space to the extent that these factors are governed by culture-specific strategies. For example, people may refrain from telephoning others after 10 pm, which is certainly the case in the Czech Republic, or from talking to others when meeting them casually in the street. Times and places are strictly set (this is sometimes referred to as 'appointments') and interaction is usually unsuccessful unless the setting strategies are adhered to.

The data collected by Müllerová *et al.* (1992) show problems with regard to settings in the case of people who call the fire-brigade concerning things in which the fire-brigade is not the appropriate agency; e.g. the hot water supply being interrupted, the lift breaking down, a person locking him/herself out of his/her apartment, etc. A similar problem of settings occurs in the case of shopping. A shopper is rudely turned down when he requires merchandise that is sold in a different department (Müllerová *et al.*, 1992: 70). In fact, there is a management routine to establish whether a place is appropriate for a particular inquiry or action. Such a routine is one type of pre-sequences through which speakers test whether basic conditions for a verbal act are satisfied. For example, at a reception desk at institutions which normally require permission to enter or an appointment, speakers typically check whether a person or an institution is located in the area.

C: *Prosím vás, sídlí tady ještě finance?* 'Excuse me, is the financial department still located here?'

S: *Ano. zapište se mně, jo? Do knihy návštěv.* 'Yes, write your name down in the guest book, OK?' (from Nekvapil, 2000e)

Unless a pre-sequence is employed, further management can take place. In the Czech Republic, checks at entrances to buildings are common. On the other hand, appointments in offices are not strictly required; for example, the immigration department is known for queues that may or may not lead to success.

Participants

In communication, many participants take part. They perform various functions and their position is often unequal. Part II presented a categorisation of communication participants in the territory of the Czech Republic from the ethnic point of view. At this point, a few more observations on some other categories of participants are provided.

Gender in language

In some languages, particularly in English, gender has become an important target of language management. Speakers note, evaluate and adjust language used differently by/to male or female speakers, or about male or female speakers.

Czech is full of gender – that is, full of grammatical gender, which may or may not refer to 'natural gender'. *Muž* 'man' is male, while *žena* 'woman' is female. In this case a natural gender distinction parallels the grammatical one. As Čmejrková (2002) has recently pointed out, there is a whole series of nouns in which the relationship between the natural and grammatical gender is more complicated. On the other hand, there are cases in which the natural gender plays no role at all. If *počítač* 'computer' is male while *lampa* 'desk lamp' is female, gender fulfils only a grammatical role and is only perceived when the nouns are personified (if that ever happens). This type of gender classification (*počítač* vs. *lampa*) is characteristic for the vast majority of nouns, unless they are neuter – the third major gender category. All adjectives also possess masculine, feminine or neuter forms, and these are used according to the grammatical gender of the noun to which they refer. Among the verbal forms it is the past participle, in particular, which distinguishes gender. While the present tense form *jdu* 'I go' is genderless, the past tense, which uses the participle, is either masculine (*šel jsem* 'I went' (m.)) or feminine (*šla jsem* 'I went' (f.)). Thus, although the pronoun *já* 'I' and *ty* 'you' are genderless, and only the 3rd person distinguishes gender, in all past tense forms, whether the pronoun is used or not, the gender distinction is clearly communicated.

Within this situation there are multiple ways in which gender can be considered as a discrimination factor. Čmejrková (1997b) highlights three cases. First, as in English and other European languages, there is the 'he' and 'she' problem, especially when a mixture of male and female participants is in question. As in English, the masculine form dominates. The second case involves the derivation of feminine forms from masculine nouns (Čmejrková, 1995, 1997b). In English, too, some nouns which refer to male subjects are the base from which feminine nouns are derived (poet→ poetess), but in Czech the number is much greater; for example, *čtenář* (m.) and *čtenářka* (f.) 'reader', or *ministr* (m.) and *ministryně* (f.) 'minister (of state)'. Third, there is the case of a predicate that refers to multiple subjects. If there is more than one subject and these subjects do not agree in gender, it is the masculine gender that prevails. If one refers to a mixture of *čtenář* 'reader (m.)' and *čtenářka* 'reader (f.)', the masculine form becomes the representative. It is necessary to realise that each of these nouns can generate a number of masculine or feminine forms in the same sentence because of the obligatory character of grammatical agreement. Hence, the consequencies are far-reaching. Čmejrková quotes an example constructed by the translator Pavel Eisner:

Její veličenstvo královna anglická a císařovna indická a řidič Pepa Žambourek vypadli z vozu. 'Her Highness the Queen of England and Empress of India and her driver, Pepa Žambourek, fell out of the car.'

The difference in status between the Queen and her driver notwithstanding, the past tense *vypadli* 'fell out' has the masculine, not the feminine form. The fact is that, in contemporary Czech, the use of the masculine form to subsume feminine referents is virtually never noted or negatively evaluated. In other words, it hardly ever becomes a language problem.

As for possible adjustment, Čmejrková (1995) quotes the sentence 'The reader is invited to find out for himself/herself about contrastive pragmatics on the basis of papers included in this volume' which, should the same strategy – using a slash – be applied, would read: *Čtenář/čtenářka je vyzýván/vyzývána, aby sám/sama odhalil/odhalila na základě příspěvků v tomto sborníku, co je kontrastivní pragmatika.* Čmejrková concludes that the issue of gender discrimination may be different in languages such as English and Czech, and that the problem of discrimination may never arise in Czech in the same way as it did in English.

The current situation is certainly peaceful, but the question is whether or not this peacefulness will endure. The basic fact to be considered is that, at the end of the 1990s, the problem of gender discrimination was only weakly noted, or not noted, in areas other than language as well. When feminism (not necessarily a militant feminism) arrives, will it be possible to guarantee that it does not also transfer to language? For the time being, language management appears neither in cases where it can be assumed that language adjustment would be difficult (as in Čmejrková's example), nor in cases where the solution would be easier (e.g. removing *slečna* 'Miss'). However, Čmejrková herself recently writes *lingvisté a lingvistky* 'linguists (m.) and linguists (f.)' (2002: 263), and there are cases of language change where feminine derivatives from masculine nouns have recently been abandoned, and forms that are felt as masculine (e.g. *advokát* 'lawyer') are used in reference to both genders. Is this the same process as replacing 'poetess' by 'poet' or rather, hypothetically, Mrs by Mr (a change that may not have been considered yet)? It is interesting to note that the derivation of feminine forms from masculine nouns has recently also been weakened in the case of proper names through the permission that, under certain conditions (see section on Form, below), Czech wives of foreigners are not obliged to change their surname to the feminine form (they can legally be *Jiřina McRae*, rather than *McRaeová*).

Features of language do not become the object of language management, simple or organised, because of some intrinsic inadequacy, but rather because an inadequacy is projected into communication from the socioeconomic sphere. Gendered language existed in English for centuries but remained unnoted and unevaluated until the 1970s. In the case of gender in Czech, the stimulus may come from the natural growth of feminism on the home soil, from the influence of language management in other languages, or from a combination of both. Or, as Čmejrková would have it, it may not come at all. In the meantime it is of interest that more and more attention is being accorded to gender distinctions in other Slavic languages as well (see van Leeuwen-Turnovcová *et al.*, 2002).

Participants' networks

Another issue related to participants is briefly mentioned: their networks. Networks are the arrangement of participants in communication. One can distinguish encounter networks, formed within a particular discourse situation, and group networks, consisting of participants who *usually* intercommunicate (Neustupný, 1978: 177).

Encounter networks can be hierarchically organised, with a pivot and marginal members of various kinds. For example, in the case of a traditional society, and in some formal situations in any society, the presence of a high status individual is strongly felt; this means that the status of participants is noted, and the way in which they 'conduct the network' may be evaluated. The authors believe that encounter networks are, at the present time, more formal than before the Velvet Revolution, or perhaps that there is a larger number of more formal networks, and that management within these networks takes place. The revaluation of the attendant/customer status can be assumed to have initially taken place in individual encounter networks.

Group networks originate in encounter networks and are basically formed through their successive overlapping. In Part III it was argued that the Roma and the Vietnamese do not frequently form group networks with members of the matrix community. Management is needed. In the popular stereotype, it is always the other community that does not enter 'our' networks by choice. In fact, the problem is often whether or not an applicant is accepted into a network – networks often have no vacancies, especially no vacancies suitable for applicants who are deviant in some respect.

Content

Content strategies form a wide category reaching from themes of communication to the meaning of individual morphemes. All these categories simply cannot be covered in this brief discussion; only a selection will be used to show the varying ways in which content becomes a problem and is managed in the case of Czech.

Politeness: *ty* and *vy* and other address terms

Politeness (the communication of social distance, see Nekvapil & Neustupný, forthcoming) is one of the important categories of content. A number of problems concerning the communication of politeness have already been discussed. The system of selection between *ty* 'you (French *tu*)' and *vy* 'you (French *vous*)' retains old features that are gradually being removed by simple management. However, in comparison with German, as spoken in Germany, more conservatism can be discerned (Ehlers & Kněřová, 1997). Jurman's survey (2001) indicates that rebuilding of the system through simple management is taking place. Consider, for example, the following discourse in which one of two female students addresses an unknown young man (about 20 years old).

> *... mohli bysme se prosím tě zeptat, jak se dostanem na nádraží?* ' ... could we ask you [a *ty* form], please, how to get to the station?'

The address uses *tě* (a *ty* form), while in the traditional system, *vy* would be used.

In this case, the new address has probably been automised, but it will be noted and possibly negatively evaluated by older speakers of Czech.

In simple management, other address modes have been managed. The address *soudruhu* 'comrade', frequently avoided (managed) even before 1989 (cf. Nekvapil & Neustupný, 2005), all but disappeared. The New Year's speeches of all four of the communist presidents in the second half of the 20th century contained the word *drazí* 'dear' (emotional) which is unusual in these situations and probably resulted through interference from the Russian (*dorogie* . . .). President Havel started with *milí* 'dear' (close relationship) and subsequently switched to *vážení* 'dear' (respected) (Hlavsová, 1997).

Politeness in service encounters

Communication of politeness in service encounters has changed radically in the 1990s. Müllerová *et al.* (1992), who collected their data at the very beginning of the decade, cite examples such as the following:

Cust.: *Skládací pláštěnky igelitový, ty průhledný* . . .
'folding raincoats, polythene, those see-through . . . '
Attnd.: *Co chcete?*
'What do you want?'
Müllerová *et al.* (1992: 70, transcription simplified)

Here the attendant reacts to a request by a customer by *co chcete* which is exactly English 'what do you want', a form managed (negatively evaluated) in similar situations throughout the Soviet-dominated period, and close to extinction now.

Management has lifted the level of politeness in other public situations as well. In train conductors' language, the optional element *prosím* 'please' appears as in the following example:

Cond.: *Dobrý večer, změna průvodčích, kontrola jízdenek, prosím.* 'Good evening, change of conductors, control of tickets, please.'

The politeness level can be further raised if the conductor finds an opportunity to use a *vy* form at the same time, as in:

C: *Dobrý večer přeji, vaši jízdenku, prosím.* 'I wish you a good evening, your (*vy*-form) ticket, please.'

This way of communication with passengers has only become manifest after the Velvet Revolution of 1989 and reflects the linguistic management of the new relationship between service personnel and customers (for details see Nekvapil & Neustupný, 2005).

Public criticism of others

The expression of indignation and criticism by first-encounter participants in public situations still occurs but is managed (negatively evaluated) by many participants. For example:

Moc si na mě, děvenko, nevyskakuj, nebo zavolám vedoucího. 'Lass, don't talk back, or I'll call the manager' (an older man speaking in a shop to a young cashier, the impolite mode of speech is reinforced by his use of *ty* rather than *vy*-forms) (Patočka, 2000: 29).

A similar case is criticism on the telephone recorded by Müllerová *et al.* (1992: 136). A fire-brigade telephone operator speaks with a customer:

Operator: *No jedině ty vodárny musíte zkoušet.* 'Well, just the waterworks, you must try again.'

Customer: *No ale když tam je to vyvěšený.* 'Well, but over there, their phone is disconnected.'

Operator: *Já za to nemůžu ale pane.* 'This is not my fault, sir'

The answer 'This is not my fault, sir' sounds critical in Czech and contradicts norms of polite conversation – as it probably does in any system of speech. This same telephonist uses an angry tone of voice and wording to other customers as well (Müllerová *et al.*, 1992: 130).

Linguistic conservatism

After 40 years of unsuccessful rule by the Communist Party, many speakers felt that the left-wing type of liberalism was undesirable. This extended to language management. In Part III, it has been stated that conservative attitudes appeared in the case of spelling. Furthermore, in the area of politeness, address using *ty* forms often gave way to address using the more formal *vy*, and titles reappeared.

Content analysis of the media

Only recently has Critical Discourse Analysis (CDA) been applied to the analysis of content within the Czech media (Homoláč, 2002). Attention has been paid to the image of ethnic minorities in central Europe, in particular to the media image of the Roma. One of the aims of the project 'Presentations of Romanies in the Central European Media', which was discussed in Part II, was to furnish an alternative portrait of the Roma (Homoláč *et al.*, 2003). Although CDA frequently refers to covert problems that are not necessarily perceived by readers and listeners, it is an important tool for discovering social problems connected with the content of the media. Such problems can further be adjusted through organised management, for example in discussion evenings with journalists or experts. It should be noted, however, that, in the contemporary situation in the Czech Republic, an old-left position, sometimes occupied by CDA analysts, is reminiscent of the immediate past and is not necessarily welcome.

Form

The category 'form' (otherwise 'message form', 'frame', etc.) refers to the various ways of ordering content in the process of communication. This includes ordering in frames of varying extension – from the life-cycle, through discourse, to the order of elements within the sentence and below (Neustupný, 1995). In an extension to this definition, the category 'form' also includes the kind and ordering of phonemes within a naming unit (such as a morph or a proper name). At each of these levels, management occurs.

Sequential organisation of talk

Turn taking presents problems. Hlavsová (1997: 29, 38) points to turn taking as a major problem in political discussions. Perhaps the political situations within the public domain are more sensitive to the problem than other situations, but the problem occurs frequently in other domains as well. In recordings analysed by Müllerová *et al.* (1992), the problem of overlaps in speech and of attempts to take turns appear everywhere. In a conversation between a woman interested in restitution of her property (H) and a cooperative official (R), the official attempts to take a turn, but H continues with her plan, and only the third attempt by R is successful (Müllerová *et al.*, 1992: 125).

Similar to turn taking is the problem of when to answer the telephone; this matter is treated in another extract published in the same collection. The issue is after how many rings to pick up the telephone: one, two . . . or 20 (Müllerová *et al.*, 1992: 192).

Another problem occurs when engaging in a request (or another speech act); should one formulate the request straight away, or should one check whether suitable conditions for the request exist; in other words whether or not to use a pre-sequence. Research has shown that such considerations are well developed in Czech (Nekvapil, 1997a).

One-word name for the Czech Republic

This issue appeared as early as 1968, when the former Czechoslovak Republic officially became a federation of the Czech Socialist Republic and the Slovak Socialist Republic. While for the latter a one-word denomination (Slovakia) was traditionally available, there was no similar term for the former. The linguist J. Bělič proposed *Česko*, not as a new coinage but as a word that had already been used in 1777. This adjustment proposal resulted in an ardent discussion in the daily press. In principle, linguists were for it, while others in the community (journalists, writers, etc.) were against. However, in the following years, the federative system of Czechoslovakia remained on paper, so that the lack of a term for one of the components was not felt to be a serious problem (Hasil, 1999).

With the break-up of the former Czechoslovakia in 1993, the problem was resurrected – but now it was more urgent than before – it was not the name of a part of a state but the name of the country. The basis of the problem is that *Czech* is an adjective in Czech, as in other languages, and it cannot become a noun naming a country. The present day Czech Republic, corresponding to the historical terri-tory of the Bohemian kings, was divided into *Čechy* 'Bohemia', *'Morava'* 'Moravia' and *Slezsko* 'Silesia' (actually only a part of Silesia); although all three used what might be called 'dialects of spoken Czech' while using the same form of written Czech, they were in fact different fiefdoms, and there was no need for a name covering all of them beyond the title *země koruny české* 'countries of the Bohemian crown', or *české země* 'the Czech lands'. This attitude, though not supported by administrative boundaries, is still alive. Note that in English, in reference to ethnicity *Czech* is used, while in territorial reference *Bohemia* is used to refer to what in Czech is *Čechy* (i.e. the western part of the Czech Republic).

Following the break-up of Czechoslovakia, discussions flared up again, and Bělič's *Česko* reappeared. Linguists pointed out again that the word had a long tradition, that its formation agreed with the rules of Czech, that it fit into a long chain of names of countries (*Rusko, Polsko, Srbsko . . .*). On the other side, the public claimed that the name was unusual, cacophonous, and lacked dignity. The difference from 1968 was that now everyone was convinced that a name should be found, because the existing situation was threatening the identity of the state. These views were strong in the camp of geographers and historians (Hasil, 1999). Nevertheless, the word *Česko* was rejected as the official name of the country. All this notwithstanding, the name *Česko* has penetrated the spoken language, but much less the written Czech, even if it can occasionally be seen in the press.

This problem also exists in other languages. In 1993, the Czech Ministry of Foreign Affairs engaged in an act of language management by recommending to Czech embassies abroad to use *Czechia* in English, *Tschechien* in German, *Tchéquie* in French, *Chequia* in Spanish, *Cechia* in Italian, and *Čechija* in Russian. The Ministry also appended a list of names that are unsuitable. The list of unacceptable terms was most extensive for German: *Böhmen und Mähren, Böhmerland, Tschechenland* and, of course, *Tschechei* which was used pejoratively in WWII by the Nazis. The list of unacceptable terms further included: Eng. *Bohemia*, Fr. *Bohême*, It. *Boemia, Cecchia* and Sp. *Bohemia* or *Bohemoravia* (Hasil, 1999: 19). One of the authors of this monograph had the opportunity in 1993 to watch how language management was being conducted in the German media. Step by step, German media were abandoning *Tschechei* and adopting *Tschechien*. The usage was also difficult for Czechs, who were not certain how to describe their place of origin in German. A discourse management strategy common for many other discourse problems, namely avoidance, was frequently used in the form *ich bin aus Prag* 'I am from Prague'.

Management of place names

One important task of organised management was to change names of places (streets, squares and, exceptionally, even cities) which in 1989 were using names and other words based on communist ideology. This was one of the few areas of Czech in which the impact of the rule of the Communist Party and the Soviet occupation was profound. There were hundreds of Lenin or Marx Streets or Squares. On the basis of a survey conducted in the city Hradec Králové it is possible to estimate that approximately one-tenth of all place names had to be changed. These acts of management altered the naming of public space in a radical way, because the undesirable names mostly involved space that was central to the settlements. The adjustment strategies employed in many instances converted the old ideology into a new one. Hence there are hundreds of Masaryk Streets and Squares. The iconic strategy (calling a long street the Long Street, etc.) was only utilised to a limited extent (Nekvapil, 1996). On the other hand, one cannot claim that all proper names introduced by the old regime were changed. For instance, names of Russian scientists, musicians or painters were retained, even if they were attached to places in order to please the Soviet Union. There is a *Náměstí I.P. Pavlova* 'I.P. Pavlov Square' (Pavlov was a Russian scientist) in a central position in Prague. Hradec Králové retained place names using the personal names of communists who were victims of WWII and who had been born in the city.

The management of proper names

A new development in the legal and administrative domain is the regulation of the form of surnames. Contemporary Czech has established a strict practice to attach feminine endings to all female surnames that appear in Czech texts; e.g. Simone Beauvoire became *Beauvoirová*, Madelene Albright became *Albrightová*, Steffi Graff became *Graffová*. This created a problem in the case of Czech women married to foreigners, since the husband and wife had different surnames. According to a new law (No. 301/2001) surnames are still entered into the official register in the Czech form, but women who possess Czech citizenship and opt for a non-Czech ethnicity, can apply to have the foreign form of their surname (without *–ová*) also entered into the register. The woman must then declare which form she will use, and she is not permitted to use the other form. The conditions are very explicit:

(1) Only Czech nationals can apply. A foreign woman who marries a Czech man and does not accept Czech citizenship cannot use her name in Czech contexts without *–ová*. (Note that the Czech marriage law allows women to keep their maiden surname on marriage.)
(2) If the woman insists that she is ethnically Czech, she must accept the Czech form of her name with *–ová* attached. Certainly, ethnicity is a matter of declaration, so she can easily declare that she is for example Danish, but some people do not want to lie.
(3) There is a relatively large fee required to change a name after the Czech name has already been registered (Zpráva, 2002: 15–16).

The legal regulations speak of the *–ová* ending as being in 'agreement with the rules of Czech grammar,' but this is a questionable claim. Such strict rules did not exist in the 19th century, and at least some native speakers of Czech feel that the *–ová* rule has a status different from the obligatory grammatical rules of Czech declension or conjugation. Certainly there are women who possess foreign nationality but who use Czech surnames without the *–ová* or other similar ending. Such a practice is not necessarily felt to be an abomination.

Channels

Channels refer to the various ways in which messages are transmitted. The basic media are the spoken, the written and the non-verbal. However, each of these can be further modified by the use of other devices; e.g. the printed language, telephones, tape recordings, video recordings, word processing and many other variants. Problems concerning channels originate in the use of these varying media and in transfer from one channel to another.

Electronic media

In the course of the 1990s, Czech society witnessed a radical diffusion of personal computers, used not only at work but also at home. The use of computers has been given considerable attention in schools, but towards the end of the 1990s, in comparison with west European countries, the situation was still alarming. The ratio in the schools was one computer for 40 students, a figure that was double that of the western European average (Možný, 2002: 78). In view of this situation, at the beginning of 2002 the Ministry of Education initiated a project called 'Internet to Schools' which is intended to ensure that at least 3620 schools will be connected to the internet through the provision of 25,240 computers and more than 2100 servers. Each school will receive a laser printer as part of the package. It is expected that this active policy will have a strong impact on schooling in the Czech Republic. Needless to say, Czech will remain the language of the instructional programmes and of communication with the computers.

In this respect, effective foundations were laid at the very outset of computerisation of the country. Czech was being used in operating systems right from the beginning; there is, of course, a Czech version of Windows. Likewise, international text editors and other office software such as *Word*, *Word Perfect* or *Excel* are used in Czech versions. A considerable number of manuals have been published to assist users. In view of the specificity of Czech script which uses diacritics to supplement letters of the Latin alphabet, a Czech word processing editor (T602) was developed at the beginning of the 1990s (by the Czech company Software 602), when other programmes failed to provide a reliable vehicle for writing Czech and Slovak. Later versions of T602 compete with programmes such as *Microsoft Word*, not only in the Czech Republic but also in Slovakia.

While word processing has been taken care of, a more complicated problem emerged with the spread of the use of e-mail and the internet. Some users apply software that enables the production and reception of texts with Czech diacritics, while others do not. Since it is not always known which addressees possess the decoding facility, frequently even those who can encode the diacritics hesitate to do so. When decoding features are included in the software, their operation is not simple and often results in gibberish that may leave at least some words unintelligible even if considerable time is spent on the task. Often diacritics can only be safely used with some fonts, but to determine which ones depends on experimentation by the user. On the other hand, Czech written without the diacritics is relatively easy to decode, even though occasional misunderstanding may occur. This claim is valid for native users of Czech; however, for non-native readers of Czech, the omission of the diacritics may create barriers to understanding. Until the emergence of e-mail, Czech had never been written without diacritics, except in the case of typewriting by expatriates who lost contact with the language. However, at present, native speakers of Czech have become accustomed to the omission of diacritics when exchanging e-mail messages. This situation is likely to last until *Microsoft* abandons its discriminative policy and decides to develop satisfactory word processing software that really works without restrictions for languages other than English.

The experience of Czech readers with the omission of diacritics is reflected in their increased tolerance to the graphic form of texts in general. In view of the number of deviations from orthographic norms in e-mail and in internet messages, misprints or spelling mistakes are not as easily noted as in other texts. Computer texts without diacritics also cause changes in language management of written texts because unusual combinations of graphemes blunt the users' norms. Müllerová (2001: 211) provides a discourse example that illustrates this process of management. Her subject X (a student at a university of technology) wrote, in an e-mail message, *Eva rykala* 'Eva said'. His younger brother, Y, commented, also without diacritics, *aspon kdyz je r s hackem, tak tam pis mekky i* 'at least when there is an r with a hook, write i after it'. X should have written *Eva rikala* , but it is possible that his spelling *rykala* was influenced by the fact that, in normal Czech, there is no syllable *ri*, only *ry*.

Another structural consequence of the absence of diacritics is the emergence of new homonyms, which are clearly distinguished in speaking and in normal orthography; for example, *horky* is used for both *horký* 'hot' and *hořký* 'bitter', or *radit* is used for both *radit* 'to advice' and *řádit* 'to rage' (Čmejrková, 1999: 118).

Even if the use of diacritics is not unusual in e-mail communication, it is virtually absent in texts sent over mobile telephones. According to the British magazine *Global Mobile*, in 2001 the Czech Republic was second in Europe in the number of mobile telephones per capita, with 80 telephones per 100 inhabitants, and the sending of written messages over this medium normally omits diacritics.

Since writing without diacritics on the computer is not automated, writers must pre-manage their process of writing, and it is not unusual for them to fail in this task and to use keys that produce letters with diacritics. Such letters in transmission may then result in gibberish. In order to prevent this from happening, many users switch from the Czech to the English keyboard that has no letters with diacritics.

Frequently, problems are noted as the text is generated; in other words 'in-management' takes place. For example, in the following sentence,

> *To zvire je podle mych skrovnych znalosti vacice (hacek nad prvnim c).* 'The animal, according to my limited knowledge, is a possum (a hook on the first c)' (Müllerová, 2001: 211),

the writer noted and negatively evaluated the absence of a diacritic on the rarely used word *vačice* 'possum', and implemented corrective adjustment by adding in brackets how to read the word: i.e. 'with a "hook" on the first *c*'. Some writers apply, as an adjustment strategy, 'cluster spelling' which was discontinued in Czech centuries ago (except for *ch*), but it has been retained in Polish. Čmejrková (1999: 17), gives an example in which a writer asks *Bohous nebo Bohousz?* 'Bohous or Bohoush?' The cluster *sz* at the end of the third word is used to replace the Czech grapheme *š*. Incidentally, a similar strategy is used in German e-mail where *Tübingen* becomes *Tuebingen*. However, in German this procedure has been to some extent alive (see the spelling *Goethe*) while in Czech the clusters function as auxiliary *ad hoc* procedures.

Since e-mail is characterised by considerable stylistic flexibility, non-standard varieties, in particular Common Czech, might occur. However, as already noted by Čmejrková (1999), informality is not the only strategy used in e-mail – another strategy is linguistic economy; for example, speakers easily apply the Common Czech form *takovýho* 'of such one' instead of the Standard *takového*, because both have the same number of letters. However, rather then using the Common Czech form *takovej* 'such one', they are not afraid to use the Standard form *takový*, which is shorter. In this way, an 'e-mail' variety of Czech is perhaps in the making. Its formation is no doubt aided by the fact that, in spoken communication, mixing Common and Standard Czech is at present a normal procedure (Hoffmannová & Müllerová, 2000; see also Part III).

The principles of informality and economy can also be identified in the trend of some writers to refrain from using upper case letters. In Czech, this practice mainly affects the beginnings of the sentences and proper names. By contrast, in German the consequences are graver. Lack of upper case letters is of course characteristic, as an optional strategy, for some e-mail styles in many languages, including English.

The dynamic and spontaneous character of electronic communication leads to the observation that most management is simple. Problems in e-mailing are solved as they appear in individual discourse by individual participants. Organised management at the level of the government concerns the accessibility of the electronic media, but not their form or content. The form of messages on the internet is, of course, carefully managed by individual organisations which use it to provide information or for advertising.

PART VI: THEORIES OF LANGUAGE MANAGEMENT

The Prague School Theory

The background

After phonology, the theory of language cultivation can be designated as one of the fundamental contributions of the Prague Linguistic Circle, an important centre of pre-war structural linguistics founded in 1926. The term 'language cultivation' refers to the Czech descriptor '*jazyková kultura*', coterminous with German *Sprachkultur*, Russian *kul'tura reči* (Daneš, 1988) or Swedish *Språkvård* (Jernudd, 1977). The Prague School version differed from these in being closely connected with the structural theories of the time (see Leška *et al.*, 1993); it provides a conceptual framework that retains considerable interest today. In the Czech Republic, other theoretical frameworks exist for language management at present (see following section) but, as far as language cultivation is concerned, the Prague School theory has not been forgotten. Although it has not survived in its original form, its individual strategies are vibrant (Daneš, 1988).

Why did this theory appear in Prague and not in Germany, Russia or Sweden? First, the social system of Czech academic life, after the country gained independence from Austrian rule in 1918, was very young and, therefore, susceptible to the growth of new paradigms. Structuralism grew up naturally on this breeding ground, not from a single source, but from many. And Prague School structuralism affected the theory of language cultivation by providing its basic concepts, primarily the concept of 'function'. Further, unlike phonology, the major and best known theory of the Prague School, language cultivation theory was almost purely Czech. It was in the Czech section of the Circle that the Early Modern nationalistic mood which fostered purism had been strongly rejected. A new approach was needed for Czech. Although the literary language was healthy and, in the work of Karel Čapek and other young authors, served as a tool of great precision, there were areas, such as the language of administration, where older patterns survived. These called for attention.

The original theory

The inquiry system

The inquiry system – in other words the identification of the objectives – of the original Prague School theory can be described with reference to three concepts: norms, noting, and evaluation (see Part I: What is Language Management).

Norms

The concept of the norm in its structuralist version was developed in Prague. The norm was not what it used to be: a normative prescription produced by grammarians. According to Havránek (1932a), all forms of language, including dialects and popular language, possess a norm which is independent of the will of the speakers. Also, it does not matter whether or not the norm is codified (Havránek, 1938).

In contrast to older conceptions of language cultivation, the Circle defined the norm as the usage of the good authors of the past 50 years. This was not intended as a universal thesis valid for all languages but rather as a rule for the Czech of the post-World-War I period. In the Czech situation, the language of literature was the first to liberate itself from the historicising norms of the first half of the 19th century and closely mirrored the contemporary spoken language morphologically as well as syntactically (see Part III). This development of the literary language intensified in the second half of the 19th century, and was virtually completed in the 1920s when the Circle formulated its theories. The new language eschewed the antiquated forms defended by the purists whose position, at the time the Prague School theory appeared, was still very powerful. In the language of non-fiction and of school textbooks, on which the purists concentrated, the process had been delayed. The definition developed by the Circle was therefore a highly political one in that it tried to exclude antiquated linguistic norms defended by the purists.

The Circle also said that the norm can be confirmed on the basic of linguistic awareness of the intellectual class and its linguistic practice (see the unsigned *General principles for the cultivation of language* in *Čeština a jazyková kultura* written by Havránek; see Havránek, 1963: 118). In this sense, too, the position of the Circle was unashamedly Modern, emphasising middle-class norms as *'language tout court'*. Language cultivation commenced programmatically with identifying the norm and noting deviations from it.

Noting

Although the concept of noting was not used, the Prague School theory was based on noting of deviations from norms that existed at the time and during the immediately preceding few decades. Due to hypercorrection practised by others, the Prague School scholars also noted those components of linguistic structure in which no adjustment was needed. There were areas in which problems obviously existed – e.g. some areas of special terminology that were the domain of German before 1918 and some areas of style.

Evaluation

Evaluation of the existing problems was in accord with the structuralist atmosphere of the time. In principle, language is good as it is. 'Leave your language alone' was a slogan formulated later in a different branch of structural linguistics (Hall, 1950), but it had already been extensively applied within the Prague School. The struggle of the Prague School against purism in 1932 and later was based on the perception that, overall, the norm of the Czech language has satisfactorily been established. It might, from time to time, need to be adjusted, but basically it must be defended against attempts of the purists to change it arbitrarily. There was no need to evaluate the norm negatively, except where problems obviously existed. Some problems, the Circle agreed, did. In the perception that a certain amount of codification and change were needed, the Prague School approach differed from the approaches of other branches of linguistic structuralism. However, a number of language problems, such as those connected with Common Czech, although noted by Havránek descriptively, did not become an object of evaluation or the focus of subsequent stages of language management in this theory. Neither did the problems of ethnic languages.

The design system

The Prague School theory of language cultivation can be seen as a system of strategies proposed for the adjustment of problems that had been noted and evaluated (in the sense of the management theory). This section will summarise the way in which the perception of language problems resulted in a prescription for change ('adjustment' strategies within the management theory).

Varieties of the theory

Understandably, the theory did not constitute a single block of strategies. The development began in the *Thèses* of the Circle, published in 1929, where the range of the theory was already impressive (*Thèses*, 1929: 15–17, 27–29); it passed through the important volume *Spisovná čeština a jazyková kultura* (*Standard Czech and the Cultivation of Language*, 1932), which embodied the struggle of the Circle against purism, and it continued in 1935 into the editorial in the opening issue of *Slovo a slovesnost*, the Czech language journal of the Circle (Neustupný, 1999). In each of these publications there were new and differing emphases. In the 1950s and 1960s, the theory underwent a gradual review, a development that will be dealt with separately under a subsequent section.

Situations for which the theory has been created

The theory is basically devoted to situations in which the Standard Language is used. Although *Spisovná čeština a jazyková kultura* (1932) included a chapter on spoken language, this chapter was not, strictly speaking, written from the point of view of the theory. However, spoken language situations are mentioned in all representative statements and, especially since World War II, these spoken situations attracted more and more attention.

Special attention was given by the Circle to situations of poetic language. In *Spisovná čeština a jazyková kultura* Mukařovský, the leading aesthetician of the Prague School, argued that poetic language performed a function different from the function of the Standard, and that the norms of the Standard could not be applied as such to the language of poetry. Distortion of the norms of the Standard Language is indispensable in poetry (Mukařovský, 1932: 22). This special condition meant that it was impossible to simply apply the management strategies applicable to the Standard to the poetic language. A different approach was needed.

Functions of management

The overall function of the Prague School theory is to manage a modern language. The following details apply:

Firstly, the role of cultivation is to make sure that the Standard Language remains adequate to fulfil its function. This task is most obvious in the area of the lexicon, where abstract words, specialised terminology and words expressing minute differences must continuously be added. In the course of enriching the lexicon, there is no need to avoid loan words. Additionally, simply elevating conversational words to the status of special terms does not necessarily work (Havránek, 1929).

Secondly, the function of language cultivation is not only to make the Standard rich, but also to make it sophisticatedly rich. In the *Thèses*, this is called *intellectualisation* of language; i.e. to make language meanings determinate and precise, and also abstract and capable of fully expressing sophisticated processes of thought (Havránek, 1932a). Intellectualisation does not affect only the lexicon. It also strongly affects the syntax, where the function of the Standard makes it imperative to be able to express minute shades of meaning. However, it would be incorrect to require a high degree of intellectualisation from all varieties of language: the degree required necessarily depends on the function of the variety.

Thirdly, cultivation grants the Standard *flexible stability* (in Czech *pružná stabilita*), a term used by Mathesius (1932) to replace the term 'la fixité' introduced in the *Thèses* (p. 27). It was considered important to emphasise that the stability required of language is not an absolute value. However, the theory claims that language, as an instrument of communication, could not work unless it was stabilised. Elements that have already been a part of the norm (such as orthography or terminology) should not be arbitrarily replaced on the basis of historical or other arguments. However, it was also emphasised, that the role of cultivation was not to achieve complete uniformity (Mathesius, 1932) and strip the language of functional differentiation (Havránek, 1932a) necessary for further development. Language changes; so does its norm, and cultivation must follow suit. *Flexible stability* differed from the 'antiquation' of language. This was not a modern strategy, and it was strongly rebuffed. The theory had Czech authors on its side – or perhaps it was on the side of the authors.

The last function of language cultivation was called '*l'originalité*' in the *Thèses*. This concept referred to the need to create language means that fit the structure of the language. It can perhaps better be called '*systemicity*'. Stich (1979b) had already pointed out that this function was dropped from the scheme. However, the criterion has more recently been defended by Jelínek (1996) who points to the fact that *systemicity* is important, though only as a criterion secondary to usage.

The application of these functional criteria has been worked out in detail and with considerable sophistication. See in particular the above-mentioned volume *Spisovná čeština a jazyková kultura*.

Settings for language cultivation

The settings (place and time) for the application of the theory were determined as use in intellectual work situations (such as academic work, creative writing) and in formal education. Office settings were also considered, but reference to industry was rare.

Participants

The agents within the theory include those who create the norm: intellectuals and writers. Codification is the work of linguists. Since, in accordance with the perception of the Modern period, all class distinctions have been removed, the theory does not in fact categorise users of language cultivation. They are the undivided 'nation'. In practice, the users were mostly conceived as the middle class. Only occasionally (see The social system) have other strata of the society been included.

Content

As Daneš emphasises (1996), the theory highlighted rational rather than emotional aspects of language management. In this sense, its 'modern' breeding ground clearly asserted itself. This was not a 19th century romantic castle with ramparts and historical flags. Perhaps the Prague School went too far in this respect. Ethical and emotional functions of language do exist and cannot be written off (Daneš, 1996). Moreover, a glance through Havránek's 1932 position papers confirms that symbolic and other social functions of language did not receive attention in the theory either.

The principal object of cultivation in the Prague School approach, as already mentioned, was the Standard and as such, in practice, the written language. In the original version of the theory, the need for the cultivation of the spoken word was postulated, and the 1932 volume had a chapter on this. However, the written language remained the focus of the theory.

Probably the widest and most enlightened description of the content of language cultivation appears in the Introduction to the Czech language journal of the Circle, *Slovo a slovesnost*. This Introduction was published in 1935 in the inaugural issue and was signed by Havránek, Jakobson, Mathesius, Mukařovský and Trnka. Language cultivation (*kultura jazyka*) is defined as an attitude toward language which considers language not as a tool but as 'the object of our attention, consideration and our emotions'. What immediately comes to mind is Fishman's (1971) formulation 'behaviour towards language' that has been adopted as the characterisation of language management in language management theory (Jernudd & Neustupný, 1987). Language cultivation, conceived in this way, was divided into three streams:

(1) Language law in theory and practice (elsewhere in the Introduction this is referred to as 'language policy').
(2) Language education (native and foreign).
(3) Language development (*výstavba*) which consisted of:
   • elaboration and codification of norms;
   • establishment of ideological and aesthetic requirements on language; and
   • application of these requirements and norms in particular discourses (language critique).

In all these streams, 'planning' takes place. The word *planning* is actually being used. What a magnificent programme for 1935! Yet, looking at the practice of the Circle, point 1 (language policy) remained undeveloped. Language policy was too big a mouthful for structural linguists, who in principle believed in the autonomy of language. Point 2 (language education) remained practically untouched. It was only Point 3, the microscopic consideration of 'corpus' problems, which was fully elaborated. Since it is very difficult to place a theory of language problems within an orthodox structuralist framework (see Neustupný, 1993a, 1999), this alone was an important achievement. The arrangement of the strategies of the theory lacks uniformity. Each edition (see Variation above) shows a different order of presentation.

Management of the theory

The theory was not rigid to the extent that it would become unmanageable. In reaction to the volume *Spisovná čeština a jazyková kultura* (1932), massive support was expressed in the community, although there were also critical voices. Daneš is undoubtedly right in saying that this criticism did not suffice to alter the theory (Daneš, 1996). During the Soviet dominated era, references to the Circle were unwelcome, and the word *structuralism* was virtually banned. Still, Havránek succeeded, in 1963, in reprinting all of his contributions to the theory in his personal volume *Studie o spisovném jazyce* (*Studies on Standard Language*). In footnotes, he mentioned, from time to time, that his current position was different.

Implementation

Nothing in the theory stipulated any particular method of implementation. One method of implementation involved contemporary authors who, thanks to the Circle, felt secure in continuing to use the language they had used. The 1941 revision of the *Pravidla českého pravopisu* (Rules of Czech spelling) (see Part III) in principle accepted Havránek's proposals (Havránek, 1963: 124). Even before World War II Havránek (with others) published a textbook of Czech for high schools that incorporated principles proposed by the Circle, and after the war, in cooperation with Alois Jedlička, he launched his *Stručná mluvnice česká* (*Short Grammar of Czech*) that became the basic codification manual for generations of Czechs. After WWII, the Institute of the Czech Language of the Academy of Sciences began, under the leadership of Havránek, to implement the principles of the theory, at least in the first decade after 1945. The four volumes of the *Slovník spisovného jazyka českého* (*Dictionary of Standard Czech*, 1960–1971) more or less followed the theory. Although Havránek was described in the Great Soviet Encyclopedia of the 1950s as a 'bourgeois linguist', he was a Party member, and he had excellent relations with the Central Committee. His influence on matters relating to the Czech language was profound; his ideas were the basic element in the lasting influence of the Prague Linguistic Circle's theories in Soviet-dominated Czechoslovakia (Novák, 1990). Anyway, since the 1960s the Prague School came to be accepted in the Soviet Union as well: in 1964, a Russian translation of Vachek's *Dictionnaire de Linguistique de l'École de Prague* appeared, and in 1967 an anthology of the work of members of the Prague Linguistic Circle was launched.

Social system

The social system underlying the theory was provided by the Prague School Circle that was, itself, located in some departments of the best universities in the country. The membership was youthful. At the time of the formation of the Circle in 1926, only Mathesius was over 40, Trubetzkoy and Mukařovský were in their mid-30s while Havránek was 33. All others who joined later, were younger.

Theories do not exist in a vacuum. They are situated within a social space, and within this space members of the Circle (apart from Troubetzkoy, who strictly speaking was not a member, and some others whose ideologies were different) were situated on the left of the political spectrum. The *Thèses* speak of the tendency of the Standard 'to become the monopoly and a characteristic feature of the dominant class' (p. 17). However, this observation has never been developed further. On the contrary, subjective feelings of the members notwithstanding, one could claim that the system of language cultivation of the Prague School was created on behalf of the middle class, to which members of the Circle belonged. What else could be expected of a system that placed so much emphasis on the principle of *flexible stability*? After WWII, Havránek (1947) once more raised the issue of the 'democratisation of language'. In that paper, he claimed that Czech was accessible to all members of the Czech ethnic group. There were few problems – such as the spelling of foreign words – but these could and would be fixed. The fact that the masses had restricted access to the active use of the Standard (see Part III) remained unnoted.

The authors of the Prague School theory were strongly opposed to nationalism and to the existing puristic networks, in comparison with which their modernity and liberalism stood out. The arch enemy was Dr Jiří Haller, the editor of the journal *Naše řeč*, who used the journal as a vehicle for attacking writers and other authors whose language did not agree with his criteria of historical purity and the notion of 'popular language'. In comparison with Haller and his like, the Circle was a bastion of progress, universalism and liberalism.

Idiom

For the idiom of the cultivation theory some terminology is of primary importance. This includes, first of all, *norm, function, intellectualisation*, and *flexible stability*. Embedding within the structuralist matrix is obvious.

Language cultivation theory after World War II

In 1969, a volume called *Kultura českého jazyka* (*Cultivation of the Czech Language*) was published, and this was followed ten years later by *Aktuální otázky jazykové kultury v socialistické společnosti* (*Topical Issues of Language Cultivation in a Socialist Society*). Daneš (1996: 311) comments that these volumes did not offer a basically different orientation, and that is certainly true. The interest of the 1979 volume (conference proceedings) lies in the fact that it documented the state of the art in most European countries of the Soviet bloc. The opening paper by Alois Jedlička showed a lack of interest in further developing the Prague School theory, but the Prague School position was clearly reflected in Kuchař's contribution (Kuchař, 1979). Some new very useful emphases emerged (e.g. Daneš' paper on attitudes and evaluation). Stich (1979b) raised an issue that had never been emphasised in classical theories of the Prague School: the social, rather than the technical (functional) aspect of language cultivation. Evaluation of language was a social, not a purely technical matter. He emphasised the need for language cultivation to acknowledge fully the right of the community to participate. Stich also provided an historical framework for language cultivation in the Czech lands: he pointed out that the term *cultivation* (*kultura*) was used by Dobrovský in 1779, but was replaced by other terms (*grinding, purification*) until *cultivation* came back in the work of the Prague Linguistic Circle in the 1930s. This, Stich claims, possibly occurred under the influence of literature such as Vinokur's *Kul'tura jazyka* (*Language Cultivation*) (1925), which circulated among members of the Circle.

A conference bearing the same name as the 1932 volume of the Circle (*Spisovná čeština a jazyková kultura*) was held in August 1993 in Olomouc, the proceedings having been published under the same name. Although the content of the proceedings is of importance, connections with Prague School theory are weak. However, an alternative theory has not yet emerged.

An interesting attempt to update Prague School theory was presented in 1996 by František Daneš, who had already published papers that transcended the traditional Prague School Approach (Daneš, 1987). Daneš noted that cultivation (and codification) occurs each time a language manual of any type appears. He tried to guess what a contemporary (post-modern) cultivation would involve. (Similarly Kraus (1996) identified a connection between post-modern heterogeneity and recent attitudes in the Czech Republic to language cultivation.) With regard to the future of language cultivation, Daneš presented in his paper the following points:

(a) Contemporary functionalism concerns not only the system of language but also the system of discourse in communicative situations. Within discourse, it pays attention to the dynamic character of language and its central and peripheral phenomena. Such a consideration of language is traditional in Prague School thought. It is essential in the present environment to design a system of cultivation that takes full account of the dynamic character of language. In this connection Daneš quotes Dokulil's 1951 words: 'not what is correct or incorrect . . . [rather] this form is productive, while another is not . . . this expression is expanding, while another expression is receding.'
(b) Cultivation must be based on a more open conception of language, including not only its Standard but also non-Standard phenomena.
(c) Cultivation cannot presently exist without extensive contacts with sociolinguistics and psycholinguistics.
(d) There is a need to include the structure of discourse (text linguistics) within the sphere of language cultivation.
(e) Cultivation must accept the current trend against fixed norms in language.

Daneš stressed the point that cultivation and codification are legitimate and necessary. The question is not 'whether or not to codify', but 'what to codify'. He also notes that cultivation is not a one way process. Language cultivation at present must aim at a more active and informed attitude of the public. This enlightened perspective should be welcome by all 'language managers' who are concerned with language cultivation.

Closing remarks

The language cultivation theory of the Prague School represents the only serious attempt at a theory of language problems within the period between the two world wars. It was an extensive and rigorous attempt that was implemented and is still influential within the Czech Republic and possibly elsewhere: especially in Slavic speaking countries, in the former GDR and also in contemporary Germany in general (see Scharnhorst & Ising, 1976, 1982).

The theory was the product of a Modern society. Its functionalism that considered language as a technical tool, rather than as a component of social life, was one of its outstanding features. Another feature was its Modern self-imposed limitation on cultivation; i.e. a microscopic level of language treatment (Neustupný, 1968), or what Kloss (1969) called 'corpus planning'. The situation of Modern thought renders it very difficult to acknowledge the existence of macroscopic problems, affecting whole varieties and their 'status'. Thus, the complicated issues of linguistic life within a country characterised by the existence of extensive ethnic minorities was virtually ignored.

For this reason, the Prague School theory cannot serve as a general theory of language problems. On the other hand, within the area of language cultivation, the theory presents a positive approach, unmarred by the structuralist tendency to claim that language should be left alone (see Kuchař, 1987). Prague School theory contains a number of conceptual tools that should not be neglected: norm, function, intellectualisation and flexible stability are the most obvious ones. There is no evidence of the existence of a theory of language cultivation that could compete with the pre-war Prague School framework.

The Communist Party Theory: Some Preliminary Observations

The background

It is beyond the scope of this monograph to provide a full analysis of the Czech Communist Party's thought on language management, to say nothing about such thought among Communist Parties in general. The aim of this section is merely to present a few observations that may be helpful in further examining the period of almost 50 years when the Party was in power. Within the world of the Soviet Union and its immediate allies, a theoretical approach was highly valued and a theory was assumed to exist, within the framework of Marxism-Leninism, for any area of human activity. The theory was expected to guide the practice of the Party within that area.

What is dealt with in this section is theory, not the practice of the Party. The practice was mentioned in the previous chapters, although attention was on the present state of affairs rather than on the past; the relation between theory and practice will be discussed again in the conclusion of this section.

The theory pertinent to language matters was the theory of ethnic relations, which is credited in principle to Lenin and Stalin. In 1913, Stalin wrote a paper entitled 'Marxism and the National Question', and the definitions presented in that paper have outlived him. The theory is dependent on folk as well as more rigorous theories that had crystallised in central and eastern Europe by the beginning of the 20th century. Because it is anchored in that space and time, it is a macroscopic theory. It did not concern language matters at the micro level, and consequently (as mentioned in the previous section) it explains why the Czech Communist Party accepted the *de facto* continuation of Prague School language cultivation. Language cultivation, which is strongly micro-oriented, was simply out of the range of interest of the Party's theory and practice.

The inquiry system

How did the Communist Party's theory perceive the problem? After the October Revolution, the Soviet government had to deal with hundreds of illiterate ethnic groups, all of them under the highly discriminatory system of tsarist Russia (Isayev, 1977). In post-World War II Czechoslovakia, the problems the Party faced were different: these problems were embodied in the multiethnic character of the country that had only partially changed after the deportation of Germans. According to the theory attributed to Lenin, the norms the party ideologues were interested in belonged to two types:

(1) Norms that would give individual ethnic groups 'equal rights' and would satisfy their interests.
(2) Norms that enabled the broadening of national and international relations and rapprochement between nations and nationalities within the framework of so-called 'proletarian internationalism'. (See Isayev, 1977: 221; Sokolová *et al.*, 1987: 7)

The theory asserts that there is a dialectical unity between national and international norms. The first norm accepts 'patriotism' as a positive phenomenon, the second rejects, in very strong terms, 'nationalism' as well as its reverse, 'cosmopolitanism' (Zvara, 1977: 530).

The application of the norms and the problems resulting from their violation were carefully monitored. It is interesting to note, for example, that, in 1966, the Czech Communist Party commissioned a representative sociological survey of three ethnic groups (Czechs, Slovaks and Poles) in the Ostrava region from the *Slezský ústav ČSAV* (Silesian Institute of the Czechoslovak Academy of Sciences) (Sokolová *et al.*, 1978: 12). A follow-up wider survey was finalised in 1981 and published in 1987 (Sokolová *et al.*, 1987). Unless this, too, was directly solicited – and we do not know – it was at least carefully considered before being approved by a top organ of the Communist Party.

Problems were evaluated with regard to the expectations of the Party; i.e. that overall, ethnic differences would gradually weaken. It was, therefore, not perceived as a tragedy if an ethnic culture or a language were not maintained, because such a phenomenon accorded with the course of history. The theoreticians and practitioners of language policy in the Soviet Union believed that, particularly in the case of small ethnic groups, 'bilingualism should be viewed as a transitional stage to monolingualism which will be reached by the small ethnic groups when their assimilation into the corresponding nations is complete' (Isayev, 1977: 200). Such a deconstruction of ethnicity was considered to be a positive development. On the surface of the theory, it was, of course, necessary to reassert that maintenance was important; but the principle of the national and international unity of the socialist nations was given priority.

Design

The design of the theory completely relied on the experience of east European communities in which, unlike western Europe, language carried particular importance (Hroch, 1999a: 77). The theory was not totally integrated, variation being prominent even between the limited number of sources available, but it is not necessary at this point to deal with this variation in detail. The situations which were assumed as targets were mostly political, rarely situations and functions of daily life or of other domains of interaction. In the context of the present territory of the Czech Republic, only a limited number of cases were encountered (mainly those of the Polish community) where the setting for policy was to be the school system.

The participants in the ethnic policy process were seen as the political representation of the community. Within the state community, the participants were strictly classified. The traditional categorisation was into *národy* 'nations' and *národnosti* 'nationalities', traditional in the Czech lands, but which, within the theory, assumed a more theoretical nature. In Soviet theory, *nations* were historically formed communities which, according to Rogachev and Sverdlin (based on Stalin), were 'characterised by a stable commonalty of economic life (and the existence of a working class), of territory, of language (particularly a literary language), of a consciousness of ethnic belonging, as well as of certain special traits of psychology, of tradition, of way of life, of culture and of struggling for liberation' (quoted from Isayev, 1977: 191). *Nations* were communities that developed into the stage of capitalism. In contrast, a *nationality* shared some of the defining features of a *nation*, but had not yet reached the stage of capitalism. In this system, there had only been *nationalities* before the industrial revolution; only following the industrial revolution did some of the nationalities develop into *nations*. After the Soviet Union was formed, *socialist nations* emerged. This historicising classification did not work and, following World War II, Marxist social scientists started using the concept of *nation* to represent ethnic communities with a majority status, while minority ethnic communities were called *nationalities*. According to this version of the theory, Czechoslovakia consisted of:

(1) two *nations* (the Czech and the Slovak), and
(2) four *nationalities* (Hungarian, Polish, Ukrainian/Ruthenian and German, the last group only being added in the 1960s – see the section in Part II).

This structure has been specified in legal documents such as the Constitutional Law 144/1968 (Kořenský, 1998a). Sokolová *et al.* (1987) claim that both categories must be considered equal and report that, in Soviet literature since the 1970s, the term *etnikum* 'ethnic group' has been used to subsume these and other groups. In the case of Czechoslovakia, Sokolová *et al.* mention Bulgarians and Greeks who, as Sokolová *et al.* say, constitute very small groups (p. 11). Note that the Roma are not mentioned, although their numbers were very large in Sokolová's and her team's home region.

Originally, language played the most important role in the consideration of *nation* and *nationality*. As Isayev (1977) argued, the purely linguistic problems within the Soviet Union were paramount. Although a wide range of references was not available, it appears that language as the main pillar of the theory receded into the background in the 1970s when the danger of anti-Soviet nationalism was real and political aspects had to be emphasised. Perhaps the process of strengthening the position of Russian in the Soviet Union also required that language had better remain unmentioned. However, Sokolová *et al.* (1987: 63), on the basis of her data, added a new aspect to the theory in emphasising that the relation between the feeling of ethnic identity and language use were not fully symmetrical. Identity was more easily maintained than language.

According to the theory, guaranteeing equal rights to all *nationalities* is not automatic even in a socialist society and must be carefully watched. Problems (obviously problems of the rights of Slovaks in Czechoslovakia) are hinted at by Zvara (1977: 525–7), although his conclusion is that basic problems have been solved.

The theory claims that, in socialist societies, and in Czechoslovakia, *nationalities* are granted certain rights which in Sokolová *et al.* (1978) are formulated as follows:

(1) the right to receive education in one's own language;
(2) the right to cultural development;
(3) the right to use language in official contact within areas inhabited by the particular *nationality*; and
(4) the right to press and media information in one's own language.

Note that the theory does not accord these rights to ethnic groups such as the Roma that are not given the status of *nationalities*. (Also note that there were special provisions for the education of Greeks and Macedonians, but these were not supported by the theory (see the section in Part II).) Leaving the situation in Slovakia aside, the only *nationality* that was in fact given its own schools was the Polish one. The theory did not touch on the relationship between the Czechs and the Slovaks. Both were *nations*, so they had higher (unspecified) rights. However, the Slovaks who lived in the Czech lands were not entitled to Slovak schools, either in theory or in practice.

The theory assumes not only that *nations* develop their own characteristics but also that *nations* and *nationalities* will grow more similar to each other and will influence each other. Lenin had said that 'as long as national and state distinctions exist among peoples and countries . . . the unity of the international tactics of the communist working-class movement in all countries demands not the elimination of variety or the suppression of national distinctions . . . ' (Lenin, *Collected Works* 31: 92). This means that, for the time being, diversity may be all right, but over long historical time ethnic distinctions will pass away. It is well known that Marx and Engels were not champions of language rights for small *nations* (Kymlicka, 1995: 69). This theory of the historical necessity of language shift coincided with the feeling of modern social scientists who were not interested in ethnic and linguistic variation. Sokolová and her team assumed that, while ethnic differentiation was a feature of pre-capitalistic societies, in capitalist and socialist societies, ethnic unification was the more characteristic phenomenon. Such unification was implemented through the processes of integration and assimilation. Integration is the result of mutual influence, while assimilation means the identification of one ethnic group with another. There is forced assimilation, which has been refuted in socialist societies. Natural assimilation is the other type, and this assimilation does not endanger ethnicity because it affects only individuals or small groups (Sokolová *et al.*, 1987: 13). In the Czechoslovak context, this was obviously intended to mean that Czech and Slovak *nations* would come close to each other (through integration), though in practice it was the Slovaks who were expected to change. How many individuals or small groups within the *nationalities* were allowed to disappear before 'the ethnic quality' of the society would suffer? And what to do about the mere 'groups of inhabitants' (term from the Czech *Encyklopedia*), such as the Roma, who are not mentioned once in a book about the *Contemporary Trends in the Development of Nationalities in the Czechoslovak Socialist Republic*?

The theory design was not available for theoreticians to change and develop. This was a highly political area which was under the direct supervision of the Party. What happened to the Sokolová *et al.* 1987 manuscript, which the authors tell us was completed in 1981 (1987: 6) but was not published until 1987, is an interesting question.

Implementation

Implementation of the theory was, of course, considered the responsibility of the Party and the government. There was little implementation of the theory in the area of education, since only Polish was the vehicle and the object of instruction. While Polish culture was served well, the Slovak *Matice slovenská* or *CSEMADOK* (Cultural Association of Hungarian Workers in Czechoslovakia) disappeared from the Czech lands.

The social system

The social system supporting the theory consisted of the Party and the government. Only occasionally were academics allowed to participate, and then only if they were members of the Party inner circles or if they possessed special skills that Party officials lacked. The close relationship with the social system of the theory guaranteed that the theory remained maximally close to the needs of the Party. So, in the 1970s and 1980s, after the occupation of Czechoslovakia, the theory emphasised the strategy of proletarian internationalism as a counter dose to the possible wave of nationalism the Party (and the Soviet Union) feared.

The idiom

The idiom of the 1970s was a hard ideological idiom, which is not a pleasure to read (especially Zvara, 1977). On the other hand, the book published by Sokolová *et al.* in 1987 is less dogmatic in form as well as in content, and, as already noted, accepts quite a few innovative features.

Conclusions

The theory is not without interest. Although it also contains much of the ideologies of the old left, and many of its claims are unacceptable to many, there are points which deserve consideration. The division of citizenship from ethnicity (called *nationality*) is systematically carried through, and this division accords with the needs and experiences of academics and others in many parts of the world. Of course, one can claim that the division is not restricted to this theoretical system. Another point is the rapprochement between different cultures and languages. If this claim is taken as an excuse for assimilation it is difficult to accept, but one knows that descriptively speaking much 'natural' assimilation does take place. Many communities, everywhere in the world, and irrespective of anti-assimilation theories being widely distributed in the societies in question, do in fact undergo assimilation. Before one declares war on the processes of rapprochement, it will be necessary to know more about their historical background.

However, in the territory of the Czech lands, the theory was a complete failure. It failed to define the boundary between rapprochement and assimilation. It was well known as early as the 1970s that Slovaks and Poles in the Ostrava region were losing their culture and language (Sokolová *et al.*, 1978: 11), and there could be no doubt that this was a more prosaic phenomenon than the fairy-tale-like process of 'socialist nationalities growing more similar to each other'. Of course, the most important testimony against the theory is its failure to solve the Roma and the Czech–Slovak problems. As soon as the political power of the Party-controlled state was removed, it became obvious that the Roma problem was still there and that it was of a magnitude previously unimagined. The Czech–Slovak relationship, managed for decades with self-professed success by the Party, resulted in a crisis which was solved by the division of the Czechoslovak Republic, a division that was amicable and did not hurt friendly relationship between Czechs and Slovaks but nevertheless resulted in a number of consequences for their ethnic relations (see Part III). It can hardly be taken as proof of the success of previous policies guided by Marxist-Leninist theories.

Contemporary Theories

The background

The background of the contemporary theories lies, of course, in the period following the Velvet Revolution. It has been marked by liberation from the Marxist-Leninist framework imposed by the Communist Party, but also by much indecision and search for new directions.

This section is being rewritten by history in an energetic fashion, and this has led to the authors' decision to leave it brief and to keep it open to the future.

The inquiry

The way in which language problems are viewed in the contemporary period has been significantly influenced by four factors. One is the pressure of language problems within the country. Such problems cannot any longer be obscured through political control. The second factor is the warning light on any theoretical stances that might be explained as a return to the left-wing ideologies of the immediate past. This sometimes includes ideologies that, in the West, would be classified as liberal. The third is related to the new situations opened for the country by the road to post-modernisation, a long-overdue go signal. The fourth, concerning the perception of language problems, has been influenced by the country's expected entry to the European Union, making it imperative to satisfy certain conditions with regard to language.

It is interesting to note that theories of language planning (Kaplan & Baldauf, 1997) have exercised only a limited degree of influence on the perception of language problems. The leading linguistic journal *Slovo a slovesnost* has occasionally published reviews and information on language planning, but not a single paper has appeared that would place itself within the range that can be described as language planning.

Design

The theory of the Prague School

The design for language management theories can be divided into a number of streams. There is a strong component called 'corpus planning' (Kloss, 1969) or the 'language cultivation approach' (Neustupný, 1978). In this context, the Prague School tradition is alive and well, in particular among linguists who deal with the problems of the Czech language. The development of the theories after World War II has been outlined and it has been pointed out that, when writing about the new 'Rules of Czech Spelling', the revision was basically governed by the principles of the Prague School. When new topics are dealt with qua language problems, as in the case of gender in language (Čmejrková, 2002), they can probably best be classified as extensions of the Prague School way of thinking about language problems (functions of language are mentioned, there is a profound grammatical treatment of the phenomena in question, etc.).

Language law theories

All remaining types of Language Management in the contemporary Czech Republic can be classified as instances of 'status planning' (Kloss, 1969) or the 'language policy approach' (Neustupný, 1978). A theory of Language Law was outlined by Stich in a lecture available in an informal version published in the bulletin *Zprávy Kruhu přátel českého jazyka* (Stich, 1979a). In this paper, Stich discussed the relationship among language law, language policy, language planning and (as was common at the time) a number of Soviet approaches. Subsequently, he presented an admirable account of the history of Czech language law from 15th century until 1945. It should be mentioned that 'language law' was already considered a legitimate area of inquiry in 19th century Bohemia (cf. Pacák, 1896) and probably elsewhere in Europe.

The language law theories lay dormant until the 1990s when the topic was reintroduced by Kořenský (1995, 1997, 1998a). Kořenský is interested both in the structure of legal documents and in the application of law in the process of language management mainly in post-World War II Czechoslovakia.

The 'laissez-faire' approach of the 1990s

The thought about language problems of the first post-Velvet Revolution governments probably does not warrant the descriptor *theory*. If one observes the language management acts of these governments, what is striking is a distinct tendency to deviate from the Marxist-Leninist theory of the preceding period. The distinction between *nation* and *nationality* has been retained in the everyday language sense of the words. However, there was no officially accepted list of *nationalities*: as early as the 1991 census respondents were required to report a *nationality* in an open-ended question, according to their choice. However, the meaning of the term *nationality* was further de-emphasised (Nekvapil, 2003c) by the interpretation of the existing laws in the sense that rights were rights of individuals, not collective rights (Frištenská & Sulitka, 1995). Consequently, each Roma could claim schooling in his/her own language, but the Roma as a community could not. As Glazer (1995) noted in a different context, within the 'rights of individuals framework' any kind of preferencing is impracticable. On the whole, there was very little activity in the governmental networks. This position reflected management ideology that was one step behind the historical situation in the Czech Republic.

Theories of the 21st century

Towards the end of the 1990s, the new Social-Democratic government, under the pressure of European institutions, and in connection with the expected entry of the Czech Republic into the EU, began to implement an active programme of management towards the non-Czech communities. This programme has been described in the final section of Part II. The person who played a very active part in this activity was Petr Uhl, the Government's Commissioner for Human Rights. Although a practitioner rather than a theorist of language management (Neustupný, forthcoming 1), he possessed a postmodern vision of the discipline, and was instrumental in drafting the new Minorities Law as well as in initiating other measures. At the present time, language management as well as its theories in the Czech Republic provide a picture of interest, a picture that reflects both the linguistic variation in the country and the tradition of the Prague School of Linguistics.

Correspondence

Any correspondence should be directed to J.V. Neustupný, School of Languages, Cultures and Linguistics, Monash University, Melbourne, Victoria 3141 Australia (jvn@neustupny.com) or to Jiří Nekvapil, Department of Linguistics, Faculty of Arts, Charles University, nám. Jana Palacha 2, CZ-11638, Prague, Czech Republic (jiri.nekvapil@ff.cuni.cz).

Notes

1. This monograph is a survey of a single country. It does not purport to be a comparative study and although occasionally references are given to literature on other countries, such references are not systematic. The authors are grateful to Bob Kaplan and Dick Baldauf for their exceptionally sensitive and effective editing of the manuscript. Our thanks are also due to friends who read individual sections and offered valuable comments: Evžen Gál (Hungarian), Milena Hübschmannová (Romani), Jitka Slezáková (Vietnamese), Marián Sloboda (Slovak, Greek and Macedonian) and Jiří Zeman (Slovak and spelling). For assistance with the processing of the maps we are grateful to Ondřej Košťál. Michael Clyne, Jiří Kraus, Peter Neustupný, Leoš Šatava and Petr Zima have provided advice on individual points. Needless to say, the authors alone are responsible for the content.

2. In Czech the question was: *uveďte národnost, ke které se hlásíte*. This was an open-ended question. The instructions emphasised that this self-categorisation is independent of the person's 'mother tongue' and the language he or she normally speaks. Although most respondents were expected to understand Czech, the Organising Committee took account of the fact that speakers of other languages might complete the questionnaires and prepared them in ten additional languages (though not in Slovak). The English translation of the question about ethnicity was 'indicate what nationality you consider yourself to be'. Since this question came after a question about the respondent's 'citizenship', those who used the English questionnaire most probably wondered why the same question was asked twice, but some of them may have figured out that 'nationality' meant 'ethnic background'. The French questionnaire suffered from the same translation problem, and the German one, using the word

Nationalität may also have presented problems to respondents who were not used to the idiom of the former regime. The Polish, Russian, Ukrainian, Chinese, Vietnamese and Romani questionnaires conveyed the same meaning as the Czech one.

The 'mother tongue' was defined as the language used in childhood by mother or other principal caretaker. Respondents were free to report more than one ethnicity or mother tongue. In the 2001 census foreigners were included if they possessed a permanent or long-term visa, but the 1991 census form covered only permanent residents. In 1991 the Czechoslovak Republic was still in existence but Table 1 only reports data for the territory of the present-day Czech Republic.

3. In total, 100,000 to 150,000 foreigners are estimated to be illegally employed in the Czech Republic (Václavíková, 2000). Many of them are Ukrainians.
4. Only after the completion of this manuscript did Uherek (2003), an important study of a number of foreign communities in the Czech Republic, come to our notice.
5. Note that the term *substandard* is used to refer here to a variety that is located between the Standard and other varieties. It has no negative connotation as in the normal use of the word in English.
6. All translations from Czech in this monograph have been provided by the authors.

References

Ajvaz, M. (1994) Proti samozřejmosti [Against obviousness]. *Literární noviny* 5 (16), 5.

Ammon, U. and McConnell, G. (2002) *English as an Academic Language in Europe*. Frankfurt am Main: Peter Lang.

Bachmann, A.R. (2002) Atlas historických německých nářečí v České republice [Atlas of historical German dialects in the Czech Republic]. *Časopis pro moderní filologii* 84, 112–13.

Bártová, A. (2002) Jsou Češi tolerantní? [Are Czechs tolerant?]. On WWW at http://www.novinky.cz/Index/Politika/10741. Accessed 15.04.02.

Bartošek, J. (1997) Jazyk žurnalistiky [Language of journalism]. In F.Daneš, J. Bachmannová, S. Čmejrková and M. Krčmová (eds) *Český jazyk na přelomu tisíciletí* (pp. 42–67). Prague: Academia.

Berger, T. (1998) Nové cesty bádání v česko-německých jazykových vztazích (na příkladu hláskosloví) [New ways of investigation into Czech-German language relationship (exemplified in the sound system)]. In *Pocta 650. výročí založení Univerzity Karlovy v Praze* (pp. 21–35). Praha: Filozofická fakulta Univerzity Karlovy.

Berger, T. (1999) Užívání češtiny jako úředního jazyka v druhé polovině 18. století na příkladě města Chrudimě [The use of Czech as the official language in the second half of the 18th century: In the case of the town of Chrudim]. In *Východočeská duchovní a slovesná kultura v 18. století. Sborník příspěvků ze symposia konaného 27.–29.5.1999 v Rychnově nad Kněžnou* (pp. 43–78). Boskovice: Albert.

Berger, T. (2000) Zur Standardisierung und Normierung des Tschechischen und Slowakischen nach der Aufteilung der Tschechoslowakei. In L.N. Zybatow (ed.) *Sprachwandel in der Slavia* (pp. 665–81). Frankfurt am Main: Peter Lang.

Berger, T. (2003) Slovaks in Czechia – Czechs in Slovakia. *International Journal of the Sociology of Language* 162, 19–39.

Bernstein, B. (1964) Elaborated and restricted codes: Their social origins and some consequences. In J. Gumperz and D. Hymes (eds) *The Ethnography of Communication* (= *American Anthropologist* 66 (6)) Part 2, 55–69.

Bezděková, E. (1988) Deutsch als Muttersprache und Fremdsprache in Böhmen und Mähren. *Germanistische Mitteilungen* 27, 115–38.

Bogoczová, I. (1994) K jazykové a komunikativní kompetenci polské dvojjazyčné mládeže na Těšínsku [On the linguistic and communicative competence of Polish bilingual youth in the Český Těšín region]. *Časopis pro moderní filologii* 76, 19–27.

Bogoczová, I. (1997) Míra interference z češtiny do primárního jazykového kódu u nejmladších členů polského etnika v České republice [The rate of interference from Czech in the primary linguistic code of the youngest members of the Polish community within the Czech Republic]. *Časopis pro moderní filologii* 79, 4–19.

Bogoczová, I. (2000) Stylizace – druhá přirozenost (K jazykové komunikaci na Těšínsku)

[Wording – the second nature: On language communication in the Těšín region]. *Slovo a slovesnost* 60, 18–29.

Bogoczová, I. (2002) České Těšínsko. Obecné a jedinečné rysy periferního regionu [The Těšín region of Czechia: General and particular features of a peripheral region]. Paper presented at the conference *Okraj a střed v jazyce a literatuře*, Ústí nad Labem, 3–5 September.

Borák, M. (1998) Problémy polské menšiny v ČR v 90. letech [Problems of the Polish minority in the Czech Republic in 1990s]. In G. Sokolová and O. Šrajerová (eds) *Národnostní menšiny a majoritní společnost v České republice a v zemích střední Evropy v 90. letech XX. století* (pp. 230–41). Opava/Praha: Slezský ústav Slezského zemského muzea/Dokumentační a informační středisko Rady Evropy.

Borák, M. (1999) Polská menšina v České republice [Polish minority in the Czech Republic]. In I. Gabal *et al. Etnické menšiny ve střední Evropě* (pp. 120–7). Praha: G plus G.

Bozděchová, I. (1997) Jazyk managementu [The language of management]. In F. Daneš, J. Bachmannová, S. Čmejrková and M. Krčmová (eds) *Český jazyk na přelomu tisíciletí* (pp. 97–104). Prague: Academia.

Brabcová, R. (1996) Škola a spisovná čeština [The school and standard Czech]. In R. Šrámek (ed.) *Spisovnost a nespisovnost dnes* (pp. 220–2). Brno: Masarykova univerzita v Brně.

Brown, P. and Levinson, S.C. (1987) *Politeness*. Cambridge: Cambridge University Press.

Budovičová, V. (1986) Literary languages in contact (a sociolinguistic approach to the relation between Slovak and Czech today). In J. Chloupek and J. Nekvapil (eds) *Reader in Czech Sociolinguistics* (pp. 156–75). Praha: Academia.

Budovičová, V. (1987a) Semikomunikácia ako faktor medzijazykovej dynamiky [Semicommunication as an aspect of interlanguage dynamics]. In *Dynamika současné češtiny z hlediska lingvistické teorie a školské praxe* (pp. 45–54). Praha: Univerzita Karlova.

Budovičová, V. (1987b) Semikomunikácia ako lingvistický problém [Semicommunication as a linguistic problem]. In J. Mistrík (ed.) *Studia Academica Slovaca* 16 (pp. 49–66). Bratislava: Alfa.

Čechová, M. (1996) Spisovnost z hlediska školy [Standard means of expression at school]. In R. Šrámek (ed.) *Spisovnost a nespisovnost dnes* (pp. 223–6). Brno: Masarykova univerzita v Brně.

Census (2001) Results of population and housing census March 1, 2001. On WWW at http://www.czso.cz/.

Chapman, R.L. (1986) Preface. In *New Dictionary of American Slang* (pp. vii–xv). New York: Harper and Row.

Chvátalová, V. (2002) Jazyková politika Evropské unie zevnitř [Language policy of the EU from within]. *Časopis pro moderní filologii* 84, 76–85.

Cink, P. (1999) Jazyková politika v nové Evropě [Language policy in a new Europe]. In H.-J. Krumm (ed.) *Die Sprachen unserer Nachbarn – Unsere Sprachen* (pp. 30–39). Vienna: Eviva.

Cipolla, C.M. (1969) *Literacy and Development in the West*. Harmondworth: Penguin.

Cizí slova v českém jazyce [*Foreign words in Czech*] (1971). Praha: Ústav pro výzkum veřejného mínění.

Clyne, M. (1991) *Community Languages. The Australian Experience*. Cambridge: Cambridge University Press.

Clyne, M. (1994) *Inter-cultural Communication at Work. Cultural Values in Discourse*. Cambridge: Cambridge University Press.

Čmejrková, S. (1995) Žena v jazyce [Woman in language]. *Slovo a slovesnost* 56, 43–55.

Čmejrková, S. (1997a) Jazyk literatury [Language of literature]. In F. Daneš, J. Bachmannová, S. Čmejrková and M. Krčmová (eds) *Český jazyk na přelomu tisíciletí* (pp. 114–32). Prague: Academia.

Čmejrková, S. (1997b) Jazyk pro druhé pohlaví [Language for the second sex]. In F. Daneš, J. Bachmannová, S. Čmejrková and M. Krčmová (eds) *Český jazyk na přelomu tisíciletí* (pp. 146–58). Prague: Academia.

Čmejrková, S. (1999) Czech on the network: Written or spoken interaction? In B. Nauman (ed.) *Dialogue Analysis and the Mass Media* (pp. 113–26). Tübingen: Niemeyer.

Čmejrková, S. (2002) Rod v jazyce a komunikaci: Specifika češtiny [Gender in language and communication: The special position of Czech]. *Slovo a slovesnost* 63, 263–86.

Čmejrková, S. (2003) The categories of 'our own' and 'foreign' in the language and culture of Czech repatriates from the Ukraine. *International Journal of the Sociology of Language* 162, 103–23.

Crown, D. (1996) Mluví se v České republice ještě česky? [Is Czech still spoken in the Czech Republic?]. *Čeština doma a ve světě* 4, 150–55.

Cunningham, K. (2001) Translating for a larger Union – can we cope with more than 11 languages? *Terminologie et Traduction* 2001/2, 22–33.

Cuřín, F. (1985) *Vývoj spisovné češtiny* [*Development of Standard Czech*]. Praha: Státní pedagogické nakladatelství.

Czech Republic (1999) Information about compliance with principles set forth in the Framework Convention for the Protection of National Minorities according to article 25, paragraph 1 of this convention. Praha (mimeo).

Daneš, F. (1987) Values and attitudes in language standardization. In J.Chloupek and J. Nekvapil (eds) *Reader in Czech Sociolinguistics* (pp. 206–45). Amsterdam: John Benjamins.

Daneš, F. (1988) Sprachkultur. In U. Ammon, N. Dittmar and K.J. Mattheier (eds) *Sociolinguistics. An International Handbook of the Science of Language and Society* (pp. 1697–703). Berlin: Walter de Gruyter.

Daneš, F. (1996) Teorie spisovného jazyka Pražského lingvistického kroužku: Pro i proti [The theory of the standard language of the Prague Linguistic Circle: For and against]. In R. Šrámek (ed.) *Spisovnost a nespisovnost dnes* (pp. 19–27). Brno: Masarykova univerzita v Brně.

Daneš, F. (1997a) Situace a celkový stav dnešní češtiny [The situation and current condition of Czech]. In F. Daneš, J. Bachmannová, S. Čmejrková and M. Krčmová (eds) *Český jazyk na přelomu tisíciletí* (pp. 12–24). Prague: Academia.

Daneš, F. (1997b) Jazyk vědy [Language of science]. In F. Daneš, J. Bachmannová, S. Čmejrková and M. Krčmová (eds) *Český jazyk na přelomu tisíciletí* (pp. 68–83). Prague: Academia.

Daneš, F. (forthcoming) Destandardization and restandardization of standard languages – ongoing processes and their problems. *International Journal of Language Management* 1.

Davidová, D. (1990) Překonávání a využití interference češtiny, slovenštiny a polštiny v komunikaci velkých podniků ostravské aglomerace [Ways of countering and utilizing interference between Czech, Slovak and Polish in communication within large companies in the Ostrava conurbation]. *Acta Facultatis Paedagogicae Ostraviensis/ Sborník prací Pedagogické fakulty v Ostravě* 121, Series D-27 (*Jazyk, literatura, umění*), 31–46.

Deutsch in der Tschechischen Republik (2000/2001). Praha: Goethe-Institut Prag etc.

Doets, C. (1994) Assessment of adult literacy levels: The Dutch case. In L. Verhoeven (ed.) *Functional Literacy* (pp. 321–32). Amsterdam: John Benjamins.

Dorovský, I. (1998) *Makedonci žijí mezi námi* [*Macedonians living among us*]. Brno: Masarykova univerzita, Společnost přátel jižních Slovanů v ČR.

Eckert, E. (2002) Variabilita, kontakt a rozklad: Jazyk náhrobních nápisů [Variability, contact and shift: Language of tombstone inscriptions]. *Časopis pro moderní filologii* 84, 1–17.

Ehlers, K.-H. and Knéřová, M. (1997) Tschechisch förmlich, unverschämt deutsch? Arbeitsbericht zu einer kontrastiven Untersuchung des Anredeverhaltens. In S. Höhne and M. Nekula (eds) *Sprache, Wirtschaft, Kultur. Deutsche und Tschechen in Interaktion* (pp. 189–214). München: Iudicium.

Elšík, V. (2000/2001) Romština jako cizí jazyk [Romani as a foreign language]. *Cizí jazyky* 44, 7–9.

Elšík, V. (2003) Interdialect contact of Czech (and Slovak) Romani varieties. *International Journal of the Sociology of Language* 162, 41–62.

Eőry, V. and Hašová, L. (2003) Hungarians in the Czech Republic. On the emergence of a 'new' linguistic minority after the division of Czechoslovakia. *International Journal of the Sociology of Language* 162, 85–102.

Fairclough, N. (1989) *Language and Power*. London: Longman. (2nd edn, 2001).

Fenclová, M. (1998/1999a) Úloha mateřštiny v didaktice cizích jazyků [The role of the mother tongue in the teaching of foreign languages]. *Cizí jazyky* 42, 3–4.

Fenclová, M. (1998/1999b) Proč se nedaří ve školách pluralitě cizích jazyků [Why the plurality of foreign languages is not successful in schools]. *Cizí jazyky* 42, 60–62.

Ferguson, C.A. (1959) Diglossia. *Word* 15, 325–40.

Ferguson, C.A. (1981) 'Foreigner talk' as the name of a simplified register. *International Journal of the Sociology of Language* 28, 9–18.

Fialová, L. *et al.* (1998) *Dějiny obyvatelstva českých zemí* [*History of the Population of the Czech Lands*]. Praha: Mladá fronta.

Fishman, J.A. (1971) The sociology of language. In J.A. Fishman (ed.) *Advances in the Sociology of Language* (pp. 217–404). The Hague: Mouton.

Fishman, J.A. (1972) Domains and the relationship between micro- and macrosociolinguistics. In J. Gumperz and D. Hymes (eds) *Directions in Sociolinguistics* (pp. 435–53). New York: Holt, Rinehart and Winston.

Frištenská, H. and Sulitka, A. (1995) *Průvodce právy příslušníků národnostních menšin v ČR* [*A Guide to the Rights of Members of Ethnic Minorities in the Czech Republic*] (2nd edn). Praha: Demokratická aliancia Slovákov v ČR.

Galtung, J. (1981) Structure, culture, and intellectual style: An essay comparing saxonic, teutonic, gallic and nipponic approaches. *Social Science Information* 6, 817–56.

Gebauer, J. (1902) Předmluva [Preface]. In *Pravidla hledící k českému pravopisu a tvarosloví s abecedním seznamem slov a tvarů* (pp. 1–6). Praha: Císařský královský školní knihosklad.

Glazer, N. (1995) Individual rights against group rights. In W. Kymlicka (ed.) *The Rights of Minority Culture* (pp. 123–38). Oxford: Oxford University Press.

Hall, R.A. (1950) *Leave Your Language Alone*. Linguistic Press. Second revised edition (1960): *Linguistics and Your Language*. New York: Anchor.

Haluková, J. (1998) Občanská sdružení a instituce slovenské národnostní menšiny a kulturní aktivity Klubu slovenské kultury v ČR [Civic associations and institutions of the Slovak ethnic minority and cultural activities of the Slovak Culture Club in the ČR]. In G. Sokolová and O. Šrajerová (eds) *Národnostní menšiny a majoritní společnost v České republice a v zemích střední evropy v 90. letech XX. století* (pp. 130–35). Opava/Praha: Slezský ústav Slezského zemského muzea/Dokumentační a informační středisko Rady Evropy.

Hancock, I.F. (1988) The development of Romani linguistics. In M.A. Jazayeri and W. Winter (eds) *Languages and Cultures: Studies in Honor of Edgar C. Polomé* (pp. 183–223). Berlin: Mouton de Gruyter.

Hasil, J. (1999) Kauza 'Česko' [The 'Czechia' issue]. In *Přednášky z XLII. běhu Letní školy slovanských studií. I. díl. Přednášky z jazykovědy* (pp. 7–30). Praha: Univerzita Karlova v Praze, Filozofická fakulta.

Hašová, L. (1996) Z výzkumu jazykové situace v Nejdku u Karlových Varů [From the study of the language situation in Nejdek by Karlovy Vary]. *Časopis pro moderní filologii* 78, 88–96.

Hašová, L. (2000). K jednomu případu česko–německé interference [One instance of Czech–German interference]. *Časopis pro moderní filologii* 82, 22–8.

Hašová, L. (2001) K problematice střídání a míšení kódů (na česko-maďarském jazykovém materiálu) [On code-switching and code-mixing as exemplified in Czech-Hungarian language contact]. *Jazykovědné aktuality* 38 (4), 52–7.

Haugen, E. (1966) Semicommunication: The linguistic gap in Scandinavia. In S. Lieberson (ed.) *Explorations in Sociolinguistics* (pp. 152–69). Bloomington: Indiana University.

Havránek, B. (1929) Funkce spisovného jazyka [Functions of the standard language]. Reprinted in Havránek (1963), pp. 11–18.

Havránek, B. (1932a) Úkoly spisovného jazyka a jeho kultura [The task of the standard language and its cultivation]. In *Spisovná čeština a jazyková kultura* (pp. 32–84). Reprinted in Havránek (1963), pp. 30–59. Partially translated into English in P.L. Garvin (1964) *A Prague School Reader on Esthetics, Literary Structure and Style* (pp. 3–16). Washington: Georgetown University Press. The English version reprinted in Vachek (1983), pp. 143–64.

Havránek, B. (1932b) Obecné zásady pro kulturu jazyka [General principles of language cultivation]. In *Spisovná čeština a jazyková kultura* (pp. 245–58). Reprinted in Havránek (1963), pp. 111–18. A German translation in Schanhorst and Ising (1976), pp. 74–85.

Havránek, B. (1938) Zum Problem der Norm in der heutigen Sprachwissenshaft und Sprachkultur. In *Actes du Quatrième Congrès International de Linguistes* (pp. 151–6). Copenhagen. Reprinted in J. Vachek (1964) *A Prague School Reader in Linguistics* (pp. 413–20). Bloomington: Indiana University Press. A slightly adapted version in Schanhorst and Ising (1976), pp. 142–9.

Havránek, B. (1947) Demokratizace spisovného jazyka. [Democratisation of the standard language]. In *Čeština v životě a ve škole* (pp. 16–20). Praha: Edice zemské školní rady v Praze. Reprinted in Havránek (1963), pp. 145–8.

Havránek, B. (1963) *Studie o spisovném jazyce* [*Studies on Standard Language*]. Praha: Nakladatelství ČSAV.

Havránek, B. (1980/1936) *Vývoj českého spisovného jazyka* [*Development of the Czech Standard Language*]. Praha: Univerzita Karlova v Praze.

Havránek, J. (2002) Rozdělení pražské univerzity roku 1882 – rozpad univerza, nebo přirozený vývoj? [Division of the Prague University 1882 – disintegration of a universe or natural development?]. In W. Koschmal, M. Nekula and J.Rogall (eds) *Češi a Němci. Dějiny – Kultura – Politika* (pp. 426–30). Praha/Litomyšl: Paseka.

Helbig, G. (1991) *Vývoj jazykovědy po roce 1970* [*Development of Linguistics after 1970*]. Praha: Academia

Heroldová, I. and Matějová, V. (1987) Vietnamští pracující v českých zemích [Vietnamese workers in the Czech lands]. *Český lid* 74, 194–203.

Hlavsová, J. (1997) Jazyk politiky [Language of politics]. In F. Daneš, J. Bachmannová, S. Čmejrková and M. Krčmová (eds) *Český jazyk na přelomu tisíciletí* (pp. 26–41). Prague: Academia.

Hoffmann, R. (1992) *České město ve středověku* [*Czech Towns in the Middle Ages*]. Praha: Panorama.

Hoffmannová, J. (1994) On the means of expressing vagueness and uncertainty in Czech discourse. In S. Čmejrková and F. Štícha (eds) *The Syntax of Sentence and Text* (pp. 219–35). Amsterdam/Philadelphia: John Benjamins.

Hoffmannová, J. and Müllerová, O. (1993) Interference češtiny a slovenštiny v mluvené komunikaci [Interference between Czech and Slovak in spoken communication]. In *Česká slavistika 1993. České přednášky pro XI. mezinárodní sjezd slavistů* (= *Slavia* 62 (3), 311–16).

Hoffmannová, J. and Müllerová, O. (2000) O českém míšení [On code-mixing in Czech]. In K. Buzássyová (ed.) *Člověk a jeho jazyk. 1. Jazyk ako fenomén kultúry* (pp. 102–11). Bratislava: Veda.

Hoffmannová, J., Müllerová, O. and Zeman, J. (1999) *Konverzace v češtině při rodinných a přátelských návštěvách* [*Conversation in Czech on the Occasion of Family and Friendship Visits*]. Praha: Trizonia.

Homoláč, J. (2002) Analýza diskursu kritická [Critical discourse analysis]. In *Encyklopedický slovník češtiny* (pp. 37–8). Praha: Nakladatelství Lidové noviny.

Homoláč, J., Karhanová, K. and Nekvapil, J. (eds) (2003) *Obraz Romů v středoevropských masmédiích* [*Presentations of Roma in Central European Media*]. Brno: Doplněk.

Horská, P. (1998) Obyvatelstvo českých zemí podle povolání [Population of the Czech lands according to professions]. In L. Fialová *et al.* (1998), pp. 227–65.

Houžvička, V. (2001) Wie Tschechen die Deutschen wahrnehmen. In K. Roth (ed.) *Nachbarschaft. Interkulturelle Beziehungen zwischen Deutschen, Polen und Tschechen* (pp. 79–97). Münster/New York/München/Berlin: Waxmann.

Hroch, M. (1999a) *V národním zájmu* [*In the National Interest*]. Praha: Nakladatelství Lidové noviny.

Hroch, M. (1999b) *Na prahu národní existence* [*On the Threshold of Becoming a Nation*]. Praha: Mladá fronta.

Hubáček, J. (1979) *O českých slanzích* [*On Czech Slangs*]. Ostrava: Profil.

Hübschmannová, M. (1979) Bilingualism among the Slovak Rom. *International Journal of the Sociology of Language* 19, 33–50.

Hübschmannová, M. and Neustupný, J.V. (1996) The Slovak-and-Czech dialect of Romani and its standardization. *International Journal of the Sociology of Language* 120, 85–109.

Hübschmannová, M., Šebková, H. and Žigová, A. (1991) *Romsko-český a česko-romský kapesní slovník* [*Romani-Czech and Czech-Romani Pocket Dictionary*]. Prague: Státní pedagogické nakladatelství.

Human Resources (2000) *Human Resources in the Czech Republic 1999.* Praha: Institute for Information on Education/National Training Fund.

Hymes, D.H. (ed.) (1971) *Pidginization and Creolization of Languages.* Cambridge: Cambridge University Press.

Hymes, D.H. (1974) *Foundations in Sociolinguistics: An Ethnographic Approach.* Philadelphia: University of Pennsylvania Press.

Isayev, M.I. (1977) *National Languages in the USSR: Problems and Solutions.* Moscow: Progress Publishers.

Ivaňová, T. (2002) *Cizinka S (Dvojjazyčná česko-slovenská komunikace)* [*Foreigner S. (On Bilingual Czech-Slovak Communication)*]. Praha: Filozofická fakulta Univerzity Karlovy, Ústav bohemistických studií (diss.).

Jabur, V. (2000) Das Rusinische in der Slowakei. In B. Panzer (ed.) *Die sprachliche Situation in der Slavia zehn Jahre nach der Wende* (pp. 117–32). Frankfurt am Main: Peter Lang.

Jakobson, R. (1960) Concluding statement: Linguistics and poetics. In T.A. Sebeok (ed.) *Style in Language* (pp. 350–73). New York: Wiley.

Jančáková, J. (1997a) Nářečí středočeské obce Dobrovíz u Prahy [The dialect of the central Bohemian village Dobrovíz by Prague]. In F. Daneš, J. Bachmannová, S. Čmejrková and M. Krčmová (eds) *Český jazyk na přelomu tisíciletí* (pp. 174–82). Praha: Academia.

Jančáková, J. (1997b) Uchování staršího nářečního úzu na jazykových ostrovech (na základě mluvy českých reemigrantů z Ukrajiny) [Maintenance of older dialectal usage in linguistic enclaves: Speech of the Czech re-emigrants from Ukraine]. In *Přednášky z XXXIX. běhu LŠSS* (pp. 50–55). Praha: Univerzita Karlova, Filozofická fakulta.

Jelínek, M. (1996) Kritérium systémovosti při kodifikaci spisovné normy [Systemicity as a criterion for the codification of the standard norm]. In Šrámek, R. (ed.) *Spisovnost a nespisovnost dnes* (pp. 36–42). Brno: PF MU.

Jernudd, B.H. (1977) Prerequisites for a theory of language treatment. In J. Rubin, B.H. Jernudd, J. Das Gupta, J.A. Fishman and C.A. Ferguson (eds) *Language Planning Processes* (pp. 41–54). The Hague: Mouton.

Jernudd, B.H. (1996) Language planning. In H. Goebl, P. H. Nelde, Z. Starý and W.Wölck (eds) *Kontaktlinguistik. Ein internationales Handbuch zeitgenössischer Forschung* (pp. 833–42). Berlin: Walter de Gruyter.

Jernudd, B.H. and Neustupný, J.V. (1987) Language planning: For whom? In L. Laforge (ed.) *Proceedings of the International Colloquium on Language Planning* (pp. 69–84). Québec: Presses de l'Université Laval.

Jesenský J. (2000) *Základy komprehenzivní speciální pedagogiky* [*Foundations of Comprehensive Special Pedagogy*]. Hradec Králové: Gaudeamus.

Jodas, J. (2001) Lexikální bohemismy v německé městské mluvě v Olomouci [Czech lexical elements in the German urban speech of Olomouc]. *Časopis pro moderní filologii* 83, 81–8.

Johnston, S.M. (2000) Multilingualism and EU enlargement. *Terminologie et Traduction* 2000 (3), 5–70.

Jurman, A. (2001) Pronominální oslovení (tykání a vykání) v současné češtině [Pronominal address forms (the use of ty and vy) in contemporary Czech]. *Slovo a slovesnost* 62, 185–99.

Kaplan, R.B. and Baldauf, R.B., Jr. (1997) *Language Planning: From Practice to Theory.* Clevedon: Multilingual Matters.

Kastner, Q. (1998) Volyňští Češi na Litoměřicku (Na základě sociologického zjišťování). [Volynh Czechs in the Litoměřice region: results of a sociological research]. In G. Sokolová and O. Šrajerová (eds) *Národnostní menšiny a majoritní společnost v České republice a v zemích střední Evropy v 90. letech XX. století* (pp. 249–56). Opava: Slezský ústav Slezského zemského muzea/Praha: Dokumentační a informační středisko Rady Evropy.

Keliš, J. (1998/1999) Nejen angličtina [Not only English]. *Cizí jazyky* 42, 62–3.

Keller, J. (2002) Romové – v bludném kruhu stigmatizace [The Roma – in the vicious circle of stigmatization]. In W. Koschmal, M. Nekula and J.Rogall (eds) *Češi a Němci. Dějiny – Kultura – Politika* (pp. 273–6). Praha/Litomyšl: Paseka.

Khubchandani, L. (1981) *Language, Education, Social Justice.* Poona: Centre for Communication Studies.

Kieval, H.J. (1988) *The Making of Czech Jewry: National Conflict and Jewish Society in Bohemia, 1870–1918.* Oxford: Oxford University Press.

Klimeš, L. (1997) *Komentovaný přehled výzkumu slangu v Československu, v České republice a ve Slovenské republice v létech 1920–1996* [*A Survey of Research on Slang in Czechoslovakia, in the Czech Republic and in the Slovak Republic in the Years 1920–1996 with a commentary*]. Plzeň: Pedagogická fakulta ZČU v Plzni.

Kloss, H. (1969) *Research Possibilities on Group Bilingualism: A Report.* Québec: International Center for Research on Bilingualism.

Kompasová, S. (1999/2000) Čeština ve vysílání slovenské televizní stanice Markíza [The Czech language in the broadcasting of the Slovak television station Markíza]. *Češtinář* 10, 156–63.

Köppen, B. (2000) Auswirkungen des Einkaufstourismus im nordböhmischen Grenzraum. *Europa Regional* 8 (2), 19–31. Leipzig: Institut für Länderstudien.

Kopřivová-Vukolová, A. (1993) Osudy ruské emigrace v ČSR po r. 1945 [History of the Russian émigré community in Czechoslovakia after 1945]. In V. Veber *et al. Ruská a ukrajinská emigrace v ČSR v letech 1918–1945* (pp. 80–94). Praha: Seminář pro dějiny východní Evropy při Ústavu světových dějin FF UK v Praze.

Kořenský, J. (1995) Tvorba právních předpisů a komunikativní problémy jejich uplatňování [Formation of legal norms and communication problems in their application]. *Slovo a slovesnost* 61, 267–75.

Kořenský, J. (1997) Jazykové právo – prostor, nebo limita? [Linguistic right – open space or a limit?] In S. Ondrejovič (ed.) *Slovenčina na konci 20. storočia, jej normy a perspektívy* (= *Sociolinguistica Slovaca* 3) (pp. 93–100). Bratislava: Veda.

Kořenský, J. (1998a) Jazykové právo a jazyková politika [Language law and language policy]. In J. Kořenský (ed.) *Najnowsze dzieje języków słowiańskich. Český jazyk* (pp. 95–101).Opole: Uniwersytet Opolski, Instytut Filologii Polskiej.

Kořenský, J. (1998b) Čeština a slovenština [Czech and Slovak]. In J. Kořenský (ed.) *Najnowsze dzieje języków słowiańskich. Český jazyk* (pp. 20–33). Opole: Uniwersytet Opolski, Instytut Filologii Polskiej.

Kraus, J. (1996) Jazyková správnost a jazyková kultura v paradigmatu současné vědy [Correct language and language cultivation in the paradigm of contemporary science]. In R. Šrámek (ed.) *Spisovnost a nespisovnost dnes* (pp. 48–51). Brno: PF MU.

Kraus, J. (1997a) Jazyk hospodářských dokumentů a písemností [Language of economic documents and texts]. In F. Daneš, J. Bachmannová, S. Čmejrková and M. Krčmová (eds) *Český jazyk na přelomu tisíciletí* (pp. 92–6). Prague: Academia.

Kraus, J. (1997b) Jaká je čeština v letech devadesátých [The Czech language in the 1990s]. In F. Daneš, J. Bachmannová, S. Čmejrková and M. Krčmová (eds) *Český jazyk na přelomu tisíciletí* (pp. 288–92). Prague: Academia.

Krčmová, M. (1993) Brněnská městská mluva – odraz kontaktů etnik [Urban speech in Brno as a reflection of ethnic contacts]. *Sborník prací filozofické fakulty Brněnské univerzity,* A 41, 77–86.

Krčmová, M. (1997) Současná běžná mluva v českých zemích [Current everyday speech in the Czech lands]. In F. Daneš, J. Bachmannová, S. Čmejrková and M. Krčmová (eds) *Český jazyk na přelomu tisíciletí* (pp. 160–72). Praha: Academia.

Kučera, K. (1990) *Český jazyk v USA* [*Czech in the USA*]. Praha: Univerzita Karlova.

Kučera, K. (2003) Rozšíření češtiny v zahraničí [Spread of the Czech language abroad]. *Přednášky z XLVI. běhu Letní školy slovanských studií* (pp. 91–98). Praha: Univerzita Karlova v Praze, Filozofická fakulta.

Kučera, M. (1998) Obyvatelstvo českých zemí ve 20. století [Population of the Czech lands in the 20th century]. In L. Fialová *et al.* (1998), pp. 311–81.

Kuchař, J. (1979) Regulační aspekt jazykové kultury [The regulatory aspect of language cultivation]. In *Aktuální otázky jazykové kultury v socialistické společnosti* (pp. 92–7). Prague: Academia.

Kuchař, J. (1987) Language treatment as an aspect of language culture. In J. Chloupek and J. Nekvapil (eds) *Reader in Czech Sociolinguistics* (pp. 246–56). Amsterdam/ Philadelphia: John Benjamins.

Kymlicka, W. (1995) *Multicultural Citizenship.* Oxford: Oxford University Press.

Lanstyák, I. (2002) Maďarčina na Slovensku – štúdia z variačnej sociolingvistiky [Hungarian in Slovakia – a study in variational sociolinguistics]. *Sociologický časopis/ Czech Sociological Review* 38, 409–27.

Leiss, E. (1985) Zur Entstehung des neuhochdeutschen analytischen Futurs. *Sprachwissenschaft* 10, 250–73.

Leška, O., Nekvapil, J. and Šoltys, O. (1993) Ferdinand de Saussure and the Prague Linguistic Circle. In J. Chloupek and J. Nekvapil (eds) *Studies in Functional Stylistics* (pp. 9–50). Amsterdam/Philadelphia: John Benjamins.

Leudar, I. and Nekvapil, J. (1998) On the emergence of political identity in the Czech mass media: The case of the Democratic Party of Sudetenland. *Czech Sociological Review* 6, 43–58.

Leudar, I. and Nekvapil, J. (2000) Presentations of Romanies in the Czech media: On category work in television debates. *Discourse and Society* 11, 487–513.

Leudar, I. and Nekvapil, J. (2004) Media dialogical networks and political argumentation. *Journal of Language and Politics* 3 (2), 247–66.

Literacy (2000) *Literacy in the Information Age. Final Report of the International Adult Education Survey.* Paris: OECD.

Lotko, E. (1994) O jazykové komunikaci polské národnostní menšiny v České republice [On language communication of the Polish ethnic minority in the Czech Republic]. *Časopis pro moderní filologii* 76, 9–19.

Lotko, E. (1998) Čeština a polština [Czech and Polish]. In J. Kořenský (ed.) *Najnowsze dzieje języków słowiańskich. Český jazyk* (pp. 33–43). Opole: Uniwersytet Opolski, Instytut Filologii Polskiej.

Magocsi, P.R. (ed.) (1996) *A New Slavic Language is Born. The Rusyn Literary Language of Slovakia.* New York: Columbia University Press.

Malý, K. (1991) Sprache – Recht und Staat in der tschechischen Vergangenheit. In J. Eckert and H. Hattenhauer (eds) *Sprache – Recht – Geschichte* (pp. 257–81). Heidelberg: C.F. Müller.

Marti, R. (1998) Sprachenpolitik im slavischsprachigen Raum. Das Verhältnis 'großer' und 'kleiner' slavischer Standardsprachen. *Zeitschrift für Slavische Philologie* 57, 353–70.

Marti, R. (1993) Slovakisch und Čechisch vs. Čechoslovakisch, Serbokroatisch vs. Kroatisch und Serbisch. In K. Gutschmidt, H. Keipert and H. Rothe (eds) *Slavistische Studien zum XI. internationalen Slavistenkongreß in Preßburg/Bratislava* (pp. 289–315). Köln/Weimar/Wien: Böhlau.

Marvan, J. (1993) Quo vadis, lingua Bohemica. *Literární noviny* 4 (42), 4.

Mattheier, K.J. (1997) Über Destandardisierung, Umstandardisierung und Standardisierung in modernen europäischen Standardsprachen. In K.J. Mattheier and E. Radtke (eds) *Standardisierung und Destandardisierung europäischer Nationalsprachen* (pp. 1–9). Frankfurt am Main: Peter Lang,

Mathesius, V. (1932) O požadavku stability ve spisovném jazyce [On the requirement of stability for the standard language]. In *Spisovná čeština a jazyková kultura* (pp.14–31). Rewritten text, published in 1947, reprinted in V. Mathesius (1982) *Jazyk, kultura a slovesnost* (pp. 65–75). Prague: Odeon. A German translation in Schanhorst and Ising (1976), pp. 86–102.

Maur, E. (1998a) Obyvatelstvo českých zemí ve středověku [Population of the Czech lands in the Middle Ages]. In L. Fialová *et al.* (1998), pp.35–73.

Maur, E. (1998b) Obyvatelstvo českých zemí v raném novověku. Třicetiletá válka. [Population of the Czech lands in the Early Modern Ages. The 30 Years War]. In L. Fialová *et al.* (1998), pp. 75–131.

McCluskey, B. (2001) Respecting multilingualism in the enlargement of the European Union – the organizational challenge. *Terminologie et Traduction* 2001 (2), 7–21.

Medgyes, P. and Miklósy, K. (2000) The language situation in Hungary. *Current Issues in Language Planning* 1, 148–242.

Mlčoch, M. (2002) K problematice česko-slovenských a slovensko-českých jazykových vztahů [On Czech-Slovak and Slovak-Czech language relationship]. *Jazykovědné aktuality* 39, 46–47.

Možný, I. (2002) *Česká společnost: Nejdůležitější fakta o kvalitě našeho života* [*The Czech Society: Basic Facts Concerning the Quality of our Life*]. Prague: Portál.

Mukařovský, J. (1932) Jazyk spisovný a jazyk básnický [Standard language and poetic language]. In *Spisovná čeština a jazyková kultura* (pp.123–49). An English translation in P.L. Garvin (1964) *A Prague School Reader on Esthetics, Literary Structure and Style* (pp. 17–30). Washington: Georgetown University Press. The English version reprinted in Vachek (1983), pp. 165–85.

Müllerová, O. (2001) E-mailová korespondence z hlediska generačních rozdílů [E-mail correspondence from the point of view of generational differences]. In M. Balowski and J. Svoboda (eds) *Język i literatura czeska u schyłku XX wieku/Český jazyk a literatura na sklonku XX. století* (pp. 205–13). Wałbrzych/Ostrava: Wydawnictwo Państwowej Wyższej Szkoły Zawodowej w Wałbrzychu.

Müllerová, O., Hoffmannová, J. and Schneiderová, E. (1992) *Mluvená čeština v autentických textech* [*Spoken Czech in Authentic Texts*]. Jinočany: H&H.

Müllerová, P. (1998) Vietnamese diaspora in the Czech Republic. *Archív orientální* 66, 121–6.

Musil, J. (1998) Česká společnost 1918–1938 [Czech society, 1918–1938]. In L. Fialová *et al.* (1998), pp. 267–309.

Musil, J. (2000/2001) Z jednání u kulatého stolu o jazykové politice [Round table talks on language policy]. *Cizí jazyky* 44, 92–3.

Musilová, K. (2000) Česko-slovenský pasivní bilingvizmus [Czech-Slovak passive bilingualism]. In S. Ondrejovič (ed.) *Mesto a jeho jazyk* (= *Sociolinguistica Slovaca* 5) (pp. 280–88). Bratislava: Veda.

Nábělková, M. (2000) Rozdelenie a 'vzďaľovanie'. Niekoľko pohľadov [Division and dissociation. Several views]. In I. Pospíšil and M. Zelenka (eds) *Česko-slovenská vzájemnost a nevzájemnost* (pp. 104–112). Brno: Ústav slavistiky Filozofické fakulty Masarykovy univerzity.

Nábělková, M. (2002a) 'K dverím ňebe se mej . . .' Bibličtina na Slovensku v 20. storočí [The language of the Bible in Slovakia in the 20th century]. In I. Pospíšil and M. Zelenka (eds) *Literatury v kontaktech (Jazyk – Literatura – Kultura)* (pp. 71–87). Brno: Ústav slavistiky Filozofické fakulty Masarykovy univerzity.

Nábělková, M. (2002b) Medzi pasívnym a aktívnym blingvizmom (poznámky k špecifiku slovensko-českých jazykových vzťahov) [Between passive and active bilingualism: Notes on the specific features of Slovak–Czech language relations]. In *Bilingvizmus. Minulosť, prítomnosť a budúcnosť* (pp. 101–14). Bratislava: Academic Electronic.

Národnostní složení (1993) *Národnostní složení obyvatelstva ČR – Výsledky sčítání lidu, domů a bytů 1991* [*Ethnic Compostion of the Population of the Czech Republic – Results of the Census of People, Houses and Flats 1991*] (= *Zprávy a rozbory* 23(2)). Praha: Český statistický úřad.

Nekovářová, H. (1999) Jazykové plánování v České republice a v zahraničí. Výuka v angličtině v ČR [Language planning in the Czech Republic and abroad. Teaching in English in the ČR]. Praha: Department of Linguistics and Finno-Ugric Studies, Charles University (mimeo).

Nekula, M. (1997) Germanismen in der tschechischen Presse und Werbung. Die Einstellung gegenüber dem Deutschen. In S. Höhne and M. Nekula (eds) *Sprache, Wirtschaft, Kultur. Deutsche und Tschechen in Interaktion* (pp. 147–59). München: Iudicium.

Nekula, M. (2002a) Kommunikationsführung in deutsch-tschechischen Firmen. In J Möller and M. Nekula (eds) *Wirtschaft und Kommunikation. Beiträge zu den deutsch-tschechischen Wirtschaftsbeziehungen* (pp. 65–83). München: Iudicium.

Nekula, M. (2002b) Česko-německý bilingvismus [Czech-German bilingualism]. In W. Koschmal, M. Nekula and J. Rogall (eds) *Češi a Němci. Dějiny – Kultura – Politika* (pp. 152–8). Praha/Litomyšl: Paseka.

Nekvapil, J. (1993) Slang and some related problems in Czech linguistics. In J. Chloupek and J. Nekvapil (eds) *Studies in Functional Stylistics* (pp. 99–111). Amsterdam/ Philadelphia: John Benjamins.

Nekvapil, J. (1996) Tschechische Medien und Mediensprache nach dem Regimewechsel. In K. Mänicke-Gyöngyösi (ed.) *Öffentliche Konfliktdiskurse um Restitution von Gerechtigkeit, politische Verantwortung und nationale Identität* (pp. 93–118). Frankfurt am Main: Peter Lang.

Nekvapil, J. (1997a) Some remarks on item orderings in Czech conversation: The issue of pre-sequences. In B. Palek (ed.) *Proceedings of LP's 1996. Typology: Prototypes, Item Orderings and Universals* (pp. 444–50). Prague: Charles University Press.

Nekvapil, J. (1997b) Die kommunikative Überwindung der tschechisch-deutschen ethnischen Polarisation. Deutsche, deutsche Kollegen, Expatriates und andere soziale Kategorien im Automobilwerk Škoda. In S. Höhne and M. Nekula (eds) *Sprache, Wirtschaft, Kultur. Deutsche und Tschechen in Interaktion* (pp. 127–45). München: Iudicium.

Nekvapil, J. (1997c) Český tisk a politický diskurs po roce 1989 [Czech press and political discourse after 1989]. In *Přednášky z XXXIX. běhu LŠSS* (pp. 86–110). Praha: Univerzita Karlova v Praze, Filozofická fakulta.

Nekvapil, J. (1997d) Tschechien. In H. Goebl, P. H. Nelde, Z. Starý and W.Wölck (eds) *Kontaktlinguistik. Ein internationales Handbuch zeitgenössischer Forschung* (pp. 1641–9). Berlin/New York: de Gruyter.

Nekvapil, J. (2000a) Sprachmanagement und ethnische Gemeinschaften. In L.N. Zybatow (ed.) *Sprachwandel in der Slavia* (pp. 683–99). Frankfurt am Main: Peter Lang.

Nekvapil, J. (2000b) Language management in a changing society: Sociolinguistic remarks from the Czech Republic. In B. Panzer (ed.) *Die Sprachliche Situation in der Slavia zehn Jahre nach der Wende* (pp. 165–77). Frankfurt am Main: Peter Lang.

Nekvapil, J. (2000c) On non-self-evident relationships between language and ethnicity: How Germans do not speak German, and Czechs do not speak Czech. *Multilingua* 19, 37–53.

Nekvapil, J. (2000d) Z biografických vyprávění Němců žijících v Čechách: jazykové biografie v rodině pana a paní S. [From the biographical narratives of Germans living in Bohemia: Language biographies in the family of Mr and Mrs S.]. *Slovo a slovesnost* 61, 30–46.

Nekvapil, J. (2000e) On the structure and production of pre-sequences in Czech conversation. Paper presented at the EuroConference on Interactional Linguistics, Spa, Belgium, 16–21 September.

Nekvapil, J. (2001) From the biographical narratives of Czech Germans: Language biographies in the family of Mr and Mrs S. *Journal of Asian Pacific Communication* 11, 77–99.

Nekvapil, J. (2002) Sociolingvistický pohled na vývoj odborných jazyků [Development of languages for special purposes from the point-of-view of sociolinguistics]. In *Přednášky z XLV. běhu letní školy slovanských studií* (pp. 117–32). Praha: Univerzita Karlova v Praze, Filozofická fakulta.

Nekvapil, J. (2003a) Language biographies and the analysis of language situations: On the life of the German community in the Czech Republic. *International Journal of the Sociology of Language* 162, 63–83.

Nekvapil, J. (2003b) O vztahu malých a velkých slovanských jazyků [On the relationship between small and large Slavic languages]. *Létopis* 50, 113–27.

Nekvapil, J. (2003c) On the role of the languages of adjacent states and the languages of ethnic minorities in multilingual Europe: The case of the Czech Republic. In J. Besters-Dilger, R. de Cillia, H.J. Krumm and R. Rindler-Schjerve (eds) *Mehrsprachigkeit in der erweiterten europäischen Union/ Multilingualism in the Enlarged European Union / Multilinguisme dans l'Union Européenne élargie* (pp. 76–94). Klagenfurt: Drava Verlag.

Nekvapil, J. and Leudar, I. (2002) On dialogical networks: Arguments about the migration law in Czech mass media in 1993. In S. Hester and W. Housley (eds) *Language, Interaction and National Identity. Studies in the Social Organisation of National Identity in Talk-in-Interaction* (pp. 60–101). Aldershot: Ashgate.

Nekvapil, J. and Neustupný, J.V. (1998) Linguistic communities in the Czech Republic. In C.B. Paulston and D. Peckham (eds) *Linguistic Minorities in Central and Eastern Europe* (pp. 116–34). Clevedon: Multilingual Matters.

Nekvapil, J. and Neustupný, J.V. (2005) Politeness in the Czech Republic: Distance, levels of expression, management and intercultural contact. In L. Hickey and M. Stewart (eds) *Politeness in Europe* (pp. 247–262). Clevedon: Multilingual Matters.

Nekvapil, J. *et al.* (2000) The presentation of Roma/Gypsies in the central European mass media. In *Přednášky z XLIII. běhu letní školy slovanských studií* (pp. 65–76). Praha: Univerzita Karlova v Praze, Filozofická fakulta.

Neustupný, E. and Neustupný, J. (1961) *Czechoslovakia before the Slavs*. London: Thames and Hudson.

Neustupný, J.V. (1968) Some general aspects of 'language' problems and 'language' policy in developing societies. In J.A. Fishman, C.A. Ferguson and J. Das Gupta (eds) *Language Problems of Developing Nations* (pp. 285–94). New York: Wiley.

Neustupný, J.V. (1978) *Post-Structural Approaches to Language*. Tokyo: University of Tokyo Press.

Neustupný, J.V. (1983) Towards a paradigm for language planning. *Language Planning Newsletter* 9 (4), 1–4.

Neustupný, J.V. (1984) Literacy and minorities: Divergent perceptions. In F. Coulmas (ed.) *Linguistic Minorities and Literacy* (pp. 115–128). Berlin: Mouton.

Neustupný, J.V. (1985) Problems in Australian–Japanese contact situations. In J.B. Pride (ed.) *Cross-Cultural Encounters: Communication and Mis-communication* (pp. 44–64). Melbourne: River-Seine.

Neustupný, J.V. (1987) *Communicating with the Japanese*. Tokyo: Japan Times.

Neustupný, J.V. (1989a) Language purism as a type of language correction. In B.H. Jernudd and M.J. Shapiro (eds) *The Politics of Language Purism* (pp. 211–23). Berlin: Mouton de Gruyter.

Neustupný, J.V. (1989b) Czech diglossia and language management. *New Language Planning Newsletter* 3 (4), 1–2.

Neustupný, J.V. (1993a) Language management for Romani in Central and Eastern Europe. *New Language Planning Newsletter* 7 (4), 1–6.

Neustupný, J.V. (1993b) *The Use of Japanese: Communication and Interaction*. Tokyo: Bonjinsha.

Neustupný, J.V. (1995) Some issues of ordering in interactive competence. In B. Palek (ed.) *Proceedings of LP'94: Item Order in Natural Languages* (pp. 10–26). Prague: Charles University Press.

Neustupný, J.V. (1996) Current issues in Japanese–foreign contact situations. In *Kyoto Conference on Japanese Studies 1994* (vol. 2) (pp. 208–16). Kyoto: International Research Center for Japanese Studies.

Neustupný, J.V. (1997) Teaching communication or teaching interaction. *Intercultural Communication Studies* 10, 1–13. Kanda University of International Studies.

Neustupný, J.V. (1999) Sociolinguistics and the Prague School. In *Prague Linguistic Circle Papers (Travaux du Cercle linguistique de Prague, nouvelle série)* (vol. 3) (pp. 275–86). Amsterdam/Philadelphia: John Benjamins.

Neustupný, J.V. (2002) Sociolingvistika a jazykový management [Sociolinguistics and language management]. *Sociologický časopis/Czech Sociological Review* 38, 429–42.

Neustupný, J.V. (2003) Japanese students in Prague. Problems of communication and interaction. *International Journal of the Sociology of Language* 162, 125–43.

Neustupný, J.V. (forthcoming 1) Language management: Theory and practice. *International Journal of Language Management* 1.

Neustupný, J.V (forthcoming 2) Language and power into the 21st century. Paper presented at the conference Language and Empowerment, organized by the Malaysian Association of Modern Languages, Petaling Jaya Hilton, Kuala Lumpur, 11–13 April, 2002.

Newerkla, S. (1999) *Intendierte und tatsächliche Sprachwirklichkeiten in Böhmen. Diglossie im Schulwesen der böhmischen Kronländer 1740–1918*. Wien: WUV.

Newerkla, S. (2000) Odvrácená tvář habsburských jazykových zákonů v Čechách

[Negative aspects of Hapsburg's language laws in Bohemia]. *Čeština doma a ve světě* 8, 233–53.

Newerkla, S. (2002) Sprachliche Konvergenzprozesse in Mitteleuropa. In I. Pospíšil (ed.) *The Crossroads of Cultures: Central Europe* (= *Litteraria humanitas* 11) (pp. 211–36). Brno: Masarykova univerzita.

Novák, P. (1990) Konstanty a proměny Havránkových metodologických postojů (se zvláštním zřetelem k jeho pojetí marxistické orientace v jazykovědě) [Constants and transformations in Havránek's methodological attitudes: With special reference to his concept of the Marxist orientation of linguistics]. *Slavica Pragensia* 34, 21–38.

Obrová, P. and Pelka, J. (2001) Translation of EC Law into Czech. *Terminologie et Traduction* 2001 (2), 95–117.

Otčenášek, J. (1998) Řecká národnostní menšina v České republice dnes [The Greek ethnic minority in the Czech Republic today]. *Český lid* 85, 147–59.

Pacák, B. (1896) *Črty k upravení poměrů jazykových v království českém* [*Essays on the Adjustment of Language Situation in the Czech Kingdom*]. Kutná Hora: Adolf Švarc.

Patočka, O. (2000) *O tykání a vykání* [*On the TY and VY Forms of Address*]. Praha: Grada.

Pauliny, E. (1983) *Dejiny spisovnej slovenčiny od začiatkov po súčasnosť* [*The History of Standard Slovak from the Beginnings up to the Present*]. Bratislava: Slovenské pedagogické nakladateľstvo.

Pěkný, T. (1993) *Historie Židů v Čechách a na Moravě* [*The History of Jews in Bohemia and Moravia*]. Praha: Sefer.

Phillipson, R. (1992) *Linguistic Imperialism*. Oxford: Oxford University Press.

Pišlová, A. (2002) *Mluva Čechů z Ukrajiny po deseti letech integrace v českém prostředí.* [*Speech of the Czechs from Ukraine after ten Years of their Integration into the Czech Milieu*]. Praha: Filozofická fakulta Univerzity Karlovy, Ústav bohemistických studií (diss.).

Polišenský, J.V. (1991) *History of Czechoslovakia in Outline*. Prague: Bohemia International.

Povejšil, J. (1975) Deutscher Dialekt und fremde Hochsprache bei zweisprachiger Bevölkerung. *Philologica Pragensia* 18, 100–110.

Povejšil, J. (1980) *Das Prager Deutsch des 17. und 18. Jahrhunderts. Ein Beitrag zur Geschichte der deutschen Schriftsprache*. Praha: Academia.

Povejšil, J. (1997) Tschechisch-Deutsch. In H. Goebl, P. H. Nelde, Z. Starý and W.Wölck (eds) *Kontaktlinguistik. Ein internationales Handbuch zeitgenössischer Forschung* (pp. 1656–62). Berlin / New York: de Gruyter.

Praha a národnosti (1998) *Praha a národnosti* [*Prague and Ethnic Minorities*]. Praha: Odbor školství, mládeže a tělovýchovy Magistrátu hl. m. Prahy.

Praha. Osobnosti (2000) *Praha. Osobnosti národnostních menšin* [*Prague. Important Names in Ethnic Minorities*]. Praha: Komise Rady hl. m. Prahy pro oblast národnostních menšin na území hl. m.Prahy.

Prokop, R. (2000) Problémy národní identity Slováků v multietnických oblastech České republiky [Problems of ethnic identity of Slovaks in the multiethnic areas of the Czech Republic]. In O. Šrajerová (ed.) *Formování multikulturní společnosti v podmínkách ČR a v zemích střední Evropy* (pp. 103–13). Opava / Praha: Slezské zemské muzeum, Slezský ústav / Dokumentační a informační středisko Rady Evropy při Evropském informačním středisku UK v Praze.

Prokop, R. (2001) Identita moravské a slezské národnosti v podmínkách České republiky se nepotvrdila [Moravian and Silesian ethnic identity in the territory of the Czech Republic failed to be confirmed]. In O. Šrajerová (ed.) *Otázky národní identity – determinanty a subjektivní vnímání v podmínkách současné multietnické společnosti* (pp. 182–93). Opava / Praha: Slezské zemské muzeum, Slezský ústav / Dokumentační a informační středisko Rady Evropy při Evropském informačním středisku UK v Praze.

Robinson, P. (1972) *Language and Social Behaviour*. Harmondsworth: Penguin.

Sadílek, P. and Csémy, T. (1993) *Maďaři v České republice – Magyarok a Cseh Köztársaságban 1918–1992* [*Hungarians in the Czech Republic 1918–1992*]. Praha: Svaz Maďarů žijících v českých zemích – Cseh-és Morvaországi Magyarok Szövetsége.

Šatava, L. (2001) *Jazyk a identita etnických menšin: Možnosti zachování a revitalizace* [*Language and Identity of Ethnic Minorities: The possibility of Maintenance and Revitalization*]. Praha: Cargo.

Sborník hesel (1999/2000) *Sborník hesel informačního bulletinu Československého ústavu zahraničního na téma Češi a jejich spolky, sdružení a instituce ve světě* [*A Collection of Short Articles from the Newsletter of the Czechoslovak Foreign Institute Concerning Czechs and their Societies, Associations and Institutions Abroad*]. Praha: Československý ústav zahraniční.

Scharnhorst, J. and Ising, E. (eds) (1976/1982) *Grundlagen der Sprachkultur. Beiträge der Prager Linguistik zur Sprachtheorie und Sprachpflege.* Teil 1, 2. Berlin: Akademie-Verlag.

Sedláček, M. (1991) K vývoji jazykové kultury češtiny v letech 1918–1945 [On the development of Czech language cultivation in 1918–1945]. *Naše řeč* 74, 169–80.

Sedláček, M. (1993) K vývoji českého pravopisu [On the development of the Czech spelling]. *Naše řeč* 76, 57–71, 126–138.

Sedláček, M. (1998) Vývoj českého pravopisu od r.1945 [Development of the Czech spelling after 1945]. In J. Kořenský (ed.) *Najnowsze dzieje języków słowiańskich. Český jazyk* (pp. 152–63). Opole: Uniwersytet Opolski, Instytut Filologii Polskiej.

Sgall, P. (1999) Issues of colloquial and standard Czech. In *Přednášky z XLII. běhu Letní školy slovanských studií. I. díl. Přednášky z jazykovědy* (pp. 57–62). Praha: Univerzita Karlova v Praze, Filozofická fakulta.

Sgall, P. and Hronek, J. (1992) *Čeština bez příkras* [*Czech without Embellishment*]. Praha: H&H.

Sgall, P., Hronek, J., Stich, A. and Horecký, J. (1992) *Variation in Language. Code Switching as a Challenge for Sociolinguistics.* Amsterdam/Philadelphia: John Benjamins.

Sherman, T. (2001) The experience of Czech–English bilingualism for Czech-American families. In O. Šrajerová (ed.) *Otázky národní identity – Determinanty a subjektivní vnímání v podmínkách současné multietnické společnosti* (pp. 268–74). Opava/Praha: Slezské zemské muzeum, Slezský ústav/Dokumentační a informační středisko Rady Evropy při Evropském informačním středisku UK v Praze.

Sherzer, J. and Darnell, R. (1972) Outline guide for the ethnographic study of speech use. In J. Gumperz and D. Hymes (eds) *Directions in Sociolinguistics* (pp. 548–54). New York: Holt, Rinehart and Winston.

Skála, E. (1977) Vznik a vývoj česko–německého bilingvismu [The rise and development of the Czech–German bilingualism]. *Slovo a slovesnost* 38, 197–207.

Skalička, V. (1979) *Typologische Studien.* Braunschweig, Wiesbaden: Vieweg.

Skwarska, K. (2001) Tykání a jeho zdvořilejší protějšek v češtině a polštině [Ty forms of address and their more polite counterpart in Czech and Polish]. In I. Vaňková (ed.) *Obraz světa v jazyce* (pp. 137–45). Praha: Univerzita Karlova, Filozofická fakulta.

Sládek, Z. (1999) České prostředí a ruská emigrace (1918–1938) [The Czech environment and the Russian émigré community, 1918–1938]. In L. Běloševská (ed.) *Duchovní proudy ruské a ukrajinské emigrace v Československé republice (1919–1939)* (pp. 7–46). Praha: Slovanský ústav AV ČR.

Slavíčková, J. (1993) Understanding Czech conversation. *Slovo a slovesnost* 54, 225–7.

Slezáková, J. (mimeo) Výzkum identity a vztahu k české veřejnosti skupiny Vietnamců v Jihlavě [A Survey of the identity of a group of the Vietnamese in Jihlava and their relationship to the Czech public].

Sloboda, M. (2000/2001) 'Až bude v Řecku mír, vrátíme se domů': O vzniku a vývoji řecké menšiny u nás – lingvistické i nelingvistické aspekty ['When there is peace in Greece, we'll go home'. On the rise and development of the Greek minority in the Czech Republic – linguistic and non-linguistic aspects]. *Čeština* 11, 112–19, 148–59.

Sloboda, M. (2003) Language maintenance and shifts in a Greek community in a heterolinguistic environment: The Greeks in the Czech Republic. *Journal of the Hellenic Diaspora* 29, 5–33.

Šlosar, D. (2002) Česko–německé jazykové kontakty [Czech–German linguistic contacts]. In W. Koschmal, M. Nekula and J. Rogall (eds) *Češi a Němci. Dějiny – Kultura – Politika* (pp. 105–9). Praha/Litomyšl: Paseka.

Šlosar, D. and R. Večerka (1979) *Spisovný jazyk v dějinách české společnosti* [*Standard Language in the History of Czech Society*]. Praha: Státní pedagogické nakladatelství.

Sokolová, G. (1991) O jazykovém zaměření Slováků a Němců žijících v severních Čechách – na základě sociologických výzkumů [On language orientation of Slovaks and Germans living in North Bohemia – based on sociological research]. *Slezský sborník* 89, 172–80.

Sokolová, G. (1999a) O vztahu k místnímu nářečí u obyvatel českého Těšínska [On the attitudes to the local dialect of the population of the Czech Těšín region.]. *Slezský sborník* 97, 211–26.

Sokolová, G. (1999b) Problematika polské menšiny v České republice a slovenské menšiny v České republice z perspektivy sociologických výzkumů [Problems of the Polish and Slovak minority in the Czech Republic from the perspective of sociological surveys]. In I. Gabal *et al. Etnické menšiny ve střední Evropě* (pp. 128–39). Praha: G plus G.

Sokolová, G. *et al.* (1978) *Současný rozvoj národnostních kultur na Ostravsku [Current Development of Ethnic Cultures in the Ostrava Region]*. Ostrava: Profil.

Sokolová, G. *et al.* (1987) *Soudobé tendence vývoje národností v ČSSR [Contemporary Trends in the Development of Ethnic Minorities in the Czechoslovak Socialist Republic]*. Praha: Academia.

Sokolová, G., Hernová, Š. and Šrajerová, O. (1997) *Češi, Slováci a Poláci na Těšínsku a jejich vzájemné vztahy [Czechs, Slovaks, and Poles in the Těšín Region and their Mutual Relationships]*. Opava: Tilia.

Spisovná čeština a jazyková kultura (1932) *Spisovná čeština a jazyková kultura [Standard Czech and the Cultivation of Language]*. Praha: Melantrich.

Šrajerová, O. (1999) Slováci v České republice. Historický pohled na Slováky v českých zemích v letech 1918–1995 [Slovaks in the Czech Republic. A historical perspective on Slovaks in the Czech lands, 1918–1995]. In I. Gabal *et al. Etnické menšiny ve střední Evropě* (pp. 139–53). Praha: G plus G.

Srb, V. (1987) Demografický profil polské menšiny v Československu [Demographic profile of the Polish minority in Czechoslovakia]. *Český lid* 74, 151–67.

Srb, V. (1988) Demografický profil německé menšiny v Československu [Demographic profile of the German minority in Czechoslovakia]. *Český lid* 75, 29–42.

Stalin, J.V. (1950) Marxismus a národnostní otázka [Marxism and the National Question]. Praha: Svoboda (2nd edn).

Staněk, T. (1993) *Německá menšina v Českých zemích (1948–1989) [German Minority in the Czech Lands, 1948–1989]*. Praha: Institut pro středoevropskou kulturu a politiku.

Staněk, T. (1998) K současnému postavení německé menšiny v České republice [On the present-day position of the German minority in the Czech Republic]. In G. Sokolová and O. Šrajerová (eds) *Národnostní menšiny a majoritní společnost v České republice a v zemích střední Evropy v 90. letech XX. století* (pp. 88–101). Opava / Praha: Slezský ústav Slezského zemského muzea / Dokumentační a informační středisko Rady Evropy.

Staněk, T. (1999) Německá menšina v českých zemích v letech 1918–1989 [The German minority in the Czech lands in 1918–1989]. In I. Gabal *et al. Etnické menšiny ve střední Evropě* (pp. 97–108). Praha: G plus G.

Statistická ročenka (2000) *Statistická ročenka České republiky 2000 [Statistical Yearbook of the Czech Republic 2000]*. Praha: Scientia.

Statistická ročenka školství (2000) *Statistická ročenka školství 1999/2000 [Statistical Yearbook of the School System, 1999/2000]*. Praha: Ústav pro informace ve vzdělávání.

Stehlíková, E. (ed.) (1997) *Čeští Němci nebo němečtí Češi? [Czech Germans or German Czechs?]*. Praha: Fakulta sociálních věd UK. (= *Biograf. Časopis pro biografickou a reflexivní sociologii* 10–11)

Stevenson, P. (2000) The ethnolinguistic vitality of German-speaking communities in Central Europe. In S. Wolff (ed.) *German Minorities in Europe* (pp. 109–24). New York / Oxford: Berghahn.

Stich, A. (1979a) Z dějin českého jazykového práva [From the history of the Czech language law]. *Zprávy Kruhu přátel českého jazyka*, leden, 1–14.

Stich, A. (1979b) K pojmu jazykové kultury a jeho obsahu [On the concept of language culture and its content]. In *Aktuální otázky jazykové kultury v socialistické společnosti* (pp. 98–108). Prague: Academia. An English translation in J. Chloupek and J. Nekvapil (eds) (1993) *Studies in Functional Stylistics* (pp. 257–71). Amsterdam / Philadelphia: John Benjamins.

Stich, A. (1993) On the beginnings of Modern Standard Czech. In J. Chloupek and J.

Nekvapil (eds) *Studies in Functional Stylistics* (pp. 92–8). Amsterdam/Philadelphia: John Benjamins.

Svobodová, J. (2000) *Jazyková specifika školské komunikace a výuka mateřštiny* [*Language Characteristics of Communication at School and the Teaching of the Mother Tongue*] Spisy Ostravské univerzity 133. Ostrava: Ostravská univerzita, Filozofická fakulta.

Tejnor, A. und Kollektiv (1982) Soziolinguistische Untersuchungen zur Sprachkultur. Probleme der tschechischen Orthographie und des Fremdwortgebrauchs im Spiegel der öffentlichen Meinung. In J. Scharnhorst and E. Ising (eds) *Grundlagen der Sprachkultur. Beiträge der Prager Linguistik zur Sprachtheorie und Sprachpflege* (vol. 2) (pp. 272–302). Berlin: Akademie-Verlag.

Thèses (1929) *Travaux du Cercle Linguistique de Prague* 1, 5–29. Translated under the title Theses presented to the first Congress of Slavists held in Prague in 1929. In Vachek (1983), pp. 77–120.

Trost, P. (1995) *Studie o jazycích a literatuře* [*Essays on Languages and Literature*]. Praha: Torst.

Turek, R. (1963) *Čechy na úsvitě dějin* [*Bohemia on the Threshold of History*]. Praha: Orbis.

Uherek, Z. (2003) Cizinecké komunity a městský prostor v České republice [Foreign communities and urban space in the Czech Republic]. *Sociologický časopis/Czech Sociological Review* 39, 193–216.

Uhl, P. (2000) Návrh věcného záměru zákona o právech etnických menšin (menšinového zákona) [Proposal concerning the legislative intention of the Act on the Rights of Ethnic Minorities (Minorities Act)]. Praha (mimeo).

Uhlířová, L. (1998) Linguists vs. the public: An electronic database of letters to the language consulting service as a source of sociolinguistic information. *Journal of Quantitative Linguistics* 5, 262–8.

Uhlířová, L. (2002) Jazyková poradna v měnící se komunikační situaci u nás [Language consulting service in the light of recent communication changes in the Czech Republic]. *Sociologický časopis/Czech Sociological Review* 38, 443–55.

Uličný, O. (1998/1999) K článku prof. Sgalla 'Neochuzujme spisovnou češtinu' [On Professor Sgall's paper 'Let's not impoverish Standard Czech'].*Český jazyk a literatura* 49 (1–2), 35–9.

Václavíková, A. (2000) Zaměstnávání cizích státních příslušníků v České republice jako jedna z forem utváření multikulturní společnosti [The employment of foreign nationals in the Czech Republic as a form of developing a multicultural society]. In O. Šrajerová (ed.) *Formování multikulturní společnosti v podmínkách ČR a v zemích střední Evropy* (pp. 193–8). Opava/Praha: Slezské zemské muzeum, Slezský ústav/ Dokumentační a informační středisko Rady Evropy při Evropském informačním středisku UK.

Vachek, J. (1939) Zum Problem der geschriebenen Sprache. *Travaux du Cercle Linguistique de Prague* 8, 94–104.

Vachek, J. (ed.) (1983) *Praguiana. Some Basic and Less Known Aspects of the Prague Linguistic School*. Prague/Amsterdam: Academia/John Benjamins.

Valášková, N. (1998) Česká minorita v Kazachstánu a její přesídlování do České republiky [The Czech minority in Kazakhstan and its resettlement in the Czech Republic]. *Český lid* 85, 161–70.

Van Els, T.J.M. (2001) The European Union, its institutions and languages: Some language political observations. *Current Issues in Language Planning* 2, 311–60.

Van Leeuwen-Turnovcová, J., Wullenweber, K., Doleschal, U., Schindler, F. (eds) (2002) Gender-Forschung in der Slawistik. *Wiener Slawistischer Almanach*, special issue 55. Vienna.

Vaňko, J. (2000) *The Language of Slovakia's Rusyns*. New York: Columbia University Press.

Vašek, A. (1976) On the problems of the isolated language. *Folia Linguistica* 9-1-4, 85–124.

Vážný, V. (1934) Mluva charvátských osad v republice Československé [Speech of Croatian settlements in the Czechoslovak Republic]. In *Československá vlastivěda* (vol. 3). Jazyk (pp. 518–23). Praha: Sfinx.

Veber, V., Sládek, Z., Bubeníková, M. and Harbuľová, Ľ. (1996) *Ruská a ukrajinská emigrace v ČSR v letech 1918–1945* [*The Russian and Ukranian émigré communities in Czechoslovakia in 1918–1945*]. Praha: Seminář pro dějiny východní Evropy při Ústavu světových dějin FF UK v Praze.

Verhoeven, L. (ed.) (1994) *Functional Literacy*. Amsterdam: John Benjamins.

Vesti (2002) *Vesti. Žurnal Russkoj Diaspory v Češskoj Respublike* [*News. Magazine of the Russian community in the Czech Republic*] Number 5.

Vinokur, G.O. (1925) *Kul'tura jazyka. Očerki linvističeskoj technologii* [*Language Culture. An Outline of Linguistic Technology*]. Moskva: Rabotnik prosveščenija.

Vrbová, E. (1993) *Language use as an aspect of ethnicity in intermarriage. A study from Czech and Slovak settings*. Praha (mimeo).

Vývojová ročenka (1999) *Vývojová ročenka školství v České republice 1989/90 – 1998/99* [*Yearbook of the Development of the School System in the Czech Republic from 1989/90 to 1998/99*]. Praha: Ústav pro informace ve vzdělávání.

Wilková, S. (1999) Romské děti berou docházku do zvláštní školy jako samozřejmost [Roma children take attending a special school as a matter of course]. *Mladá Fronta Dnes* (15 July), 6.

Zeman, J. (1988) K jazykovým kontaktům mezi češtinou a slovenštinou [On language contacts between Czech and Slovak]. In J. Nekvapil and O. Šoltys (eds) *Funkční lingvistika a dialektika* (= Linguistica 17 (1)) (pp. 172–5). Praha: Ústav pro jazyk český ČSAV.

Zeman, J. (1994) K problému výzkumu česko-polského kontaktu z hlediska komunikace [On Czech-Polish contact from the point-of-view of communication]. In *Kształcenie porozumiewania się* (pp. 115–20). Opole: Wyższa szkoła pedagogiczna.

Zeman, J. (1997a) Czech-Slovak. In H. Goebl, P.H. Nelde, Z. Starý and W. Wölck (eds) *Kontaktlinguistik. Ein internationales Handbuch zeitgenössischer Forschung* (pp. 1650–55). Berlin/New York: de Gruyter.

Zeman, J. (1997b) K výzkumu percepce slovenské kultury Čechy po rozpadu Československa [Research on perception of Slovak culture by Czechs after the dissolution of Czechoslovakia]. *Český lid* 84, 175–8.

Zeman, J. (1999/2000) Seminář o výuce slovenštiny [A workshop on the teaching Slovak]. *Čeština* 10, 164–6.

Zich, F. (2001) *The Bearers of Development of the Cross-border Community on Czech-German Border* (= Sociologické texty 1 (4)) Praha: Sociologický ústav Akademie věd České republiky.

Zilynskyj, B. (1995) *Ukrajinci v Čechách a na Moravě (1894) 1917 – 1945 (1994)* [*Ukranians in Bohemia and Moravia, (1894) 1917 – 1945 (1994)*]. Praha: X-egem.

Zilynskyj, B. (1996) Ukrajinci u nás – problémy minulé i současné (I), (II) [Ukranians in this country – problems of the past and of the present]. *Most* 2 (11–12), 4–5, *Most* 2 (14–15), 4–5.

Zimek, R. (1999/2000) O Rusínech a rusínštině [The Ruthenians and the Ruthenian language]. *Čeština* 10, 8–15.

Zimová, L. (2001) Začátky multietnické komunikace v české škole [Beginnings of multiethnic communication in Czech schools]. In *Naše a cizí v interetnické a interpersonální jazykové komunikaci* (pp. 183–9). Ostrava: Ostravská univerzita, Filozofická fakulta.

Zpráva (2002) *Zpráva o situaci národnostních menšin v České republice za rok 2001* [*Report on the Situation of Ethnic Minorities for 2001*]. Attached to the Resolution of the Government of the Czech Republic from 12 July 2002, No. 600. On WWW at http://www.vlada.cz/urad/urad_postaveni.htm.

Zvara, J. (1977) Princípy národnostnej politiky komunistických a robotníckych strán pri výstavbe socializmu a komunizmu [Principles of ethnic policy of communist and worker's parties while constructing socialism and communism]. *Filozofický časopis* 30, 520–34.

Appendix
TABLE OF CONTENTS

- Part I: *Language Management in Czech Society: Target and Models* (p. 16)
  This introductory part provides a justification for discussing Czech language management at this length and describes the model used in the monograph.
  - The Target Society and Languages (p. 16)
    (Why Czech?, The neighbourhood, Czechs and the Czech language, Other ethnic communities, Czechs abroad)
  - What is Language Management (p. 19)
    (Simple and organised language management, The management process, Socioeconomic, communicative and linguistic management, Interests, power and management, Levels of management)
  - The Object of Language Management (p. 22)
    (Participant strategies, Language variation strategies, Situation strategies, Function strategies, Setting strategies, Content strategies, Form strategies, Channel strategies)

- Part II: *Communities* (p. 24)
  This Part of the paper concentrates on facts about communities, which reside in the territory of the Czech Republic, rather than narrowly on their language problems. It closes with a discussion of the ethnic policy of the Czech State.
  - Introduction (p. 24)
    (Overall census figures, Distance between the communities)
  - The Czechs (p. 25)
    (The Czech, Moravian and Silesian communities, Czech-speaking and other-speaking communities throughout history, Returnee communities)
  - The Slovaks (p. 33)
  - The Roma (p. 37)
  - The Poles (p. 41)
  - The Germans (p. 43)
  - The Ruthenians, Ukrainians and Russians (p. 46)
  - The Vietnamese (p. 48)
  - The Hungarians (p. 50)
  - The Greeks and Macedonians (p. 51)
    (Greeks, Macedonians)
  - Other communities (p. 52)
  - Communities: A Summary (p. 55)
    (Types and size of the communities, The phenomenon of assimilation, Interests and power, What to do?)
  - Ethnic Policy of the Czech State (p. 58)
    (Legal norms: The ethnic minority law, Management agencies, Management acts)

- Part III: *Management of Language Varieties* (p. 61)
  In Part III, the most extensive in the study, the language situation and problems of individual languages spoken in the Republic are given detailed attention.

Some general trends, such as a massive shift of speakers of other languages to Czech, are discussed at the end of this Part.

- The Czech Language (p. 61)
  (The Czech language: A brief history of its management, The problem of Standard and Common Czech, The problem of dialects, Slang, Language of returnees, Written language and spelling, Literacy)
- The Slovak Language (p. 91)
  (Situation, problems, Simple management, Organised management)
- The Romani Language (p. 99)
  (Situation, problems, Multilingualism of the Roma, Simple management, Organised management, Romani at primary level, Secondary and adult education, University courses, Textbooks, Standardisation and elaboration, Governmental level management, Further management)
- The Polish Language (p. 105)
  (Situation, problems, Simple management, Organised management)
- The German Language (p. 108)
  (Situation, problems, Language biography of Mr S, Simple management, Organised management)
- Ruthenian, Ukrainian and Russian (p. 116)
- The Vietnamese Language (p. 117)
  (Situation, problems, Simple management, Organized management)
- The Hungarian Language (p. 121)
  (Situation, problems, Simple management, Organised management)
- Greek and Macedonian (p. 124)
  (Greek, Macedonian)
- Foreign Languages in the Czech Republic (p. 125)
  (Competence in foreign languages, Simple management in the use of foreign languages, Organised management: The teaching of foreign languages at primary schools, Organised management: The teaching of foreign languages at the secondary level, Prognosis, Languages at tertiary level)
- Languages and Czech Entry to the European Union (p. 131)
  (European Union Languages for the Czech Republic, Czech for other EU countries)
- Languages of Instruction (p. 134)
- Language Varieties: A Summary (p. 135)
  (Languages other than Czech, Types of languages, Maintenance and shift, Language management in the EU, Language policy of the Czech State, Education policy, Language cultivation)

- Part IV: *Management of Situations* (p. 138)
  This Part deals in a preliminary way with a topic little noted in literature about language management so far: management of language in individual 'situations' within individual domains of language use.
  - The Framework (p. 138)
  - Management in the Daily Life Domain (p. 139)
  - Management in the Family Domain (p. 141)
    (Problems of intergenerational usage, 'Indeterminacy of expression')

- Management in the Friendship Domain (p. 142)
  (Parties, The *ty* ritual)
- Management in the Education Domain (p. 144)
  (Changes in educational situation sets, Children of refugees)
- Management in the Work Domain (p. 145)
  (Example of a meeting, Communication in joint ventures)
- Management in Public Domain (p. 147)
  (Language of politics, Language of law and administration)
- Management in the Cultural Domain (p. 148)
  (Science and humanities, Literature, Media, Book/periodicals reading situations, Religion)
- Management in Contact Situations (p. 150)
  (Czechs and foreigners in external contact situations)
- Problems of Situations: A Summary (p. 152)

- Part V: *Management of Functions, Setting, Participants, Content, Form and Channels* (p. 153)
Problems concerning functions, settings, participants, content, form and channels of communication receive attention in this Part of the paper. Problems such as those of the electronic media are included.
  - Problems in Functions (p. 153)
    (The communicative function, The symbolic function, The bridging function)
  - Problems in Settings (p. 156)
  - Participants (p. 156)
    (Gender in language, Participants' networks)
  - Content (p. 159)
    (Politeness: *ty* and *vy* and other address terms, Politeness in service encounters, Public criticism of others, Linguistic conservatism, Content analysis of the media)
  - Form (p. 161)
    (Sequential organisation of talk; One-word name for the Czech Republic, Management of place names, Management of proper names)
  - Channels (p. 164)
    (Electronic media)

- Part VI: *Theories of Language Management* (p. 167)
The final Part analyses theories that are of particular importance for understanding language management in former Czechoslovakia and the present day Czech Republic.
  - The Prague School Theory (p. 167)
    (The background, The original theory, Language cultivation theory after World War II)
  - The Communist Party Theory: Some Preliminary Observations (p. 175)
    (The background, The inquiry system, Design, Implementation, The social system, The idiom, Conclusions)
  - Contemporary Theories (p. 180)
    (The background, Inquiry, Design)
References (p. 183)

The European Union, its Institutions and its Languages: Some Language Political Observations

T.J.M. van Els

University of Nijmegen, Uniceflaan 47, 6525 JL Nijmegen, The Netherlands

The present 15 member states of the European Union have acknowledged 11 languages as the 'official and working-languages' for use within the organisation. In principle these languages are fully equal. The future expansion with new member states may bring the number of 'official and working-languages' to over 20. It is expected that institutional communication within the European Union – which is not without problems under the present circumstances – will become more and more laborious with each additional language. These circumstances raise a major question for the European Union – whether to consider the restriction of the number of official and working-languages. This monograph puts forward linguistic insights that may be pertinent both to reconsidering the desirability and tenability of the principle of plurilinguistic equality and to the day-to-day practice of multilingual institutional communication. Central to the discussion are: (1) a number of 'myths' surrounding the phenomenon of language; (2) domains of language use; (3) quality of (multilingual) communication; and (4) the handicaps experienced by natives and non-natives in multilingual communicative settings.

Editors' Introduction

Professor Theo van Els has been one of the leading figures in Applied Linguistics in Europe since the early 1970s. In 1965 he joined the faculty of the University of Nijmegen, and soon thereafter he was appointed director of the then recently established Institute of Applied Linguistics. In 1981 he was appointed to the Chair of Applied Linguistics at the University of Nijmegen, and from 1994 till his retirement in 2000 he was Rector of the University. His efforts to establish Applied Linguistics as an academic discipline led first to the development of a course in Applied Linguistics (as a subsidiary subject) and later to the creation of a full programme of study. For this course, van Els and his colleagues wrote a handbook that was published in Dutch in 1977 and later, in a revised form, in English (1984). As a result of his extensive work at both the European and the Dutch national levels in foreign language teaching, in 1989 he was designated chair of a task force set up by the Netherlands Ministry of Education to develop, and in 1992 was appointed chair for the implementation of, a National Action Programme for Foreign Languages. A more complete biographical note can be found in de Bot (1999).

In some parts of the academic world, including The Netherlands, 'Professor' is not a position one acquires by having a substantial number of publications, by securing many grants or through promotion. Only a limited number of professorial positions or chairs exist providing leadership roles for disciplines. Van Els has been both Professor and Chair of Applied Linguistics. A new Professor's appointment is heralded by an inaugural speech in which individuals outline their plans for the future or speak about the needs of their field. Upon leaving a chair (usually upon retirement) one is expected to deliver a formal farewell speech or 'Final Public Lecture' in which one either looks back at what has been achieved during one's tenure or makes a summary political statement relating to one's field.

The following monograph is a slightly expanded version of Professor van Els' 'Final Public Lecture', delivered on 22 September 2000 at the University of Nijmegen as part of a symposium in which there were five participants: Professor van Els, a participant from the Dutch Parliament, one from the European Parliament, and a former ambassador and leading civil servant from Brussels. The topic of the symposium was the complex issue of the language situation in the European Union. The editors are pleased to be able to make Professor van Els' final lecture available to a wider audience as a monograph in *Current Issues in Language Planning*'s polity studies.

Introduction

In many ways, but certainly in terms of its policy with regard to the use of languages in its organisation, the European Union (EU) is the odd one out. No other international organisation in the public or private sphere has recognised so many languages as its 'official and working languages'. There are now 11 of them and – if the current policy remains the same with the entry of new member states – their number will increase to more than 20 in the near future.

With 11 official and working languages, life is not particularly easy – as you will soon see – but every addition to this number makes it harder and harder. Each time, further pragmatic solutions will need to be thought up, which will all more or less be in conflict with the fundamental equality that again and again is solemnly proclaimed with regard to the national languages brought in by the member states.

Many experts say that something needs to be done about it. Some of them are convinced that 'muddling on' will no longer do, and that alternatives to the principle of equality will need to be considered (Haarmann, 1991b: 9). Countries with a mosaic of languages have always found it difficult to draw up an adequate language policy (Lambert, 1999: 15). Therefore, especially the European Union's multilingualism is regarded – with some irony – as one of the most fascinating challenges in current language politics (Grin, 1996: 27).

On the other hand, the EU itself shows considerable hesitancy when it comes to bringing its official policy up for discussion (see, e.g. Bos, 1999; Wright, 2000: 120; Truchot, 1994). It is easier to talk about butter mountains, wine lakes or the common currency, and find solutions to these problems, than to tackle the language policy and discuss the possibility of one common working language (Coulmas, 1991b: 22). Also in the recent, controversial contributions by Joschka Fischer, the German Minister of Foreign Affairs, and Jacques Chirac, the President of France, on, among other things, the streamlining of the decision-making process, which is becoming increasingly time-consuming, one will look in vain for a reference to the language problem.[1]

Not only are the present policy and practice often very inefficient; they can also slow down procedures to a considerable degree (de Swaan, 1999: 13). There are many stories going around about how matters in the European Parliament are held up by members who 'open up their box of tricks'. As a prominent Dutch member of this parliament recently said in an interview: 'If you don't like some-thing, you go by the book and refer to the rules'.[2] As in this specific case, it often involves rules and regulations regarding the availability of written or verbal translations.

What is worse, however, is that there is still no real community of communica-tion within the EU. According to Wright (2000: 8), such a community of commu-nication might help the EU to develop democratic structures and legitimacy and give meaning to its policies of free movement. De Swaan (1999: 16) holds a simi-lar view: there is 'a lack of veritable public space in Europe, where the political, social and cultural issues are discussed'. In an interview he further commented that Europe 'is suffering from a shortage of democracy due to the non-existence of a public platform'.[3]

According to de Swaan, the development of such a platform is seriously hindered by the fact that the EU has not just one common language, or, for that matter, two or three. Wright (2000: 122) agrees that real progress on the way to political integration is impossible without 'profound linguistic consequences'. If it should prove possible without any linguistic consequences, the EU would instantaneously become a new kind of 'political animal'!

Be that as it may, the EU's language problem remains a very important subject. And as such it is very suitable for a final public lecture, even though it is by no means an easy matter! It is also very suitable for a final lecture because it is such an emotionally charged theme that is considered 'very explosive'. A final public lecture is an excellent occasion to state a number of things very clearly for a change: one has already left the stage before anything can blow up in one's face!

As a linguist specialising in applied linguistics, I am very aware that language policy is more than just a question of weighing a number of linguistic arguments (Paulston, 1998: 5; Herriman & Burnaby, 1996: 13). Therefore, I make no preten-sions to being able to reformulate the EU's language policy or save the situation through this discussion. However, as an expert in applied linguistics, I can make a contribution by commenting on linguistic aspects of the problem. Although, in some circles, people automatically assume linguists to be proponents of plurilingualism ('the more languages, the better') (Wright, 2000: 246) – just as laymen expect them to speak many languages! – part of my contribution will consist of unravelling the myths that are and have been woven around language. Language is first and foremost a means to establish and maintain communication between people (Coulmas, 1991b: 27). And, as you will see, one should not attach great value to linguistic diversity too easily or a priori (see also Grin, 1996: 29).

I will first go into some of the background, including the EU and its institu-tions, the EU's current language policy and practice and a number of questions that are generally related to language use. In the subsequent section, I will discuss the central linguistic considerations. In particular, these involve the qual-ity of communication in multilingual contexts, the handicaps that participants in these contexts may experience in connection with their knowledge of languages, and the situation that will evolve if the EU should decide to opt for one working language, be it English or another language. The final section contains some concluding observations from the linguistic perspective as to which direction the EU might or perhaps should take.

Background

In this section, I would like initially to describe the organisation of the EU followed by a brief description of the language situation in the EU. Next, I will describe the policy and practice regarding the use of languages in the EU institutions and say a few words about the EU's non-institutional language policy. Subsequently, I will go somewhat deeper into a few aspects of the principles that determine the EU's language policy and briefly discuss a number of other models of language use in international organisations. In the final part of this section, I will look at the question of whether the development of an explicit language policy is really necessary.

The European Union and its institutions

With the 1958 Treaty of Rome, the EU commenced as three Communities: the European Economic Community, Euratom and the European Coal and Steel Community. In 1967, these three were united and continued as the European Economic Community. This lasted until 1979 when the members of the European Parliament were first elected directly by the citizens and the emphasis on co-operation gradually began to include more than strictly economic motives. Therefore, from then on, the participants preferred to speak simply of the European Community. With the signing of the Maastricht Treaty in 1993, the creation of the European economic union was completed and the member states had definitely opted for – and already given shape to – the route towards further political and social integration. From then on, the community was called the European Union (see Figure 1).

Originally, there were six countries that participated in the Communities: the three Benelux countries (Belgium, The Netherlands and Luxemburg), Germany, France and Italy. These were joined by Denmark, Ireland and the United Kingdom in 1973, Greece in 1981, Portugal and Spain in 1986, and Finland, Austria and Sweden in 1995. Currently, the EU is negotiating with a number of countries from Central and Eastern Europe and Turkey about their possible entry.

It is beyond the scope of this monograph to give a detailed description of the operations of the EU and its institutions, but some of the key EU-institutions are as follows:

- The three major bodies for the management and administration of the EU are the Council of Ministers, the European Parliament and the European Commission.
    - The Council of Ministers is the policy-making body on which one representative from each member state has a seat.
    - The European Parliament (EP) has a controlling and legislative function. Its 650 members are elected by the citizens of the 15 member states, and the number of representatives from each country varies according to the number of inhabitants. The EP resides in Brussels and Strasbourg, and has its own administrative system.
    - The European Commission (EC) is the executive body, which also provides support to the Council of Ministers. The EC and its administration reside in Brussels. In total, there are just over 20 European Commis-

Figure 1 States forming the European Union

sioners – one for each country and two for the large countries – and an
  independent chairman.

- All the member states have a permanent representative in Brussels. The
  ambassadors prepare, among other things, the meetings of the Council of
  Ministers.
- Furthermore, the EU has a number of institutes and agencies, most of which
  are not situated in Brussels. Best known are the European Court of Justice in
  Luxemburg and the European Central Bank in Frankfurt.
- The work of the EU in the broadest sense is supported by a large number of
  permanent and *ad hoc* commissions and advisory bodies.

The language situation in the European Union

The 15 countries that constitute the European Union together represent a very
complex and historically interesting collection of languages. They may be
grouped under a limited number of language-families, the main groups being
the Romance, the West Germanic and the Scandinavian ones, but there are also
outsiders like Finnish, which belongs to the Finno-Ugrian languages. Almost all
the languages involved form language-families of their own, with their subdivi-

Table 1 The languages of the European Union and its member states

Member States	Official National Languages	Autochthonous Languages	Official and Working Languages of EU
Austria	German		Danish
Belgium	Dutch, French, German		Dutch
			English
Denmark	Danish		Finnish
Finland	Finnish, Swedish	Sami	French
France	French	Breton, Flemish, Occitan	German
			Greek
			Italian
Germany	German	Frisian	Portuguese
Greece	Greek		Spanish
Ireland	English, Irish		Swedish
Italy	Italian		
Luxemburg	French, German, Letzebuergesh		
The Netherlands	Dutch	Frisian	
Portugal	Portuguese		
Spain	Spanish	Basque, Catalan, Galician	
Sweden	Swedish	Finnish, Sami	
United Kingdom	English	Gaelic, Welsh	

Table 2 Numerical strength of EU languages around 1990 (in millions) (adapted from Ammon, 1991: 245)

Official National Languages	Speakers	Autochthonous Languages	Speakers
German	63	Catalan	10.0
English	60	Basque	1.0
French	60	Breton	0.9
Italian	58	Irish	0.7
Spanish	39	Frisian	0.5
Dutch	22	Welsh	0.5
Portuguese	11	Letzebuergesh	0.4
Greek	10	Gaelic	0.1
Danish	5		

sions into many distinct dialects, sociolects and idiolects. Only a few of these many languages and sub-languages have gained the status of 'national' language. How they attained that status is beyond the scope of this study. To one aspect of it, i.e. the role the 'national' language has played in European nation-state building, we will return later. Table 1 provides a list of all the official national languages and most of the other 'autochthonous' or indigenous languages of the fifteen member states of the EU; Table 2 gives approximative

Table 3 Estimated numbers of inhabitants of Maghreb and Turkish origin in twelve EU countries, January 1994 (Eurostat, 1997; adapted from Extra, 1999: 72)

EU Countries	Maghreb	Turkey
Belgium	161,588	88,302
Denmark	3,952	34,658
Finland	910	995
France	1,393,165	197,712
Germany	133,945	1,918,395
Greece	827	3,066
Italy	115,675	3,656
The Netherlands	167,887	202,618
Portugal	302	65
Spain	64,940	301
Sweden	3,284	23,649
United Kingdom	7,000	41,000
TOTAL	2,053,505	2,514,417

figures for the numbers of native speakers for some of these languages around 1990. It is again beyond the scope of this discussion to examine the differences in status that exist both between the various national languages and between the various autochthonous languages in the countries concerned. (But, see Baker & Prys Jones, 1998: 398ff) We will return to the position of all these languages within the EU organisation in a following section.

Europe has always been the scene of much migration. New languages and language-groups have constantly moved across and into the continent. The language situation has never been stable for long. Thus, there have also been great changes in the half-century since World War Two. For a variety of reasons millions of migrants from a great many different corners of the earth have moved into all the countries of the European Union, and that is still going on. Immigration has taken place from former British, Dutch, French, Portuguese and Spanish colonies. Immigrants have brought with them a multitude of allochonous languages and related foreign cultures. In The Netherlands, for example, at least 20 new languages were brought into the country in recent times; the total non-Dutch population numbers 2.5 million as against a total indigenous population of about 15 million (see Broeder & Extra, 1997: 161ff). Individual countries have been affected to different degrees and in different ways. This may be demonstrated by examining the detailed figures relating to migration into a number of EU countries of people from the Maghreb (i.e. Algeria, Morocco, Tunisia) and from Turkey (see Table 3).

The third aspect of the language situation that is of relevance to our discussion is the 'second' language competence of EU citizens. It is of great importance to the EU, at all levels, that its citizens have a command of more languages than just the language they grew up with. 'Other' languages may be acquired in different ways, i.e. in bilingual settings, in the country where the language in question is spoken or in a 'foreign' setting. People may attain competence at a variety of levels and they may also acquire competence in more than one 'second' language. Table 4, neglecting all these distinctions, gives some insight into the 'second' language competence of citizens of the various EU countries in English, French, German and Spanish. It is interesting to see how the amount of 'second' language competence differs for the four languages over the individual countries and what developments there have been between 1990 and 1998. From figures presented by Ammon (2000: 483) it appears that, in all the EU member states in the late 1980s, approximately 19 million pupils were learning English in school, about 9 million French, about 3 million German and just over 200,000 Spanish.

Language policy and practice

It is imperative to distinguish between the 'institutional' and 'non-institutional' sides of the EU's language policy and practice. By *institutional* is meant the use of languages within and between the EU institutions themselves and in their communications with the member states and their citizens, and the world outside the EU. By *non-institutional* is meant the use of languages within and between the member states and between their citizens mutually, without the EU institutions being party to this.

Institutional

The foundation for all regulations concerning the institutional use of languages is Article 217 of the Treaty of Rome. This states that all regulations shall be drawn up by the Council of Ministers. This happened for the first time in 1958 when it was decided that German, French, Italian and Dutch – the national languages of the first six member states – would count equally as 'official and working languages' of the Communities.[4] With each subsequent expansion of the EU, another national language was added as an official and working language on the basis of the equality principle. Thus, Danish, English, Finnish, Greek, Portuguese, Spanish and Swedish all became languages of the EU institutions.

It should be noted that not all the national languages of the member states gained the status of official and working language. For example, Ireland also has Irish as a national language, and Spain has, in addition to Castilian (which is called 'Spanish' in the EU regulation), Catalan, Galician and Basque.[5] So far, separate arrangements have been made for two of the approximately 30 national languages that were not given 'EU status', namely Irish and Catalan (Labrie, 1996: 5). The EU also provides translations of official documents, wholly or partly, in these two languages.

Language practice is not such that all EU languages are in fact always used. In day-to-day practice, ample use is made of the possibility that seems to be contained in the dual and equivocal formulation 'official and working language'

Table 4 Knowledge of English, French, German and Spanish as a 'second' language (in per cent, by member state; adapted from European Commission, 1999: 111)

EU Countries	*Language*	*1990*	*1998*	*Difference*
EU all over	English	23	31	+8
	French	11	12	+1
	German	7	8	+1
	Spanish	5	4	−1
Belgium	English	32	41	+9
	French	32	38	+6
	German	18	14	−4
	Spanish	3	3	0
Denmark	English	68	77	+9
	French	7	10	+3
	German	45	49	+4
	Spanish	2	3	+1
Finland	English	–	49	–
	French	–	3	–
	German	–	13	–
	Spanish	–	1	–
France	English	26	32	+6
	German	9	9	0
	Spanish	12	11	−1
Germany	English	34	41	+7
	French	8	11	+3
	Spanish	1	3	+2
Greece	English	25	38	+13
	French	6	7	+1
	German	4	5	+1
	Spanish	1	0	−1
Italy	English	18	27	+9
	French	16	19	+3
	German	3	3	0
	Spanish	2	4	+2
The Netherlands	English	62	77	+15
	French	14	15	+1
	German	55	59	+4
	Spanish	2	2	0
Portugal	English	23	21	−2
	French	23	18	−5
	German	2	2	0
	Spanish	7	7	0

Table 4 *(cont)*

EU Countries	Language	1990	1998	Difference
Spain	English	10	17	17
	French	9	8	–1
	German	1	1	0
Sweden	English	–	75	–
	French	–	5	–
	German	–	24	–
	Spanish	–	4	–
United Kingdom	French	16	14	–2
	German	6	5	–1
	Spanish	2	2	0

to get around having to use all 11 languages under all circumstances and on each occasion. As it happens, the original regulation does not explicitly specify the difference between the terms 'official language' and 'working language'. This leaves room for an interpretation that seems to go more or less as follows: 'official' is a quality that each EU language has and continues to have under all conditions; 'working language' is a quality that *may* be assigned to a language, but which it does not need to have under all conditions. As it has also been stipulated that each institute is to regulate its own language regime, provided that it is in accordance with the regulation of the Council of Ministers, there is now considerable diversity in language use practice (Coulmas, 1991b: 6; Labrie, 1996: 6).

All official documents are translated into all the official EU languages and are valid in a member state only when they are in the officially recognised language of that member state. Generally, the European Commission will only address the governments of the member states in the language of the governments concerned.[6]

All citizens, for their part, can address themselves to the EU in their 'own' language and are entitled to receiving a response from 'Brussels' in that language. Something similar applies to the communications between the EU institutions themselves.

Finally, it should also be noted that the EU's terminology database only gives full coverage in the languages designated as official EU languages (Labrie, 1996: 5).

As for internal communication within the individual EU institutions, the 11 languages do not all equally qualify as working language. The Council of Ministers and the European Parliament are the bodies that come closest to the 'ideal' situation in the sense that they use all the 'official' languages as 'working languages' on certain occasions.

The fact that often only certain languages, English and French in particular, are used as working languages in actual practice, and that certain other languages are only used as such when this use has a symbolic meaning, has not yet led to a formal distinction between the languages as working languages (Labrie, 1996: 6).

What is actual practice within the EU institutions? In the formal meetings of the Council of Ministers, all the EU languages are used as working languages and all the documents that form the basis for decisions are made available in advance in all those languages. Preparing the agenda and documents for these formal meetings can therefore be very time-consuming and usually there is hardly any room to put an additional item on the agenda at short notice.

In the informal meetings of the Council of Ministers, normally only three working languages are used: English, French and the language of the country that fills the presidency. Also in the preliminary meetings of the permanent representatives, i.e. the ambassadors of the member states, the languages used are limited to English, French and German (Duthoy, 1993: 31).

In the plenary sessions of the European Parliament, all the EU languages are working languages. All the official documents are available in the 11 languages and interpreters provide simultaneous translations in each language. Some members of parliament occasionally choose not to use their own language in a plenary session, which often leads to considerable irritation among their compatriots or people that speak that same language.

Simultaneous translation does of course involve translation *from* and *into* all languages. With the current number of languages, this practice often leads to a very laborious process. Therefore, with a view to future developments, it is being investigated whether variants with fewer language combinations can be used. One obvious variant, which is already used, involves translation *from* each language, but not *into* all other languages. This may be said to be a case in which there is 'asymmetry': speakers of the 'minor' languages are dependent on the translations into one of the 'major' languages (Coulmas, 1991b: 7; Duthoy, 1993: 42). Another conceivable variant involves translating both from and into all languages, but then in such a way that the route from one 'minor' language to another 'minor' language is no longer a direct translation, but one that goes via one of the 'major' languages available. This is known as 'relay interpretation' and often means a double delay in reception for speakers of the 'minor' target languages (Labrie, 1993: 105).[7]

In all the other plenary sessions of the European Parliament, the language use practice is completely different. Although the EP repeatedly stated that any limitation whatsoever of the number of languages will fundamentally damage the democratic character of the Parliament, it is regularly agreed *ad hoc* in meetings at commission level to work with a drastically reduced number of languages in written and/or verbal communication. This limitation may occasionally also result in the exclusion of the languages of some of the members involved in the consultations (Coulmas, 1991b: 7). In corridor chats and informal consultations between people from various language groups, it is very common to speak only French or English.

In the European Commission and its offices, which accommodate civil servants from all the member states, English or French, and sometimes German, is often used in internal communications, as has become clear from a number of surveys among civil servants. Over the last few years, the verbal use of English appears to have increased, which may particularly have affected the use of German, a language that was not used very frequently to begin with. There are indications of an increasing divergence in this 'duopoly' of English and French among civil servants (and members of the European Parliament): whereas those from the northern member states prefer to use English, those from the southern member states prefer to use French (Gehnen, 1991: 56ff; Haselhuber, 1991: 43ff; Labrie, 1993: 111; Quell, 1997: 63ff; Schlossmacher, 1994: 11ff; Wright, 2000: 169ff).

Internal memos and drafts of official documents are drawn up in one or both of these languages. If the official documents are meant for consideration in an advisory body or commission, the European Commission makes them available in all EU languages. However, for deliberations in such commissions, the number of languages is often limited, usually on an *ad hoc* basis. This is often also necessary due to the limited availability of conference rooms equipped with translation facilities. Whether or not a language belongs to the 'drop-outs' usually depends on the position of that language in the 'language pecking order' (together with Italian and Spanish, Dutch belongs to the 'middle group' that comes after the 'big three') and on the availability of qualified interpreters (Duthoy, 1993: 32ff; Fasol, 1994b).

Finally, of the many institutes and agencies that work for the EU but are usually not situated in Brussels, the European Court of Justice in Luxemburg and the European Central Bank in Frankfurt should also be mentioned here.

The European Court has worked out its own language regime in which three levels of language use can be distinguished. Firstly, it is at least officially so that all EU languages as well as Irish can be used in litigation; the choice of language is left to the plaintiff, unless this is one of the EU bodies itself, in which case the choice of language is left to the defendant. In practice, the working language of the Court itself, i.e. French, is often used as well. At this level, i.e. the second, French has always been the sole language from the very beginning, and has maintained this position despite the strong advance of English elsewhere in the EU. The third level is that of the Court's official publications. All the Court's decisions are eventually published in every EU language, and, in case of doubt later on, the text in the language used during the proceedings is considered authentic (Koch, 1991: 155–6).

The recently established European Central Bank uses only English for internal communication (at both board and staff levels). It also uses this language to communicate with the outside world, no matter whether it concerns institutions and bodies inside or outside the EU. However, at a later stage, all relevant documents are translated into every EU language. It would not be feasible to use another language than English, or even next to English, in international banking. This regime of the European Central Bank is generally accepted, no matter how sensitive an issue the language problem may otherwise be in the EU.

All in all, it may be clear that, even with the pragmatic interpretation of the fundamental equality of EU languages, a very large effort, costly in terms of money and time, has to be made to translate written and verbal texts. An extensive machinery has been set up to facilitate the translation work for such 'bulk consumers' as the Council of Ministers, the European Commission, the European Parliament and the European Court of Justice. In 1991, it was estimated that between 15% and 20% of the office staff of these institutions were engaged in these types of tasks and that about 40% of the budget available for administration, i.e. almost 2 billion guilders (US$1 billion), was spent on the EU's multilingualism (Coulmas, 1991b: 22ff).

In what light other budgetary costs may or should be seen will be discussed below. As far as the money question is concerned, there are still a few things that need to be said. First of all, there is still considerable uncertainty about the estimates that are made in various places. Moreover, the fact remains that the costs in question constitute only 2% of the total budget of the European Commission and should also be set off against the benefits of this policy (Coulmas, 1991b: 24ff). That, in addition to the 'economic value', the subjective value that various actors attach to multilingualism should also be taken into account does not, of course, make the estimations any simpler. However, this does make clear that, when it comes to costs, some people tend to jump the gun and start using exaggerated 'crisis rhetoric'. The fact that translation costs may be assessed as 'high' does not warrant the conclusion that they are 'too high' (Grin, 1996: 30; Pool, 1996: 162). It is, of course, very possible to maintain that the total costs of translation are not the real problem (de Swaan, 1999: 16). In any case, for some, the value that is subjectively attached to an equal treatment of all EU languages is in itself of greater importance than the financial efforts made by the EU in this respect.

'Non-institutional'

While discussing the 'institutional' side of the EU's language policy, we have looked at both the internal communication within the EU organisation as well as that between the EU and the outside world. Now, we will have a look at a number of aspects of this policy that concern the language use by citizens, focusing on foreign language teaching and minority languages.

Foreign language teaching. Almost by definition, the implementation of a multi-language policy requires that specific attention is given to the learning and teaching of foreign languages. However, regarding foreign language teaching, the EU adheres to the principle that the autonomy of the member states should be honoured insofar as possible in matters related to culture and education. The EU has therefore no real policy on foreign language teaching in the true sense of the word. It is not the EU that determines which foreign languages may and/or should be taught, by which citizens, at which age, with which methods or by which means.

However, the EU does of course have an interest in improving the mobility of its citizens for reasons of employment and/or study. Knowledge of relevant foreign languages is vital for this kind of mobility. The EU may therefore regard it as its duty to deal with possible obstructions to mobility at the supranational level if it is to be expected that such obstructions will not be removed by actions of the individual member states. In the mid-1970s, there was a growing awareness that the EU also has its own task to perform with regard to the smaller issues in educational policy (Coulmas, 1991b: 9ff).

It was against this background that, for example, the LINGUA programme was eventually set up. This programme, which started in 1990, was initially created for a period of five years, but then was continued as part of the new SOCRATES programme.

The fact that it did not always prove to be easy to stick to the programme objectives in the discussions on and implementation of LINGUA aptly illustrates which kinds of dilemmas confronted the EU due to the complex language problem. Let me give one example. It is in the interest of the EU that the improvement of employment- and education-related mobility involves all the EU member states and not just the larger ones. Currently, the situation in the EU is such that knowledge of the languages of the 'smaller' states is in general rather poor; Danish, Dutch, Greek and Finnish are examples of 'less-commonly taught languages'. There is often no teaching tradition with regard to these languages and, more concretely, hardly any suitable teaching materials are available. It is therefore appropriate that the promotion of the teaching of these languages is one of the special objectives of the LINGUA programme. But what happens? This component of LINGUA is regularly justified by pointing out the necessity to protect the 'minor' languages as such against a possible weakening of their position. However, this line of reasoning has nothing to do with the need for mobility improvement, but only with the wish to maintain language diversity – a point which I will come back to later on.

Minority languages. As I have already mentioned, the EU, and the European Parliament in particular, have repeatedly been shown to have great respect for the cultural diversity in the community of member states. Multilingualism is an essential part of this. Resolutions of the European Parliament have not always been well received by the European Commission, but, all in all, the minority languages have benefited considerably from the existence of the EU. For example, the EU set up a permanent Bureau for Lesser Used Languages in Dublin[8] and provided a special budget to subsidise activities – such as publications, research and conferences – that are somehow connected with minority languages. Curiously enough, Brussels has always been more willing to give a sympathetic ear to the cause of the minority languages than the governments of the states in which these languages are spoken (Coulmas, 1991b: 14ff).

I will come back to these aspects later on. For the sake of clarity, I would like to point out here that I am talking solely about native-born populations and not about immigrants. The languages of immigrants have, oddly enough, never been given the same amount of political attention at the European level. It is very rare that people bring 'cultural diversity' forward as an argument for the teaching of immigrant languages (Extra, 1999: 78–9).

Other models of institutional language use

As I have already mentioned, the language use model of the EU is 'plurilinguistic' – several languages are used, which, in principle, are all treated equally as 'official and working languages' of the organisation. However, I also explained that, in practice, there are various regimes in which this fundamental equality is virtually non-existent. Before commenting on this, I would first like to describe a number of other models and discuss the ways in which other international organisations solved their institutional language problems.

Although very interesting comparisons can be made between the situation in the EU and many other countries that are characterised by a more or less great diversity of languages (within a federal context or otherwise), these will merely be alluded to when discussing 'international organisations'. Of the language problems of countries such as Australia, Canada, India and South Africa, those at the national institutional level have often been given the least attention (see, e.g.

Lo Bianco, 1987; Churchill, 1998; King, 1997; Webb, 1999). For our discussion, these do not offer any special reference points at the moment. An in-depth analysis of the situations and developments in these countries might, however, lead to important insights, particularly with respect to future EU language policy at the non-institutional level.

Language use models

The plurilinguistic model of the EU is said to be 'non-restrictive', i.e. there is no restriction in the sense that each member state may use its own national language. However, there may also be variants of this non-restrictive model in which the required language and translation arrangements are structured differently. The EU model is based on the idea that everyone should be enabled to speak their own language and that translations should be provided from and into all languages, but it is also very possible to single out one language as target language for translation: all persons can then use their own language 'productively', while all translations are solely made into this 'pivotal or intermediate languages'. This pivotal language may be the language of one of the member states or an external language, for example, an 'artificial' language such as Esperanto (Grin, 1996: 33).

There are basically two types of restrictive models: either one language or a small number of languages are chosen to work in; all the excluded languages cannot be used. Furthermore, the chosen language may be the language of one of the member states or an external language, whether artificial or not.

It may of course also be possible to develop variants of this restrictive model. When they were negotiating their entry into the EU in 1972, the Danes seriously proposed that only English and French be used as working languages, provided that the English would speak only French and the French only English (Duthoy, 1993: 39). I will come back to this variant when discussing the handicaps that become apparent when people have to use a language that is not their own.

Analysis of these diverse models and their variants does not provide a straightforward answer as to which one is the best. In order to compare them with each other, an integral 'cost-benefit' analysis of each model needs to be made. This should not only include things that can be expressed in terms of money such as the costs of the required translation facilities and possibly required language learning and teaching efforts, but also the preferences and priorities of the citizens, as a group and individually. The latter does of course make a comparison very complicated. But even if only the first type of costs are taken into account, none of the models can be said to be 'obviously preferable' (Grin, 1996: 34).

Language use in other international organisations

As I have already mentioned at the beginning, the EU with its plurilinguistic model and 11 official and working languages is certainly the odd one out. All the other organisations that were confronted with such a number of languages spoken by its members opted for a restrictive model (see, e.g., Coulmas, 1992: 154ff).

The Council of Europe, to which belong all the EU member states, as well as Cyprus, Malta, Russia, Turkey and Switzerland, opted at the very beginning for English and French as official languages. It is an organisation that primarily seeks to realise cultural and educational objectives, but certainly no economic ones. It is located in Strasbourg.

The United Nations in New York uses six 'official' languages: Arabic, Chinese, English, French, Russian and Spanish. Two of these, i.e. English and French, have a separate status as 'working languages'. This means that verbal translations are only made into these two languages and that the administration is conducted in English and French. All the official documents are published in the six official languages. By the way, if member states express the wish to address the general meeting in their own language or receive certain documents in their own language, this wish is always granted, provided that they bear the translation costs themselves.

Other economic and/or political organisations that are more active at the regional level project a varied image, but they all impose language restrictions on themselves to some degree. The Association of South-East Asian Nations (ASEAN) and the European Free Trade Association (EFTA) use only English as a working language, and there are no interpreters present at their meetings. The Organisation of African Unity (OAU), on the other hand, uses Arabic, English and French as working languages, whereas the Organisation of American States (OAS) allows itself four working languages: English, Spanish, Portuguese and French.

I might of course complete this picture by also sketching the situation of sports organisations such as the International Olympic Committee or aid organisations such as the International Red Cross, but I will confine myself to saying a few words on international businesses, also known as multinationals. Multinationals are of course confronted with more language problems than merely the institutional ones. Companies need to sell their products and also purchase materials. Which language can be used best for this purpose depends on the actual situation, but many of them will have come to the conclusion – possibly from bitter experience – that sales are best made in the language of the customer (Vandermeeren, 1998: 67).

Institutional language use in international business also has an external and internal side. The former usually involves contacts with local and regional governments, for example, those in which the company's own language cannot be used.

Multinationals that are confronted with a highly differentiated staff in terms of language background will never opt for a plurilinguistic model such as that of the EU.[9] Companies always opt for one corporate language, often within the context of their local branches in combination with a relevant regional or national language. Which corporate language is chosen sometimes depends on where, i.e., in which country, the parent company is or was located. However, the more global the scope of the company, the sooner it will opt for English as its corporate language. For example, only recently, the originally Dutch-speaking ABN/AMRO Bank adopted English as its corporate language, which is the obvious choice given the current situation in banking. It may be clear this choice will not all of a sudden solve all the problems for this multinational.

One other aspect, namely the quality of the communication in English, will be discussed later on.

Discussion of the EU's language policy and practice

After this extensive sketch of the language policy and practice of the EU, I would like to comment on a few aspects of policy and practice that either have emerged gradually from the situation or were agreed upon. Most of these comments will be of a linguistic nature. The aspects in question relate to more general matters; they involve the prominent principle of plurilingualism, the notion of 'domains of language use', questions concerning the application of the principles adhered to, and the question whether it is actually necessary for the EU to draw up an explicit institutional language policy.

In the final section, the linguistic observations will all concern the language communication process itself.

Plurilingualism

There are a number of well-founded arguments that support the EU's choice in favour of plurilingualism. These may be founded on the analysis of the language communication processes involved or on the more general wish to treat all the citizens of all the member states as equally as possible. Some regard this principle as 'admirable in its idealism and concern to maintain equality between groups, but utopian' (Wright, 2000: 7). For many, though, it is such a solid starting point that it no longer needs to be put forward for discussion. The fact that people accept this principle without question (see, e.g., Laver & Roukens, 1996; Wright, 2000: 120) may have to do with the European tradition in which 'one language, one state, one people' seems firmly rooted (Wright, 2000: 1). I will come back to this later on, and then I will also discuss the associated problem of the relation between language and culture.

I would first like to say something about the arguments that are often brought forward to defend multilingualism, specifically in the European Parliament, and that apparently are regarded as incontestable by many.

First of all, the 'people back home' should be able to identify with their representatives when these speak publicly in Parliament. This requires that these representatives are allowed to speak in their own language, if they so desire (de Swaan, 1999: 21).

Consequently, if there is a discrepancy between the languages of the EU institutions and those of the peoples they represent, this might cause the people to turn against these institutions, leading eventually to the disintegration of the EU (Mamadouh, 1999a: 160). The relativity of this line of argument is evident. After all, there are large groups of minorities in the EU that never hear their language in the EU forum, even though it is officially recognised in their country. Be that as it may, the possible 'loss' suffered as a consequence of abolishing this largely symbolical use of a number of 'minor' languages should be offset against the 'profit' that might be made by the European Parliament in terms of communicative quality (see below), efficiency and credibility in general.

Another popular argument brought forward to justify plurilingualism and considered even more incontestable is that it would infringe the democratic rights of citizens, if, with regard to the knowledge of foreign languages, certain conditions were to be attached to the membership of the EU (see, e.g., Working Party, 1999: 5).

Several points need to be raised with regard to this argument. Firstly, this is to a certain extent just as relative as the previous argument: many official languages of the member states are *not* represented in the EP; it is now already the case that some Members of Parliament have to 'get by' in what they undoubtedly consider a second / foreign language. Secondly, as we have already seen, there do exist all kinds of language restrictions for the non-plenary activities in the EP. A Member of Parliament who has insufficient command of English and / or French will not be able to function as such at all. People whose mother tongue is not English or French have long come to the conclusion that they should learn to master at least one of these two languages if they are to gain a seat in the EP. Why should the EU not assume that every Member of Parliament has command of a limited number of foreign languages? And why should it not be allowed to design a regulation of limited language use in the EP on the basis of this assumption? Such a regulation of language use may be drawn up without attaching any explicit conditions to membership with regard to the command of the languages concerned. A parallel can be found in the expectation that every Member of Parliament can read: literacy is not a condition for membership, but the activities of the EP are such that anyone who cannot read would in fact be totally out of place.

The relation between language, state and nation. For the peoples of this world, language is an important means in the struggle for prosperity. Lack of a good means of communication can seriously impede social intercourse and may result in the exclusion of certain people. More in particular, it can lead to people being denied their rightful share of 'the goods of this earth'. This in itself does not mean that language is a natural binding element in the struggle for economic and non-economic prosperity of ethnic groups or peoples, or that language loyalty is essentially inherent to group formation. However, one regularly sees that the native language is used consciously for this purpose (Paulston, 1998: 22).

In the past, language was often used for this purpose in Europe, and this makes the language problem such an emotionally charged issue for the EU and many people (Coulmas, 1991b: 4). During the Enlightenment period, 'elevation' of the mother tongue, as an alternative to the Latin of the literate and the Church, was an important lever in the struggle to undermine the educational lead of the nobility and clergy and therewith the social position of the elite (Coulmas, 1991b: 18ff). In the early 19th century, the French Revolution and the German Romantic Movement turned this instrumental and rational approach to language into a very ideologically oriented vision of language, in which it was considered of essential importance to the forming of the nation. Thus, the care of language was no longer a social concern, but became a major patriotic issue. All over Europe, language became the key symbol of nationalism.

These sentiments still exist and continue to affect the EU even today. If the EU cannot distance itself from linguistic nationalism, which Coulmas (1991b: 27) calls 'the ideological dead weight of the nineteenth century', and cannot replace it by a pragmatic view on multilingualism, it will never be able to instil a sense of European identity in the citizens (Wright, 2000: 122).

And, again according to Coulmas (1991b: 27), it is particularly up to the 'educators and the media to see to it that the Europeans once again conceive of language as a tool rather than a myth'. As a linguist, I consider myself to be one of those educators who may help reduce mythologisation.

The relation between language and culture. It is obvious that language and culture are related. Language is embedded in culture; language utterances cannot be made outside the context of a certain culture nor be fully interpreted as separate from this culture. On the other hand, culture can only thrive thanks to its relation with a certain language; culture requires expression in language.

In European rhetoric, language and culture are always mentioned in one breath, and the diversity of cultures is practically always immediately related to the diversity of languages. This is always done in a positive way: it always concerns the 'great wealth' of languages and cultures, a treasure that is considered the highest good. Subsequently, this necessarily leads to the proposition that it is an essential duty to maintain and promote the multiformity of cultures as well as to honour the variety of languages.

We have already seen that, in this respect, people tend to think only or primarily of the national languages that were recognised as official EU languages. What I would like to do here is to make a few critical remarks with regard to this presupposed *close* relationship between language and culture.

First of all, language as a phenomenon has many forms. Well known are the variants that are called dialects of the 'main language'. There are also dialects that are associated with social groups, from vernacular to 'chic' and 'posh'. There are also specialised languages or language variants; almost every occupational group has its own specific variant to a certain degree, which in any case distinguishes itself from other variants by its own jargon.

In all these variants, there is a relation between language and culture, which can also manifest itself in various subcultures of a clearly individual nature. However, the relation with culture, as well as that with a culture or subculture that is specific for that language or variant of that language, can vary considerably in strength. The culture-specific content can be very limited in many technically specialised languages, particularly when the language in question is used all over the world by that occupational group. For example, the manuals used in the aircraft industry are written in what is called 'controlled English', for which very precise guidelines were drawn up with regard to the vocabulary and sentence structures to be used. Also in the world of Internet communication, people use internationalised English, which is always some form of 'reduced English'. And this 'reduction' does not only involve the elements of language but also the underlying structure or the cultural embedding.

This reduction does not in itself necessarily have to cause any problems, but the fact remains that the receiver has to be acquainted with those reductions. The reader of, or listener to, 'reduced' texts should not enrich the message again with the cultural load of which it was stripped on purpose. The fact that the backgrounds of people from different cultures colour the 'international' language they jointly use – be it English or some artificial language such as Esperanto – causing unsuspected misunderstandings, will be further discussed later on. Certain American Internet companies have by now come to understand that they need to 'localise' their English messages, i.e. adapt them to the cultures of the individual regions in which they operate, if they want to get their messages across.

We therefore may state as a fact that there are limits to the 'deculturalisation' of language. However, what I want to indicate here first and foremost is that there are many gradations in the strength of the relation between language and culture.

There is also another aspect of the relation between language and culture that may have become clear to you by now. As much as languages have their variants or 'sublanguages', cultures have their variants or subcultures. Therefore, when discussing, for example, the Dutch language, we do not actually talk only about a conglomerate of language variants, but rather, also about the various cultures that are expressed in that one language. On the other hand, when discussing Dutch culture, we talk not only about a conglomerate of culture variants, but also again about various languages in which that culture is expressed. And just as dialects of one and the same language will not always be mutually intelligible, so the subcultures in question may sometimes be miles apart.

The defence of the position of Dutch or of one of the other national languages recognised as an EU language merely or primarily on the basis of the specific cultural load or cultural embedding of the language is thus placed in a different light. Particularly the claims that multilingualism and cultural diversity as such are treasures and resources of inestimable value should perhaps be viewed with slightly more reserve than is usual in European rhetoric (Grin & Vaillancourt, 1997: 48ff). Those who speak of these things in such terms should have the courage to go beyond metaphoric language use and also indicate what they really mean by 'resources'. Anyone who considers this issue properly will understand that profits also involve costs, and this is also applicable to linguistic and cultural diversity. For example, maintaining the full range of languages requires specific measures in the fields of education and social service. Diversity of language and culture, no matter how highly appreciated subjectively, has its price and requires sacrifices, naturally at the expense of something else (Grin, 1996: 29; see also Grin, 1997).

Domains of language use

Language is always used within certain contexts, which are also known as 'language use domains'. The characteristics of a certain domain or the cultural environment co-determine the meaning and form of the language, as may have become clear from the previous discussion. There are of course many language domains. Within the EU context, de Swaan (1999: 14) distinguishes three:

- the 'official, public domain', including the EP and the external language use of the EC;
- the domain of EU bureaucracy;
- the domain of the European citizens.

In the previous discussion, the first two were classified under 'institutional' and the third under 'non-institutional' domains. It will be clear that other distinctions can be made or that, within each of these three domains, there are subdomains with their own characteristics.

I am not so much interested in distinguishing domains as such; rather, I am far more interested in two related factors. The first is that the language policy with regard to the EU institutions does not need to be the same for all domains or subdomains. I have already described the differences in the current practice of the EU institutions. The second factor, which requires a little more attention, is the question to what extent language policy and language practice within one domain have certain consequences for language policy and practice within the other. Let me illustrate this with a quotation. In one of its publications, the Dutch Language Union pays considerable attention to the worrisome fact that the use of Dutch in the day-to-day practice of the EU is gradually being reduced. The final conclusion is: 'This erosion process may have far-reaching consequences for Dutch in the long term. Something will have to be done to prevent the Dutch language from being degraded to a linguistic curiosity' (Duthoy, 1993: 48; de Bot, 1994: 14–15).

The conviction that measures in the institutional domain of the EU may and *will* have dramatic consequences for the 'home situation' of the languages in question is fairly widespread (see, e.g. Mamadouh, 1999b: 119). This is more or less in line with the commotion that the Dutch Minister of Education caused a number of years ago when he suggested that certain parts of university education be offered in English. Italian newspapers thereupon reported that the Dutch, those barbarians, had abandoned their own language.[10] What should one think of that? Is there really more to it than swollen rhetoric?

Language use in one domain can influence language use in another. This influence may of course be characterised by a multitude of contexts and modalities. I would like to confine myself here to discussing the situation in which one language or a very limited number of languages would be singled out for institutional language use in the EU: what would then be the influence on the non-selected EU languages in other domains?

Two types of effects can be distinguished. The first type involves language developments to which the chosen EU languages *would* contribute and the 'shelved' languages *would not*. For example, just think of the terminological databank in all official languages of the EU, or the imbroglios in 1993 that were the result of the initial decision of the Council of Ministers to limit the language use in the Trademark Office of the EU (located in Spain) to English, French, German, Spanish and Italian (Fasol, 1994d: 58). In cases such as these, languages that are 'not allowed to participate' run the risk of falling behind in their development as a language in these domains.

In both cases, concrete solutions were found to minimise this risk. However, this did not mean that all the languages were granted fully equal status as official languages within the institutes in question.

The situation in which non-selected languages, as a result of this type of exclusion, lose their capability to perform certain functions – e.g. as a means of communication for international trade or diplomacy – will not occur for those European languages, which are already highly developed for these functions.

The other type of effects involves cases in which the non-selected languages are affected or 'contaminated' by or via the selected languages. Most of the activities of the EU institutions are carried out in isolation and, for that simple reason, the risk of contamination will be very small. However, there is always the risk that something will spread unchecked. Take for example the EU tenders. The outside world – in this case the subsidy-oriented industry – does adjust its language use to that of the EU bureaucracy. In these cases, the risk of 'contamination' is certainly present. However, the question is: does this matter? It is in any case a phenomenon that has always existed. There is no language that has not absorbed elements from other languages. Even the lines that I quoted from the publication of the Dutch Language Union show traces of this. And would English be what it is today without the many loan words from the Romance languages? It is all puristic squabbling, because this type of influence, too, has existed throughout the centuries. This bickering will no doubt also continue when elements of Eurospeak enter the Dutch language.

The next pressing question is then: does Dutch not run the risk of being entirely pushed aside in the long run? And would that not be truly tragic? I will come back to this when discussing the position of English as lingua franca. All I want to say here about it is that experts generally rule out the possibility that the languages of the EU will become entirely extinct. The fear that other languages in the EU, particularly the 'minor' ones, run the risk of being marginalised is exaggerated, according to some (Graddol, 1997: 2; Scheffer, 1999: 2). After all, the conditions that occurred in the known cases of 'language death' are absent for these languages, even if a process of gradual adaptation is involved (see, e.g. Baker & Prys Jones, 1998: 150ff; Sirles, 2000). The most important motives (there must be very large personal, economic advantages attached to it, and the dominant language should have tremendous social prestige) are lacking to a sufficient degree (Paulston, 1998: 20). The reference to what happened to the languages of the conquered peoples in the Roman Empire does not apply here. Even if it was a question of true 'language death' in these cases, the democratic standards of the present EU would never allow such conditions as occurred in those days (Haarmann, 1991b: 18).

A counterexample can perhaps also be found in present-day Switzerland. In the Federal Office, where the civil service is composed in accordance with the ratios of the language groups in the country, practically all communication is conducted in German (contrary to the agreements); the other languages (French, Italian and Rhaeto-Romanic) are hardly used (Dürmüller, 1996: 20). However, this does not mean that German has developed into the national language, the language that every Swiss from the other three language groups learns and speaks as a second language or, for that matter, that every non-German-speaking Swiss would trade in his own language for German. It is absolutely inconceivable that one of the four national languages will develop into a single national language for the whole of Switzerland (Dürmüller, 1996: 74). Surveys show that a large majority of the Swiss, particularly the young, would sooner have English as their official national language! Mind you, this does not mean that they would actually prefer to have English as their official national language for that would be taking things a bit too far (Dürmüller, 1996: 76–7).

Application of the EU language principles

More than once, doubts have arisen as to how conscientiously the EU actually applies the sacred principle of plurilingualism. There is a clear discrepancy between what member states aver, at the EU level, about linguistic diversity – in order to defend the equal status of 'their' national language – and how these member states treat minority languages in their own countries. I have already mentioned this and it is not my intention to discuss at length the policies of the member states with regard to minority languages, either those of the natives or those of immigrants.

I merely wish to point out how easily one can get caught in one's own rhetoric about the 'richness of a plurilinguistic and pluricultural Europe'. After all, in their internal policies, member states have always displayed a strong tendency towards linguistic and cultural homogeneity, and this is a tendency they *still* have (Coulmas, 1991b: 14; Phillipson, 1995: 105). Weighty arguments that support this were and are still found in the necessity to create or preserve the unity of the state.

Some have quite rightly pointed out that the 'multiple identity' that member states apparently expect from the minorities within their own borders should also be realisable at EU level. Would it not be possible to make a clear distinction between the subjective value attached to one's own national culture and language, on the one hand, and the practical needs of European intercommunication, on the other (Haarmann, 1991a: 111–12)?

By the way, there is quite a bit of 'historical irony' in the fact that, at EU level, member states have jointly adopted a much more liberal and friendly attitude towards well-known minority languages such as Frisian, Welsh and Catalan than they have ever done internally (Coulmas, 1991b: 14; see also Baker & Prys Jones, 1998: 343). Up till now, the languages of the more recent ethnic minorities such as Turkish and Arabic have not really benefited from this more liberal attitude at EU level (Extra, 1999: 78).

Active institutional EU language policy?

We have seen that the willingness among politicians to reconsider seriously the language policy or language practice of the EU institutions is not very great, particularly when the principle of plurilingualism is at issue. On the other hand, a survey did show that more than three-quarters of the EU officials and about 40% of the members of the European Parliament were in favour of a clear and limiting regulation. However, within these groups, there is absolutely no agreement about what the actual content of this limitation should be. For example, it is rather striking to see that 65% of the officials would not mind a limitation that would leave only English and French, whereas the Members of Parliament are not particularly keen on this idea (Schlossmacher, 1994: 115ff). Moreover, 20% of the trainees (the future officials?) prove to have a preference for English only (Quell, 1997: 65).

In the meantime, the problem has also drawn the attention of a number of experts, particularly in the light of the coming expansion of the EU. It looks as if the EU itself will let the matter rest, perhaps because it has no other option; but what do experts say about the possibility and/or necessity to pursue an active policy with regard to the institutional language use of the EU?

Experts think that the EU should and will introduce a limitation of the number of working languages (Grin, 1996; de Swaan, 1999; Mamadouh, 1999a; Wright, 2000), but they do not agree on how many working languages there should be. Some think the number will be limited to just one language, i.e. English. Others think that, besides English, French will also maintain its strong position.

There is also disagreement about whether or not the EU should pursue an active policy in this matter or should let developments take their course. There are some who, on the one hand, indicate that the EU can no longer hide its head in the sand, but, on the other, eventually seem to opt for an unplanned development towards strong limitation, which, so they think, will then go in the direction they advocate (de Swaan, 1999; Wright, 2000). This could just be common sense, because explicit regulations that go against the existing socio-cultural forces in this precarious and highly explosive matter are doomed to fail (Paulston, 1998: 4).

On the other hand, some also point out that a language policy which is more or less the result of an ordinary market mechanism will not necessarily be the best or optimal solution (Grin, 1996: 31ff). Language is a 'public property'. Those who are convinced that language diversity in the EU is of great importance will have to take action and should pursue an active policy, because it seems inevitable that the 'spontaneous' result of a 'linguistic laissez-faire' will be absolute dominance of the English language (see also Quell, 1997: 73).

I, for my part, think that an explicit policy of limitation with regard to the EU working languages is highly preferable to the current situation. The consequences of such a limitation for the various parts of the institutional domain should be examined separately. For each different situation, an individual variant will need to be developed.

However, in order for such a policy to be successful, many obstacles that have to do with the mythologisation of language will need to be removed. I sincerely hope that the following observations about a number of linguistic aspects of the matter may contribute to this.

Linguistic Considerations

In this section, I will go into the relevance of linguistic insights for drawing up an institutional language policy. Then, I will discuss two very important points, namely the quality of communication processes and the handicaps that participants in the communication process may be confronted with in various models of language use. Finally, I cannot avoid paying attention to English, especially to English as a lingua franca.

Relevance of linguistic insights

Linguistic insights have already been discussed to some extent in the previous section, particularly those of a socio-psychological nature related, among other things, to the attitudes towards language and language identification. In choosing a certain language use model and the realisation thereof, it may also be useful to know its value in communicative terms.

The aim of language communication is to exchange messages, to transfer meanings and feelings, and to understand, convince and correct one another. Particularly with regard to the effectiveness of the communication process and the extent to which participants can contribute to this, a number of things can be said from the linguistic angle. Two major perspectives from the linguistic point of view are, on the one hand, the quality of communication and, on the other, the handicaps that participants in the process may be confronted with in various designs.

It is rather striking to see that these linguistic aspects get hardly any attention (or no attention) at the micro-level in the literature on the language policy of the EU, not even when the range of possible restrictive models is discussed in detail (see also Haarmann, 1991b: 21ff). Most authors do not go any further than to state that little is known about the actual language use within EU institutions and its consequences for the decision-making process (Mamadouh, 1999a: 161).

Linguistic insights are not the only insights relevant to policy decisions. Nor are they only meaningful when explicit policy decisions have to be made. They can also be relevant when a policy gradually evolves or comes to the fore automatically. In those cases, they may be useful in decision-making concerning the concrete design of the language use situation.

Quality of communication

The observations I wish to make about the quality of communication are presented in two separate sections. The first section deals with the 'non-restrictive' model, the second with the 'restrictive model'.

'Non-restrictive'

'Non-restrictive' means that none of the languages brought in as working languages by participants in an international organisation are dropped as such. All languages are considered equal. The EU with its plurilinguistic foundation adheres in principle to the non-restrictive model.

Many people think it is always possible to make arrangements that will guarantee an optimal quality of communication, even when an organisation uses a plurilinguistic model with several working languages. Is this assumption correct? Let us have a look at three such 'arrangements'.

The first 'arrangement' implies that, when the number of languages is very limited, these languages are used interchangeably and simultaneously. Each person speaks his own language and the others are able to understand him, even when this language is not the mother tongue of the listener. Everyone has at least a good passive knowledge of the other languages. This model is also known as the polyglottic model, or the *Partnersprachen-Modell* in German (Dürmüller, 1996: 81).

Implementation of this model in the EU – while simultaneously maintaining the plurilinguistic principle – is of course out of the question. It is impossible to have at least a passive knowledge of 10 languages. However, this variant has been suggested – and perhaps it is used occasionally in practice – for situations in which the parties have agreed to limit the number of languages to two or three working languages: in this case the parties concerned have to acquire a passive knowledge of only one or two other languages, and simultaneous translations will then not be necessary. Experience does show that it is very difficult, in organisations and even in a multilingual country such as Switzerland, to get people to engage in polyglottic dialogues (Dürmüller, 1996: 81; Vandermeeren, 1998: 47).

It is usually assumed that the equality of languages is guaranteed as long as there are sufficient translation facilities. This is the second arrangement on which I would like to comment. First of all, I would like to go into the simultaneous translation of what is said at meetings and discussions. There are aspects of this facility that affect the progress and quality of the communication process, one of which particularly concerns the speakers of the 'minor' EU languages.

I am not referring here to the quality of the translation as such which, naturally, is seldom perfect and often not optimal. But that is a given fact you may learn to live with, provided that you keep in mind that the translation does not always convey exactly what is being said.

The time lags that occur between the moment of utterance and the moment of hearing during simultaneous translations are known to be rather annoying for both speaker and listener, for example when there is no synchrony between utterance or message conveyed and the facial expression of the partner(s) in communication. Furthermore, there are of course the costs of the entire procedure. The direct financial costs do not necessarily have to be a problem when plurilingualism is given first priority, but the costs in terms of time consumption and loss of efficiency may become very troublesome when a large number of languages is involved.

There is another matter which also impedes the normal process of communication and of which many are often unaware. Speakers who are more familiar with the situation know that simultaneous translation is no easy task for the interpreters, and as they are aware that what they say can often not be rapidly translated literally or very precisely, they tend to simplify their texts as much as possible in order to make the job easier for the interpreters. They adapt their language, leave out mixed metaphors and jokes, speak in short sentences and use direct language. Thus, subtle distinctions get lost, things are said in plain terms and, although not intended, the message may hit the listener very hard.

This phenomenon has been mentioned in the literature, but not very often (Abélès, 1999: 113). So far, no empirical research has ever been conducted to investigate the extent and the possibly very negative effects of this phenomenon.

Additionally, I would like to stress one thing in particular. It, too, has never been investigated, but my own experience of it is in any case confirmed by others.[11] Not all that is brought forward at meetings is necessarily interesting. Often much of the same is said, particularly when there are many speakers, who also, each in turn, have to deliver the official standpoint or view of their countries and/or parties. This type of meeting can take very long and participants regularly feel the need to let their attention wander, particularly when they have to listen to many messages in translation. What happens then is that they only listen to the languages of which they have passive knowledge and ignore the translations as far as possible. Thus, the speakers of the 'minor' languages, of which practically no one has passive knowledge, become the victims of this practice for their message is not heard at all.

Now the original intention was that, by enabling them to speak in their own language, the contribution of the speakers of the 'minor' languages would come across clearly, and not in some second-hand way through a foreign language. In this manner, simultaneous translation leads to serious discrimination, especially against the 'minor' languages. And matters may even become worse if, in the future, cost-saving variants will be introduced in which, as I have already mentioned, the translation into the 'minor' languages will take place via one of the 'major' languages. Apparently, so much importance is attached to the plurilinguistic principle that, astonishingly enough, people are willing to embrace these types of variants that have a disastrous effect on communication (Duthoy, 1993: 42; Working Paper, 1999).

Finally, what may we expect in the near future of the third arrangement, which involves the developments in machine translation and voice technology? Much money has been invested in the research into machine translation of written texts, including funding by the EU. Some successes have been achieved, although not the major success that some had expected or predicted. Non-prepared texts or texts that have not been written in 'controlled language' cannot be translated fully or perfectly by computers. Translation programmes do lend themselves very well for the translation of standardised texts and screening the general content of texts so that people can determine whether or not translation of the full text is desirable or useful.

Speech technology has made considerable advances in the field of automatic recognition and processing of speech. It has now become possible to render automatically an utterance in one language into an utterance in another language, but only in 'controlled language'. There is still a long way to go before workable procedures have been developed for this in each EU language. It is naive to expect that speech technology will ever be developed, let alone in the coming decades, that will be able to replace completely the current system of simultaneous translation.

'Restrictive'

From the linguistic perspective, quite a number of objections may therefore be raised to practices based on the plurilinguistic principle. What about the models in which one language or a small number of languages are selected as working languages?

The main problem of any restrictive model is that those people whose language was not selected will be more or less seriously handicapped in comparison with those whose language *was* selected as a working language. People usually have a much poorer command of a foreign language than of their mother tongue. How serious this handicap is will be discussed separately.

I would now like to go into some aspects of the communicative situation in which a group of people, or a number of people in that group, have to communicate in a language that is not their mother tongue. For the sake of convenience, the mother-tongue speakers will be called the 'natives', and the others the 'non-natives'. The situations concerned may differ considerably. The participants can opt for using just one working language, i.e. either the language spoken by one of the participants or groups of participants or a language that is not the mother tongue of any of the participants, or they can opt for using a few languages. What the consequences of this may be for the participants whose mother tongue is not selected will be discussed in the following material.

Let us first look at the situation in which only one working language is used. In such a situation, the imbalance between the natives and the non-natives in terms of language proficiency will have a negative effect on the quality of communication. The extent of the negative effect depends to a large degree on the non-natives' proficiency in the foreign language. This proficiency will usually not approximate that of the natives. Although there is no empirical evidence that corroborates this, experience shows that the communicative performances of the non-natives are co-determined by the degree of confidence with which they participate in the communication. Furthermore, the confidence of many non-natives is much greater when they use a foreign language that is not the mother tongue of any of the participants. In such a case, non-natives addressing each other feel that they do not have to bother so much about whether what they say is formulated or pronounced correctly, and they can therefore concentrate on the message they want to convey.

It is important to realise that language skills consist of a number of sub-skills. When there are problems with communication and the message cannot be conveyed properly, laymen usually ascribe this to a poor knowledge of the language in a restricted sense, i.e. to a lack of grammatical knowledge and vocabulary. But, as we have already seen, language is always embedded in culture. Every language community has its own way of approaching the surrounding world and also its own way of expressing it in or through language. This means that language proficiency does not only include a purely linguistic component consisting of grammar and a vocabulary, but also a socio-cultural component (see Knapp & Knapp-Potthoff, 1987).

Some researchers have studied what is known as cross-cultural communication, or interlanguage pragmatics, i.e. situations in which non-natives are involved in communication. Their research has shown that many misunderstandings occur in these situations; in other words, there is much 'non-communication'. To be on the same wavelength communicatively is often a problem in groups that, from a cultural point of view, are of a homogeneous composition, but it is even more so in groups of mixed composition (Garcia & Otheguy, 1989: 1; see also Kasper & Blum-Kulka, 1993; Vandermeeren, 1998: 45). It must be said that the research in question is rather limited. Up to now, for example, the focus has been on how culturally different ways of expressing gratitude or offering apologies has led to misunderstandings in the communication between natives and non-natives. Large-scale research into how differences in language and cultural skills affect the quality of communication in international organisations has not yet been conducted (Graddol, 1997: 13). This also applies to the EU (Mamadouh, 1999a: 161).

In this respect it is essential that more attention should be paid to the role of natives in cross-cultural communication. Should we take it for granted, as people usually do, that natives have no problems communicating with non-natives, and that they always function optimally?

The first problem with natives may be that they are not sufficiently aware of the problems that non-natives may have. To start with, they do not always take into consideration that the non-natives they are speaking to may sometimes have difficulties understanding what has been said. In this case, the natives do not always realise that, when non-natives answer their questions with 'yes' or 'no', they may actually not have understood the question at all. Non-natives usually do not like to admit that they do not entirely understand something (Munter, 1993: 75; see also McArthur, 1998: 211). Natives also do not always realise that non-natives may be tempted to use what little vocabulary they have to just say what they can say and, consequently, do not always say what they wanted to say.

Natives can have even more problems with the socio-cultural side of the matter (Munter, 1993: 69). When they hear utterances in their own language, they too hastily assume that these will have the cultural load that is normal in their language. They do not realise that the 'yes' they hear may mean 'no' to the non-native who makes the utterance. Thus, the misunderstanding is not only a disadvantage for the non-native, but also for the native (Verschueren, 1989: 34).

It has been said that there is a lot of 'pseudo-understanding' in the communication between natives and non-natives. Particularly with regard to the use of English as an international language, the following observation was made: 'a serious consequence of the spread of English has been that it has created a false sense of mutual intelligibility' (Garcia & Otheguy, 1989: 1–2).

Yet another aspect – and this makes the whole issue even more difficult to understand – is that natives, especially those who are aware of their language, do sometimes adapt their language to the actual communicative situation and, more importantly, to the poorer proficiency of the non-natives with whom they are communicating. This results in what is known as 'foreigner talk', of which the main feature is simplification of formal and functional aspects of a language (see, e.g., Gass, 1999: 574–5). In certain situations, it also happens that non-natives pretend to have a poorer proficiency in the foreign language than they actually have in order to make their non-native status very clear (Davies, 1991: 46ff, 70).

Handicaps

It is evident that people are at a disadvantage when they have to communicate in a foreign language. This disadvantage can of course vary considerably depending on the foreign language proficiency of those involved, and may also vary in accordance with the extent to which natives are aware of the imbalance in the communication situation. But the disadvantage for the non-natives *vis-à-vis* the natives cannot be ignored.

Certainly in the EU where, for the member states, great economic and political interests are at stake, such a language handicap can have serious economic consequences. As the EU's point of departure is that no one should be at a disadvantage as a result of having a different language background, it is quite understandable that it opted for the plurilinguistic principle. On the other hand, the EU also defends the viewpoint that 'the right to freedom from discrimination on the basis of language' does not necessarily have to lead to 'the right to use your language(s) in the activities of communal life' (Ricento, 1996: 137). And de Swaan (1999: 10) adds that the right to freedom of expression, *if* this were to include the right to express oneself in any given language, does in any case not mean that others are obliged to listen.[12]

However, with regard to the EU working languages, the relevant question is not so much *if* restrictions have to be made, but rather *what* restrictions need to be made. When the necessary choices are to be made, the decision-makers will also want to reduce the handicaps for the participants to an absolute minimum or at least spread them as evenly as possible.

It may be interesting to note that the disadvantage for the non-natives will naturally be greater when not one but two or three languages will be selected as working languages. In this case, the non-natives need to have a good passive and/or active knowledge of more than one foreign language, and should also be able to deal with the associated cultures. Moreover, the cultural mix in communication would become much more obscure for everyone and the natives would dominate the communication situation even more.

If the EU should choose to abandon plurilingualism, reducing the number of working languages to just one is actually the only feasible option. There is an additional reason for this, which, generally speaking, does not get enough attention in these types of discussions. In an organisation with many members, who 'bring in' many different languages, the type of dominance that naturally and normally falls to the natives will become less and less. The large majority of non-natives will take control of the communication situation, and the natives will no longer be automatically the ones to take the lead. In a sense, the non-natives will gradually begin to take possession of the language, or at least they become co-creators of the specific variant of the working language required in that organisation. The natives are then no longer in possession of their own language. I will come back to this interesting phenomenon when discussing the English language separately.

Finally, I would like to go into one more variant of the restrictive model. We have just seen that a restriction to a few languages is more disadvantageous for the non-natives than the restriction to one language. However, there is also a variant of that 'few-languages model' in which the handicaps are spread more evenly among all the participants in the communication. In this variant, the speakers of the selected languages – which, in the EU context, will probably be German, English and French – are expected to speak in another language than their own. The English will speak only in German or French, the French only in German or English, and the Germans only in English or French.

As I have already mentioned, this model was brought forward by the Danes when negotiating their entry into the EU in the early 1970s, as they wanted only English and French as working languages (Duthoy, 1993: 39). This proposal was unsuccessful. The English and French were also against it, thus – according to some – betraying the great advantage they already had as a result of the stealthily growing monopoly of their languages in the present situation; they probably expected this to continue as long as no changes were made in the fundamental equality of all the languages (Wright, 2000: 174).

This idea rarely meets with warm approval, and it is only its simplicity that occasionally elicits a friendly cry of surprise, which is then soon followed by qualifications such as 'unnatural', 'charming', 'idealistic' and 'naive', or 'rationalistic' and 'purely analytical, functional'. In connection with the last two qualifications, the adherents to this idea are even considered 'misguided and misguiding', for anyone may know that no one can be motivated to support such an arrangement, nor, for that matter, to adopt 'nobody's language, e.g. Latin or Esperanto' as a working language (Grin, 1999: 148).

Is there *nothing* to be said in its favour? How people got the idea that no one is likely to endorse this model remains a mystery to me. It is of course quite understandable that those people whose mother tongue is selected as working language in this model will not particularly like it. They would after all be saddled with a considerable handicap, one that they did not have until then. And, indeed, many people consider it 'unnatural' not to speak in their own language, while others do use it in that same situation. We have already seen this in the discussion of the polyglottic model. But all the other people in the EU whose language is hardly functioning as a working language at present – whatever the plurilinguistic principle may say about this – will surely not have any problem with it–or will they? An additional advantage is that it would also put an end to the objectionable habit of a number of purely monolingual English and French in the European Parliament who use the principle of equality as an excuse for not speaking any other language than their own, even in informal situations (Wright, 2000: 177).

The advantages of this variant are not limited merely to a more just distribution of handicaps. For it is to be expected that this variant will improve the general quality of communication. This will undoubtedly come as a surprise to you. Is it not so that *everyone* will then be condemned to use a foreign language and be saddled with the handicaps of a poorer proficiency? Yes, of course. But, if you look on the positive side, there is, first of all, the advantage that the natives will no longer dominate the communication, and secondly, *all* participants in the communication process will be aware of the obstacles that prevent clear communication in the very complicated situation of the multilingual and multicultural EU. Everyone would then be equally willing to make efforts to understand others and to express themselves clearly. This might reduce considerably the chances of miscommunication.

English as a 'lingua franca'

Expectations are that, eventually, English will become the only working language for the EU institutions, and proposals have been made to select English explicitly for this purpose. Sometimes the expectations and proposals go even beyond the institutional domain. It is envisaged that, in the long term, English will be the sole official language for all international communication in Europe. Some even think it will replace all the national languages.

So far I have confined myself to discussing the language use of the EU institutions. I will also mainly do so in this section, but an occasional digression into other language use domains may be necessary to prove my point.

First of all, I will go into the expectations and proposals for English as the only working language of the EU. Next, I will discuss the phenomenon of the 'lingua franca'. And finally, I will describe the way the English language developed over the past century.

The English language in the EU

There are two things I would like to say initially. Firstly, I am now no longer talking about the question as to whether the EU should let developments take their course or devise a truly new policy. I will now confine myself to giving a brief outline of what the actual outcome will be regardless of which of these two processes will actually take place. Secondly, when statements are made with regard to this matter, the essential distinction between domains and subdomains is often not made or remains vague. This is, however, not the place to discuss this issue.

Anyone who makes statements about an 'autonomous' development and expects that just one language will remain will, without exception, come to the conclusion that this will most likely be English (Fishman, 1994: 67; Mamadouh, 1999b: 125).

In any case, most people have this expectation as far as the EU institutions are concerned, although some will also include language use outside these institutions. With regard to the latter, there are some who explicitly rule out the outcome that English will be the sole language used everywhere (Fishman, 1994: 71). Recent research among the officials of various Euregions (regional administrative bodies with restricted authority, across the borders of two adjoining EU member states) shows that these use the language of their 'European neighbours' in official communications, both in writing and speech (Gellert-Novak, 1994: 126). At this level, English has therefore not yet replaced the languages of the member states.

Those who think that a change of policy is imperative have more problems with working out in detail the choice of language. Their proposals can be categorised depending on whether they have a preference for a combination of languages (and thereby, usually quite emphatically, reject English as sole language) or just one language (rarely indicating another language than English).

We have seen above that a myriad of factors are involved in deciding on the candidates for the position of EU working language, although many people often take only the psycho-social factors into account and tend to disregard other factors, especially the linguistic ones. Someone who put much effort into this is Ulrich Ammon. He also compared the EU languages in terms of their position and suitability for being used as working language in the EU (Ammon, 1995: 28ff; Ammon, 1996: 244ff). The criteria he used were, among other things, the numerical strength of the language in terms of the number of mother-tongue speakers, the economic strength in terms of, for example, the gross national product, the strength of the language as 'official' language in terms of the number of countries in which the language has this status, the number of people who learn the language as a foreign language, and the use of the language in industry, science and diplomacy. On the basis of his analyses, Ammon (1994: 10) devises a model that he characterises as 'English generally', excluding 'English only'. In this model, everyone masters English and uses this language as lingua franca, but certain people also use other languages as lingua franca in certain domains. The position of English will remain strong in the EU, but Ammon (1995: 50) expects that German will become increasingly important at the expense of French (see also Fishman, 1994: 68).

Others have developed similar constructions, usually with the help of different terminology; they talk, for example, about 'selective multilingualism'. This involves a concrete proposal for just the working languages of the EU bureaucracy: English and French are given a central position, and, for certain purposes, German and Spanish are also used (Haarmann, 1991b: 21ff). There are also a few who expect that the position of French will remain stable next to English as long as the major EU institutions remain based in areas where French is spoken, no matter how biased people may become in favour of English as sole language (Dollerup, 1996: 32).

There are also some people who explicitly opt for one language, namely English. This does not always mean that it is their personal preference, for some of them add that it is in any case inevitable (Scheffer, 1999: 2). In such a situation, it may also happen that English is expressly labelled 'lingua franca' in order to indicate that the other languages will keep their functions outside the EU institutions (Dürmüller, 1994: 62ff.; Dürmüller, 1996: 81). De Swaan (1999: 19ff), who occasionally intimated that he is in favour of using only English at the institutional level as he deems the development towards this situation inevitable, opts for a mixed model: plurilingualism for the public debate in the EP, English and French for informal use, and a limited number of languages for use in the bureaucratic system.

There is no one who opts for any language other than English as sole language. There does exist some resistance to the use of English, by which the importance of other languages, especially French and German, is also brought to the fore (see, e.g., Ammon, 1996: 263). But in that case the other language is never highlighted as the exclusive EU working language.

In the discussions about the language dilemmas confronting the EU, opting for a non-EU language is also occasionally mentioned as a solution. However, this option has never included one of the other world languages such as Arabic, Russian or Chinese. It has always involved either Latin – a dead language – or Esperanto, one of the artificial languages.

Although Latin has a long history as an international language – even long after it ceased to be a 'living' language – and as the language of the Catholic Church (Haarmann, 1991b: 11ff), it was never considered as a serious option, except in the proposal of Patijn and Van der Hek, two Dutchmen who were members of the European Parliament in the 1970s (Coulmas, 1991b: 6).

The use of Esperanto was proposed more than once, but primarily by Esperantists. Of the many artificial languages developed, Esperanto is the most successful.[13] Speakers of Esperanto can be found all over the world; in Hungary it is a subject in secondary education. Once it even drew the official attention of UNESCO. In a sense it has now passed the stage of being merely an artificial language, and Esperantists therefore prefer to call it 'the international language'. However, there is no international political organisation that uses this language. Its use is limited 'to circles of enthusiasts who believe in values of universality' (Haarmann, 1991b: 12–13). It has never been seriously considered for use in international political organisations, although members of the European Parliament did once render assistance to a conference on this issue.[14]

Why are linguists particularly so easily inclined to put Esperanto aside as not a feasible option? Davies (1999: 110ff) sums it up as follows. The supporters always tend to look from a purely linguistic perspective at Esperanto as a possible solution to language problems. In this light, there seems to be nothing wrong with Esperanto, although a few questions might be in order here (1999: 110). However, experts in applied linguistics know that more factors need to be taken into account than only the purely linguistic ones when looking at language problems. When calling to mind the cultural, psychological, sociolinguistic, educational and political factors, one will rarely get the idea that something can be done with an artificial language (Davies, 1999: 111).

Lingua franca

In the following three subsections, I will elaborate on this important subject from three different perspectives.

Definition. 'Lingua franca' has generally meant any language that is used as an exchange language for communication between people with different native-language backgrounds. In the Middle Ages, when the term was introduced, a lingua franca was always a mix of elements from different languages, which sailors used to communicate with people who did not speak their language. Nowadays the term is used to refer to any language that can be used as an international medium of communication. The fact that a language used frequently in this way, such as English, will gradually begin to bear the marks of it is no prerequisite for referring to it as a lingua franca (Ammon, 1995: 25; Christ, 1997: 130ff).

In this sense, 'lingua franca' can therefore be denoted as an international language. I do not follow those who only wish to speak of 'lingua franca use' with respect to communication between non-natives only (Ammon, 1995: 26). Nor do I want to follow the Esperantists who wish to reserve the term 'international language' exclusively for their artificial language.

A language that is used as a lingua franca will undergo the influence of being a lingua franca. I have already mentioned that when a language is used as a lingua franca by non-natives from a diversity of linguistic backgrounds, the 'ownership' of the language will be transferred to the non-natives, i.e., the natives become '"minority stakeholders" in the global resource' (Graddol, 1997: 23). We have seen that some research has been carried out with regard to the problems that arise in native/non-native communication and the situations in which only non-natives take part. Various things are known about the strategies that non-natives adopt to overcome their communication problems, and some insight has been gained into the use of lingua franca (Firth, 1996: 242ff; Vandermeeren, 1998: 45–6). The important point here is that any language used systematically as a lingua franca will undergo such changes that the dominance that natives normally have via their language is affected in some way.

Linguistic imperialism. This automatically leads to a discussion of the question whether a reduction of the number of working languages in the EU institutions can be equated to what is known as linguistic imperialism, particularly when the remaining languages are French and English, two languages whose spread in the past was partly the result of their 'colonial' positions. Does not a similar pursuit of dominance lie hidden behind the seemingly inevitable development towards, and generally felt need for, a limitation of the number of working languages, i.e. a pursuit of dominance that should be particularly associated with the spread of English, also in the more recent post-imperialistic period?

It is very tempting to go deeper into this subject, particularly where the authors who made in-depth and often very critical analyses of the linguistic imperialism of English have begun to discuss the current language-political issues of the EU in the same vein (Phillipson & Skutnabb-Kangas, 1999: 22ff; see also Phillipson, 1992; Phillipson & Skutnabb-Kangas, 1994; Phillipson & Skutnabb-Kangas, 1999).[15]

It is, however, not my intention to discuss this subject at length. The arguments in this matter are predominantly of a socio-economic and political nature, and others have already conclusively invalidated the doom scenarios that were drawn up (see, e.g. Conrad, 1996: 22ff). In the compilation edited by Fishman *et al.* (1996) with the revealing title *Post-Imperial English*, the position and development of the English language in nearly twenty former British and American colonies are critically examined (Fishman, 1996a). Almost all of the authors examine this position and development in the light of Phillipson's ideas on linguistic imperialism. Fishman (1996b: 640) finally comes to the conclusion that the spread of English in these countries has everything to do with their participation in the modern global economy and hardly anything with the direct interference of their former colonial masters.[16] The choice in favour of English is one made by the people themselves, who considered it the best way to acquire a place in the global economy. When people speak of linguistic imperialism in this context, it is mere rhetoric of western intellectuals (Chew, 1999: 38).

It has also been observed that, whereas English as a lingua franca is becoming increasingly important for the 'global arrangements' in these countries, life at the local level remains strongly connected with the national and regional languages and cultures (Fishman, 1996b: 640). Where English actually becomes the official language of a country, the people themselves choose to adopt the language. But, in the ideological worldview of the adherents to linguistic-imperialistic theory, it is inconceivable that the language of the former colonials – in this case the English – 'can be ever truly considered an adopted African or Asian language' (Chew, 1999: 41). The adoption of English, however, did not cause the local cultures to disappear. Countries such as Singapore did adopt English, but say emphatically 'no' to western cultural values (Chew, 1999: 42).

Thus, one single language, no matter how much it is used as a lingua franca worldwide, becomes 'the courier of many cultures and sub-cultures, of myriad values and sets of values, of different religions and of antagonistic political systems' (see also Graddol, 1997: 3). The fear that the possible adoption of English as a lingua franca in the EU, or as only a working language of the EU institutions, will seriously threaten the diversity of languages and cultures appears to be completely without foundation.

English. Supposing the EU were to allocate the role of lingua franca to English, what kind of language would this be then? I have already said something about this, partly by implication, when discussing the phenomenon of the lingua franca. Let me add a few other points that, in my opinion, are relevant to the theme of EU language policy at the institutional level.

Currently, English is clearly *the* language of the world.[17] When it is compared with other languages using the criteria developed by Ammon (1996: 244ff), English turns out to be the most widely used language. It is *the* language in the non-English-speaking world for what is called 'informal metaphorical usage'. As such, it can be found in every shop window and advertisement. It is also the 'met-aphorical indicator of being young, carefree, technically competent, in touch with the current world and its distinctive problems and opportunities' (Fishman, 1994: 70).

Does English owe this position to its special intrinsic qualities? And is it there-fore the best candidate for the position of lingua franca in the EU? There are indeed people who are really convinced that English is the best language in the world. English is said to have the largest vocabulary and the simplest syntax. It is supposed to be very flexible and thereby able to absorb much from other languages. And this would of course have to do with the fact that the English – unlike, for example, the French – are themselves so democratic and flexible (Pennycook, 1998: 129ff). When the Berlin Wall was torn down, Douglas Hurd, who was Secretary of State for Foreign Affairs at the time, proclaimed that English should now become the first language of Europe, the lingua franca of what he called 'the changed economic and political circumstances'. In documents of the British government, it was stated in plain terms: 'English skills have been identified as a major factor in the process of reconstruction and transition to democracy' (Phillipson & Skutnabb-Kangas, 1994: 733–74).

These types of claims can of course also be made for other languages besides English – even for Dutch, despite the fact that its speakers are supposed to have such a great contempt for their own language (Hagen, 1999). But these claims are totally unfounded, for Dutch as well as for English.[18]

The phenomenon of 'English as a World Language' has been the object of study for some time now (see, e.g. Kachru, 1982; Alatis, 1990). It is acknowledged that English functions in 'pluralistic contexts' in many cultures, that English as a lingua franca has a distinctive 'international' variant, and, consequently, that there exists a diversity of 'World Englishes' (Kachru, 1997: 67; Davies, 1991: 68). English has certainly not developed into one uniform world language, nor will it do so in the near future.[19]

We have seen that, in the development of the lingua franca, in native/non-native communication, the natives may eventually lose their status of 'owners' of the language. This certainly does not mean that the English and Americans 'have lost their English' as some people think (Graddol, 1997: 3; Cenoz & Jessner, 2000: vii). This applies only (partly?) to the international variant, but of course not to the British and American varieties.

We have also seen that adoption of a lingua franca does not need to be accompanied by cultural erosion. On the one hand, adopting a language as lingua franca does not necessarily need to involve adopting the cultural load as well. The lingua franca may very well be enriched with a new cultural content (Chew, 1999: 42; Widdowson, 1994: 382). On the other hand, adoption of a lingua franca does not mean that all the other languages have lost their functions, certainly not when the lingua franca is only used in the institutional domain (Chew, 1999: 43; Graddol, 1997: 2). The lingua franca does not become a type of 'overlanguage', and there certainly does not exist 'a hierarchy of languages, the lingua franca being the superior one and all others being subordinate', as some people fear in the EU context (Christ, 1997: 131). In international business, most multinationals, *if* they have a lingua franca as corporate language, also use one or more other national or local languages besides this (Labrie, 1999: 136).

In all this, no conclusive argument can be found for the adoption of English as the sole working language for EU institutions. However, as apparently many people are afraid that the adoption of, and creeping development towards, one lingua franca, in this case English, will have serious consequences, these considerations may help them to develop a more balanced view on the matter. And perhaps the 'undeserved' gains that the native speakers of the selected language, or their culture and society, may make in terms of symbolic capital (see de Swaan, 1999: 19) can also be put into perspective.

There is still another comment I would like to make with regard to the possible hegemony of English and the speakers of this language. When English is the only means of communication in a certain institution, which is often the case in multinationals, all the non-native speakers of English taking part in the communication have the advantage that they are at least bilingual. In such a case, it will regularly happen that the British and Americans who are monolingual – and this is certainly not a small group – will be at a disadvantage. Bilingual or multilingual people are generally more flexible in the communication process and are better able to empathise with others. In addition they often have the opportunity to 'come to an understanding' by resorting to another language than the lingua franca, which is something the monolingual speakers of English cannot do. The latter are thus excluded and will then feel trapped inside the bastion of their own language. Graddol (1997: 57) perhaps overstates the case by writing: 'mono-lingualism may become a liability which offsets any economic advantage gained from possessing extensive native-speaker resources in the global language'.

Should one language, i.e. English, eventually become the only official internal language of the EU, then the following can be said about the external institutional language use in the EU. In the communication with the outside world, English will also be the exchange language in many cases, perhaps even in the majority of cases. But not in all parts of the world with which the EU maintains connections does English hold the position that it already holds elsewhere. I was struck by a photograph of President Clinton, which showed him addressing the Russian Duma. He did so in English, of course. About 20 members of the Duma sitting in the first rows were also visible. Of these 20 members, almost two-thirds used their headphones to listen to Clinton's speech, which was being simultaneously translated, I presume. The EU as an organisation would do well to face the world with a competence in more languages than just English. There are also other important languages in the world, and, at least for the time being, their share in global communication will sooner increase than decrease (Graddol, 1997: 3).

In the EU, communication is of course not limited to the EU institutions. The individual member states are responsible for the policy on language use outside the institutions. Neither the current position of English as a working language in the EU, nor a possible monopoly as such in the future can guarantee that all communications between and within the member states will take place in English. In this respect I have already mentioned the language use in the admin-istrative system of a number of Euregions. However, many people, politicians among them, are of the opinion that such communication should also be conducted exclusively in English. Let me repeat what I have so often stated with regard to the Dutch situation: it is absolutely not true that, within Europe, the foreign language needs in industry, diplomacy and social intercourse between citizens in general are fully covered by merely learning English (see, e.g., van Els & van Hest, 1990; van Els, 1993; van Els, 1994a; van Els, 1994b).[20] This is of course especially true for the countries where the 'minor' languages are spoken, but nonetheless also for countries speaking the 'major' languages, even Great Britain (see, e.g. Hagen, 1994).

In order to develop a sound policy on foreign language teaching, it is neces-sary to catalogue the actual needs of the country and the citizens; making vague general statements on the importance of teaching foreign languages is not enough. This is what the EU tends to do, usually also stressing that *all* officially recognised languages of the EU should be taught, as if many citizens in the EU would benefit from learning Dutch, and as if it is a crying shame that the majority of the citizens choose not to do so, whatever the EU may say. Diversity as such is no concern of the citizenry (van Els, 1994b: 40; Wright, 2000: 3).

What about the proficiency in English of the Dutch people? Let me just say two things about this. First of all, the Dutch are said to be good at languages, especially English. But this only means that the Dutch are in general better at expressing themselves in English compared to others. The Dutch may have a larger vocabulary and also a better command of the language than they used to, especially orally, but this is no reason to become complacent about it. There are sufficient examples illustrating that our proficiency in English is not good enough. This is not surprising, and also not a terrible thing, because something can be done about it. However, because we get so many compliments, and because we switch to English whenever we get the chance to avoid having to speak German or French, which are languages that generally suit us less, the real problem may be that we think we do not have any problem with English at all, and turn a blind eye to the fact that only very few are able to achieve a level of proficiency that approximates the native or native-like level.

Second, the rapid spread of English as an international language has changed a number of things, also in the teaching of English in The Netherlands. Particularly the learning objectives in English language teaching have changed. The first aspect that should be mentioned in this context is that the orientation of Dutch education towards British English is no longer a matter of course. In the past few years, more room has been created for the American variant.

A second related aspect is that Dutch people are increasingly required to use English in international situations which involve native/non-native communication. For a number of years now, it has been common practice in education to focus additionally on what are known as communicative language strategies, this in addition to the purely linguistic component. These strategies also include those that are used to bridge possible gaps in language competence, also known as avoidance strategies (Bialystok, 1990; Poulisse *et al.*, 1990; Poulisse, 1999). I think the time has come to demand that attention be given to the recognition and application of strategies that may be essential prerequisites for success in communication between natives and non-natives, or among non-natives. As I have already indicated, this is still very much uncharted territory, but it has now become imperative to pay more attention to it, particularly in certain areas of education (see, e.g. Firth, 1996: 243; McArthur, 1998: 212; Munter, 1993).

Concluding Observations

I started this monograph with an extensive sketch of the current language use policy and practice in EU institutions. To put it briefly, it is quite a complicated matter. It is therefore with some trepidation that I view future developments that will increase the present number of official and working languages of the EU to more than 20. EU politicians usually do not like to get their fingers burnt over this sensitive language issue, but many of them are now beginning to realise that the cherished principle of equality for all EU languages as official and working languages will come under tremendous pressure in the near future. To make choices that are not in line with this principle can be very risky for politicians.

In the last few years, scientists and other experts have begun to pay more and more attention to this matter. At conferences dedicated to this subject, you see an increasing number of politicians and other people who are closely associated with the European Commission. In February 2000, the European Commission itself organised a conference on multilingualism and the expansion of the EU.[21]

My contribution is intended to serve the same purpose as the conferences on this subject. What is needed in this phase is a debate that should be open and 'unfettered by political or ideological constraints' (Bos, 1999: Foreword). This debate should eventually lead to recommendations that, as far as possible, are based on empirical and scientific insights and should give shape to the EU's institutional language policy in the near future. My contribution to this is primarily of a linguistic nature, and not of a political or socio-scientific one.

The final decision is up to the politicians, in this case the political authorities that represent the EU member states in the Council of Ministers. There are matters in which it is not wise to force decisions and the better option is to let things take their course. Some people think that the language issue is such a matter. Again, it is up to the politicians to assess whether this is actually the case.

Looking from the perspective of an applied linguist, I have come to the conclusion that a decision *should* be made. The exercise that I have reported on in this monograph has convinced me that current institutional language practice has too many drawbacks; reorganisation of this practice may lead to a considerably higher quality of communication.

The core problem is the fundamental equality of all EU languages as EU working languages. There is no linguistic insight that opposes the abandonment of this principle. Neither are the arguments for maintaining this principle tenable from a linguistic perspective.

There are many who assume that linguists are always staunch supporters of the principle of equality for all languages. They expect that linguists cherish each language as a precious and valuable commodity and that they will help to terminate or adjust the course of any development that can be regarded to constitute a threat to one of these languages. It is assumed that they are idealistic plurilinguists (Wright, 2000: 246). And that is what they should be, according to some. If a language group, for reasons of its own, decides to leave their language as it is, it is considered 'aberrant behaviour' when a linguist simply accepts this (de Bot, 1994: 13).

It is a myth that the great diversity of languages and cultures as such is a good thing and that, consequently, its present manifestation in the EU represents a great richness, a treasure that should be defended at all costs. It is one of the myths that co-determine current EU policy on institutional language use. Diversity is in itself not a good thing, certainly not the concrete manifestation of it at the present moment. Neither is diversity of language and culture a constant factor, for they are forever changing: what disappears is replaced by something new, if people so desire. We have also seen that people do not accept extreme homogenisation in the field of language.

Of course the diversity of languages and cultures should be defended – also the present one – if the interests of the people to whom these languages and cultures belong are threatened. These interests most certainly also include the subjective value that people attach to language and culture, or more specifically, to their own language and culture. But when defending this diversity, the weight of all these interests should be offset against the disadvantages that may also be inherent in this diversity of languages and cultures, for example, in the case that an efficient design of institutional language use is required.

Another myth is that changes in language policy in one domain, in this case the EU institutions, should necessarily have consequences for other domains, in this case particularly for the language use in the member states themselves. Yet another myth that plays an important role in the European perception of language is that language and nation or state are closely linked. Measures that are taken within EU institutions regarding a certain language are soon regarded as an infringement of the sovereignty of the member state concerned. And yet another myth involves the assumed close one-to-one relationship between language and culture.

I hope the linguistic observations in the previous sections will contribute to a partial unravelling of these myths and will help people to place the issues concerned in perspective. On the basis of these observations and the related further analysis of aspects of the quality of communication and of the handicaps that play a role in language use situations in which natives and non-natives meet, it is possible to indicate from the linguistic perspective what kind of adaptations will have to be made in the language policy of the EU institutions.

The following points may be elements in this adaptation of EU language policy:

- the principle of equality for all 'official' languages, also as 'working languages' of the EU, will be abandoned formally;
- the basic principle will be, or remains, that none of the crucial interests of any member state or citizen of the EU may be harmed as a result of their language background;
- another basic principle will be that individual pragmatic solutions will be sought for the language communication problems in each of the sub-domains of the EU organisation.

This is neither the time nor the place to elaborate on what these solutions will actually look like, but let me just say a few words about them. With regard to the language use in writing, the current regime may be continued to a large extent, particularly where it concerns documents that are sent 'outside' to, for example, the member states and their citizens. Internally, a limited number of languages may be used, for example, just German, English and French, especially when the documents do not relate to the final stages of decision-making.

Oral language use should be drastically restructured in a number of subdomains and situations. Using all the EU languages in meetings of the Council of Ministers and the European Parliament for symbolic reasons should be limited to the absolute minimum. In all other meetings, the number of working languages should be reduced substantially. A maximum of three languages may be considered for the function of working language; these will be, in order of their priority: English, French and German.

For the non-natives, whose languages are not eligible for the function of working language in any given situation, a limitation to two working languages instead of three may be better, although just one working language would be optimal. This only applies if the speakers of the two or three working languages are not prepared to speak any other language than their own mother tongue in those situations.

We have seen that such an 'unnatural' arrangement may lead to a considerable improvement of the quality of communication. I still have hope that this variant of the restrictive model will be perceived as more 'natural' than many people now think, once everyone has got rid of the myths woven around language *and* has come to realise that the communication problem should be solved jointly. Would it not be just common decency if the speakers of the 'major' languages were to refrain from exploiting their advantageous position in the language situation and abide the rules of 'linguistic etiquette' (Mamadouh, 1999b: 161)?

We have seen that in the event that this variant is not chosen, the non-natives will have to overcome considerably fewer handicaps in these situations if there is just one working language, for example, English. They should therefore do everything in their power to ensure that this option is chosen.

I do understand that unravelling myths or presenting empirically proven insights with regard to the communication process is in itself not enough to convince people immediately, let alone to create sufficient public support for the kind of changes suggested in this monograph.

Firstly, I am fully aware that we still do not know precisely how the communication processes in the EU institutions take place and, more specifically, to what extent the effectiveness and 'impartiality' of the decision-making process are affected.

Secondly, and most importantly, it is essential that there should be the political will to continue towards the goal of European integration. It is then particularly important that there should be an 'elite' that will do its utmost to bring about the required change (Wright, 2000: 30). I think it would be nice if a relatively small country such as The Netherlands were to take the lead in this. The risk of sustaining political damage in this matter is not very high, unless of course the language issue is toyed with as it is being played with now, i.e. not because it is difficult to reach a decision on this issue, but merely because the route towards further integration of the EU can thus be blocked without revealing this intention (Wright, 2000: 175).

Acknowledgements

The research reported on in this lecture would not have been possible without the help and support of many colleagues and respondents. I was given the opportunity to have penetrating and very informative talks with experts in this field from the following international organisations, institutions and companies: The European Commission (including the *Service Commun Interprétation Conférence*), the European Parliament, the European Central Bank, the World Bank, the United Nations, ABN-AMRO and Shell International.

In addition, I had the privilege of exchanging views with many colleagues at the AAAL Annual Conference in Vancouver, Canada, and during my stay as Visiting Scholar at the National Foreign Language Center (NFLC) in Washington, DC. Furthermore, I had many enlightening conversations with colleagues from the Center for Applied Linguistics (CAL) and Georgetown University, both also located in Washington, DC, the Carnegie Mellon University and Pittsburgh University, both in Pittsburgh, Pennsylvania, and the Ontario Institute for Studies in Education (OISE) in Toronto, Canada.

It is impossible to mention by name all the people to whom I owe many thanks, but I would like to make an exception here for all those who have given me their special help in establishing the necessary contacts and realising the research. These are (in alphabetical order): Jim Alatis (Georgetown University), Kees de Bot (University of Nijmegen), Dick Brecht and his staff (NFLC), Heidi Byrnes (Georgetown University), Donna Christian (CAL), Stacy Churchill (OISE), Jacqueline Hofland (University of Nijmegen), Bob Kaplan (University of Southern California), Dick Lambert (NFLC), Frans Lander (Dutch Ministry of Education, Culture and Sciences), Mary McGroarty (Northern Arizona University), Christina Bratt Paulston (University of Pittsburgh), Merrill Swain (OISE) and Dick Tucker (Carnegie Mellon).

The research was partly funded by the Board of the University of Nijmegen Foundation, for which I would also like to express my gratitude here.

Correspondence

Any correspondence should be directed to Professor T.J.M. van Els, Emeritus Professor of Applied Linguistics, University of Nijmegen, Uniceflaan 47, 6525 JL Nijmegen, The Netherlands (t.vanels@mailbox.kun.nl).

Notes

1. I presume this reluctance to pay attention to the language problem is as such not directly linked to an aversion to policy-making. Although, now I come to think of it, Pompidou, Chirac's predecessor, once seems to have said that there are three ways in which a politician can ruin his career: 'by womanizing, by taking bribes and by policy-making'. The first is said to be the most pleasant way, the second the fastest, and the third the surest! (Paulston, 1998: 39).
2. Ria Oomen said this in an interview with Geert-Jan Bogaerts in *De Volkskrant* of 27 June 2000.
3. In Dirk van Delft's article entitled 'The more languages, the more English' in *NRC Handelsblad* of 22 May 1999.
4. The texts of the relevant regulations can be found in Coulmas 1991b: 38–43; Duthoy, 1993: 16–18; Fasol, 1994c.
5. When in 1984 the Duchy of Luxemburg proclaimed Letzebuergesh its national language in addition to German and French, the country decided not to apply to the EU for the status of treaty language for this language (Labrie, 1996: 4).
6. By the way, it happens increasingly that all member states are invited to submit tenders only in English and French or that the forms in these two languages are available sooner than those in the other languages. Those who submit tenders are increasingly inclined to draw up the tenders in English and not in their own language, because they suspect that the tenders in English will be read first and processed sooner (Quell, 1997: 64). Despite repeated protests against it, this phenomenon seems ineradicable. It is said that this has to occur with the pressure of time under which matters are put out to tender.
7. Within the context of the consultations for the future expansion of the EU, the EP is currently discussing variants of this, such as the 'hub-and-spoke' system (the 'hub', or central language, is always the same one) (Working Party, 1999).
8. It has now obtained the status of Non-Governmental Organisation (NGO) from the Council of Europe and the United Nations (Extra, 1999: 78).
9. Multinationals that essentially evolved out of two parent companies sometimes opt for using the two languages in question as internal corporate languages, especially when these languages are closely related, for then they may choose to use the system that is also known as the 'polyglottic dialogue': each person uses his/her mother tongue productively and is able to understand the other language (Vandermeeren,

1998: 47). When they negotiated the merger of Hoogovens in The Netherlands and Hoechst in Germany (which eventually failed), the parties decided to use Dutch and German as working languages at the headquarters.

10. The Dutch are often reproached for trading in their language too easily. The critics usually refer to the ease with which Dutch immigrants in countries such as the USA, Canada, Australia and New Zealand have taken on a new identity and new language (see, e.g. Broeder & Extra, 1997). Dutch officials and members of the EP are also regularly confronted with the reproach, especially from the Flemish, that they treat their own language unscrupulously (see also Duthoy, 1993: 13, 48). However, the results of national and international surveys show that there is no proof for the claim that the Dutch have such an indifference to their own language. Is this another instance of mythologisation? (De Bot & Weltens, 1997: 154; Weltens & Coppen, 2000: 88).

11. Partly for this reason, Michiel van Hulten, a Dutch member of the EP, regularly decides not to use Dutch in plenary meetings of the EP.

12. An extensive discussion of linguistic rights is beyond the scope of this monograph. For the relevant literature, see Paulston (1997), Spolsky and Shohamy (1999; 2000), and also de Varennes (1996). A Universal Declaration of Linguistic Rights was accepted at a world conference of international NGOs in Barcelona in 1996. Up until now, a number of regional governments have signed this declaration. This declaration, too, distinguishes between individual and group rights. There are generally no objections to language measures being taken, provided that these do not harm the civil rights of the individuals concerned or that provisions have been made to remedy sufficiently any possible harm caused (Spolsky & Shohamy, 2000: 21). However, neither the individual rights nor the group rights should obstruct the possible integration with the wider language community. I did not find an explicit statement or case anywhere that would prove that those who defend language diversity on the grounds of linguistic rights might even go so far as to defend the idea that languages as such have a right to exist. Nevertheless I have the strong impression that some of the prominent advocates of language diversity do have this idea at the back of their minds. In any case, a few years ago, a French judge pronounced that French legislation protects first and foremost the French language and not so much the francophones themselves. The case in question concerned the use of 'un-French' words such as 'hamburger' by a French company. The company was previously acquitted by a lower court, by the way (Paulston, 1997: 76).

13. Artificial languages were constructed as early as the Middle Ages and the Renaissance (Haarmann, 1991b: 11).

14. The Hans Seidel Stiftung organised a conference entitled 'The communication and language problem in the European Community – to what extent can an 'artificial language' contribute to the solution?' in Brussels in September 1993.

15. As far as French is concerned, this subject was already discussed extensively by Calvet (1998; originally published in French in 1987). English and, more in particular, its 'colonial' background, were subject to critical observations in the publications of Pennycook (1994, 1998). The theme of the first publication was that the spread of English cannot be regarded as 'natural, neutral and beneficial' as everyone seems to think. The second book analysed 'how language and practices developed in different colonial contexts' and wanted to show 'how the discourses of colonialism still adhere to English' (Pennycook, 1998: 2).

   People often wonder why Dutch in the former Dutch colonies, for example Indonesia, never acquired a status similar to that of French and English elsewhere. This is generally connected to a certain characteristic indifference of the Dutch *vis-à-vis* their own language (see note 10). As colonials, the Dutch would have been more concerned with making profits than with the spread of their language and culture (Willemyns, 1994: 16). Regarding Indonesia, de Waard observes that the most striking feature in the colonial history of Indonesia is the total lack of government interference with language politics. According to de Waard (1999: 121), the main reasons for the fact that Dutch did not 'catch on' were that, when the Dutch took over the colony, Portuguese was already well established as a language in the archipelago, and that, for a considerable period of time, the Dutchmen who were sent there were not allowed to bring along Dutch women. These men therefore married native women and their children were raised in an environment in which Malay and Portuguese were the dominant languages.

16. There are also other authors who speak negatively about the linguistic imperialism theory. Spolsky and Shohamy (1999: 38, 2000: 26) think it is a 'conspiracy theory' and find it to be 'oversimplified to offer a simple, power-based, conspiratorial explanation of language policy', which does absolutely no justice to the complexity of the problem (see also de Swaan, 1999: 18–19).

17. There is a very nice anecdote that John Adams (1735–1826), the second President of the United States, predicted that English would become the 'most respectable language in the world, the most universally read and spoken' in the next century, if not before the end of the nineteenth century (see Kachru, 1982: 2).

18. It is not only demagogic politicians who participate in these types of eulogies on individual languages. Otto Jespersen, the well known Danish linguist, was of the opinion that the grammar of English was more efficient than those of other languages (Alatis, 1990: 52).

19. The various Englishes and their variants may differ considerably. Some people are afraid that they will grow so far apart that their mutual intelligibility is bound to get lost, if this is not the case already (Widdowson, 1994: 383). In the 19th century, Henry Sweet, another great linguist, predicted that this would happen before the end of the 20th century (see McArthur, 1998: 183). However, so far, this has not happened, as at least one experiment proved (Graddol, 1997: 56).

    By the way, those who are afraid extreme uniformisation of the world language will eventually result in the survival of only one single language should realise that language has always been in a state of flux throughout the history of mankind. It is a historical fact that a long period of simplification and uniformisation is always followed by a period in which the people once again begin to call for differentiation (Aitchinson, 1991; Widdowson, 1994: 384). This is a phenomenon that can also be observed today. New variants of languages evolve, whereby certain subcultures wish to distinguish themselves from the standard culture. Interesting examples of what the Dutch call 'street language' can be seen emerging in various European cities (Appel, 1999). A recent development in France is 'verlan', which is characterised by an often very ingenious reversal of the syllables in words: 'verlan' = 'l'envers' (reverse) (Doran, 2000).

20. My arguments have never been based on anything other than the importance that the Dutch attach to mastering certain languages. It is in the interest of The Netherlands that many Dutch people not only master English but also at least German and French. I never based my line of reasoning on the interests of those other languages as such or of the speakers of those languages, as Phillipson and Skutnabb-Kangas (1997: 143) have suggested.

21. A preliminary version of the final report of the conference entitled 'Multilingualism and EU Enlargement' is now available. It was drawn up by a group of EU trainees under the supervision of Rosalie Bongers.

References

Abélès, M. (1999) Multiculturalism and multilingualism in the European institutions. In N. Bos (ed.) *Which Languages for Europe?* (pp. 111–117). Amsterdam: European Cultural Foundation. [Report of the conference held in Oegstgeest, The Netherlands, 9–11 October 1998.]

Aitchinson, J. (1991) *Language Change: Progress or Decay?* (2nd edn). Cambridge: Cambridge University Press.

Alatis, J.E. (1990) On English as a world language. *Journal of Applied Linguistics* 6, 48–58.

Ammon, U. (1991) The status of German and other languages in the European Community. In F. Coulmas (ed.) *A Language Policy for the European Community. Prospects and Quandaries* (pp. 241–54). Berlin/New York: Mouton de Gruyter.

Ammon, U. (1994) The present dominance of English in Europe. With an outlook on possible solutions to the European language problems. *Sociolinguistica* 8, 1–14.

Ammon, U. (1995) To what extent is German an international language? In P. Stevenson (ed.) *The German Language and the Real World. Sociolinguistic, Cultural, and Pragmatic Perspectives on Contemporary German* (pp. 25–53). Oxford: Clarendon Press.

Ammon, U. (1996) The European Union (EU – formerly European Community): Status change of English during the last fifty years. In J.A. Fishman, A.W. Conrad and A. Rubal-Lopez (eds) *Post-Imperial English. Status Change in Former British and American Colonies, 1940–1990* (pp. 241–67). Berlin/New York: Mouton de Gruyter.

Ammon, U. (2000) Die Rolle des Deutschen in Europa [The role of German in Europe]. In A. Gardt (ed.) *Nation und Sprache. Die Diskussion ihres Verhaeltnisses in Geschichte und Gegenwart* [*Nation and Language. A Discussion of their Relation in Past and Present*] (pp. 471–94). Berlin/New York: Walter de Gruyter.

Appel, R. (1999) Straattaal. De mengtaal van jongeren in Amsterdam (Street language, the mixed language of young people in Amsterdam). *TTWiA* 62, 39–55.

Baker, C. and Prys Jones, S. (1998) *Encyclopedia of Bilingualism and Bilingual Education.* Clevedon: Multilingual Matters.

Bialystok, E. (1990) *Communication Strategies.* Oxford: Blackwell.

Bongaerts, T. and de Bot, K. (eds) (1997) *Perspectives on Foreign-Language Policy. Studies in Honour of Theo van Els.* Amsterdam/Philadelphia: John Benjamins.

Bos, N. (ed.) (1999) *Which Languages for Europe?* (Report of the conference held in Oegstgeest, The Netherlands, 9–11 October 1998). Amsterdam: European Cultural Foundation.

de Bot, C.L.J. (1994) *Waarom deze Rede Niet in het Engels is?* [*Why this Speech is not Done in English*] 'sHertogenbosch-Nijmegen: Katholieke Universiteit Nijmegen.

de Bot, K. (1999) van Els, T. (1936). In B. Spolsky (ed.) *Concise Encyclopedia of Educational Linguistics* (pp. 793–94). Amsterdam: Elsevier.

de Bot, K. and Weltens, B. (1997) Multilingualism in the Netherlands. In T. Bongaerts and K. de Bot (eds) *Perspectives on Foreign-Language Policy. Studies in Honour of Theo van Els* (pp. 143–56). Amsterdam/Philadelphia: John Benjamins.

Broeder, P. and Extra, G. (1997) Minority groups and minority languages in the Netherlands. In T. Bongaerts and K. de Bot (eds) *Perspectives on Foreign-Language Policy. Studies in Honour of Theo van Els* (pp. 157–79). Amsterdam/Philadelphia: John Benjamins.

Calvet, L.-J. (1998) *Language Wars and Linguistic Policies.* Oxford: Oxford University Press. [Translated from French: *Guerre des Langues et les Politiques Linguistiques*, 1987.]

Cenoz, J. and Jessner, U. (eds) (2000) *English in Europe. The Acquisition of a Third Language.* Clevedon: Multilingual Matters.

Chew, P.G.-L. (1999) Linguistic imperialism, globalism, and the English language. *AILA Review* 13, 37–47. [Graddol, D. and Meinhof, U.H. (eds) *English in a Changing World.*]

Christ, H. (1997) Foreign language policy from the grass roots. In T. Bongaerts and K. de Bot (eds) *Perspectives on Foreign-Language Policy. Studies in Honour of Theo van Els* (pp. 129–41). Amsterdam/Philadelphia: John Benjamins.

Churchill, S. (1998) *New Canadian Perspectives. Official Languages in Canada: Changing the Landscape.* Toronto: Canadian Studies Program.

Conrad, A.W. (1996) The international role of English: The state of the discussion. In J.A. Fishman, A.W. Conrad and A. Rubal-Lopez (eds) *Post-Imperial English. Status Change in Former British and American Colonies, 1940–1990* (pp. 13–36). Berlin/New York: Mouton de Gruyter.

Coulmas, F. (ed.) (1991a) *A Language Policy for the European Community. Prospects and Quandaries.* Berlin/New York: Mouton de Gruyter.

Coulmas, F. (1991b) European integration and the idea of the national language. In F. Coulmas (ed.) *A Language Policy for the European Community. Prospects and Quandaries* (pp. 1–43). Berlin/New York: Mouton de Gruyter.

Coulmas, F. (1992) *Die Wirtschaft mit der Sprache. Eine sprachsoziologische Studie* [*The Economics of Language. A Sociolinguistic Study*]. Frankfurt: Suhrkamp.

Davies, A. (1991) *The Native Speaker in Applied Linguistics.* Edinburgh: Edinburgh University Press.

Davies, A. (1999) *An Introduction to Applied Linguistics*. Edinburgh: Edinburgh University Press.

Dollerup, C. (1996) English in the European Union. In R. Hartmann (ed.) *English Language in Europe* (pp. 24–36). Oxford: Intellect.

Doran, M. (2000) Speaking Verlan: Performing hybrid identity in suburban Paris. Paper presented at AAAL Annual Conference, Vancouver, March.

Dürmüller, U. (1994) Multilingual talk or English Only? The Swiss experience. *Sociolinguistica* 8, 44–64.

Dürmüller, U. (1996) *Mehrsprachigkeit im Wandel. Von der viersprachigen zur vielsprachigen Schweiz* [*Changing Multilingualism. From a four-language to a multi-language Switzerland*]. Zürich: Pro Helvetia.

Duthoy, W. (1993) *Het Nederlands in de instellingen van de Europese Gemeenschap* [*Dutch in the Institutions of the European Community*] (2nd printing entirely revised by P.W.H. Fasol). Den Haag: Nederlandse Taalunie.

van Els, T.J.M. (1993) Foreign language teaching policy: Some planning issues. In K. Sajavaara, R.D. Lambert, S. Takala and C.A. Morfit (eds) *National Foreign Language Planning: Practices and Prospects* (pp. 3–14). Jyväskylä: Institute for Educational Research.

van Els, Theo J.M. (1994a) Foreign language planning in the Netherlands. In R.D. Lambert (ed.) *Language Planning Around the World: Contexts and Systematic Change* (pp. 47–68). Washington, DC: National Foreign Language Center.

van Els, Theo J.M. (1994b) Planning foreign language teaching in a small country. *The Annals of the AAPSS* 532, 35–46. [R.D. Lambert (ed.) *Foreign Language Policy: An Agenda for Change*.]

van Els, T., Bongaerts, T., Extra, G., van Os, C. and Janssen-van Dieten, A. (1984) *Applied Linguistics and the Learning and Teaching of Foreign Languages*. London: Edward Arnold.

van Els, T.J.M. and van Hest, E. (1990) Foreign language teaching policies and European unity: The Dutch National Action Programme. *Language, Culture and Curriculum* 3, 199–211.

European Commission (1999) *Eurobarometer. Public Opinion in the European Union*. Report no. 50. Brussels: European Commission.

Extra, G. (1999) Immigrant minority groups and immigrant minority languages in European education. In N. Bos (ed.) *Which Languages for Europe?* (Report of the conference held in Oegstgeest, The Netherlands, 9–11 October 1998) (pp. 69–80). Amsterdam: European Cultural Foundation.

Fasol, P.W.H. (ed.)(1994a) *De toekomst van het Nederlands in de Europese Unie* [*The future of Dutch in the European Union*]. Den Haag: Staatsdrukkerij.

Fasol, P. (1994b) Het Nederlands in de instellingen van de Europese Unie [*Dutch in the Institutions of the European Union*]. In P.W.H. Fasol (ed.) *De toekomst van het Nederlands in de Europese Unie* [The future of Dutch in the European Union] (pp. 39–44). Den Haag: Staatsdrukkerij.

Fasol, P. (1994c) De officiële regeling van het taalgebruik [The official regulation of language use]. In P.W.H. Fasol (ed.) *De toekomst van het Nederlands in de Europese Unie* [*The Future of Dutch in the European Union*] (pp. 65–9). Den Haag: Staatsdrukkerij.

Fasol, P. (1994d) Een blik op de toekomst? De verwikkeling rond Eurokorps en het Merkenbureau [A glance into the future? The complications surrounding Eurocorps and the Patent Office]. In P.W.H. Fasol (ed.) *De toekomst van het Nederlands in de Europese Unie* [*The Future of Dutch in the European Union*] (pp. 57–59). Den Haag: Staatsdrukkerij.

Firth, A. (1996) The discursive accomplishment of normality: On 'lingua franca' English and conversation analysis. *Journal of Pragmatics* 26, 237–59.

Fishman, J.A. (1994) 'English Only?' in Europe? Some suggestions from an American perspective, *Sociolinguistica* 8, 65–72.

Fishman, J.A. (1996a) Introduction: Some empirical and theoretical issues. In J.A. Fishman, A.W. Conrad and A. Rubal-Lopez (eds) *Post-Imperial English. Status Change in Former British and American Colonies, 1940–1990* (pp. 3–12). Berlin/New York: Mouton de Gruyter.

Fishman, J.A. (1996b) Summary and interpretation: Post-imperial English 1940–1990. In J.A. Fishman, A.W. Conrad, and A. Rubal-Lopez (eds) *Post-Imperial English. Status Change in Former British and American Colonies, 1940–1990* (pp. 623–41). Berlin/New York: Mouton de Gruyter.

Fishman, J.A., Conrad, A.W. and Rubal-Lopez, A. (eds) (1996) *Post-Imperial English. Status Change in Former British and American Colonies, 1940–1990*. Berlin/New York: Mouton de Gruyter.

Garcia, O. and Otheguy, R. (eds)(1989) Introduction. In *English Across Cultures. Cultures Across English. A Reader in Cross-Cultural Communication* (pp. 1–10). Berlin/New York: Mouton de Gruyter.

Gass, S.M. (1999) Second language acquisition: Conversation. In B. Spolsky (ed.) *Concise Encyclopedia of Educational Linguistics* (pp. 572–7). London: Pergamon.

Gehnen, M. (1991) Die Arbeitssprachen in der Kommission der Europäischen Gemeinschaften unter besonderer Berücksichtigung des Französischen [The working-languages in the Commission of the European Communities with special reference to the French language]. *Sociolinguistica* 5, 51–63.

Gellert-Novak, A. (1994) Die Rolle der englischen Sprache in Euregionen [The role of the English language in the Euroregions]. *Sociolinguistica* 8, 123–35.

Graddol, D. (1997) *The Future of English? A Guide to Forecasting the Popularity of the English Language in the 21st Century*. London: British Council.

Graddol, D. and Meinhof, U.H. (eds)(1999) English in a changing world. *AILA Review* 13.

Grin, F. (1996) Current problems and dilemmas of language strategies for Europe. An economist's perspective. In P. Ó Riagáin and S. Harrington (eds) *A Language Strategy for Europe. Retrospect and Prospect* (pp. 27–36). Dublin: Bord na Gaeilge.

Grin, F. (1997) Gérer le plurilinguisme européen: Approche économique au problème de choix [How to handle European plurilingualism: An economics approach to the problem of choice]. *Sociolinguistica* 11, 1–15.

Grin, F. and Vaillancourt, F. (1997) The economics of multilingualism: Overview and analytical framework. In W. Grabe *et al.* (eds) *Annual Review of Applied Linguistics* 17 (pp. 43–65). Cambridge: Cambridge University Press.

Grin, J. (1999) Which languages, when and where, for Europe? Why and how to consider a research project as an exercise in political judgement. In N. Bos (ed.) *Which Languages for Europe?* (Report of the conference held in Oegstgeest, The Netherlands, 9–11 October 1998) (pp. 147–53). Amsterdam: European Cultural Foundation.

Haarmann, H. (1991a) Language politics and the new European identity. In F. Coulmas (ed.) *A Language Policy for the European Community. Prospects and Quandaries* (pp. 103–19). Berlin/New York: Mouton de Gruyter.

Haarmann, H. (1991b) Monolingualism versus selective multilingualism – on the future alternatives for Europe as it integrates in the 1990s. *Sociolinguistica* 5, 7–23.

Hagen, A.M. (1999) *De Lof der Nederlandse Taal* [In praise of the Dutch language]. Nijmegen: Katholieke Universiteit Nijmegen.

Hartmann, R. (ed.) (1996) *English Language in Europe*. Oxford: Intellect.

Haselhuber, J. (1991) Erste Ergebnisse einer empirischen Untersuchung zur Sprachensituation in der EG-Kommission (Februar 1990) [First Findings of an empirical investigation into the language situation of the European Commission]. *Sociolinguistica* 5, 37–50.

Herriman, M. and Burnaby, B. (eds) (1996) Introduction. In *Language Policies in English-Dominant Countries. Six Case Studies* (pp. 1–14). Clevedon: Multilingual Matters.

Hoffmann, C. (ed.) (1996) *Language, Culture and Communication in Contemporary Europe*. Clevedon: Multilingual Matters.

Kachru, B.B. (ed.) (1982) *The Other Tongue. English Across Cultures*. Oxford: Pergamon Press.

Kachru, B.B. (1997) World Englishes and English-Using Communities. In W. Grabe *et al.* (eds.) *Annual Review of Applied Linguistics* 17 (pp. 66–87). Cambridge: Cambridge University Press.

Kasper, G. and Blum-Kulka, S. (eds) (1993) *Interlanguage Pragmatics*. Oxford: Oxford University Press.

King, R.D. (1997) *Nehru and the Language Politics of India*. Dehli: Oxford University Press.

Knapp, K., Enninger, W. and Knapp-Potthoff, A. (eds) (1987) *Analyzing Intercultural Coomunication*. Berlin/New York: Mouton de Gruyter.

Knapp, K. and Knapp-Potthoff, A. (1987) Instead of an introduction: Conceptual issues in analyzing intercultural communication. In K. Knapp, W. Enninger and A. Knapp-Potthoff (eds) *Analyzing Intercultural Coomunication* (pp. 1–13). Berlin/New York: Mouton de Gruyter.

Koch, H. (1991) Legal aspects of a language policy for the European Communities: Language risks, equal opportunities, and legislating a language. In F. Coulmas (ed.) *A Language Policy for the European Community. Prospects and Quandaries* (pp. 145–61). Berlin/New York: Mouton de Gruyter.

Labrie, N. (1993) *La Construction de la Communauté Européenne* [*The Construction of the European Community*]. Paris: Honoré Champion.

Labrie, N. (1996) The historical development of language policy in Europe. In P. Ó Riagáin and S. Harrington (eds) *A Language Strategy for Europe. Retrospect and Prospect* (pp. 1–9). Dublin: Bord na Gaeilge.

Labrie, N. (1999) La constellation des politiques linguistiques dans l'Union Européenne [The state of affairs of language policies in the European Union]. In N. Bos (ed.) *Which Languages for Europe?* (Report of the conference held in Oegstgeest, The Netherlands, 9–11 October 1998) (pp. 135–40). Amsterdam: European Cultural Foundation.

Lambert, R.D. (ed.) (1994a) *Language Planning Around the World: Contexts and Systematic Change*. Washington, DC: National Foreign Language Center.

Lambert, R.D. (ed.) (1994b) Foreign language policy: An agenda for change. *Annals of the AAPSS* 532.

Lambert, R.D. (1999) A scaffolding for language planning. *International Journal of the Sociology of Language* 137, 3–25.

Lambert, R.D. and Shohamy, E. (eds) (2000) *Language Policy and Pedagogy. Essays in Honor of A. Ronald Walton*. Philadelphia/Amsterdam: John Benjamins.

Laver, J. and Roukens, J. (1996) The global information society and Europe's linguistic and cultural heritage. In C. Hoffmann (ed.) *Language, Culture and Communication in Contemporary Europe* (pp. 1–27). Clevedon: Multilingual Matters.

Lo Bianco, J. (1987) *National Policy on Languages*. Canberra: Australian Government Publishing Service.

Mamadouh, V. (1999a) Concluding remarks. In N. Bos (ed.) *Which Languages for Europe?* (Report of the conference held in Oegstgeest, The Netherlands, 9–11 October 1998) (pp. 155–71). Amsterdam: European Cultural Foundation.

Mamadouh, V. (1999b) Institutional multilingualism: An exploration of possible reforms. In N. Bos *Which Languages for Europe?* (Report of the conference held in Oegstgeest, The Netherlands, 9–11 October 1998) (pp. 119–25). Amsterdam: European Cultural Foundation.

McArthur, T. (1998) *The English Language*. Oxford: Oxford University Press.

Munter, M. (1993) Cross-cultural communication for managers. *Business Horizons* 36 (3), 69–79.

Ó Riagáin, P. and Harrington, S. (eds) (1996) *A Language Strategy for Europe. Retrospect and Prospect*. Dublin: Bord na Gaeilge.

Paulston, C.B. (1997) Language policies and language rights. *Annual Review of Anthropology* 26, 73–85

Paulston, C.B. (1998) *Linguistic Minorities in Multilingual Settings*. Amsterdam/Philadelphia: John Benjamins.

Pennycook, A. (1994) *The Cultural Politics of English as an International Language*. London: Longmans.

Pennycook, A. (1998) *English and the Discourses of Colonialism*. London/New York: Routledge.

Phillipson, R. (1992) *Linguistic Imperialism*. Oxford: Oxford University Press.

Phillipson, Robert (1995) Review of Labrie 1993. In R. Phillipson and T. Skutnabb-Kangas (eds) *Papers in European Language Policy, Rolig Papir* 53 (pp. 103–6). Roskilde: Universitets Center. (Reprinted from *International Journal of the Sociology of Language.*)

Phillipson, R. and Skutnabb-Kangas, T. (1994) English, Panacea or Pandemic. *Sociolinguistica* 8, 73–87.

Phillipson, R. and Skutnabb-Kangas, T. (eds) (1995) *Papers in European Language Policy, Rolig Papir* 53. Roskilde: Universitets Center.

Phillipson, R. and Skutnabb-Kangas, T. (1997) Lessons for Europe from language policy in Australia. In M. Pütz (ed.) *Language Choices. Conditions, Constraints, and Consequences* (pp. 115–59). Amsterdam/Philadelphia: John Benjamins.

Phillipson, R. and Skutnabb-Kangas, T. (1999) Englishisation: One dimension of globalisation. *AILA Review* 13, 19–36. [Graddol, D. and Meinhof, U. H. (eds) English in a changing world.]

Pool, J. (1996) Optimal language regimes for the European Union. *International Journal of the Sociology of Language* 121, 159–79.

Poulisse, N. (1999) Communication strategies. In B. Spolsky (ed.) *Concise Encyclopedia of Educational Linguistics* (pp. 484–9). London: Pergamon.

Poulisse, N., Bongaerts, T. and Kellerman, E. (1990) *The Use of Compensatory Strategies by Dutch Learners of English.* Dordrecht: Foris.

Pütz, M. (ed.) (1997) *Language Choices. Conditions, Constraints, and Consequences.* Amsterdam/Philadelphia: John Benjamins.

Quell, C. (1997) Language choice in multilingual institutions: A case study at the European Commission with particular reference to the role of English, French, and German as working languages. *Multilingua* 16 (1), 57–76.

Ricento, T. (1996) Language policy in the United States. In M. Herriman and B. Burnaby (eds) *Language Policies in English-Dominant Countries. Six Case Studies* (pp. 122–58). Clevedon: Multilingual Matters.

Sajavaara, K., Lambert, R.D., Takala, S. and Morfit, C.A. (eds) (1993) *National Foreign Language Planning: Practices and Prospects.* Jyväskylä: Institute for Educational Research.

Scheffer, P. (1999) A lingua franca for the European Union? In N. Bos (ed.) *Which Languages for Europe?* (Report of the conference held in Oegstgeest, The Netherlands, 9–11 October 1998) (pp. 1–3). Amsterdam: European Cultural Foundation.

Schlossmacher, M. (1994) Die Arbeitssprachen in den Organen der Europäischen Gemeinschaft. Methoden und Ergebnisse einer Empirischen Untersuchung [The working-languages in the institutions of the European Community. Methodology and findings of an empirical investigation]. *Sociolinguistica* 8, 101–22 .

Sirles, C. A. (2000) A sociolinguistic typology of cases of language decline and death. Paper presented at AAAL Annual Conference, Vancouver, March.

Spolsky, B. (ed.) (1999) *Concise Encyclopedia of Educational Linguistics.* London: Pergamon.

Spolsky, B. and Shohamy, E. (1999) *The Languages of Israel. Policy, Ideology and Practice.* Clevedon: Multilingual Matters.

Spolsky, B. and Shohamy, E. (2000) Language practice, language ideology, and language planning. In R.D. Lambert and E. Shohamy (eds) *Language Policy and Pedagogy. Essays in Honor of A. Ronald Walton* (pp. 1–41). Philadelphia/Amsterdam: John Benjamins.

Stevenson, P. (ed.) (1995) *The German Language and the Real World. Sociolinguistic, Cultural, and Pragmatic Perspectives on Contemporary German.* Oxford: Clarendon Press.

de Swaan, A. (1999) The European Language Constellation. In N. Bos (ed.) *Which Languages for Europe?* (Report of the conference held in Oegstgeest, The Netherlands, 9–11 October 1998) (pp. 13–23). Amsterdam: European Cultural Foundation.

Truchot, C. (ed.) (1994) *Le Plurilinguisme Européen. Théories et Pratiques en Politique Linguistique (European Plurilingualism. Theory and Practice in Language Policy).* Paris: Honoré Champion.

Vandermeeren, S. (1998) *Fremdsprachen in Europäischen Unternehmen. Untersuchungen zu Bestand und Bedarf im Geschäftsalltag mit Empfehlungen für Sprachenpolitik und Sprachunterricht (Foreign Languages in European Enterprises. Investigations into Existing and Lacking Competence in Day-to-day Business with Recommendations for Language Policy and Language Teaching*). Waldsteinberg: Heidrun Popp Verlag.

de Varennes, F.J. (1996) Language, minorities and human rights. PhD thesis, University of Maastricht, Maastricht.

Verschueren, J. (1989) English as an object and medium of (mis)understanding. In O. Garcia and R. Otheguy (eds) *English Across Cultures. Cultures Across English. A Reader in Cross-Cultural Communication* (pp. 31–53). Berlin/New York: Mouton de Gruyter.

de Waard, M. (2000) Language policies in Dutch Indonesia. *University of Pittsburgh Working Papers in Linguistics* 5, 71–124.

Webb, V. (1999) Language policy and language politics in a pluralist democracy: The South African case. Paper presented at Second International Symposium on Language Policy, Tel Aviv, November.

Weltens, B. and Coppen, P-A. (2000) Taalmythe: De Nederlander minacht zijn taal [Language myth: The Dutch look down on their own language]. *Onze Taal* [Our Language] 4, 84–8.

Widdowson, H.G. (1994) The ownership of English. *TESOL Quarterly* 26, 377–89.

Willemyns, R. (1994) Het Nederlands in Europa in het licht van de integratie van Nederland en Vlaanderen [Dutch in the light of the integration between the Netherlands and Flanders]. In P.W.H. Fasol (ed.) *De toekomst van het Nederlands in de Europese Unie* [The future of Dutch in the European Union] (pp. 11–17). Den Haag: Staatsdrukkerij.

Working Party (1999) On multilingualism within the context of enlargement. Final Report (manuscript). Brussels: European Parliament.

Wright, S. (2000) *Community and Communication. The Role of Language in Nation State Building and European Integration*. Clevedon: Multilingual Matters.

An Update on the European Union, its Institutions and its Languages: Some Language Political Observations

T.J.M. van Els
Nijmegen 2004

On May 1, 2004 ten new Member States joined the European Union (EU). On that day the number of eleven *official and working languages* of the Institutions of the EU that the first fifteen Member States had got accustomed to using over the years, all at once rose to twenty. Thus, the question of whether the number of official and working languages should be restricted, has not lost any of its importance and urgency since it formed the central issue of the 2001 monograph. This Update focuses exclusively on the topic of *institutional language usage in the EU*. Two sides of this issue will be highlighted. Firstly, have any changes in policy – or practice – come about or are they being considered by the EU since the monograph was written? Secondly, what attention has been devoted to the topic in the literature, scholarly or otherwise?

Compared to the situation of around the year 2000 described in the 2001 monograph, *the EU policy* with regard to the institutional use of the official and working languages has not undergone any change, nor has a change of policy been seriously considered recently. Language use in the EU Institutions was not an issue in the negotiations leading up to the entry of the ten new Members States as such, nor did it recently figure on the agenda of the European Convention on the Future of Europe. The Convention was convened by the EU at the end of 2001 to draw up proposals on a number of subjects vital to the future of the –enlarged – Union. The European Council, i.e., the meeting of Prime Ministers of the Member States, had asked the Convention, among other things, to draw up proposals on 'how to organise politics and the European political area in an enlarged Union' and 'how to develop the Union into a stabilising factor and a model in the new world order'. And although the Convention has worked out 'measures to increase the democracy, transparency and efficiency of the EU . . . by simplifying the decision-making processes, and by making the functioning of the European Institutions more transparent and comprehensible', in the draft text of the *Constitution for Europe*, adopted by the Convention in the summer of 2003, changes in the existing institutional language policy are not foreseen, it seems (European Convention, 2003). Besides sex, race, colour and other such conditions, language is named as a ground on which discrimination is forbidden (Article II–21), and the following Article of the draft Constitution prescribes that 'The Union shall respect cultural, religious and linguistic diversity' (European Convention, 2003: 65). The only specification of this to be found in the Constitution is where it is explicitly stipulated that every citizen of the Union 'has the right to address the institutions or advisory bodies . . . and to have an answer' in any of the official and working languages (European Convention, 2003: 84). These languages, in the text also referred to as 'the languages of the Constitution', are also explicitly summed up (Article IV–10, European Convention, 2003: 267). As for the languages regimes of the individual Institutions, the Convention, having stated that they each should adopt – and publish – their own Rules of Procedure, more in particular requires that 'The Council of Ministers shall adopt unanimously a European regulation laying down the rules governing the languages of the Union's institutions, .. .' (Article III-339, European Convention, 2003: 259). Restriction of the number of official and working languages, thus, lies within the competence of the Council of Ministers. Whether the Council will actually consider changing present-day practices or, for that matter, show an inclination to embark on a discussion of the principles of policy holding so far, is very unlikely to happen in the foreseeable future. There is no indication that the issue of institutional languages has ever been prominent in the Convention's deliberations when it was working on measures to 'simplify the decision-making processes' of the EU. For the time being, Institutions will continue making the best of things and devising such practical solutions on a day-to-day basis as have been described in the 2001 monograph for the communication problems they encounter under the present multi-lingual regime. Especially the European Parliament, where the subject of languages has always been a most sensitive subject and which has a tradition of trying its hardest to comply with a strict application of the full equality of all official and working languages, will be the first to experience the communicative problems created by the present great expansion of the EU. That there is an awareness of the seriousness and the acuteness of the language communication problems that the Administration of the EU and its Institutions are confronted with, one can see from the fact that mid-2003 a Colloquium was organised by the European Commission, at the initiative of a number of European language institutions such as the British Council and the *Goethe Institut* (Bliesener, 2003: 79ff). At the colloquium the idea of restricting in a sensible and acceptable way the unqualified application of the principle of full equality was put forward as a serious option by the Secretary General of the Commission. But, as Bliesener (2003: 83) reports, the expert deliberations at the colloquium in general showed 'a competitive situation in which everybody is against everybody else while looking after his individual interests irrespective of what would be beneficial to Europe and all Europeans.' The lack of rational deliberation at the Colloquium, once again ignoring the real language needs both of the EU as a political unit and of its citizens, will not have readily convinced the EU authorities of the necessity of seriously undertaking steps to produce a coherent language policy of and for the EU.

While *scholarly discussion* of EU institutional language use may not have had any substantial influence on actual policy and practice in the time that has elapsed since 2001, it has not come to a standstill either. The most notable publication, no doubt, has been Phillipson (2003), but let us first address issues raised in a number of other publications.

In his comprehensive and insightful introduction into the field of language policy Spolsky (2004) dwells on the EU as an example of supra-national groupings which have great difficulty coping with a very complex internal language situation. He shows how in drawing up the bureaucratic language policy of the EU, for example, a solution has to be found for 'the conflict between pragmatic and symbolic considerations' (Spolsky, 2004: 53ff). But Spolsky does not explicitly suggest any particular direction. In a similar way, but from the point of view of the French language, Truchot (2001: 25ff) discusses the EU institutional language policy and practice. Ammon (2001, 2003a) and Weinacht (2001) do so from a German language perspective, without expressing any specific preference for one particular solution or another for the institutional language problems of the EU either. Lever (2003), former British Ambassador to Germany, on the other hand, does express firmly his conviction that the EU Institutions will have to opt for one common working language, if 'we really want the EU to be a political union,…, more than just an association of nation states' (Lever, 2003: 110). And for Lever there is no doubt that 'the only language which can aspire to this role is English'. Such a restriction to one common language, however, would not necessarily also apply to the non-institutional domains, and, moreover, where one language should become the sole medium of communication it does apply, it would not carry with it the notion that all people using it would of necessity be brought to think in the same way or to have a common view of the world (Lever, 2004: 109). Lever's views clearly coincide with those expressed in the 2001 monograph. The insight that, for different domains of language use different regimes may and should be developed, is also expressed by Bliesener (2003: 96), and also – extensively – by Mackey (2001). Neither of these two authors, however, explicitly favours a particular mode of restriction for the EU. Finally, Seidlhofer (2003) discusses and defends the notion that, should English become the common language for the EU Institutions, and that the ownership of the language would more and more fall to the large majority of the non-native speakers. They would turn it into a European variety of English as an International Language (EIL). Seidlhofer (2003: 136) 'advocates an **adaptation into** European English rather than an **adoption of** English for Europe'.

   Thus, substantive new arguments for EU language policy development have not been put forward in the literature that has been reviewed, nor are new insights or new arguments to be found in Phillipson (2003) either, the first full-scale monograph on the subject of EU language policy. The book presents an extensive and detailed coverage of the various aspects of the subject. The author has consulted a great many published and unpublished documents, and he has spoken to many people who have taken part in and / or have witnessed internal communication processes of the EU. Yet, despite this wealth of information, of the often stimulating analyses the author undertakes and of the thought-provoking suggestions that he makes, in the end the book falls short of presenting a well-reasoned and rational language policy outline for the EU (Ammon, 2003b; Van Els, 2004). Phillipson's pre-occupation with the dangers of the possible dominance that one common language, in his case invariably English, would be posed to all other languages prohibits him from taking a rational approach to solving the practical language communication problems of such international organisations as the EU. His conception of a language policy is that it should primarily 'ensure that all languages can flourish' (Phillipson, 2003: 3). The single language situation, he is convinced, will inevitably endanger linguistic and cultural diversity. For Phillipson it can hardly be 'compatible with principles of equity, language rights, and human rights' (2003: 2). Phillipson too readily thinks that linguistic human rights – i.e., the right to use one's own language, in particular the right *not* to be discriminated against when a person exercises that right – as such require the automatic preservation and maintenance of all languages. This pre-occupation leads him inadequately to consider such basic issues in language policy development as the concept of language use domains (e.g., institutional *versus* non-institutional language use) and the various aspects of the quality of communication in international, i.e., multilingual, settings (e.g., the effects of different types of simultaneous interpretation). Thus, he also fails sufficiently to assess the impact that the use of one common language by speakers with different native language backgrounds may have on the development and use of the language in question. Although Phillipson does discuss this aspect of English as a lingua franca, he is unable to see it as an attractive option for international communication purposes. His fear of dominance by the Anglo-Americans is so strong that he is convinced that their mother-tongue norms will prevail in forming the lingua franca, thereby rejecting the premise that the ownership of this new brand of the language will reside with non-native speakers. Instead, he puts Esperanto forward as a serious option (Phillipson, 2003: 166) in full agreement with the position taken by Skutnab-Kangas (2000: 284). On the basis of the criteria of equality, cultural and linguistic diversity, non-discrimination, democracy and efficiency Skutnab-Kangas concludes, without further argumentation, that, when a decision has to be taken on what the common language for institutional use is to be in the EU: 'There is no doubt in my mind that a solution with English does not fulfil any of the criteria. Esperanto does.'

In his monograph Phillipson (2003: 190) correctly anticipates that language policy is unlikely to be high enough on the agenda in the negotiations in connection with the expansion of the EU for the Union to reconsider its present language use regimes. So far this assertion has proved correct. But, should the need for an active EU language policy eventually arise, it is to be hoped that in such discussions Phillipson's views will be treated with the critical scepticism they deserve.

References

Ahrens, R. (ed.) (2003) *Europäische Sprachenpolitik* [*European Language Policy*]. Heidelberg: Universitätsverlag Winter.

Ammon, U. (2001) Deutsch als Lingua franca in Europa [German as lingua franca in Europe]. *Sociolinguistica* 15, 32–41.

Ammon, U. (2003a) The decline of German and the rise of English as international languages of the sciences. In R. Ahrens (ed.) *Europäische Sprachenpolitik* [*European Language Policy*] (pp. 215–23). Heidelberg: Universitätsverlag Winter.

Ammon, U. (2003b) Review of Phillipson (2003) *Language Problems and Language Planning* 27, 289–94.

Bliesener, U. (2003) European language policy – Frustration and hope. A personal view of the state of affairs. In R. Ahrens (ed.) *Europäische Sprachenpolitik* [*European Language Policy*] (pp.75–98). Heidelberg: Universitätsverlag Winter.

European Convention (2003) *Treaty Establishing a Constitution for Europe. Draft*. Luxembourg: Office for Official Publications of the European Communities.

Lever, P. (2003) The future of Europe: Will we all speak English? In R. Ahrens (ed.) *Europäische Sprachenpolitik* [*European Language Policy*] (pp. 101–12). Heidelberg: Universitätsverlag Winter.

Mackey, W. (2001) Conflicting languages in a united Europe. *Sociolinguistica* 15, 1–17.

Phillipson, R. (2003) *English-Only Europe? Challenging Language Policy*. London/New York: Routledge.

Seidlhofer, B. (2003) English for Europe, or European English? In R. Ahrens (ed.)

Europäische Sprachenpolitik. [*European Language Policy*] (pp. 121–38). Heidelberg: Universitätsverlag Winter.

Skutnab-Kangas, T. (2000) *Linguistic Genocide in Education – or Worldwide Diversity and Human Rights?* Mahwah, NJ: Lawrence Erlbaum.

Spolsky, B. (2004) *Language Policy*. Cambridge: Cambridge University Press.

Truchot, C. (2001) Le français langue véhiculaire en Europe [French as a language of communication in Europe]. *Sociolinguistica* 15, 18–31.

van Els, T. (2004) Review of Phillipson (2003). *Sociolinguistica* 18, 4–10.

Weinacht, P.-L. Das Recht auf die eigene Sprache und die Pflicht zur Verständigung: Deutsch in Europa [The right to one's own language and the obligation of mutual understanding: German in Europe]. In R. Ahrens (ed.) *Europäische Sprachenpolitik.* [*European Language Policy*] (pp. 225–42). Heidelberg: Universitätsverlag Winter.

Language Planning in Northern Ireland

Diarmait Mac Giolla Chríost
Llechwedd, 23 Gerddi'r Twyn, Ffordd y Coleg, Caerfyrddin, Wales UK

This monograph offers an overview of the background of and current language policy and planning matters related to the language situation in Northern Ireland with reference to the full range of linguistic diversity in the polity. Particular attention is paid to the Irish language, due to the size of the Irish-speaking community in the region and the historical and political profile of the language. The current policy and planning framework for Irish is analysed and recommendations are provided on how effective progress in this area might be made in the short to medium term. The development of a community-based approach is suggested, drawing upon the Welsh model.

Keywords: Minority languages, Irish language, Northern Ireland, language policy, language planning, language rights

Introduction

The political entity that is Northern Ireland (NI) is situated in the northeastern part of the island of Ireland (Figure 1) and covers 5452 sq. miles (14,121 km^2).] The polity comprises the six counties of Armagh, Antrim, Down, Fermanagh, Londonderry and Tyrone. These counties, along with the counties of Cavan, Donegal and Monaghan, form the historical province of Ulster. The two main urban centres in NI are the cities of Belfast, in the east of the province, and Londonderry (or Derry) in the west. According to the 2001 Census, the population of NI is just over 1.6 million. NI came into being in 1921 as the greater part of Ireland exited from the British Empire. Until the early 1970s NI, while a part of the United Kingdom (UK), possessed a powerful form of self-government, seated at Stormont, through which the pro-British and largely Protestant Unionist Party exercised virtually unchallenged political hegemony. Subsequent to the failure of the Unionist regime to respond to an increasingly vociferous campaign for equality of access to the full range of resources of the state, largely driven by mostly Catholic Irish Nationalists, the British Government imposed direct rule from London over NI. This remained the case, without significant interruption, until 1998 when almost all of the political parties reached an agreement, variously described as 'The Belfast Agreement' or 'The Good Friday Agreement', through which power would be shared between the different parties and also through which the Republic of Ireland and the UK would share political sovereignty in a substantial manner. Despite recent and profound political difficulties, this arrangement remains in place.

Until the 1990s and the advent of the current political 'peace' process, language issues were not considered to be a significant feature of NI. This point was reinforced when the matter of language, and in particular the Irish language, emerged as an area of serious political interest during the multi-party discussions which culminated in the Good Friday Agreement in 1998, much to the surprise of many commentators and, indeed, some policy-makers. Notwithstanding the unexpected nature of this manifestation, a more measured approach towards language issues was, at that point, made

Figure 1 Map of Ireland showing international boundary, county boundaries and main towns
Source: Adapted from Foster, 1988

more difficult by the paucity of reliable sociological data regarding languages other than English in the polity. At the point of writing, the volume of available primary evidence is greater, although it remains limited and is almost wholly concerned with the Irish language. Data are drawn together in this paper from a number of sources including the full results of the 1991 Census, the Euromosaic study and a 1998 survey by the author. The results from the 2001 Census will only be available later in 2003. (Early headline figures show that 10.35% of a population of 1,617,957 have some knowledge of Irish (www.nisra.gov.uk).) Objective and quantitative information on the other languages of NI is non-existent. In two recent volumes on language issues in NI, the Republic of Ireland and Scotland (Kirk & Ó Baoill, 2000, 2001) a number of contributors referred to the case of various other languages, including Albanian, Arabic, Bengali, Cantonese, Farsi, Hindi, Mandarin, other Chinese, Punjabi, Sign and Ulster Scots, without being able to demonstrate the sociological extent of any of

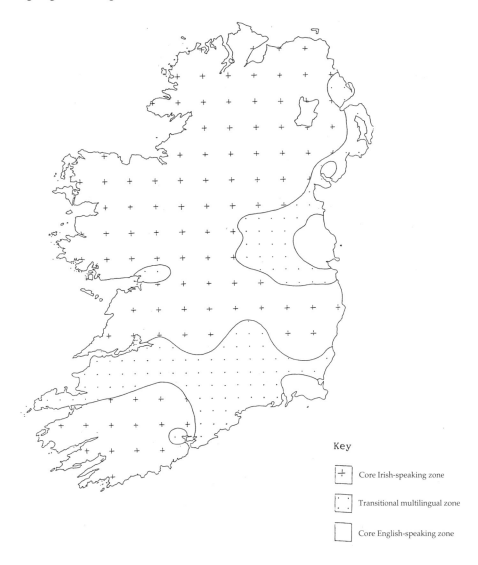

Figure 2 The ethno-linguistic situation in Ireland *c.* 1500

them. Data provided to the author by the Equality Commission for Northern Ireland (personal communication, 8 April 2003) estimate that there exist small numbers of speakers of various languages associated with diverse communities of peoples of Chinese (8000), African (1600), Indian (1500), Arabic (1500), Irish Traveller (1500), Pakistani (1000), Portuguese (700), Bangladeshi (500), Filipino (350) and Persian (350) origins. In the same correspondence it is noted that it is almost impossible to estimate numbers of Ulster Scots speakers due to the paucity of information. This lack of adequate data is similarly reflected here. While necessarily limited as a result of the paucity of objective data, this monograph may, however, be considered a contribution towards the construc-

tion of a more informed public discourse on language issues and the development of a more responsive policy process. The position of the Irish language is
explored in some depth.

The Irish Language in the Modern Period until 1991

The dynamics of language shift in what is now Northern Ireland have their
origins in the Early Modern Period. Historical sources (Nicholls, 1972; Ó Cuív,
1976) indicate that the Irish language was by far the dominant language in this
part of Ireland at the outset of the 16th century (Figure 2). Almost all of the northern part of the island lay within what was described by some at the time as 'The
Great Irishry'. In this area of Ireland, the Irish language was pre-eminent in all
domains and was replacing Latin as the language of the learned classes, secular
and ecclesiastical. Only in pockets along the eastern seaboard was the English
language in use. The English language is associated with the Anglo-Normans,
who had invaded Ireland in the 12th century, but it was probably merely one of a
number of languages in use by the Anglo-Normans. During the course of the
Medieval Period, many of the Anglo-Normans acquired Irish and, like many of
their European peers, were in all probability multilingual. For example, the Late
Medieval library of the Lords of Desmond was known to have contained literature in a number of languages including English, French, Irish and Latin. This
pattern of language shift was to be transformed by increasing intervention by the
English state in Ireland during the course of the 16th century, the origins of which
may be traced to the publication by Henry VIII in 1534 of the 'Ordinances for the
Government of Ireland'. The immediate effect of this intervention by the Tudor
state was that the English language began to make significant inroads into the
area of 'The Great Irishry' (Crawford, 1993). The ambiguous attitude of native
Irish lords towards the Tudor administration was a key feature of this process.
Minor Irish lords in particular became ever more eager to better secure their
claim to territorial possessions through gaining recognition of their ownership in
English Common Law (Duffy, 1981; O'Dowd, 1981). The Irish word for the
English language, *Béarla*, was used at this time to mean 'technical language',
perhaps reflecting the special function of English in the domain of law. At this
time the English language was also displacing both French and Latin as the sole
language of official records of the Tudor state (Bliss, 1976). As well as featuring
prominently in the domain of law, the English language also began to penetrate
other domains of language use. For example, in order to make their fealty to the
English monarch explicit, Irish lords sent their sons on fosterage to their new
overlord, as was native practice (Welch, 1996). As a result, many of the heirs of
Gaelic lordships received a significant part of their education in the English
court. As relationships with the English monarchy became increasingly important, so the status of the English language too rose, and only the most vehement
opponents of England prided themselves on their lack of mastery of that
language (Cahill, 1938).

Towards the close of the 16th century, Tudor policy in Ireland became
increasingly aggressive, eventually culminating in open warfare. Under the
leadership of Hugh O'Neill, the Earl of Tyrone, the historical province of Ulster
in the northern part of the Great Irishry was the focal point for this war, and this

was to have far-reaching consequences for the fate of the Irish language (Barnard, 1993). At this point, the Irish language was regarded as a useful medium for proselytising the Catholic Irish. However, the tighter enforcement of the 1560 Act of Uniformity prohibited Irish Catholics from attending the English universities of Oxford and Cambridge, and the deepening deprivations of war saw the retreat of Irish culture and learning from Ireland. Schools of Gaelic learning emerged on the European continent in response and quickly began to produce both secular and religious texts in Irish for consumption in Ireland (Millett, 1976; Ó Cuív, 1976; Ó Dushlaine, 1987; Silke, 1976). Had O'Neill been successful in his war with the Tudor state in Ireland, the Irish language may well have been able to recover from such dislocation. His defeat and the subsequent settlement of Ulster by colonists from Britain, and Scotland in particular, had dramatic consequences for the Irish language. Initially, some elements of Gaelic society survived, for instance, the *filíd* (poet class) were found to be useful as advisers on land ownership, law and land claims (Ó Buachalla, 1983). As the 17th century progressed, however, many of the features of traditional Gaelic society were abandoned as the adjustments considered necessary for modern Ireland were made in the areas of language, religion and lifestyle (Dunne, 1980; O'Riordain, 1990).

The geography of language in the northern part of Early Modern Ireland is complex. Using a variety of sources (Adams, 1958, 1964, 1967, 1970; Braidwood, 1969; Gregg, 1972; Robinson, 1989) it is possible to outline the distribution of the various languages spoken following this period of conquest and colonisation. The territory of Ulster, the former heartland of the Great Irishry, is marked by several zones of penetration by other languages (Figure 3). One zone follows the course of the Lagan valley from where Belfast is now sited to the south of Lough Neagh. A second zone comprises the area to the north and east of the lake of Fermanagh and a third zone stretches from south Antrim into the modern county of Londonderry. The linguistic composition of these zones is complex as a number of different languages, namely English, Scots Gaelic and Scots or Lallans, are known to have been variously spoken by the incomer groups which were central to the process of colonisation known as the Plantation of Ulster. Linguistic research suggests that English speakers were very numerous in most of the areas of the Plantation and especially so in the Plantation towns of Londonderry and Coleraine. That said, it is very likely that Scots or Lallans speakers comprised the greater part of the body of incomers. Scots Gaelic speakers were much less numerous and were probably confined to the east of Ulster and to the coastal parts of north Antrim in particular. Aside from the movement of such groups into the northern part of Ireland, significant numbers of Irish speakers were forcibly resettled in Connaught in the west of Ireland, further threatening the continuity of the Irish language in Ulster. Also, native attitudes continued to contribute to the new direction of language shift. Historical sources show that, while the English language was seen as one of the defining characteristics of the colonisers, its acquisition was desired by many native Irish (Caerwyn Williams, 1958; Canny, 1982; Ó Rahilly, 1952; O'Riordain, 1990; Williams, 1981). For example, the poet Cúndún (late Medieval) records among his achievements mastery over chess, the harp, hunting, riding, spear throwing, the Spanish language and the English language. Poetic displeasure towards the English

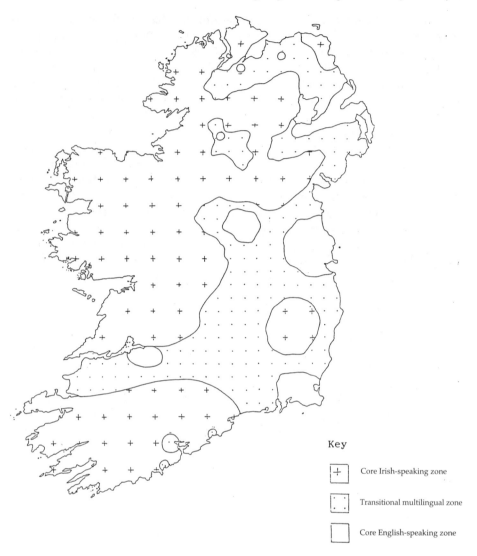

Key

$\boxed{+}$ Core Irish-speaking zone

$\boxed{\cdot\,\cdot}$ Transitional multilingual zone

$\boxed{}$ Core English-speaking zone

Figure 3 The ethno-linguistic situation in Ireland *c.* 1700

language, as evidenced in historical sources, appears to bear more upon the elitist disdain of Cundun, and those of his class, towards the low socioeconomic status of most of the incomers. Also, they viewed with contempt those of a social status inferior to their own in native Irish society who sought to better their station in the world through acquiring a modicum of the English language.

The acquisition of the English language by the Irish speakers of Ulster appears to have been accompanied by their abandonment of the Irish language. Drawing from the work of Fitzgerald (1984) (Figure 4), it can be seen that by the second half of the 18th century the Irish language was reduced to an isolated pocket in the north of Antrim. The beginnings of its isolation in central Ulster can also be

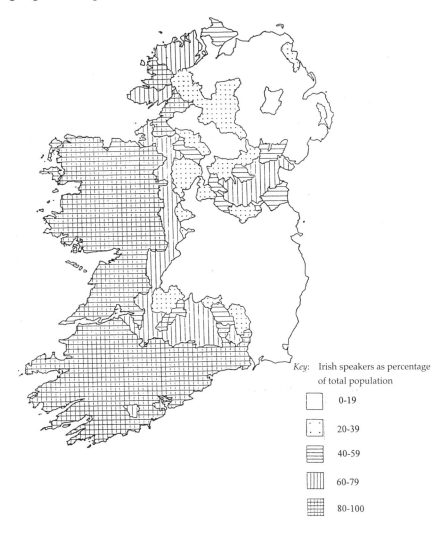

Figure 4 The Irish language in Ireland by Barony, late 18th century
Source: Adapted from Fitzgerald, 1984

discerned. By the first quarter of the 19th century (Figure 5) the language was reduced to isolated pockets in several parts of Ulster. By the close of the century, only in the western county of Donegal did it retain any resemblance of its former vitality. Traditionally, the advent of the National Schools during the second half of the 19th century and the human tragedy of the Irish Famine, 1845–49, are seen to have been largely responsible for the rapid decline of the Irish language throughout Ireland in this period (Brown, 1985; Ó Tuathaigh, 1972; Wall, 1969). The abandonment of the language by the Irish is an act, however, which is not explicable in terms of the necessity of the acquisition of the English language. As Lee (1989) points out, many other language communities have acquired another language

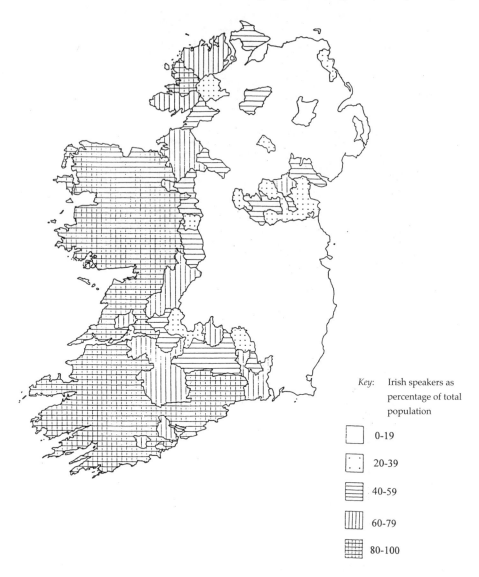

Key: Irish speakers as
          percentage of total
          population

          0-19

          20-39

          40-59

          60-79

          80-100

Figure 5 The Irish language in Ireland by Barony, early 19th century
Source: Adapted from Fitzgerald, 1984

while maintaining their indigenous tongue. The Census returns from the 19th century suggest that it is more likely that these events merely contributed to the momentum of a process that was already underway. The causes of the decline of the Irish language in much of Ireland, and in Ulster in particular, are longer term and relate much more closely to the structures of modern Irish society which emerged during the course of the warfare, plantation and colonisation experienced in Ireland from the close of the 16th century (Ní Mhurchada, 1984; Ó

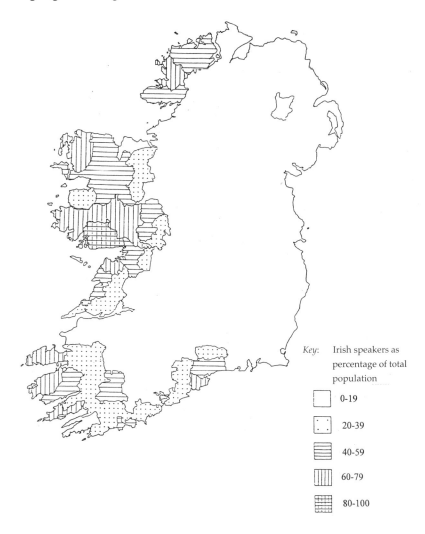

Key: Irish speakers as percentage of total population

☐ 0-19

⋮ 20-39

▤ 40-59

▥ 60-79

▦ 80-100

Figure 6 The Irish language in Ireland by Barony, early 20th century
Source: Adapted from Coimisiún na Gaeltachta, 1926

Murchú, 1992). The totality of the language shift by the 20th century is also partly explained by the acquiescence of the native Irish in the process from the outset.

Until 1991, the last Census question on the Irish language in the part of Ireland now known as Northern Ireland was in 1911. Northern Ireland came into being in 1921. In this Census, 28,729 individuals were enumerated as Irish speakers in the area of the six counties which subsequently comprised Northern Ireland (Figure 6). At that time, small Irish-language communities were to be found in the area of Red Bay in the north-east of Ulster, in Central Ulster to the west of Lough Neagh and in the southern reaches of the counties of Armagh and Down. Pockets of Irish speakers were also to be found in southern and western Tyrone, within striking distance of the still significant Irish-language community of Donegal, and in south

Table 1 Irish speakers by age in the six northern counties of Ireland, 1901 and 1911

Age	1901 (percentage)	1911 (percentage)
< 3	0.2	0.4
3–9	3.4	7.5
10–17	10.9	25.9
18–29	21.4	23.3
30–59	38.2	25.7
60+	25.8	17.2

Source: Adapted from Máté, 1997

Fermanagh where they bordered on large Irish-speaking communities in neighbouring counties to the south which subsequently became a part of the Irish Free State (later the Republic of Ireland). The remains of an Irish-language community centred on the mountains of Mourne in County Down were also evident.

Given the dearth of data resulting from the absence of a Census question on the Irish language in Northern Ireland until 1991, the history of the Irish-speaking community in Northern Ireland in this period may only be partially illuminated. It is the case that the sets of Census data for 1901 and 1911 suggest a reversal of the relentless contraction of the Irish-speaking community in the modern era. The total number of Irish speakers jumped from a figure of 21,432 in 1901 to 28,729 in 1911 in the territory that was to comprise Northern Ireland (Table 1). The data show that both numbers and proportions of Irish speakers increased among the younger age cohorts (under 29 years) while the actual numbers and proportions of Irish speakers falled markedly in older age groups. This is probably the result of the 'Gaelic Revival', characterised by the activity of a number of social and cultural organisations including *Conradh na Gaeilge*, the Gaelic League.

Following the Government of Ireland Act (1920) and the eventual ratification of the Anglo-Irish Treaty, the Irish Free State (now Republic of Ireland) came into being, leaving the six counties of the province of Northern Ireland within the United Kingdom of Great Britain and Northern Ireland. From this point onwards, until 1991, no question on the Irish language was asked in any subsequent Census in Northern Ireland. Little other evidence exists with regard to the fate of the Irish language in the region in this period; thus it is difficult to discern with total confidence the dynamics of the language shift that took place. Commentators (Hindley, 1990; Maguire, 1991) commonly point to the fact that the German academic, Wagner, noted the ruins of the Irish-speaking community on Rathlin Island during the 1950s, and that Ó Murcada (1951), an Irish-speaking native of Tyrone, described that parlous condition of the Irish language in central Ulster in the same decade, as powerful indicators of the death of the Irish language in Northern Ireland some time prior to the Census of 1991. Some caution should be exercised with regard to this, as Irish speakers were most unwilling to advertise their ability in the Irish language as it was regarded as the language of Irish nationalist separatism as well as being strongly associated with economic backwardness and therefore alien to the values of Northern Ireland.

The Irish Language 1991–2001

The Irish language in NI in recent years has been of increasing interest to Government. In 1987, the first significant government publication on the subject appeared (Sweeny, 1987). In 1988, the Irish language was incorporated in the National Curriculum (DENI, 1988) and in 1991 questions on the Irish language were included in the Census in NI (DHSS/RGNI, 1991). Government policy towards the Irish language in NI, while undergoing some development, remains ill-defined (CAJ, 1993; Pritchard, 1990). In recent years, the central Government set its policy in the context of culture: 'The Government regards the language as an important strand in the complex cultural inheritance of Northern Ireland which should be valued as such by all sections of the community' (CCRU, 2 June 1997). This approach is regarded as open and non-political. The policy itself is described as follows: 'The Government's policy is to respond positively, where practical, to soundly based requests for assistance' (CCRU, 2 June 1997). The focal point for policy would appear to be the Ultach Trust, founded in 1989, a body whose main aim is 'to widen the appreciation of the Irish language and culture throughout the community in Northern Ireland' (CCRU, 2 June 1997). Through this trust the Government makes available monies for a variety of projects with an Irish-language dimension, including schools. In 1995–96, the trust received some £426,000 in financial support out of total government expenditure of £2.9m on projects with an Irish-language dimension.

The Government would also appear to be encouraged by increased Irish-language programming in radio and television broadcasting under the auspices of the BBC and the Independent Broadcasting Companies and the progress of negotiations to improve the reception of the output of *Radio Telefis Éireann* (*RTÉ*), the national broadcasting corporation in the Republic of Ireland, as well as the Irish-medium television channel *Teilifis na Gaeilge* (now *TG4*). The CCRU also notes that the Government made available £1,161,000 to the Department of Education for Northern Ireland during 1995–96 for the funding of Irish-medium schools and curriculum materials. Other sources note that the Government had also begun to fund Irish-medium education in a much more direct manner (*Lá*, 13 April 1995 – an Irish-language weekly newspaper). Support was also given in that year to the Irish language via the Londonderry Development Office and Making Belfast Work (£296,000), the Training and Employment Agency, Enterprise Ulster and the Northern Ireland Tourist Board (£463,000). Some £36,300 is expended on the provision of education and translation facilities for prisoners. Grants are also provided by the Arts Council of Northern Ireland for Irish-language projects; this includes £494,000 available from the National Lottery funds. The 1949 legislation banning street names in Irish has been repealed. Members of the public who write to Government departments in Irish will have their letters translated and be replied to in English. Policy during much of this period, however, varies little from that which is criticised by the authors (CAJ) of a report on Government policy on the language published in 1993. Features of the policy are also contrasted with more positive examples elsewhere in the UK, particularly in relation to the Welsh language in Wales and Scots Gaelic in Scotland (Mac Póilin, n.d.).

The context in which the language is set in the document arising from the political agreement of Good Friday 1998 entitled 'The Agreement' offers the prospect for firming up language policy in some respects. Significant parts of the text, however, are ambiguous. In the section entitled 'Rights, Safeguards and Equality of Opportunity: Economic, Social and Cultural Issues', it is noted that while all the participants in the talks 'recognise the importance of respect, understanding and tolerance in relation to linguistic diversity' (NIO, 1998: 19), it is only the British Government which is committed to the most significant statements on the Irish language and this commitment by the British Government is conditional upon 'the context of active consideration currently being given to the UK signing the Council of Europe Charter for Regional or Minority Languages' (NIO, 1998: 19) and also upon determining 'where appropriate and where people so desire it' (NIO, 1998: 19). The most important commitments are in the areas of education and broadcasting. The first relates to bringing the statutory obligations of the Department of Education with regard to Irish-medium education into line with that for integrated education. The second relates to broadening support for televisual broadcasting and production in the Irish language including making readily available *Teilifís na Gaeilge* (now *TG4*) in Northern Ireland. The taking of action upon these, as well as the other more general commitments, is dependent upon a new Assembly for NI. The potential for difficulties arising from implementing any of these commitments is suggested in the final point of Part 4 in which the government will 'encourage the parties to secure agreement that this commitment will be sustained by a new Assembly in a way which takes account of the desires and sensitivities of the community' (NIO, 1998: 20). Similarly, Part 5 of the same section notes the need for sensitivity with regard to the use of symbols for public purposes. The Irish language has fallen foul of Fair Employment legislation regarding this issue. A commitment is made to set in motion arrangements for monitoring this issue with a view to determining 'what action might be required' (NIO, 1998: 20). A leaked communication between the NIO and a minister of state publicised in *Lá* (30 April 1998), an Irish-language weekly newspaper, would suggest that these commitments are vulnerable to considerable differences of interpretation.

The attitudes of local government vary significantly. Belfast City Council, for example, has maintained a very negative attitude towards the language. Although noting that the Unionist parties have lost their majority in Belfast City Hall following the local government elections of 1997, Irish-language groups in the city are intending to exert pressure on the other political parties represented on the council to develop a more favourable policy with regard to the Irish language (*Lá*, 30 April 1998). At the other end of the spectrum, Newry and Mourne District Council has appointed an Irish-language officer and is positive in its support of Irish-language activities. Derry City Council has created a cultural sub-committee and is seeking ways in which to develop policy on the Irish language. Whatever the positions of institutions and individuals in relation to the language over the last decades, Irish was deemed to be sufficiently significant to have a question on it inserted in the 1991 Census in NI, and it is to this that attention is now turned.

The 1991 Census

As with the other parts of the UK, the 1991 Census was taken in NI on 21/22 April. The data on which this analysis is founded are derived from the NI Census 1991 Irish Language Report.[1] The statistics recorded indicate the numbers of people aged three years and over in the 566 Census Wards of NI who have some knowledge of the Irish language, with subdivisions according to abilities to speak, read and write Irish, and show also the data by religion, economic activity, social class, highest academic qualification, sex and age.

The question posed on the Irish language was question number 14 on the Census form and was worded as follows: 'Can the person speak, read or write Irish?' Four boxes were to be ticked as appropriate for each of the four statements as follows:

i.   Can speak Irish   ☐
ii. Can read Irish   ☐
iii. Can write Irish   ☐
iv. Does not know Irish   ☐

As a result, in terms of language proficiency, it is possible to differentiate all combinations of ability to speak, read and write Irish. The Census did not ask whether or not persons were able to speak English, so the number, if any, of Irish monoglots cannot be determined. The question on the Irish language in Northern Ireland is the same as that posed for Welsh in Wales and Scots Gaelic in Scotland.

The base resident population of NI for the 1991 Census is derived from information on the whereabouts and usual address given for each person listed on the Census form. This includes the population present on Census night (present population), which is a count of all people recorded as spending Census night in the area regardless of whether or not this was where they usually lived; the usually resident population, being a count of those people recorded on the forms for the area as usually living 'at this address' whether or not they are present on Census night.

Analysis and mapping of the Irish language is affected by the nature of the administrative units employed. For the purposes of the Census, the territory of NI comprises 4 Regions, 26 Local Government Districts (LGD) (Figure 7) and 566 Census Wards. The effective analysis and illustration of areal patterns is made more complex by the variations which exist in the geographical size of units and the populations they contain. Rural Census Wards, for example, tend to be more extensive and less populated than urban Census Wards which tend to be compact and heavily populated. There are large variations between LGDs and the numbers of Census wards they contain; Belfast, for example, contains 51 wards while others comprise just 15 (Tables 2–4).

The 1991 Census records a total Irish-speaking population of 131,974, representing 8.8% of the total resident population aged three and over. Table 5 and Figure 8 illustrate the distribution of the language by Census Region and LGD. Clearly, the language enjoys a significant presence in all four Census Regions. Irish speakers are most strongly represented in the Southern and Western Regions, while actual numbers of Irish speakers in the Eastern Region are very high, and 31.7% of all Irish speakers actually reside in this region. They are also

Figure 7 Northern Ireland: Census Regions and Local Government Districts
Source: HMSO Belfast, 1992

strongly represented in the two largest urban centres in NI, the cities of Belfast and Londonderry (Table 6). Mapping the distribution of Irish speakers at the level of Census ward highlights some exceptional features of the distribution of Irish speakers (Figure 9). Higher than expected levels of Irish speakers may be noted in central Ulster to the south-west of Lough Neagh, an area centred on where the boundaries of the LGDs of Cookstown, Dungannon and Omagh meet and extending into Magherafelt LGD. In Cookstown LGD, two wards with relatively high proportions of Irish speakers are Dunnamore (27.6%) and Pomeroy (26.3%). In Dungannon LGD the wards with high proportions of Irish speakers are Altmore (26.4%), Coalisland North (52.8%), Coalisland South (45.4%), Coalisland South and New Mills (34.2%), Mullaghmore (30.4%) and Washing Bay (62.5%). The ward of Termon in Omagh LGD contains the highest proportion of Irish speakers (44.4%). Two wards in Magherafelt LGD stand out, namely Lower Glenshane (29.9%) and Swatragh (26.4%). Higher than expected levels of Irish speakers are also to be found in the western part of Newry and Mourne LGD. Wards with relatively high proportions of Irish speakers are Camlough (30.1%), Creggan (28.3%) and Silver Bridge (30.4%). The western parts of the cities of Belfast and of Londonderry (Derry LGD) also return high proportions of Irish speakers. Belfast wards with a high proportion include Andersonstown (28.8%), Falls Park (29.6%), Glen Colin (27.7%), Glen Road (30.3%) and Upper Springfield (27.4%). Wards in Derry LGD with similarly high proportions include Ballynashallog (27.6%) and Strand (27.6%).

On the whole, the Irish-speaking population is young, with 48.0% aged 24 or less (Table 7). A breakdown of the 3–14 age group (Table 8) would appear to indicate that, while there are very many young Irish speakers, the actual number who

Table 2 Numbers of Census Wards by Local Government Districts and Census Regions, NI 1991

	Number of Census Wards
Northern Region LGDs	
Antrim	19
Ballymena	23
Ballymoney	16
Carrickfergus	15
Coleraine	21
Cookstown	16
Larne	15
Magherafelt	15
Moyle	15
Newtonabbey	25
Eastern Region LGDs	
Ards	20
Belfast	51
Castlereagh	21
Down	23
Lisburn	28
North Down	24
Southern Region LGDs	
Armagh	22
Banbridge	15
Craigavon	26
Dungannon	22
Newry & Mourne	30
Western Region LGDs	
Derry	30
Fermanagh	23
Limavady	15
Omagh	21
Strabane	15

acquire the language via parental transmission is limited and that the greater number acquire the language in school, particularly at secondary level.

In Tables 9–11, the incidence of Irish speakers is related to highest academic qualification, social class and economic activity. No attempt has been made to deduce spatial patterns. Table 9 indicates that Irish speakers tend to be overrepresented in the higher levels of academic attainment and are particularly

Table 3 Local Government Districts by population, NI 1991

Total population	Number of LGDs	As % of total number of LGDs	As % of total population NI
< 15000	1	3.8	1.0
15000–24999	1	3.8	1.5
25000–34999	7	26.9	14.5
35000–44999	3	11.5	8.6
45000–54999	4	15.4	13.5
55000–64999	3	11.5	11.7
> 65000	7	26.9	49.3

Table 4 Census Wards by population size, NI 1991

Total population	Number of wards	As % of total number of wards	As % of total population of NI
< 1000	11	1.9	0.6
1000–1499	23	4.1	2.1
1500–2499	300	53.0	41.0
2500–3499	150	26.5	28.7
3500–4499	32	5.7	8.9
4500–5499	29	5.1	10.1
> 5500	21	3.7	8.5

overrepresented in level 1, the highest level of academic attainment. There is a notable blip at level 5 indicating qualifications at GCSE level and equivalent. There is no significant variation between the sexes; the Irish-speaking population conforms with NI as a whole in that males tend to predominate at both the very top and bottom ends of the scale and females to be slightly more heavily represented at level 3 (GCE A level and equivalent) and also at level 5.

An exploration of the incidence of Irish-speaking by social class reveals some interesting relationships (Table 10). Both male and female Irish speakers are significantly overrepresented in the top two social classes. Those are the professional occupations and the managerial and technical occupations respectively. Females are especially overrepresented in the latter social class. Also, males in particular are overrepresented in the class 'no paid job within the last 10 years'. Relationships between the language and economic activity are more complex again (Table 11). Male Irish speakers tend to be more likely to be out of employment than their non-Irish-speaking counterparts and much more likely than female Irish speakers to be in this category. However, male Irish speakers, as with their female counterparts, are more likely to be professional employees than the rest of the resident population in NI. Female Irish speakers are overrepresented among the economically active population and are, as a result,

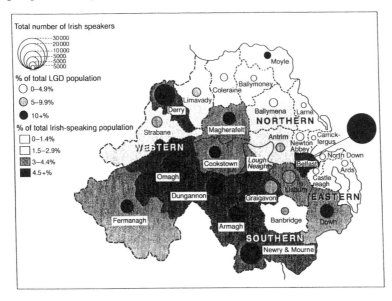

Figure 8 Irish speakers in Northern Ireland by Census Region and Local Government District

Table 5 Irish speakers by Census Region, NI 1991

Census Region	Number of Irish speakers	As % of total population of Census Region	As % of total Irish-speaking population
Northern	22,236	5.9	16.8
Eastern	41,846	6.9	31.7
Southern	37,352	13.6	28.3
Western	30,540	12.4	23.1

Table 6 Irish speakers by main urban centres, NI 1991

Urban centre	Total population	As % of total population of NI	Number of Irish speakers	As % of total Irish-speaking population of NI
Belfast	266,384	17.7	27,430	20.8
Derry City	59,712	4.0	9,731	7.4
Total	326,096	21.7	37,161	28.2

overrepresented among those who are both in and out of employment. Irish speakers of both sexes are much more likely to be pursuing further or higher education than the rest of the population. They are also very substantially underrepresented among the retired, confirming the young age structure of the Irish-speaking population.

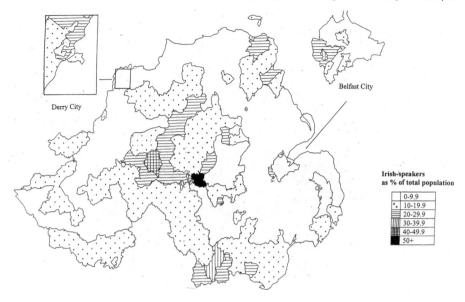

Figure 9 Irish speakers in Northern Ireland by ward

Table 7 Irish speakers by age, NI 1991

Age group	Number of Irish speakers	As % of total population of age group	As % of total Irish-speaking population
3–14	30,903	10.0	23.4
15–24	32,426	12.8	24.6
25–44	39,784	9.2	30.1
45–64	19,861	6.5	15.0
65+	9,000	4.5	6.8

Table 8 Irish speakers by age 3–14, NI 1991

Age group	Number of Irish speakers	As % of total age group	As % of total Irish-speaking population of NI
3–4	1,586	3.0	1.2
5–9	7,648	5.9	5.8
10–14	21,669	16.9	16.4

The levels of literacy (Table 12) of this young Irish-speaking population vary little throughout NI. The overall profile of literacy would suggest two significant levels of literacy, the first, comprising 55.6% of the total population with any knowledge of Irish attaining the highest level of literacy, and the second,

Table 9 Irish speakers by highest academic qualification and gender, NI 1991

Level of qualification by gender	Number of Irish speakers	As % of Irish speakers	Number of non-Irish speakers	As % of non-Irish speakers
1 Male	7,308	16.0	34,926	6.8
Female	6,961	13.7	27,302	4.9
Total	14,269	14.8	62,228	5.8
2 Male	1,365	3.0	13,538	2.6
Female	687	1.4	3,893	0.7
Total	2,052	2.1	17,431	1.6
3 Male	4,720	10.3	24,487	4.8
Female	6,019	11.9	35,716	6.4
Total	10,739	11.1	54,847	5.1
4 Male	1,060	2.3	11,534	2.2
Female	663	1.3	5,109	0.9
Total	1,723	1.8	16,643	1.6
5 Male	8,648	18.9	69,768	13.6
Female	12,386	24.4	97,929	17.5
Total	21,034	21.8	167,697	15.7
6 Male	1,365	3.0	18,532	3.6
Female	1,297	2.6	19,296	3.5
Total	2,662	2.8	37,828	3.5
7 Male	21,351	46.6	340,569	66.3
Female	22,709	44.8	374,156	67.0
Total	44,060	45.6	714,725	66.7

comprising 31.9% of the population with any knowledge of Irish only being able to speak the language. It is worth pointing out at this stage that, in the 1981 Census in the Republic of Ireland, just over 31% of the population aged three and above were reported as having some competency in Irish (Ó Murchú, 1992) whereas in the 1991 Census in NI (DHSS/RGNI, 1991) the comparable figure was around 10%. Clearly the dynamics of the Irish language communities in the two parts of Ireland are very different.

A significant difference between the Census questionnaire for NI and for the rest of the UK in 1991 was the absence of a question on ethnic identity. In NI, a question on religious denomination fills this gap (Openshaw, 1995). The Census data on the Irish language in relation to religion (Table 13) show the overwhelming majority of Irish speakers are Roman Catholics. Over 89% of all Irish speakers stated that they were Roman Catholics. This means the Roman Catholics are grossly overrepresented among Irish speakers. Not all Roman Catholics are Irish speakers; however, 20.6% of Roman Catholics stated that they spoke Irish. Other religious denominations are grossly underrepresented among Irish speakers. Irish speakers who represent the three main Protestant denominations (Presbyterian, Church of Ireland and Methodist) comprise less than 3% of the Irish-speaking community. Fewer than 2% of all respondents identifying themselves as belonging to one of the three main Protestant traditions returned themselves as Irish speakers. Those respondents who returned

Table 10 Male and female Irish speakers by social class, NI 1991

Social class and gender	Number of Irish speakers	As % of Irish speakers	Number of non-Irish speakers	As % of non-Irish speakers
1 Male	2,449	7.5	15,385	4.1
Female	792	3.2	3,640	1 .5
2 Male	8,772	26.6	79,017	21.1
Female	9,447	38.6	57,087	22.8
3 Male	11,531	35.2	153,253	41.0
Female	7,822	32.0	102,602	40.9
4 Male	3,383	10.3	52,112	13.9
Female	3,052	12.5	44,206	17.6
5 Male	1,345	4.1	20,292	5.5
Female	1,037	4.2	22,634	9.0
Armed forces etc.				
Male	633	1.9	14,462	3.9
Female	307	1.3	3,493	1.4
Training scheme etc.				
Male	890	2.7	7,759	2.1
Female	496	2.0	4,100	1.6
No paid job in 10 yrs				
Male	3,771	11.5	31,511	8.4
Female	1,523	6.2	13,056	5.2

themselves in the 'None' and 'Not Stated' categories comprised 6.9% of the total Irish-speaking community. This figure indicates that respondents of this nature are underrepresented among Irish speakers.

Interpretation and analysis

At present it is very difficult to talk about meaningful trends in relation to the Irish language in NI because of the statistical hiatus between 1911 and 1991. In time, successive results from the Censuses (including those of 2001 when available) will facilitate the development of a body of evidence which may be subjected to complex interrogation. It is possible, however, to draw a number of insights from the data set as it stands. The results of various programmes of research can be brought to bear on the Census data in order to better understand the place of the Irish language in NI. The meaning of the term 'Irish-speaking' as used in the 1991 Census requires some qualification. The form of the question in the Census does not allow for any indication of levels of ability in the language. Some of those respondents who described themselves as Irish-speaking may possess very limited competence in the language. Regarding the Census figures, Mac Póilin offers the following insight: 'Responses appear to have ranged from the over-scrupulous to the over-optimistic, so the figures underestimate the numbers who have some knowledge of Irish, but probably exaggerate the number of fluent speakers' (Mac Póilin, 1996: 153). Data which throw some light on this may be derived from the Euromosaic survey (www.uoc.es/euromosaic).

Table 11 Economic activity by male and female Irish speakers, NI 1991

Economic activity and gender	Number of Irish speakers	As % of Irish speakers	Number of non-Irish speakers	As % of non-Irish speakers
Total economically active				
Male	32,733	71.4	373,993	72.9
Female	24,476	48.3	250,818	44.9
Total economically inactive				
Male	13,084	28.6	139,361	27.1
Female	26,246	51.7	307,227	55.1
Total in employment				
Male	24,634	53.8	304,766	59.4
Female	21,497	42.4	224,053	40.1
Total out of employment				
Male	8,099	17.7	69,227	13.5
Female	2,979	5.9	26,765	4.8
Self-employed				
Male	5,103	11.1	58,664	11.4
Female	846	1.7	9,102	1.6
Managers				
Male	2,500	5.5	29,528	5.8
Female	1,198	2.4	11,603	2.1
Foremen & supervisors				
Male	858	1.9	12,552	2.4
Female	856	1.7	8,995	1.6
Professional employees				
Male	1,596	3.5	11,868	2.3
Female	678	1.3	3,092	0.6
Other employees				
Male	13,687	29.9	184,395	35.9
Female	17,422	34.3	187,162	33.5
Students				
Male	6,362	13.9	28,884	5.6
Female	7,940	15.7	31,343	5.6
Training				
Male	890	1.9	7,759	1.5
Female	496	1.0	4,100	0.7
Retired				
Male	3,586	7.8	73,106	14.2
Female	4,785	9.4	99,299	17.8

Table 12 Literacy profile of Irish speakers, NI 1991 (in percentages)

Speak Irish only	Speak and read but not write Irish	Speak, read and write Irish
34.4	5.0	59.9

Table 13 Irish speakers by religion, NI 1991

Religion	Number of Irish speakers	Percentage of religious denomination who speak Irish	Percentage of total Irish-speaking population
Roman Catholic	118,009	20.6	89.4
Presbyterian	1,383	0.4	1.0
Church of Ireland	1,747	0.7	1.3
Methodist	265	0.5	0.2
Other	1,459	1.2	1.1
Not stated	6,739	6.3	5.1
None	2,372	4.3	1.8

This is a project which has as its primary aim the quantification of the potential for the production and reproduction of minority language groups in the European Union including the Irish language in NI. The results of this survey, conducted entirely among Irish speakers, showed that 28% considered themselves to be 'very good' in their ability to speak the language, 32% considered themselves to be 'quite good', 39% considered themselves to have only a 'little' Irish, while 1% even reported that they spoke no Irish whatsoever. Should one accept the representativeness of these results then one could approximate the size of the functional Irish-speaking population from the 1991 Census at something in the region of 36,000 ('very good' level of ability) up to around 79,000 ('quite good' level of ability). Only 3% of respondents recorded the Irish-language as their first language. As the survey was conducted among an adult population of an unknown age range but being at least over 18 years of age none of these respondents would have acquired their Irish since 1980. Most commentators, and especially those within the Irish-language community, argue that it was only during the 1980s that the regrowth of the Irish language community took off. Levels of incidence of the Irish language as a first language may well be higher than the 3% recorded by Euromosaic.

The distribution of Irish speakers in NI as derived from the 1991 Census is related entirely to the distribution of Catholics in the region, according to the author of the Euromosaic report *Irish in the North of Ireland*. It is stated in the report: 'Given that the two religious groups are not randomly dispersed within the region there are also geographical variations in the number of speakers that are evident' (www.uoc.es/euromosaic). Nic Craith and Shuttleworth (1996) contradict this assertion in a brief exploration of the data from the 1991 Census. They note that the distribution of those with a knowledge of Irish is not entirely related to the distribution of Catholics in the region. They point to the high density of Catholics (61.8%) in Strabane but the relatively low level of those with a knowledge of the language (9.39%) in contrast with the Belfast urban area where the proportion of those with a knowledge of Irish is much higher despite the fact that the proportion of Catholics is much lower. While refraining from a substantial analysis of the data, they suggest that the higher incidence of knowledge of the language in Belfast may be related to generally higher levels of politicisation in Belfast as opposed to other parts of NI and also, perhaps, to the greater concentration of Irish-language activity which may be seen in Belfast. Such an analysis would not explain the concentrations of Irish speakers noted in other parts of NI unless one were to translate the higher levels of politicisation noted for Belfast to those other parts as well. It is significant that in other parts of NI such as Crossmaglen Census Ward, an area which may be characterised in a fashion similar to west Belfast, the Irish-speaking population (24.1%) is not much greater than that which would be expected from within the Catholic community as a whole (*c.* 21%). Examples of similar cases can be found elsewhere in the region; for example, the levels of Irish speakers are much lower in the wards of Creggan Central (18.1%) and Creggan South (16.6%) in the western half of the city of Londonderry where it could be said that the overwhelmingly nationalist community is highly politicised in a fashion similar to west Belfast. In other words, the geography of the Irish language in NI is not to be explained simply in terms of the distribution of the Catholic population, nor in terms of the location of highly politicised nationalist communities. The presence of Irish speakers in some parts of society and their relative scarcity in others must be explained with reference to a more diverse sociopolitical context. The attitudinal data presented in this paper allow for some light to be thrown on this issue.

Mapping of the data at Census Ward level (Figure 9) shows that there may be some evidence for some very limited continuity between the Irish-speaking community as recorded in 1911 and in 1991. For example, the age structure of Irish speakers in Glendun Census Ward, Moyle LGD (Table 14) shows that over 17% of Irish speakers in that ward were 65 years old or older. The proportion in this age group within the Irish-speaking population across NI as whole is 6.8%. Glendun Census Ward, Moyle LGD is located within the Red Bay area of north-east Antrim which, in 1911, contained a significant Irish-speaking community. Due to changes in the administrative units between the two censuses in 1911 and 1991, this apparent pattern should be treated with some caution. But it is nonetheless suggestive of the survival of some individuals from the Irish-speaking community recorded in 1911. These vestiges, which may be described as *relict Gaeltachtaí*, are remarkable in that they appear to confound those well-received notions on the death of the Irish language during the middle part of this century.

The figure in Glendun Census ward is in contrast to the much younger profiles for the high concentrations of Irish speakers found in some other parts

Table 14 Irish speakers by age in Glendun Census Ward, Moyle LGD, NI 1991

Age group	Number of Irish speakers	As % of total age group	As % of Irish-speaking population
3–14	25	11.2	12.4
15–24	51	26.4	25.4
25–44	42	16.0	20.9
45–64	48	23.0	23.9
65+	35	17.3	17.4

Table 15 Irish speakers by age in Coalisland South Census Ward, Dungannon LGD, NI 1991

Age group	Number of Irish speakers	As % of total age group	As % of Irish-speaking population
3–14	259	50.4	30.4
15–24	209	56.5	24.6
25–44	241	45.0	28.3
45–64	113	38.3	13.3
65+	29	18.6	3.4

of NI. The age profile of the Irish speakers recorded in the 1991 Census indicates a general rejuvenation of the language. This rejuvenation is located in some areas in which an Irish-speaking population was recorded in 1911, including parts of central Ulster and southern Armagh but not the area of Red Bay. It is also to be found in other parts of NI in which no significant Irish-speaking population whatsoever was recorded in 1911. This includes the urban centres of Belfast and Londonderry and the rural district around Coalisland on the south-western corner of Lough Neagh. Maguire (1987) used the term *neo-Gaeltacht* to describe the Irish-speaking community of west Belfast whose growth during the 1980s she recounted more fully in 1991 (Maguire, 1991). This term could equally be applied to those other emergent Irish-speaking communities in NI whose presence the mapping of the data from the 1991 Census makes more salient. The process of rejuvenation is clear in these cases. The Irish-speaking population in the cluster of wards around Coalisland in Dungannon LGD contain a much lower proportion of Irish speakers in the age group 65 years old or older than does Glendun Census Ward. For example, in Coalisland South Census Ward, 3.4% of Irish speakers are in the age group 65 years old or older, and 30.4% are in the age group 3 to 14 years of age; indeed, 55% of all Irish speakers in this particular ward are to be found in the age range of 3 to 24 years old (Table 15). Some Irish-speaking populations in other wards – for example, Falls Park, Belfast LGD – contain no speakers whatsoever in the older age groups.

The data from the 1991 Census suggest that language acquisition may centre on the educational system rather than on intergenerational transmission. The results of the Euromosaic survey appear to reinforce this analysis. Besides the low number of respondents recording the Irish language as their first language, the use of the language within family units is sporadic: 'the degree of language reproduction, which we have defined in terms of inter-generational transmission is limited to 17% or less' (www.uoc.es/euromosaic). From the total survey population of 284, only seven cases (3%) were reported in which the sole language of the family was Irish, and a further 12 (4%) were reported in which the Irish language was the main language of the family. In 16% of cases, English was recorded as the main language of the family with some use of Irish as well. Also, 80% of respondents in the survey claimed to have acquired their Irish at school.

The socioeconomic patterns derived from the Census data are interesting in that they appear to confirm some historical beliefs about the Irish language, and more importantly in that they may also indicate ways in which the language has broken with its historical past characterised by decline and marginalisation. Also, the potential for certain features of the contemporary socioeconomic context of the language in NI to further promote the resurgence of Irish is not inconsiderable. As pointed out elsewhere (Aitchison & Carter, 1987), much of the literature on minority languages, and the case of the Irish language in NI is no exception, is influenced by Hechter's (1975) ideas on 'internal colonisation' and 'the cultural division of labour'. What this means is that groups which are peripheral to the core of any given state are differentiated by such features as religion, culture and language and as a consequence experience differential access to the resources of the state. Because of this view, such groups become disadvantaged and marginalised. This does characterise much of the experience of Irish speakers throughout Ireland during the last century and in NI for much of this century. Several sources (Andrews, 1991; Maguire, 1991; O'Reilly, 1995) point to the indifference, if not hostility, of the state in NI to the Irish language and the subsequent effect on the Irish-speaking population.

The socioeconomic profile of the Irish-speaking community in NI may well confirm this legacy in that Irish speakers are overrepresented in the lowest socioeconomic class, the long-term unemployed. Regarding the potential for the growth and development of the Irish-language community, it is very significant that Irish speakers are overrepresented in the urban-dwelling, well-educated, professional, managerial and technical classes. This profile is confirmed, though not analysed, in the brief exploration of aspects of the SARs pertaining to the 1991 Census in NI by Nic Craith and Shuttleworth (1996).

The appearance of Irish speakers in the higher socioeconomic classes may be explained by turning to the wider socioeconomic context. The historic support of the Irish language in limited sectors of the education system in NI (Andrews, 1991; Pritchard, 1990) is one factor. The recognition by central government of Irish-medium schools (Mac Póilin, 1992; Nic Craith, 1996/7), increasing recognition of the language at the level of local government and the increasing provision of Irish language broadcasting on English-medium radio and television have given significant stimulus to the language. Since 1991 the creation of *Teilifís na Gaeilge* and increasing recognition of Irish-medium education have provided further stimulus. Similar developments in Wales during the 1980s, including the establishment of *Sianel 4 Cymru* (Welsh language television channel) and the passing of a Welsh Language Act, appear to prompt the increasing instrumentality of the Welsh language resulting in the appearance of Welsh speakers in greater proportions in higher socio-economic classes, especially in Cardiff – a transformation described as a 'quiet revolution' (Aitchison & Carter, 1987).

The literacy profile for the Irish speakers recorded in the Census is similar to that for Gwent in south-eastern Wales. This area was an English-speaking part of the country for many generations but has witnessed a rejuvenation of the Welsh language since the 1980s (Aitchison & Carter, 1987). The Euromosaic survey on *Irish in Northern Ireland* suggests that levels of literacy among Irish speakers are 'relatively high' (www.uoc.es/euromosaic) although the figures presented indicate that 52% of respondents recorded themselves as having 'little' ability or 'none' with regard to the reading of Irish, and 57% described themselves as having 'little' ability or 'none' in the writing of the language. Indeed, such a profile contrasts with that of Welsh-speaking populations in traditionally Welsh-speaking parts of Wales in which the language has been transmitted intergenerationally over a very long period. The literacy profile for the Irish-speaking community from the language information currently available would suggest modest levels of literacy, reflecting the recent acquisition of the language on the part of the overwhelming majority of the community and the limited education in Irish for the Irish speakers surveyed in the Euromosaic project. Indeed, other results from the Euromosaic survey confirm that only 4% of the respondents experienced Irish-medium education at primary level, with even smaller proportions at higher levels of education. Considering the growth of the Irish-medium sector during the 1980s and 1990s, one would expect to see greater proportions of the population under 18 years of age experiencing Irish-medium education, and one would expect that the literacy profile in this age group would show greater levels of ability in the reading and writing of Irish.

The growth of the Irish-language community in the region may also be related to increasing levels of awareness of ethnic identity (Maguire, 1991; O'Reilly, 1995). The very low numbers of Protestants recorded as Irish speakers by the 1991 Census and the higher densities of Irish speakers in areas such as west Belfast may be seen as prima facie support to this view. Some authors argue that the recent political history of NI has reinforced awareness of senses of Irish ethnic identity in the region, the Irish language being a very powerful medium for articulating this identity. A parallel may be drawn for this in the Republic of Ireland around the turn of the century where a strong relationship between senses of Irish ethnic identity and the Irish language presaged the political independence of the 26 counties and a violent political landscape.

The relationship between the language and Irish ethnic identity is described by O'Reilly (1995: 14) as:

> the primary symbol of Irish ethnicity, the Irish language has become an important emblem to many Catholics in west Belfast. Under the unique circumstances of partition and the current conflict, it is a marker which distinguishes them from the British and at times from Protestants as well.

O'Reilly suggests (1995: 8) that the prolonged nature of the 'troubles' in NI may well have created the sociological conditions for this more intense sense of ethnic identity. She perceives a close relationship between the language and nationalism, as does Maguire (1991: 99). Pritchard (1990: 30) quotes a survey carried out by *Glór na nGael* in West Belfast during 1984–1985 in which 61% of respondents stated that the H-Block protests of Irish Republican prisoners was the main factor which encouraged them to learn Irish. In another Euromosaic document, *Irish in the North of Ireland*, it is contended that, 'it [NI] is a territory which is subject to different political claims and much of the salience of the Irish language within this area pertains to this contentious issue' (www.uoc.es/euromosaic) and, 'As might be expected given the ideological importance of Irish for those who claim to speak it, links with the Republic of Ireland are strong' (www.uoc.es/euromosaic). Mac Póilin (1996: 158) asserts that:

there is no doubt that political nationalism often provides the stimulus for involvement in the language movement in Northern Ireland, and is in fact, the source of much of the vitality of the present phase of the movement there.

Others (de Baroid, 1990; Jarman, 1993) note that the practice of renaming of streets in Irish in nationalist areas, a practice which dates from the 1980s, is an act of opposition to British rule. During the 1992 British General Election, Proinsias Mac Aonghusa, President of *Conradh na Gaeilge* and Chair of *Bord na Gaeilge* (Irish Language Board), encouraged voters in the constituency of West Belfast to vote for Gerry Adams of *Sinn Féin* (*Anois*, 5 April 1992). A more recent President of *Conradh na Gaeilge*, Gearoid Ó Cairealláin, was noted to have given a triumphalist nationalist speech during the *Ard-Fheis*, the most important event in the calendar of the society being held in Belfast for the first time (*The Irish Times*, 21 May 1996; *Lá*, 23 May 1996). This was despite the explicitly non-political opening speech of John Robb, for example: '*Tá sé in am cuimhneamh go bhfuil an Ghaeilge os cionn na polaitíochta. Déan an Ghaeilge a choinneáil scartha on pholaitíocht náisiúnta agus deanfaidh an teanga an tír a aontú*' (It is time to remember that the Irish language is above politics. Make the Irish language keep clear from nationalist politics and the language will unite the country) (*Lá*, 23 May 1996). Previous British governments would appear to have recognised a link between the language and nationalist politics. On the granting of a substantial grant to Ultach Trust, a Junior Minister remarked that: '[language] has been torn out of the cultural context and has become a political weapon' (*The Irish Times*, 4 April 1991). At the same time, *Glór na nGael* in Belfast lost substantial government funding as it was seen to be: 'improving the standing and furthering the aims of paramilitary groups' (*The Irish Times*, 4 April 1991). In may be in the context of intervention of this nature that many within the Irish language community form their opinions of the nature of the commitment to the Irish-language on the part of the Government in NI. The results of the Euromosaic survey show that most respondents believed that the language was of little interest to the Government; 47% of respondents gave the Government the lowest possible rating. Of the various institutions in this aspect of the survey, the Government was perceived to have the least interest of all in the Irish language.

Despite this, there is a body of evidence which suggests that the case for the ethnic value of the Irish language in Northern Ireland is overstated. Such evidence suggests that relationships between the Irish language and socio-cultural identity possess a higher degree of complexity. For example, research by Northover and Donnelly (1996) among Catholic adult learners of the language shows that their pursuit of the language is not motivated in particular by any enhanced sense of Irish ethnic identity. They note that 'those who do not learn Irish are not essentially different in their self-perception of ethnic identification from learners' (Northover & Donnelly, 1997: 45). Furthermore, the Euromosaic document *Irish in Northern Ireland* notes the following from the survey data derived from the Euromosaic project: 'What is surprising is that a substantial number do not feel that the language makes one "more Irish" than non-speakers. That is, the symbolic value of the language is limited' (www.uoc.es/euromosaic). Most respondents (54%) did not feel that having Irish was essential to being Irish.

A minority (26%) of respondents agreed with the assertion that being able to speak Irish was essential to being Irish. This feature of the Euromosaic dataset seems to have confused the author of this document, something which is clear in the conclusion:

> Irish is one of the symbolic element[s] around which the very close knit, highly politicised community is constituted. Yet as a symbol of being Irish it is by no means universal. This is probably a realistic reflection on the nature of Irish society and of the place of both the language and the respondent in such a society. Being a member of the Irish language community (that is, those selected for interviews) involves not being British much more than it does being able to speak Irish. That is, personal identity is much more highly politicised than it is bound with the embeddedness of language in its symbolic context. Language is only one of the objects around which the notions of Ireland and Irishness is assigned meaning. (www.uoc.es/euromosaic)

The difficulties the author of this document has in interpreting the data from the Euromosaic survey would be surmounted in part by reference to other language surveys on this question in both the Republic of Ireland, and also, on a more modest scale, in NI. The difficulties are compounded by the way in which the idea of national or ethnic identity is perceived by Euromosaic. The survey is clearly grounded in a simplistic bi-polar British-Irish understanding of identity. Five categories of identity were employed in the survey, namely Irish, British, English, European and Other. This range of choices does not appear to be informed by any other social survey of significance. Indeed, the inclusion of the category 'English' is bizarre, especially as the various categories are, according to the document, overlapping to some extent. A broader and more sophisticated conception of national or ethnic identity would have facilitated a clearer understanding of this key issue. Also, there are important structural reasons for the low levels of competence in the Irish language among Protestants, the almost total absence of the language from the curriculum of state schools (hence largely Protestant) made the language greatly inaccessible to Protestants. The exclusion of non-Irish speakers from the Euromosaic survey meant that very little, if any, material was collected during the course of the survey which could reliably inform on attitudes which were representative of the Protestant population in any sense of the word. The relationship between Protestants and non-nationalists and the language is taken as read.

A significant problem arises from an uncritical reading of the significance of the Irish language in the sociocultural landscape of NI and in particular from a failure to move beyond the political rhetoric. That problem is the development of an understanding of the relationship between the Irish language and society as a whole in NI. The societal well-being of the language is naturally in the hands of the whole of the community in NI and a close association between the Irish language and Irish nationalism frustrates an identification by others with the Irish language (Stephens, 1976: 137–8). At the same time, there has been a considered effort on the part of Ultach Trust in particular to ensure the accessibility of the Irish language to the Protestant and Unionist community in NI (Mac Póilin, n.d.; Mistéil, 1994; Ó Snodaigh, 1995). This unresolved issue of the direction of the development of the Irish-language in relation to Irish ethnic identity has given rise to not inconsiderable tension within the Irish language community (Ó Muirí, 1994a, 1994b; Mac an Fhaili, 1994). Considering the full range of evidence in its broadest context, it appears to be useful to distinguish between the Irish language movement on the one hand, which is politicised to a considerable degree, and the Irish-speaking community on the other, it being a diverse and complex phenomenon which confounds many traditional preconceptions in the region.

Language use is another key issue, and it may be explored with reference to the Euromosaic survey and other academic sources. O'Reilly relates the use of the language to the politics of ethnic identity: 'The two functions become entangled in a situation where the language is being actively revived, making it difficult to say where symbolism ends and simple communication begins' (O'Reilly, 1995: 11). Her difficulty may be resolved by accepting that the token manipulation of the language as an ethnic symbol does not constitute language use other than in a political meaning of the term. Maguire moves closer to the substance of the issue. She maintains that it is possible to make use of the Irish language in Belfast in a variety of domains (Maguire, 1991). Some evidence is presented to support her statement that 'it [the Irish language] has been established as a viable medium of communication during everyday interactions in the city (Belfast)' (Maguire, 1991: 230). Her attempt to quantify the extent of use is limited; indeed, her evidence that very limited use is made of the language in the homes of her subjects would encourage one to form a very different conclusion to that which she herself reaches (Maguire, 1991: 117–23).

Other data on language use are available from the Euromosaic survey. The data on language use within the immediate family suggest that 'about 7 per cent use Irish exclusively in the home, while a further 16 per cent use at least some Irish' (www.uoc.es/euromosaic). Only 3% of respondents claimed that Irish was the only language used when communicating with their parents, and a further 4% claimed that Irish was the main language of communication in this relationship. Only 6% of partners used Irish together exclusively while a further 16%, according to the survey, used some Irish in communicating with their partner. The use of language with the children of the household is more extensive: 'about 12% use Irish exclusively with their children, and a further 27% use some Irish with their children' (www.uoc.es/euromosaic). Perceptions of ability within the family suggests a decline in the levels of competency in Irish across three successive generations – grandparents, parents, children.

For the majority of Irish speakers, the use of Irish beyond the home appears to be located within a number of closely defined spheres, in particular sporting and cultural activities, but English and not Irish has normative status. For others, Irish is the main language of a small, close-knit network of Irish speakers. Despite the problems with the way in which the questions related to the data presented in Table 9 in the report in the Euromosaic survey, the results can be used to cast some light on language use among the respondents. The data appear to show that the respondents' use of Irish in the community depended to a great extent on interpersonal knowledge. The language was most used in social interaction in the pub, in children communicating with the teacher and in communicating with the priest and with the local councillor. In contrast, very little use of Irish was noted in relation to state and semi-state organisations or their representatives; for example, 'driving test','water bill', 'department of social security' and 'tax office' all scored zero. Other results indicate that various activities, while they are not conducted entirely through the medium of Irish, provide opportunities for use of Irish, including theatre visits, the church, the Gaelic Athletic Association, choir and drama groups, local politics and the local *Feis* (cultural festival). Also, over a third of respondents listened to Irish language radio broadcasts, and over 40% watched Irish-language television broadcasts. Around 20% regularly read Irish-language books, and a similar proportion read Irish-language newspapers. According to the respondents, Irish-speaking children's activity through the medium of Irish centred largely on educational activities, particularly the local *Feis* and the annual sojourn to the *Gaeltacht* to improve language skills. Various cultural events such as traditional festivals and musical and theatrical events appear to provide a vehicle for some level of bilingual interaction. Sporting events and Sunday school register very low on the scale and are largely English-language experiences.

Besides testing the ethnocentricity of attitudes towards the language, the Euromosaic survey also explored a number of other attitudinal questions. Perceptions of the instrumentality of the Irish language surprised the author of the report in that they were higher than anticipated. Some 21% of respondents claimed that the ability to speak Irish was essential to their work; a further 20% claimed that it was useful to be able to speak Irish in their work. Despite the quite misleading interpretation offered in the report, most respondents (57%) felt that the Irish language was not a dying language and disagreed in large proportions with assertions that the language was not modern (51%), that it was not for the modern world (79%), nor was it for science or business (66%). Most respondents (58%) did not consider Irish to be 'necessary for social mobility' – considering the use of the word 'necessary', it is surprising that the figure was not higher; use of 'advantageous' or 'useful' would have been more revealing. In this respect it is worth noting that most respondents (81%) did not feel that Irish was indicative of a low class.

The results of a 1998 survey are of value in relation to the acquisition of the Irish language, the use of the language and attitudes towards the language (Mac Giolla Chríost, 2001). It would appear to be the case that few respondents acquired Irish as their first language and that, for many, the language was first made accessible to them via the educational system. This is particularly so for younger respondents. Many others of the adult respondents appear to have acquired the language beyond the normal pathways of formal education at any level. The diverse ways in which the language has been acquired is, perhaps, reflected in the modesty of the claims in levels of ability in the language. A minority of Irish speakers return themselves as having better than average ability in the language. These modest levels of ability translate into limited use of the language in very clearly defined networks centring on the immediate family, friends, the school, the church and, for adults, the workplace. Use of the Irish language among young Irish speakers is confined to certain domains. The data indicated that very few households are wholly Irish speaking (Table 16). Only 3.2% indicate that they always use Irish in communication with their parents and only 1.1% always use Irish in communicating with their siblings. In addition to this, 6.3% 'often' use Irish with their parents, and 11.7% claim the same level of usage

Table 16 Percentage of Irish speakers by use of Irish in domestic relationships

Relationship	Extent to which Irish is spoken				
	Never	Seldom	Sometimes	Often	Always
Young people 16–18					
Parents	55	15	21	6	3
Siblings	39	20	28	12	1
Ext. family	58	17	19	6	–
Friends	27	22	34	15	2
Adults 18+					
Parents	72	14	7	5	2
Partner	61	19	16	4	–
Children	36	17	33	9	5
Siblings	66	11	13	7	3
Ext. family	68	15	8	7	2
Friends	47	13	25	10	5

with their siblings. On the other hand, 54.7% 'never' use Irish with their parents, and 39.4% 'never' use Irish with their siblings. Levels of use are slightly lower in contacts with relatives. No young respondents claim to use the language all the time with relatives, and only 6.3% claim to use Irish 'often'; 57.9% 'never' use Irish to communicate with relatives. More use is made of Irish with friends. Only 26.6% claim 'never' to use Irish with their friends; 2.1% 'always' do so, and 14.9% 'often' communicate with their friends in Irish. The results of the survey indicate that the use of the Irish language among adult Irish speakers is limited. Few adult respondents (5.2%) indicate that they 'always' use Irish in communication with their children, and a further 8.6% claim to use the language 'often' in this context; 36.2% 'never' use Irish with their children. Levels of use with children are none-theless greater than levels of use with the older generation. Only 1.8% of adult respondents claim to 'always' use Irish with their parents and a further 5.4% claim to use Irish 'often' in this context. Levels of use are lower still with partners. No adult respondents claim to 'always' use Irish with their partner, and only 7.4% claim to use Irish 'often' in this context. Reported levels of use of Irish on the part of adult respondents with siblings are quite low with 3.3% claiming to 'always' use Irish and 6.5% claiming to use Irish 'often' in this context. Further, 65.6% claim 'never' to use Irish with siblings. The profile of use of Irish with siblings is very similar to that for other relatives of the adult respondents; 68.3% claim 'never' to use Irish, 6.7% claim to 'often' use Irish and 1.7% claim to 'always' use Irish with other relatives. The greatest levels of use of Irish among adult respondents are to be found in relation to friends; 4.9% report that they 'always' use Irish with their friends, and a further 9.8% claim that they 'often' do so.

Among young Irish speakers, the language appears to enjoy frequent use in relation to school (Table 17). Only 20.4% claim 'never' to use Irish in school in contrast to 39.8% doing so 'often' or 'always'. The language is used less often in

Table 17 Percentage of Irish speakers by use of Irish in public settings

Public setting	Extent to which Irish is spoken				
	Never	*Seldom*	*Sometimes*	*Often*	*Always*
Young people 16–18					
Church	47	16	26	8	3
Banks	95	3	2	–	–
Shops	63	24	12	1	–
Disco/Club	74	7	9	8	2
School	20	10	30	38	2
Adults 18+					
Church	64	13	15	5	3
Banks	90	3	7	–	–
Shops	71	19	10	–	–
Place of work	66	12	9	9	4
School	62	8	13	12	5
Council	88	7	3	1	–

Table 18 Percentage of Irish speakers by use of Irish language media

Medium	Extent to which Irish is spoken				
	Never	*Seldom*	*Sometimes*	*Often*	*Always*
Young people 16–18					
Mag/Paper	38	21	21	13	7
Book	39	15	27	11	8
Radio	37	23	18	11	11
TV	15	13	40	18	14
Society	63	13	13	7	4
Adults 18+					
Mag/Paper	42	23	16	6	13
Book	42	27	15	5	11
Radio	39	14	16	13	18
TV	26	16	30	13	15
Society	57	13	16	6	8

other contexts beyond the school; 73.9% 'never' use Irish in discos or clubs, and 63.4% 'never' use Irish in shops. Use of the language is slightly more prevalent in relation to the church with 10.8% using Irish 'often' or 'always' in the church, and 47.3% 'never' make use of the language in church; 11.0% of young Irish speakers claim to attend an Irish-language club or society either 'often' or 'very often' (Table 18). Passive use of the Irish language is significant (Table 18); 19.4% of young Irish speakers read an Irish book and magazine 'often' or 'very often'; 21.7% listen to Irish medium radio broadcasts 'often' or 'very often', and 32.2% watch Irish medium television broadcasts 'often' or 'very often'. Use of the language beyond personal relationships by adult speakers varies according to the domain. The highest levels of use are to be found in relation to school, with 4.9% 'always' using Irish and 11.5% 'often' using Irish. Similar levels of use are to be found in relation to the place of work; 5.2% report that they 'always' use Irish in their place of work. A further 8.6% report that they 'often' do so. Slightly lower levels of use are reported in relation to the church; 3.3% of adult respondents claim to 'always' use Irish, and 5% 'often' do so. Levels of use with the council, shops and banks are significantly lower with overwhelming majorities claiming to 'never' to use Irish – 88.1%, 71% and 90.2% respectively (Table 17). Levels of participation in Irish-medium activities are modest with 14.5% of adult respondents frequenting an Irish-language club or society 'often' or 'very often', while 56.5% 'never' do so. The survey results indicate that some of the more passive language activities are enjoyed by a significant minority of adult Irish speakers; 16.1% of adult Irish speakers read Irish-language books 'often' or 'very often', and 19.4% read Irish language newspapers or magazines. Additionally, 30.6% listen to Irish-language radio broadcasts 'often' or 'very often', and 27.4% watch Irish language television broadcasts 'often' or 'very often' (Table 18).

In addition to issues regarding language use, the 1998 (Mac Giolla Chríost, 2001) survey yields information which touches upon a range of attitudinal matters. For example, among younger respondents, perceptions of the nature of the Irish-speaking community vary according to senses of ethnic and religious identity and whether they speak Irish or not. British-identifiers, Protestants and non-Irish speakers are more conservative than other respondents in their measure of the extent of the Irish-speaking community and its likely growth. Younger respondents of all types are supportive of the language in general terms and would seek its maintenance though not to the extent of attempting to shape a bilingual society of any sort in NI. Attitudes among younger respondents in relation to the language in political context vary according to a number of factors. While respondents of all types agree that there is too much politics in the language in NI, Irish, Northern Irish-identifiers, Irish speakers and, to a lesser extent, Catholics are more likely to contend that the Government does not do enough for the language and that the place of the Irish language in school curricula should be broadened. The views of younger respondents of all types concur in rejecting the idea of being Irish-speaking as offering a more authentic sense of Irishness. Irish and Northern Irish-identifiers, Catholics and Irish speakers are clear in their belief that the Irish language belongs to all the people of NI and that the language is a part of their cultural identity and tradition. The attitudes of British-identifiers, Protestants and non-Irish speakers are much more ambiguous. Many respondents in these categories agree that the language does belong to all the people of NI. Many Protestants identify with the language as a part of their cultural identity and heritage as well. The clearest rejection of the latter concept is amongst young British-identifiers and non-Irish speakers, although significant minorities in these categories also express such an identification with the language.

The attitudes of adult respondents tend to be more complex than those of younger respondents. Additional factors, such as gender, occupation and education, play a greater role. There is very little variation among adult respondents with regard to perceptions of the extent and growth of the Irish-speaking community. One variation of note is that respondents with lower levels of education tend to believe most strongly of all in the likely future growth of the Irish-speaking community. Respondents of all types are in agreement as to the value of the Irish language in general terms and are convinced of the necessity of its preservation. Some variation is to be found with regard to the development of a bilingual society in NI. Only among female respondents is there a majority in favour of bilingualism and that with English as the main language. Irish-identifiers, Irish speakers and respondents with a professional occupation are more likely to concur in this than are respondents of any other type, though only to a small degree. Those with a managerial occupation are clearest in their opposition to such developments.

Identifications with the language among adults vary according to senses of ethnic and religious identity, gender, occupation and highest academic qualification (HAQ). Most respondents of all types agree in their rejection of the idea of Irish-speaking being necessary to an authentic sense of Irish identity. Irish-identifiers, Northern Irish-identifiers, and Catholics are more likely to agree that the Irish language belongs to all the people of NI than are British-identifiers and Protestants. Respondents with the latter two characteristics are much more ambiguous in relation to this issue, with substantial proportions in agreement and also in disagreement with the proposition. Female respondents are most assertive of all in their very strong levels of agreement that the language belongs to all in NI. Attitudes towards the language as a feature of cultural identity and heritage are more clear cut in relation to senses of ethnic and religious identity. Irish-identifiers, Northern Irish-identifiers and Catholics firmly identify with the language in this way while British-identifiers and Protestants tend to reject this notion. Further variation on this issue is to be found in relation to gender, occupation and HAQ. Females are more likely than males to identify with the language as a part of their cultural identity. Respondents with a professional occupation or in the lower occupation groups are also more likely to concur in this than are respondents with other occupations. Similarly, respondents with the highest and lowest levels of education are more likely to concur than are those with middle levels of education.

Before moving on to discuss some matters relating to language policy and planning it is pertinent to indicate the very limited nature of the structural support for the Irish language in the region in those domains not already touched upon. In a recent overview (Ó Murchú, 1999) of the Irish language in both the Republic of Ireland and Northern Ireland, the domains of education and, to a lesser degree, the arts and culture are underlined as providing more support to the language, relative to other areas of activity. For example, it is noted that 13 primary schools and two postprimary schools are supported by the state. The total number of pupils attending these schools is less than 2000 (Ó Murchú, 1999: 23). It is also noted that the Irish language is taught as a subject in many other schools in the region. With regard to the arts and culture, it is noted that the Northern Ireland Arts Council supported a range of Irish language activities during the period 1998–1999. This included musical events, community festivals, activities of cultural centres, theatre groups and literary activities. Total expenditure was in the order of £132,700 (Ó Murchú, 1999: 37).

Some Considerations for Language Policy and Planning in Northern Ireland

The formulation, implementation and evolution of a comprehensive and successful language policy needs to be informed by reliable and robust insights into these issues of language knowledge, use and attitude, while recognising that the complex cultural matrix of NI makes for difficulties in doing so. The language-driven ethnic congruencies and the potential the language possesses for transcending the divisions which are at the heart of the conflict in NI are of significance to practical matters of Irish language policy and planning in the region. The translation of the commitments to the Irish language in the articles of the political agreement in NI into policy and practice is a critically sensitive issue in the region. In October 2000, David Trimble, leader of the Ulster Unionist Party, described language matters as 'a political battleground' (*The Irish Times* 7 October 2000). It is argued here that some of the results of this study, indicating a potential role for the Irish language in achieving conflict resolution, could usefully inform and even guide political discourse on language matters. In doing so, the language may be located within a policy framework which would facilitate the realisation of this potential. In working towards this goal, Haarmann's view of language and ethnicity in a network of ecological relations and, in particular, the basic model of ecological relations (Haarmann, 1986) is employed as the framework in which the significance of the results with regard to language policy and planning is measured. This allows for the highlighting of those features of Irish in NI which are of greatest relevance to this purpose.

The discussion, at this point, is moved beyond theory and into application through a close analysis of the nascent institutional framework in NI. One of the newly created institutions resulting from the political settlement in NI, the implementation agency, the North/South Language Body (*An Foras Teanga*), is highlighted as a body with a pivotal role to play in the short to medium term for the Irish language in the region. The multilevelled and consociational features of the dynamics of *An Foras Teanga* are highlighted as features which may serve to ensure that language issues do not become ensnared in broader political concerns. It is also argued that the successful management of the politics of the Irish language must be coupled with the effective delivery of policy at local levels. This is critically analysed with regard to the Welsh model of *Mentrau Iaith* (Language Initiatives). It is suggested that a similar strategy could be adopted in NI and that such *Fiontair Teanga* (Language Initiatives) would succeed in realising the positive engagement between the new regional institutions of government in NI and local Irish-speaking communities.

The Irish language in a network of ecological relations: Variables for planning

It is to be understood from Haarmann that intervention in the field of language planning will be more effective if the ecology of the language to be the subject of this planning is understood. One is confronted by some limitations in seeking to accomplish this. Haarmann (1986: vii, 257), for example, recognises that his treatment of some pertinent issues is not definitive and that the model of ecological relations requires further elaboration. Also, the empirical evidence relating to the Irish language in social context in NI upon which one might rely is not as comprehensive as one would wish it to be. That said, it is possible to identify a number of ecolinguistic variables which require the careful attention of policy makers and planning agencies. These are outlined according to the categories defined by Haarmann (1986: 11–16).

Ethnodemographic variables

In the first place, it is clear that the Irish-speaking community is of a modest size. The results of this study suggest that the functional Irish-speaking community is much smaller than the total number of Irish speakers identified in the NI Census of 1991, or for that matter the Census of 2001. The data on levels of ability in speaking Irish indicate that about 33% of adults and about 37% of young people claim better than average ability. If such levels of ability can be taken to mean that such respondents are functional Irish speakers, and if this survey is taken to be representative of the Irish speakers of NI as a whole, it gives a body of functional Irish speakers of the order of 40,000 to 45,000, with some 13,000 to 15,000 (about 10% of the Census population of Irish speakers) possessing fluency in the full range of language skills. The analysis of the 1991 Census data shows that this modest Irish-speaking community is dispersed across NI. Although fragmented, this Irish-speaking community is characterised by a number of emergent cores of Irish speakers that can be identified in a number of locations in the region. The urban centres of Belfast and Derry and the more rural locations of the areas of Dungannon, Magherafelt and Newry and Mourne all contain relatively high concentrations of Irish speakers, commonly constituting over 30% of the total population in some parts. The ethnic heterogeneity of NI does not facilitate the transcending of this fragmentation as the ethnic mosaic which is NI means that local Irish-speaking communities and networks are largely confined within small, clearly defined sociopolitical enclaves. The results of this survey also indicate that actual use of the Irish language is limited to closely defined and personally immediate networks of Irish speakers. Key tasks must focus on increasing the size of the functional Irish-speaking community by improving the language skills of those who claim some proficiency in the language and also by gaining greater numbers of newcomers to the language from across traditional ethnic and sociopolitical divides, where levels of goodwill exist. The diffuse geography of the Irish-speaking communities in NI suggests that local, community-based language planning activities would be more effective than a regional, macro approach to intervention in the field.

Ethnosociological variables

The historical fact of the segmented cultural division of labour in Ireland (Hechter, 1975) and the inimical attitude of the Unionist-dominated Stormont Government towards the Irish language in NI (Andrews, 1997) are major factors in shaping the contemporary condition of the language in the region. In the light of this, the preponderance of Irish speakers in certain of the higher socioeconomic classes is a phenomenon of significance. This preponderance would indicate that the language, despite perceptions (especially amongst Protestants and young non-Irish speakers according to the results of this study), possesses some instrumental value. The over-representation of Irish speakers in the very lowest socioeconomic class as well suggests a polarity of experience within the Irish-speaking community. Although this polarity of experience does not appear to inform negative perceptions of the instrumentality of the Irish language, it does appear to be the case that perceptions of linguistic instrumentality are cross-cut by socioeconomic status. It is in the lower and in the top socio-economic classes that the most affirmative responses to the instrumentality of the language are to be found. The results also show that adult females are significantly more persuaded of the instrumentality of Irish than are their male peers. Gender appears to be a factor of wider significance in understanding the nature of the Irish-speaking community in the region. The greater representation of females than males in this survey reflects a pattern noted in the 1991 Census data that females are more likely to be actively engaged in language matters than are males. The greater involvement of females in the language will be critical in strengthening the reproduction of the language in the domain of the home. The results of this survey also suggested that females were generally more optimistic regarding the future prospects of the language and were keener to see greater levels of government intervention in the field and a more substantial presence for the language in the education system. Adult females were also more prepared to see the further politicisation of language issues. A further issue is the low level of intermarriage between Catholics and Protestants in NI. This phenomenon is an important factor in preventing greater levels of inter-group empathy in the region (Whyte, 1986) and is also another contributory factor to the more limited development of the Irish language among Protestants, as the results of the survey show that the intergenerational transference of the language as the first language in NI exists to some extent among Catholics but not among Protestants.

Ethnopolitical variables

The most important factor in this context is the partial autonomy which has been devolved to NI and is characterised by a consociational sharing of political power by the various political parties from across the ethnic divides in the region. A feature of the recent sociopolitical conflict in NI has been the marked alienation of many sections of the population from the various institutions of government. The myriad of sociopolitical relationships between individual, group, society and state in the region have the potential to be transformed as a result of this recent political settlement, and it is certain that the Irish-speaking community will also feel the weight of these changes to political culture as the range of new institutions is shaped to better reflect the diversity of aspirations and identities in NI. The results of the survey reveal a complexity of attitudes towards the role of government in language issues and the embedding of the Irish language in society in NI. There is some evidence that considerable polaris-ation exists regarding the desired extent and nature of government intervention in this field and that this polarisation conforms to the archetypal divisions in the region. There is other evidence again that suggests broad levels of support and attachment to the Irish language which confounds these traditional cleavages and, where polarisation is manifest, it centres on points of detail in relation to possible government policy and intervention in particular. The unfolding political framework will be critical in shaping the institutional status of the Irish language and in reinforcing the reproduction potential of the language. Commitments made as part of the political settlement in NI to extending administrative usage of Irish and to the funding of Irish-medium education will, if fulfilled, raise the status of the language in the region. Policy and planning initiatives should be proactive in this process of transformation as many individuals from across the traditional sociopolitical cleavages in NI make various positive identifications with the Irish language. *An Foras Teanga* will be of central importance in this regard and also in approaching the increasingly pressing issue of language rights. In attempting successfully to achieve the overarching language policy and planning goals, *An Foras Teanga* will have to engage with the local Irish-speaking communities, the critical nodes in the Irish-speaking network which have been identified in this study.

Ethnocultural variables

The two main ethnic groups in NI, the Irish and the British, can be distinguished because of their specific cultural traditions. Despite differences in ethnocultural patterns, the social distance (Haarmann, 1986: 14) between the two groups is not strong in some key areas, and the most important of these is the Irish language. The historical overview, which comprised the opening section of this study, as well as the results of this survey, show that many from various groups positively engaged with the language in the past and that many from the two ethnic groups currently make positive identifications with the language. The Irish language is an important vehicle for cultural exchange in interethnic contact in NI. The promotion of the interests of the Irish language and of the Irish-speaking community requires that the cultural and political organisations which take upon themselves such a role be informed by the full range of identifications which are made with the language. The *ausbau* status of the Irish language is also of some relevance in this context as some Unionists are attracted to the Ulster dialect of the language (*Let's Talk* 23 June 1998, BBC2 NI). The management of the identity of the Ulster form of Irish is a key task. This might include promotional and/or educational campaigns, or perhaps the production of teaching materials, especially for adult learners of Irish, which are in the Ulster dialect and reflect the plural identity of Ulster and NI.

Ethnopsychological variables

Haarmann (1986: 26) points out that the ethnopsychological variables which affect group behaviour can only be detected indirectly. Factors of this nature and their potential influence can be read in relation to the results of this survey regarding issues of attitude and in particular the perceptions of ethnic group ownership of the Irish language. The results show that attitudes towards this issue are immensely complex. According to Irish nationalist rhetoric, the language is central to definitions of being Irish. Attitudes towards the language among Unionist British-identifiers are also filtered through various categorisations and identifications which, for many of them, are grounded in assumptions that conform with traditional Irish nationalist views on the language. Yet, the majority of the respondents in the survey, including Irish speakers, did not regard being Irish speaking as constituting an enhanced sense of being Irish. In some contexts, this might be seen as something which weakens the vitality of a language, but in the immediate post-conflict situation in NI this is a potentially useful feature of the language. Too close an identification with a particular ethnic group alienates other ethnic-group members from the language. It is a strength of the language that it authenticates a range of senses of group identity in NI, albeit differentially. This strength could be nurtured. The maintenance of the language should be seen as a measure of the vigour of the new forms of non-inimical ethnic interaction. Exceptionally, two sections of the survey population – adult females and Irish speakers who claimed the highest levels of ability in the language – were more likely than any other section to assert the view that speaking Irish made one more Irish. The ethnopsychological factors implicated in the dynamics of interethnic group relations in this study are informed in part by a very public discourse on language–identity relationships which conforms to the traditional sociopolitical rhetoric in NI, but at a deeper level a very significant range of nuances in attitude which confound the sociopolitical stereotypes of this discourse may be discerned.

Interactional variables

The Irish language has a very low public presence. The broadening of this presence has been frustrated, in part, by a legislative framework which, while designed to protect against discrimination on the grounds of religious belief or political opinion, is not appropriately sophisticated for effective application to language matters. Certain ethnopolitical variables may well have a substantial positive impact on this state of affairs. Government commitments on the Irish language in education, the media and administration, made as a part of the recent political settlement in NI, promise as much. There is some scope for extending the public presence of the Irish language. Intervention on behalf of the Irish language in public domains, however, must be an initiative which commands the support of the Assembly in NI as the results clearly indicate some sensitivities on this issue among certain sections of the population, largely Protestant, British-identifying and of low/mid socioeconomic status. The available data indicate that certain types of intervention are more likely to be acceptable and desirable than others. A public profile for the language in the day-to-day affairs of the Assembly itself could serve to facilitate the extension of the Irish language beyond its present almost complete restriction to domestic and private domains. It is clear from the evidence that, within the latter domains, the use of the language is largely confined to tightly defined and personalised networks of Irish speakers. Effective intervention at this level requires that local Irish-speaking communities take ownership of language policy and planning via agencies which are both based in and led by local communities.

Ethnolinguistic variables

A number of language-specific characteristics come into play as factors in the ecology of the Irish language in NI. Linguistic distance (Haarmann, 1986: 15) is a factor of some influence. The relative distances between the Irish, English and Ulster-Scots languages in NI variously affect the status of Irish and Ulster-Scots. The relatively short distance between English and Ulster-Scots causes many not to recognise the latter as a language at all, but to regard it as a degenerate variation of English. The relatively large distance between Irish and English means that it is easily recognised as a distinct form of language. Some useful work has been completed by Maguire (1991) on other language-specific characteristics. Maguire shows that the Irish language as spoken in west Belfast is very heavily influenced by English-language vocabulary and syntax. This feature of the Irish language as spoken in NI has made it vulnerable to politically motivated attacks on the purported revived and artificial nature of the Irish-speaking community in NI. The very low public profile of native speakers of Irish in the region – that is, of Irish as a first language – serves only to reinforce this vulnerability. Increasing interaction with the extensive pool of native Irish speakers in the Ulster *Gaeltacht* of Donegal could help to address this. The varied levels of competency in the range of language skills among Irish speakers is also a factor in understanding the condition of the Irish language in NI. In this study, the literacy profile of the Irish-speaking population is shown to compare with that of other regions in which very long-term language shift appears to be being reversed.

Regional policy issues: *An Foras Teanga*

It is obvious that the emergent institutional framework is of central importance to the prospects of the Irish language in NI in the short to medium term. Mac Póilin (1998), writing in the period following the signing of The Agreement and prior to the drawing together of The Implementation Bodies Agreement, was concerned that the Irish language would be drawn into the political landscape in such a way that it would serve merely to reinforce traditional political tensions. Similar views were also voiced by the representatives of Ultach Trust in the semi-structured interview with the organisation conducted as a part of the fieldwork for this study. The representatives of Ultach Trust were keen to underline the inclusive nature of both their board of trustees and the mission statement of the organisation itself. At this time it was feared that the Irish and the Ulster-Scots languages would be written into a new framework as Nationalist and Unionist sops respectively. The potential for the specific translation of the broader sociopolitical conflict in the region into domains of culture was first highlighted by Miller (1994: 74–9). He noted the origins of such a shift in the late 1980s in relation to the work of the Community Relations Council. Summarising his line of argument very briefly, it appeared that the simple structuring of core cultural values in the institutional framework for the two main cultural traditions in NI would serve merely to reinforce the political divide, as political representatives of the two traditions set crude measures of government support for their communities through the support given to project bids from cultural activists within their electorate. The solution, as Miller saw it, lay in addressing issues of power: 'In the community relations approach all cultures are equal; in reality, some cultures are more equal than others' (Miller, 1994: 76). A recognition of this reality sidesteps simplistic readings of parity of esteem. The fact of the incorporation of both languages into the legislative framework communicates the parity of esteem afforded to them both in general terms, but the broader remit for the Irish language reflects the greater awareness of the Irish language across society as a whole in NI and also the recent historical pressure in favour of the language in certain key domains.

Under The Implementation Bodies Agreement, a cross-border implementation body for language, known as The North-South Language Body (in Irish *An*

Foras Teanga, in Ulster-Scots *Tha Boord o Leid*) is to be established (NIO, 1999: Article 1). Two separate parts of this body, in a consociational coupling, have the function of serving the interests of the two languages. The remit for the Irish language includes the promotion of the language in general, encouraging, facilitating and advising upon the use of the language in private and public domains, supporting Irish-medium education and undertaking research and the development of corpus status. This is clearly set in the context of Part III of the European Charter for Regional or Minority Languages (NIO, 1999: Part 5). The remit for Ulster-Scots is much narrower, being confined to the 'promotion of greater awareness of the use of Ullans and of Ulster-Scots cultural issues, both within NI and throughout the island' (NIO, 1999: Part 5). The necessity of such action is reflected in the low status of Ulster-Scots and in the ambiguity surrounding its status as a distinct form of language at all (Mac Póilin, 1998). This has remained the case despite activity to promote the language including the publication of an Ulster dialect dictionary (Macafee, 1996) and the occasional polemical piece in Unionist newspapers (e.g. *The Belfast Telegraph*, 28 July 2000).

The sections of the act entitled 'Exercise of Functions and Structures' are critical in understanding the dynamics of *An Foras Teanga*. Two distinct agencies of the body will service the needs of the two languages. Sixteen members with a perceived interest in the Irish language will be appointed to the board of *An Foras Teanga* by the North-South Ministerial Council (NSMC), the body with overall responsibility for the range of cross-border implementation bodies. These members will exercise the functions of the Irish language agency, and a chairperson for the agency will be appointed by the NSMC from among their number. The other eight members of the board of *An Foras Teanga* will be similarly appointed, in this case due to their perceived interest in the affairs of Ulster-Scots. These eight members will include a chairperson for the Ulster-Scots agency. The two co-chairpersons will serve jointly as Chairpersons of *An Foras Teanga*.

The institutional suture in which the two languages find themselves is likely to serve to foster greater cooperation between representatives of the two languages and to arrest the potential for competition between these groups, thereby decreasing the vulnerability of both of the languages to inimical political interest. Favell and Martiniello, in a discussion of the governance of Brussels, highlight some of the possibilities in such systems. The inherent advantage of consociationalism is described as follows:

> Whilst the consociational elements of Belgian politics perpetuate a situation of permanent 'crisis' and potential gridlock between two rival linguistic communities, it also ensures that progress is only made at the mutual benefit of both parties and is never zero-sum (Favell & Martiniello, 1999: 9–10).

The potential risk of the complete internalisation within elite organisations of decision-making and the resultant distancing from popular participation is a matter of concern. The multi-levelled features of the new institutional framework for NI have a role to play in addressing this concern. These features include the NI Assembly, the North-South Implementation Bodies, the NSMC and the British-Irish Council functioning in relation to each other and also in relation to other existing local polities such as City and District Councils. For *An Foras Teanga*, the translation of macro policy on the Irish language to micro levels across NI requires that a local hurdle be overcome on the measurement of local aspirations and sensitivities. That said, it is in such a complex interlocking and overlapping of powers and competencies that Favell and Martiniello see further opportunities:

> Producing different kinds of access points for actors and the expression of interests, which also widen the potential forms of interest representation and aggregation, enabling new forms of non-traditional and unconventional political activity to find a place and take root (Favell & Martiniello, 1999: 9).

Thus, those promoting the interests of Ulster-Scots could forge energising linkages with the Scots language community in Scotland. Likewise, the dynamics of the Irish-speaking community in NI could be informed by conceptions of an island-wide language community characterised by regional and local variations in the nature of the different Irish-speaking communities in NI and in the Republic of Ireland and also within and outside the *Gaeltacht*. Such structures would also constitute a useful vehicle for the operation of informed connections with Celtic-speaking communities elsewhere in the UK, and in this way language planners at micro levels in Ireland could fashion dynamic synergies with their peers in other parts of the Celtic UK. More importantly, the development of community-based planning initiatives in the Irish language, akin to the *Mentrau Iaith* of Wales, could form an integral part of such synergies.

A matter of concern remains regarding the momentum of change in this critical field in NI. On the announcement of the Implementation Bodies Agreement, British government sources noted that 'the commitments in the Agreement in relation to economic, social and cultural issues, including as regards the Irish language, are being carried forward, though much of this work is inevitably long term' (BBC Online Network < http://bbc.co.uk >, 1 April 1999). The idea of 'long term' contains within it the prospects of little happening in the short to medium term, and it is within this timescale that the new institutions and the political settlement will be seen to work, or otherwise. The continuing procrastination on the part of the British Government on the signing of the European Charter is indicative of this telescoping of implementation (*The Irish Times*, 19 May 1999). The Irish language must be positively and immediately embedded in the institutional framework as an integral and animated feature of the implementation process in order to realise its potential in facilitating the resolution of the conflict in NI. Policy commitments must have an impact on the place of the Irish language in society in NI in general terms and also on the Irish-speaking community in the various parts of the region from the outset.

The hesitations of the British Government, despite its commitment to promote the Irish language generally through 'resolute action' and also to 'seek to remove, where possible, restrictions which would discourage or work against maintenance or development of the language', indicate uncertainty in the realisation of policy at a practical level. This view on the position of the Government with regards to Irish-language matters finds reinforcement in information derived from the semi-structured interview with the CCRU. On this occasion the representative, a civil servant, was unable to describe the implementation stage with much clarity of vision or purpose. In contrast, the process by which the commitments to the language were arrived at was outlined with considerable confidence. The uncertainty appears to be related to concerns regarding attitudes towards the Irish language across the community in NI. In The Agreement, the Government undertakes to encourage the commitments to the language to be met 'where appropriate and where people so desire it' and that actions in this field be measured according to 'desires and sensitivities of the community'. Recent difficulties, prior to the political settlement, have turned on the matter of the Irish language in the public domain, and in the workplace in particular.

According to Ruane and Todd (1996: 194–5, 202–3), the contestation of public space is deeply embedded in NI. They suggest that the historical experiences of conquest and colonisation have submerged native Irish cultural signifiers; for example, place names once Gaelic are now anglicised. Because of this, Nationalists are obliged to excavate, metaphorically, the cultural landscape in order to trace their sense of national identity in its structure and symbols. Unionists, due to their geographic location in Ireland, are determined that the public sphere should appear and feel British and that this includes, among other things, the exclusion of the Irish-language. Some (Capita, 1997) suggest that the Irish language functions in the public sphere to discriminate against members of the community in NI who are from Unionist and Protestant backgrounds. As a result, the language has fallen foul of the Fair Employment (NI) Act 1989. The argument runs that, on encountering Irish-language signs in public places, some feel uncomfortable to the extent that they experience a 'chill factor'. This term is defined by the Fair Employment Code of Practice as a 'problem of attitude' arising from which individuals from certain backgrounds are discouraged or even prevented from seeking and gaining employment with a company which appears to be associated with a particular other form of religious or political identity (DED, 1989: 2). The ongoing situation in the Students' Union building in The Queen's University, Belfast, arises from the coincidence of the underrepresentation of Protestants on the workforce within the Students' Union and the public presence of Irish-language signs in the same building. Under the Fair Employment in Northern Ireland Code of Practice (1989) certain symbols and emblems can and do cause offence, amounting to actual discrimination on the grounds of religious belief and/or political opinion. It is in this respect, as a symbol of religious belief and/or political opinion, that the Irish language in public domains runs contrary to the legislative framework.

Recent research (Scullion, 1999) indicates something of the nature of this problem of attitudes which underlies this issue. Employees from a range of socioeconomic classes and from across the community as a whole were surveyed in their workplaces in the Dungannon area of Northern Ireland in the period immediately following the elections to the NI Assembly. In general terms, the data

Table 19 Attitudes towards English–Irish bilingualism in public domains, NI, 1998

Field in the public domain	Level of support among Catholics (%)	Level of support among Protestants (%)
Personal	90	63
General environment	72.5	30
Workplace	60	13

suggest a broad level of support for increased use of the Irish language in various fields within the public domain throughout NI. Among Protestant respondents, support is high, at over 63%, for bilingual (English–Irish) facilities which do not have an immediate and clear visual impact, such as application forms, etc. This support declines to 30% with regard to bilingualism of a greater public profile, such as signage in public places. Only a small minority of Protestant respondents, 13%, were in favour of significant levels of bilingualism within their workplace. Levels of support for the same were much higher in all cases among the Catholics surveyed (Table 19). The nature of these findings is broadly reflected in further research (PERU, 2001).

Also according to the survey, attitudes towards the Irish language amongst Protestants are cross-cut by socioeconomic factors. Protestants at the top and bottom ends of the socioeconomic scale are very much closer to their Catholic peers in their attitudes towards the language. The greatest and sharpest division, tending towards polarisation, occurs among respondents with managerial and skilled occupations and also among those educated to GCE 'A' level or its equivalent (NI Census Highest Academic Qualification level 3). This division is at its clearest in the 34–41 age group. The small size of this survey (71 questionnaires) limits the broader significance of the data, but they are nonetheless suggestive of some of the complexity of attitudes towards the Irish language. Read solely as a symbol of Nationalist political ideology (O'Reilly, 1996), the language is rendered vulnerable to the tensions which underscore the divisions within society in NI and are at the heart of cases of discrimination on the grounds of religious belief and political opinion. The results of this work suggest that the Irish language merits, prima facie, a more inclusive reading in relation to such issues. The successful implementation of policy requires the facilitating of linguistic pluralism within harmonious working environments. The delivery of the commitments to the Irish language at local levels is likely to be further frustrated if the Fair Employment (NI) Act (1989) continues to be deployed in this manner when clearly this piece of legislation is not wholly adequate for dealing with such language issues in an appropriately sophisticated manner.

The research commissioned by the Linguistic Diversity Branch within the Department of Culture, Arts and Leisure (PERU, 2001) on the matter of establishing demand for services and activities in the Irish language in NI may be viewed as a potential point of departure from such restrictive interpretations of the legislative framework and the provision of public services according to language choice. In this report an attempt is made to define what could be held to constitute reasonable demand with regard to the Irish language and public services. Four particular perspectives are explored comprising the following different views:

- that those who speak Irish have a fundamental right to services;
- that there is an unanswerable case for strong and well-resourced support for the Irish language;
- that there are a number of language groups who must be taken account of with regard to the delivery of public services;
- that there is no need for public offices to have any special regard for any minority language.

The report indicates very little common ground between public officials, on the one hand, and Irish speakers, on the other. Unfortunately, the report does not venture beyond the descriptive and does not offer firm recommendations with regard to policy development and implementation. Filling this policy tools gap is a major problem for language issues in NI. This is likely to feature the development of a policy approach similar to the Irish Action Plans adopted by public authorities in the Republic of Ireland or the Welsh Language Schemes adopted by public authorities in Wales. Through a similar such tool:

- the Irish language would be situated in public services in NI with regard to the corporate identity of public authorities;
- methods would provide for dealing with correspondence, meetings and other contact with Irish speakers;
- staffing needs would be defined; and
- requirements for the translation of documents as well as the relationship between the language and other policies, strategies and initiatives pursued by public authorities would be defined (Mac Giolla Chríost, 2003).

The effective development of policy processes and the realisation of culture change in large-scale public organisations with regard to language issues can only be realised over the medium term; the case of Wales, for example, tells us as much. For the Irish language in NI, therefore, it is likely to be of more immediate value to focus resources upon community-based activity where the language is already experiencing some renewed vigour. That said, community-based activity also requires a strategic framework if the investment of public resources is to be cost-effective. It is to such a framework that attention is focused next.

Local policy issues: *Fiontair Teanga*

The evidence suggests that the Irish language is beginning to take root in a number of locations in NI. These emergent Irish-speaking cores require careful cultivation if the language is to prosper in the region. A key task for *An Foras Teanga* will be to see through the implementation of the broad commitments of the political settlement in NI while ensuring that this has a real impact at local levels in the region. The translation of macro policy to micro levels is a difficult affair in most systems of government, and in the context of the resolution of the conflict in NI, this is likely to be even more the case. Indeed, some of the results presented in this monograph indicate that the successful attainment of policy goals will require a sophisticated and informed engagement with the community. It is clear that there exists a broad, cross-community platform of goodwill towards the language in a general sense. It is equally clear that, beyond this, attitudes are more varied on a range of specific issues. The bridging of this gap between macro and micro levels is a critical issue.

Community-based initiatives in the Irish language, or *Fiontair Teanga*, akin to the *Mentrau Iaith* of Wales, could be a part of the answer to this problem. These *Fiontair Teanga* would serve the enabling of broad policy commitments to local levels in a manner similar to the *Mentrau Iaith*. The geographical analysis of the Irish-speaking community derived from the Census data of 1991 highlights a number of locations in NI in which *Fiontair Teanga* could function most effectively. These locations are characterised by proportions of Irish speakers rising from 20% to over 50% of the local population in parts of the locality. They include the cities of Belfast and Londonderry and the rural areas of Newry and Mourne LGD and Dungannon LGD. Omagh LGD and Moyle LGD also appear to offer contexts in which an Irish-language initiative could usefully function. That is not to say that such initiatives might not be successfully established in other parts of the region – merely that these are the locations for which the strongest cases can be made.

The strength of the *Mentrau Iaith* in Wales lies in the fact that they are community-based initiatives which have originated in, and evolved according to, the desire of local people to see an increase in the use of Welsh in their local community. *Mentrau Iaith* are engaged in a holistic form of language planning at micro levels. For example, they offer advice and support relating to the use of the language to the public, and to private and voluntary organisations. They also ensure opportunities for people, especially children and young people, to socialise through the medium of Welsh. They also provide services in developing projects for tourists, for non-Welsh speakers and for Welsh learners. By 2000, there was a network of 20 *Mentrau Iaith* across Wales, financed by the Welsh Language Board, local authorities, National Lottery charities, European funds and other sources (*Bwrdd yr Iaith Gymraeg*, 1999).

A great advantage of the *Mentrau Iaith* is their flexibility. There is no single model; each *Menter Iaith* reflects its local situation and responds to the social and language needs of its local community. According to Williams and Evas (1997), in proffering advice to the Welsh Language Board, the main reasons for supporting *Mentrau Iaith* in the Welsh context are as follows:

> In situations which are characterised by strong language potential but weak socio-linguistic networks, they offer a significant socio-psychological fillip for maintaining the Welsh language in contexts which would otherwise lead to fragmentation ... In respect of their remit as local language planning bodies, they can function as a focus to create a new set of partnerships between the central government (in the form of the Welsh Office), the Welsh Language Board, local government, statutory public bodies, health trusts and a variety of other voluntary agencies and private companies, so as to extend the opportunities to use Welsh (Williams & Evas, 1997: 30).

Fiontair Teanga in NI could imitate this pattern and thus be the hubs for the development of the Irish language at a local level in the region. This would give to the language a community-based and holistic form of language planning which would be economically engaged and socially inclusive. Local adaptations would be necessary, but the main elements of the general rationale for *Mentrau Iaith* would apply equally to *Fiontair Teanga*. These are:

> to create social conditions that will nurture positive attitudes towards Welsh and an increase in its use;
>
> to normalise the use of Welsh as a medium of social and institutional communication; and
>
> to highlight the close relationship between language and attitudes which relate to quality of life issues, the environment and the local economy (Williams & Evas, 1997).

Beyond these, adaptations in the intended functions of *Fiontair Teanga* would be necessary in order to address the sociopolitical and linguistic nuances of particular locations and contexts in NI. The data presented in this monograph indicate that language agencies have work to do in areas of language acquisition, attitudes and use. *Fiontair Teanga* could play an important role in strengthening the means by which the Irish language is acquired in the community in NI. Language reproduction within the Irish-speaking community is diffused across a number of mechanisms. Of the Irish speakers surveyed, just under 10% of adults and just over 11% of young people claimed the Irish language as their first language. The education system is of critical importance in the reproduction of the language. Many more younger Irish speakers have had some of their education through the medium of Irish than to adult Irish speakers. The fact of experiencing one's education through the medium of Irish appears to effect a confidence in self-perceptions of ability in the language. For example, young Irish speakers who have experienced Irish-medium nursery education are more likely to return themselves as Irish speakers of the highest ability later in life. Acquisition of the language by Protestants is frustrated by the absence of the language from school curricula. Adult Protestants encounter difficulties in their attempts to acquire the language as classes are often held in locations within what are perceived as Nationalist parts of the locale.

Fiontair Teanga could play an important role in addressing concerns, shared by the community as a whole in NI, regarding the politicisation of the language. They should be explicitly non-political in their constitution and mission. The lower regard for the instrumental value of the Irish language among Protestants could be addressed by highlighting the success of cultural tourism ventures such as Tí Chúlainn in south-east Ulster (a centre that is host to a wide range of Irish language and cultural activities). A wider sense of community ownership of the Irish language could be facilitated by *Fiontair Teanga*. They could engage in the drawing together of cultural resources relating to the language for use by the local community, including schools and other organisations.

Use of the Irish language is limited to very clearly defined networks centred on the immediate family, friends, the school, the church and, for some adults, the workplace. *Fiontair Teanga* could liase with a range of institutions, groups and individuals in encouraging the provision of opportunities for use of the language in a more extensive range of domains. Public bodies may be seen to have a particular responsibility in this regard. *Fiontair Teanga* could also strengthen networking between local Irish-speaking communities in NI and the Ulster *Gaeltacht* of Donegal. This would serve to knit the Irish-speaking community of NI into a wider Irish-speaking community while not compromising local identities. This could also serve to improve the levels of ability of Irish speakers in NI and counter the almost overwhelming influence of the English language on the vocabulary and syntax of the Irish popularly spoken in NI. This in turn would raise the prestige of the language as it is spoken in NI within the Irish-speaking community on the island of Ireland as a whole and also within the broader community of NI itself.

Possible aims for *Fiontair Teanga* could include the following:

- to encourage and facilitate community (including cross-community) owner-ship of the Irish language;
- to increase levels of awareness of the language among non-Irish speakers;
- to broaden accessibility to the Irish language across the community as a whole;
- to increase opportunities to use the language beyond the domains of the home and school;
- to offer practical help to families whose language of the home is not Irish but whose children are attending Irish-medium schools;
- to offer practical help to learners of Irish as a second language;
- to liase with local employers with regard to expanding the role of the Irish language in workplaces;
- to liase with other Irish-language agencies in the field so as to facilitate the knitting together of a holistic approach to language planning issues;
- to increase the public profile and status of the Ulster dialect of Irish;
- to strengthen networking between the local Irish-speaking community and the *Gaeltacht* of Donegal.

The impact and efficacy of *Fiontair Teanga* will depend, to a great degree, on the initial situation of the Irish language in the local community. As such, it is very desirable that the momentum for *Fiontair Teanga* come from within specific local communities rather than such initiatives being introduced as external agencies. The gap of experience and understanding between emergent cores of the Irish-speaking community in NI and the *Mentrau Iaith* of Wales could be bridged via a series of seminars through which the possibilities and opportunities opened up as a result of the political settlement could be explored in partnership between *An Foras Teanga* and the Irish-speaking community.

Conclusions

Language policy is on the cusp of what is, potentially, a radical new departure in NI. The autochthonous minority languages of Irish and Ulster-Scots have gained a certain niche in the arena of public discourse but have yet to command a position of conviction on the public policy agenda. A critical issue regarding the prospects for the Irish language in NI is identified at the macro/micro interface, the point at which the broad commitments to the language crystallise and impact upon the daily affairs of local communities. *Fiontair Teanga*, similar to the *Mentrau Iaith* of Wales, are identified as a possible mechanism for ensuring the cohesion of this interface and the successful translation of regional language policy in local Irish-speaking communities. A range of indicators from various sources of data show that Catholics and Protestants make a range of positive identifications with the Irish-language. The embedding of the language in the institutional structures of the political settlement will contribute to the decons-truction of historical structures of 'dominance, dependence and inequality' (Ruane & Todd, 1996: 316). The emergent legislative framework has the potential to facilitate the more effective institutional expression of the identity of the Irish language community in its broadest sense. In the medium term, tensions will remain in relation to the translation of aspirations into realities, of policy into practice, especially if political discourse on the language continues to be determined by traditional Nationalist and Unionist narratives. Moving beyond these narratives requires a more informed understanding of the significance of the Irish language beyond the political landscape, in its wider environment, in the fullest meaning of the term. Only in this way will the Irish language gain the civic identity that is already claimed by Welsh and Scottish Gaelic, its Celtic cousins, as languages of citizenship in the UK. For Ulster-Scots, on the other hand, it is another dimension to status that is the most pressing issue. Given the continuing debate regarding the identity of Ulster-Scots as a language, the thrust here for language planners should be with regard to corpus development, awareness raising and education. With a fuller sense of the nature of the language as a distinct entity, the case will be stronger for undertaking more detailed sociological research and also for the inclusion of a question on the Census, thereby generating the kind of data which would enable the implementation of a more comprehensive approach to policy and planning for Ulster-Scots. In general terms, however, both the Irish language and Ulster-Scots present important issues of equality and merit being matters for proactive approaches to language policy and planning in Northern Ireland.

Correspondence

Any correspondence should be directed to Diarmait Mac Giolla Chríost, Llechwedd, 23 Gerddi'r Twyn, Ffordd y Coleg, Caerfyrddin, Wales SA31 3EJ, UK (DiarmaitMGC@aol.com).

Note

1. Statistics provided by the Census Office for NI, Ad Hoc Request ITG364.

References

Adams, G.B. (1958) The emergence of Ulster as a distinct dialect area. *Ulster Folklife* 4, 61–73.
Adams, G.B. (1964) *Ulster Dialects*. Cultra: Ulster Folk and Transport Museum.
Adams, G.B. (1967) Northern England as a source of Irish dialects. *Ulster Folklife* 13, 69–74.
Adams, G.B. (1970) Language and man in Ireland. In D. McCourt and A. Gailey (eds) *Studies in Folklife Presented to Emyr Estyn Evans* (pp. 140–71) Cultra: Ulster Folk and Transport Museum.
Aitchison, J. and Carter, H. (1987) The Welsh language in Cardiff: A quiet revolution. *Transactions of the Institute of British Geographers* NS 12, 484–92.
Andrews, L.S. (1991) The Irish language in the education system of Northern Ireland: Some political and cultural perspectives. In R.M.O. Pritchard (ed.) *Motivating the Majority: Modern Languages in Northern Ireland* (pp. 89–106). Coleraine: Northern Ireland Centre for Information on Language and Teaching Research.
Andrews, L.S. (1997) 'The very dogs in Belfast will bark in Irish': The Unionist government and the Irish language, 1921–43. In A. Mac Póilin (ed.) *The Irish Language in Northern Ireland* (pp. 49–94). Belfast: Ultach Trust.
Barnard, T.C. (1993) Protestants and the Irish language *c.*1675–1725. *Journal of Ecclesiastical History* 44 (2), 243–72.
Bliss, A. (1976) The English language in early modern Ireland. In T.W. Moody, F.X. Martin and F.J. Byrne (eds) *A New History of Ireland iii: Early Modern Ireland, 1534–1691* (pp. 546–60). Oxford: Clarendon Press.
Braidwood, J. (1969) *The Ulster Dialect Lexicon*. Belfast: Queen's University Press.
Brown, T. (1985) *Ireland: A Social and Cultural History, 1922–1985*. London: Fontana Press.

Bwrdd yr Iaith Gymraeg (1999) *Mentrau Iaith Cymru. Datblygu'r Gymraeg yn y Gymuned* [*Wales' Language Ventures. Developing the Welsh Language in the Community*]. Cardiff: Bwrdd yr Iaith Gymraeg [Welsh Language Board].

Caerwyn Williams, J.E. (1958) *Traddodiad Llenyddol Iwerddon* [*Ireland's Literary Tradition*]. Cardiff: University of Wales Press.

Cahill, E. (1938) The Irish language and tradition, 1540–1691. *Irish Ecclesiastical Record* 54, 591–617.

CAJ (Committee on the Administration of Justice) (1993) *Staid agus Stádas Gaeilge i dTuaisceart na hÉireann* [*The Condition and Status of the Irish Language in Northern Ireland*]. Belfast: CAJ.

Canny, N.P. (1982) Identity formation in Ireland: The emergence of the Anglo-Irish. In N.P. Canny and A. Pagden (eds) *Colonial Identity in the Atlantic World, 1500–1800* (pp. 159–212). New Jersey: Princeton University Press.

Capita, (1997) *The Queen's University Belfast Students' Union Bilingual Policy Review, Final Report.* Belfast: Capita Management Consultants.

CCRU (Central Community Relations Unit) (1997) Personal correspondence, 2 June.

Crawford, J.G. (1993) *Anglicizing the Government of Ireland: The Irish Privy Council and the Expansion of Tudor Rule, 1556–1578.* Dublin: Four Courts Press.

de Baroid, C. (1990) *Ballymurphy and the Irish War.* London: Pluto.

DED (Department of Economic Development) (1989) *Fair Employment in Northern Ireland Code of Practice.* Belfast: HMSO.

DENI (Department of Education Northern Ireland) (1988) *Education Reform in Northern Ireland: The Way Forward.* Belfast: HMSO.

DHSS/RGNI (Department of Health and Social Services / Registrar General Northern Ireland) (1991) *The Northern Ireland Census 1991: Irish Language Report.* Belfast: HMSO.

Duffy, P.J. (1981) The territorial organisation of Gaelic landownership and its transformation in Co. Monaghan, 1595–1640. *Irish Geography* 14, 8–21.

Dunne, T.J. (1980) The Gaelic response to conquest and colonisation: The evidence of poetry. *Studia Hibernica* 20, 14–26.

Favell, A. and Martiniello, M. (1999) Multi-national, multi-cultural and multi-levelled Brussels: National and ethnic politics in the 'Capital of Europe' WPTC-99-04. On WWW at http://www.transcomm.ox.ac.uk.

Fitzgerald, G. (1984) Ireland's identity problems. *Études Irlandaises* 1, 135–42.

Gregg, R.J. (1972) The Scotch-Irish dialect boundaries in Ulster. In M.F. Wakelin (ed.) *Patterns in the Folk Speech of the British Isles* (pp. 109–39). London: Athlone Press.

Haarmann, H. (1986) *Language in Ethnicity: A View of Basic Ecological Relations.* Berlin: Mouton de Gruyter.

Hechter, M. (1975) *Internal Colonialism: The Celtic Fringe in British National Development, 1536–1966.* London: Routledge and Kegan Paul.

Hindley, R. (1990) *The Death of the Irish Language: A Qualified Obituary.* London: Routledge.

Jarman, N. (1993) Intersecting Belfast. In B. Bender (ed.) *Landscape: Politics and Perspectives* (pp. 107–38). Oxford: Berg.

Kirk, M.K. and Ó Baoill, D.P. (eds) (2000) *Language and Politics. Northern Ireland, the Republic of Ireland, and Scotland.* Belfast: Queen's University Press.

Kirk, J.M. and Ó Baoill, D.P. (eds) (2001) *Linguistic Politics. Language Policies for Northern Ireland, the Republic of Ireland, and Scotland.* Belfast: Queen's University Press.

Lee, J.J. (1989) *Ireland 1912–1985, Politics and Society.* Cambridge: Cambridge University Press.

Macafee, C.I. (ed.) (1996) *Concise Ulster Dictionary.* Oxford: Oxford University Press.

Mac an Fhaili, F. (1994) No language heavies. *Fortnight* 333, 34.

Mac Póilin, A. (1992) *Irish-medium Education in Northern Ireland. A Preliminary Report.* Belfast: Ultach Trust.

Mac Póilin, A. (1996) The Irish language movement in Northern Ireland. In M. Nic Craith (ed.) *Watching One's Tongue: Aspects of Romance and Celtic Languages* (pp. 137–62). Liverpool: Liverpool University Press.

Mac Póilin, A. (1998) The Charter and the Belfast Agreement: Implications for Irish in Northern Ireland. *Contact Bulletin* 15 (1), 3–4.

Mac Póilin, A. (n.d.) Mr Priestly's priorities. *Fortnight* 316, 28–30.

Mac Giolla Chríost, D. (2001) Implementing political agreement in Northern Ireland: Planning issues for Irish language policy. *Journal of Social and Cultural Geography* 2 (3), 297–313.

Mac Giolla Chríost, D. (2003) Local councils and the Welsh experience. A presentation as part of Language Rights and the Local Council. An Information Day for Councillors, Council Chief Executives and Senior Officers, Belfast.

Maguire, G. (1987) Language revival in an urban neo-Gaeltacht. In G. MacEoin *et al.* (eds) *Third International Conference on Minority Languages: Celtic Papers* (pp. 72–88). Clevedon: Multilingual Matters.

Maguire, G. (1991) *Our Own Language: An Irish Initiative.* Clevedon: Multilingual Matters.

Máté, I. (1997) Changes in the Celtic-language-speaking populations of Ireland, the Isle of Man, Northern Ireland, Scotland and Wales from 1891–1991. *Journal of Multilingual and Multicultural Development* 18, 316–30.

Miller, D. (1994) The new battleground? *Planet. The Welsh Internationalist* 102, 74–9.

Millett, B. (1976) Irish literature in Latin, 1550–1700. In T.W. Moody, F.X. Martin and F.J. Byrne (eds) *A New History of Ireland iii Early Modern Ireland, 1534–1691* (pp. 561–86). Oxford: Clarendon Press.

Mistéil, P. (ed.) (1994) *The Irish Language and the Unionist Tradition.* Belfast: Ulster People's College and Ultach Trust.

Nic Craith, M. (1996/7) The Irish language in primary and post-primary education: North and south of the border. *Irish Studies Review* 17, 35–9.

Nic Craith, M. and Shuttleworth, I. (1996) Irish in Northern Ireland: The 1991 census. In M. Nic Craith (ed.) *Watching One's Tongue: Aspects of Romance and Celtic Languages* (pp. 163–75). Liverpool: Liverpool University Press.

Nicholls, K.W. (1972) *Gaelic and Gaelicised Ireland in the Later Middle Ages.* Dublin: Gill and Macmillan.

NIO (Northern Ireland Office) (1998) *The Agreement: Agreement Reached in the Multi-Party Negotiations.* Belfast: HMSO.

NIO (Northern Ireland Office) (1999) *Agreement between the Government of the United Kingdom of Great Britain and the Government of Ireland Establishing Implementation Bodies.* Belfast: HMSO.

Ní Mhurchada, M. (1984) Pleanail teanga i leith na Gaeilge, 1800–1922 [Language planning with regard to Irish, 1800–1922]. Unpublished PhD thesis, Trinity College, Dublin.

Northover, M. and Donnelly, S. (1996) A future for English/Irish bilingualism in Northern Ireland? *Journal of Multilingual and Multicultural Development* 17, 33–48.

Ó Buachalla, B. (1983) Na Stiobhartaigh agus an t-aos léinn: Cing Seamas [The Stewarts and the literati: King James]. *Proceedings of the Royal Irish Academy* 3c(4).

Ó Cuív, B. (1976) The Irish language in the early modern period. In T.W. Moody, F.X. Martin and F.J. Byrne (eds) *A New History of Ireland iii Early Modern Ireland, 1534–1691* (pp. 509–45). Oxford: Clarendon Press.

Ó Dushlaine, T. (1987) *An Eoraip agus Litríocht na Gaeilge, 1600–1650. Gnéithe den Bharócachas Eorpach i Litríocht na Gaeilge* [Europe and Irish Literature, 1600–1650. Aspects of the European Baroque in Irish Literature]. Dublin: An Clóchomhar.

O'Dowd, M. (1981) Gaelic economy and society. In C. Brady and R. Gillespie (eds) *Natives and Newcomers: The Making of Irish Colonial Society, 1534–1641* (pp. 120–49). Dublin: Irish Academic Press.

Ó Muirí, P. (1994a) Cumhacht don phobal [Power to the community]. *Fortnight* 331, 36.

Ó Muirí, P. (1994b) Pumping up the fuaim. *Fortnight* 332, 38–39.

Ó Murcada, M.S. (1951) Gaeilge dutcais Tir Eogain [The Native Irish of Tyrone]. *An tUltach* 28 (5), 1–3 & 8.

Ó Murchú, M. (1992) Aspects of the societal status of modern Irish. In M. Ball (ed.) *The Celtic Languages* (pp. 471–90). London: Routledge.

Ó Murchú, H. (1999) *Irish. Facing the Future.* Dublin: European Bureau for Lesser Used Languages.

Openshaw, S. (ed.) (1995) *Census Users' Handbook.* Cambridge: Geoinformation.

Ó Rahilly, C. (1952) *Five Seventeenth Century Political Poems*. Dublin: Institute for Advanced Studies.

O'Reilly, C. (1995) The company of strangers. Ethnicity and the Irish language in west Belfast. *Fortnight* 336. Supplement.

O'Reilly, C. (1996) The Irish language – litmus test for equality? Competing discourses of identity, parity of esteem and peace process. *Irish Journal of Sociology* 6, 154–78.

O'Riordain, M. (1990) *The Gaelic Mind and the Collapse of the Gaelic World*. Cork: Cork University Press.

Ó Snodaigh, P. (1995) *Hidden Ulster: Protestants and the Irish Language*. Belfast: Lagan.

Ó Tuathaigh, G. (1972) *Ireland Before the Famine, 1798–1848*. Dublin: Gill and Macmillan.

PERU (Policy Evaluation and Research Unit) (2001) *Establishing the Demand for Services and Activities in the Irish Language in Northern Ireland*. Belfast: Department of Culture, Arts and Leisure.

Pritchard, R.M.O. (1990) Language policy in Northern Ireland. *Teangeolas* 21, 26–35.

Robinson, P. (1989) The Scots language in 17th century Ulster. *Ulster Folklife* 35, 86–99.

Ruane, J. and Todd, J. (1996) *The Dynamics of Conflict in Northern Ireland. Power, Conflict and Emancipation*. Cambridge: Cambridge University Press.

Scullion, P. (1999) Attitudes to the public presence of the Irish language in Northern Ireland: Cross-community perspectives. Unpublished MA dissertation, University of Wales.

Silke, J.J. (1976) The Irish abroad, 1534–1691. In T.W. Moody, F.X. Martin and F.J. Byrne (eds) *A New History of Ireland iii Early Modern Ireland, 1534–1691* (pp. 587–633). Oxford: Clarendon Press.

Stephens, M. (1976) *Linguistic Minorities in Western Europe*. Llandysul: Gomer Press.

Sweeny, K. (1987) *The Irish Language in Northern Ireland, 1987. A Preliminary Report of a Survey of Knowledge, Interest and Ability*. Belfast: Policy and Planning Research Unit.

Wall, M. (1969) The decline of the Irish language. In B. Ó Cuív (ed.) *A View of the Irish Language* (pp. 81–90). Dublin: Stationery Office.

Welch, R. (ed.) (1996) *The Oxford Companion to Irish Literature*. Oxford: Clarendon Press.

Whyte, J. (1986) How is the boundary maintained between the two communities in Northern Ireland. *Ethnic and Racial Studies* 9 (2), 219–34.

Williams, C.H. and Evas, J. (1997) *The Community Research Project. Summary of a Report Prepared for the Welsh Language Board*. On WWW at http://www.bwrdd-yr-iaith.org.uk. Accessed 19.7.00.

Williams, N.J.A. (1981) *Pairlement Chloinne Thómais* [The Parliament of the Thomas Clann]. Dublin: Institute of Advanced Studies.

An Update on Language Planning in Northern Ireland

Diarmait Mac Giolla Chríost
Llechwedd, 23 Gerddi'r Twyn, Ffordd y Coleg, Caerfyrddin, Wales UK

Despite recent substantial political difficulties, both the British and the Irish governments reaffirmed their commitment to the Irish language with regard to 'Rights, Equality, Identity and Community' in their 'Joint Declaration' of 2003. Under Paragraph 30 it is noted that; 'The British Government will continue to discharge all its commitments under the Agreement in respect of the Irish language'. The signing of the European Charter for Regional and Minority Languages in March 2000 (in force by July 2001) by the British government may be regarded as a step towards the realisation of some of these. The Department of Culture, Arts and Leisure in Northern Ireland [DCALNI] has been identified as the lead body with regard to the implementation of the European Charter. It is in this role that DCALNI have issued guidance (in draft form in January 2004) for public bodies on meeting the UK government commitments in respect of the European Charter. In this DCALNI communicate no sense of mission nor declare any aims with regard to policy on the Irish language. The emphasis on 'UK government commitments' as opposed to any engagement by the administration in NI may be regarded as an indication that the Irish language is undergoing a process of institutionalisation on the basis of legitimation at UK state level but in the absence of legitimation at a local level within NI.

Through the signing of the European Charter and the recognition of the Irish language with respect to Part III, a number (38) of commitments were made with regard to Irish in the areas of education (9), media (7), public administration (9), judicial authorities (1), cultural (9), social and economic activities (1), and, transfrontier exchanges (2). The Code of Courtesy included in the guidance indicates those areas in which DCALNI anticipates greatest demand – the use of Irish language versions of personal names and addresses, and the exercise of language choice in face-to-face meetings, telephone calls and letters. With regard to the Irish language in relation to questions of citizenship, equality and rights it is noted in the guidance provided by DCALNI that 'the Charter does not establish any individual or collective rights for the speakers of regional or minority languages' and that the purpose of the European Charter is 'cultural' (DCALNI, 2004: 3). Although, it is also noted that the European Charter 'commits the UK government to ensure that authorities, organisations and persons concerned are informed of the *rights and duties* (my italics) established by the Charter' (DCALNI, 2004: 5).

Elsewhere in the 'Joint Declaration', under the section entitled 'Rights, Equality, Identity and Community', the two governments point out that a number of important steps have been taken. These include the setting up of the Northern Ireland Human Rights Commission [NIHRC], established by legislation in 1998. This body was charged with the task of advising upon the creation of a Bill of Rights for Northern Ireland. It is clear that language issues are important in this context. For example, its consultative document of 2001 featured the following clause specific to language rights (NIHRC, 2001):

> Clause 13. Language Rights
> 1. Everyone has the right to use his or her own language for private purposes and all languages, dialects and other forms of communication are entitled to respect.
> 2. Everyone has the right to communicate with any public body through an interpreter, translator or facilitator when this is necessary for the purposes of accessing, in a language that he or she understands, information or services essential to his or her life, health, security or enjoyment of other essential services.
> 3. The State shall make suitable provision for assisting communication between members of different linguistic communities. 4. In relation to the Irish language and Ulster-Scots, legislation shall be introduced to implement the commitments made under the Belfast (Good Friday) Agreement and the European Charter for Regional or Minority Languages.
> 5. Without prejudice to the foregoing provisions, legislation shall be introduced to ensure for members of all linguistic communities, where there is sufficient demand, the following rights in respect of their language or dialect:
> > a. The promotion of conditions necessary to maintain and develop it;
> > b. The right to use it in dealings with public bodies;
> > c. The right to use one's name in it and to be officially recognised under it;
> > d. The right to display signs and other information in it;
> > e. The right to display local street and other place names in it;
> > f. The right to learn it and to be educated in and through it.

While it is the view of DCALNI that the European Charter does not confer any specific language rights, the NIHRC notes that in 'The Agreement' under the section entitled 'Rights, Safeguards and Equality of Opportunity' that the UK government committed to 'a recognition of linguistic diversity coupled with specific commitments for the protection and promotion of the Irish language' and that associated with that was the commitment of both the UK government and the government of the Republic of Ireland to 'the protection of civil, political, social, economic and cultural rights' and that thereby the inter-relationship between economic, social and cultural rights, on the one hand, and civil and political rights, on the other hand, was identified in 'The Agreement' (NIHRC, 2002: Section 7). Thus, tension in the area of rights and of their embedding in the post-conflict institutions and policy processes are delineated by the NIHRC as follows:

> One of our [NIHRC] statutory functions is precisely that of providing human rights assessments, on request or at our discretion, in relation to legislation that has effect in Northern Ireland. We are also routinely consulted on a very wide range of policy initiatives, and endeavour to respond in every instance where we have identified human rights concerns. The Committee should, however, note that we are not consulted on *all* legislation, even where there are clear human rights concerns, and

when we do make recommendations they are much more often than not disregarded. (Section 5, Paragraph h.)

For an authoritative assessment of the human rights compliance of legislation and policy it is at least desirable that reference of such initiatives be made by the executive or legislature to an appropriately empowered and resourced independent human rights institution. (Section 5, Paragraph i.)

Clearly there are some substantial challenges to be met with regard to embedding the equality and rights agenda more generally in policy processes. With regard to language, according to the NIHRC, the approach so far adopted with regard to the European Charter is very restrained. For example, in their submission of April 2002 to the UN Committee on Economic, Social and Cultural Rights, the NIHRC underlines the relevance of the European Charter to language rights but is critical of the level of commitment to the European Charter:

The formal status of Irish has also improved with the United Kingdom's application of the European Charter for Regional or Minority Languages ... However, the Committee should note that although the UK has identified 36 Charter paragraphs which it intends to apply to Irish (compared with 59 for Welsh), these are (where options are available within the Charter framework) the minimal provisions in each area, and even then they have not been implemented in full. (Section 5, Paragraph e.)

With regard to specific language rights in the area of education, one of the main thrusts of the UK government commitments to the Irish language in 'The Agreement', NICHR signposted their concerns in this area:

The international human rights standards require that parents should be free to send their children to schools that are in conformity with their own beliefs, and this Commission therefore believes that public funding should be made available on an equitable basis to schools in all sectors. Equitable in this context does not mean equal: there should be additional funding where required to target social need, to redress the historic underfunding of many schools, and to meet the start-up costs of new schools, for example in integrated and Irish-medium education (the main 'minority' sectors). We would wish to see a situation where every family that wanted to avail of integrated or Irish-medium education had the right and the freedom to do so. (Section 5, Paragraph f.)

Language equality and rights has further developed as a discursive strategy among advocates of the Irish language in NI during this period. The evidence from the NIHRC consultative process of 2001 on a Bill of Rights indicates as much. In general terms, the range of views is summarised as follows:

In terms of scope, the main tension seems to be between on the one hand adequate protection for what is thought 'particular to Northern Ireland', and for disadvantaged groups (as highlighted by language and human rights NGOs) and on the other hand the logistics of implementing such rights (as mentioned in submissions from state controlled bodies and two political parties). In relation to identity, there is also friction between an approach that treats all languages the same and one that recognises special protection for the dominant cultural or linguistic communities. (NIHRC, 2003: 76).

According to the NIHRC report many of the submissions on the Irish language argue for the recognition of legally defined rights: 'These submissions maintain that the Irish language is indigenous to Northern Ireland and should therefore have protection that reflects international standards, together with a state duty to implement protective legislation' (NIHRC, 2003: 76). It is also noted that of the minority opposed to the granting of language rights formulated their objections on the grounds of cost and not on the substantive matter of equality and rights: 'Their arguments are more concerned with how the government would absorb the cost' (NIHRC, 2003: 76). Some submissions, they note, claim that the implications of the granting of language rights would be 'a financial nightmare' (NIHRC, 2003: 79). The recognition of rights can be costly, of course, but is certainly no more costly than discrimination.

References

DCALNI (Department of Culture, Arts and Leisure Northern Ireland) (2004) *The European Charter for Regional and Minority Languages. Code of Courtesy.*
NIHRC (Northern Ireland Human Rights Commission) (2003) *Summary of Submissions on a Bill of Rights.*
NIHRC (Northern Ireland Human Rights Commission) (2002) *Submission to the United Nations Committee on Economic, Social and Cultural Rights on the UK's Fourth Report.*
NIHRC (Northern Ireland Human Rights Commission) (2001) *Making a Bill of Rights for Northern Ireland: A Consultation.*

Biographical Notes on Contributors

Jiří V. Neustupný was born and educated in Prague where he received his PhD (CSc) in 1964. From 1966 to 1993 he taught Japanese sociolinguistics and applied linguistics at Monash Univeristy in Melbourne. Then he continued teaching in Japan (Osaka University, Chiba University, and Obirin University, Tokyo). After ten years he came back to Australia and joined the Monash University. Among his publications are *Post-Structural Approaches to Language* (University of Tokyo Press 1978), *Gaikokujin to no komyunikeeshon* [Communicating with Foreigners] (Iwanami shoten 1982), *Communicating with the Japanese* (The Japan Times 1987), *Atarashii Nihongo kyoiku no tamen ni* [Towards New Directions in Japanese Language Teaching] (Taishukan 1995) and *Kyo to ashita no Nihongo kyoiku* [Japanese Language Teaching Today and Tomorrow] (ALC 2000).

Jiří Nekvapil teaches sociolinguistics, conversation analysis, and pragmatics at the Department of General Linguistics at Charles University, Prague. His research interests lie in the issues of language interaction. Recently he has published a series of papers dealing with the Czech mass media, interethnic relationships, and language planning in Central Europe. He is the author of the intercultural training module *Sprechen überPersonen: Soziale Kategorisierung im tschechisch-deutschen Kontakt* (Hof 1999; CD-ROM + video). His current research focuses on the language biographies of Czech Germans, language management theory and an ethnomethodologically-based analysis of media discourse. He is also member of an international team studying to what extent, how and why Czech, German and English are used in multinational companies operating in the Czech Republic.

Theo J.M. van Els (1936) studied English Language and Literature at the Universities of Nottingham (England) and Nijmegen (The Netherlands). At the latter University he did a PhD on Old English Phonology (1972). At the University of Nijmegen, he developed a programme of applied linguistics (i.e., the learning and teaching of foreign languages) and in 1981 he was appointed there to he first Chair of Applied Linguistics in The Netherlands. Van Els has served on a great many committees in – and boards of – national and international organisations in the field of foreign language teaching and of applied linguistics in general. He was initiator and Chairman of the Dutch Government Task Force that developed the Dutch National Action Programme for Modern Foreign Languages (1989–1990). He held a number of positions in the (academic) administration of the University of Nijmegen. Before his retirement in 2000 he held the position of 'Rector Magnificus' (i.e., Provost) of the University.

Diarmait Mac Giolla Chríost (PhD) is a lecturer in the School of Welsh at Cardiff University, Wales, the UK. He is a native of Ireland and an authority on linguistic minorities and language planning. He has a range of research interests including: the situation of the Irish language, and, the nature of the relationship between language and conflict from a comparative, European perspective, and also, language in city contexts. He has a number of publications in Irish studies, the social sciences, human geography, and the sociology of language. These include a number of substantial articles in various scholarly journals and two single-author books – *Language, Identity and Conflict* (Routledge, 2003) and *The Irish Language in Ireland* (Routledge, 2005). He was educated at The Queen's University Belfast, The University of Wales Aberystwyth, The Open University and The London School of Economics and Political Science. He is a Fellow of The Royal Geographical Society.